Dictionary of the Politics of the People's Republic of China

Dictionary of the Politics of the People's Republic of China

Edited by
Colin Mackerras
with
Donald H. McMillen and Andrew Watson

London and New York

First published in 1998
by Routledge
11 New Fetter Lane, London EC4P 4EE
29 West 35th Street, New York, NY 10001

© 1998 Routledge

Typeset in 9/11pt Palatino by RefineCatch Limited, Bungay, Suffolk

Printed in Great Britain by TJ International Ltd, Padstow, Cornwall

Printed on acid-free paper

British Library Cataloguing in Publication Data
A catalogue record for this book is available from the British Library

Library of Congress Cataloging-in-Publication Data
A catalog record for this book is available on request

ISBN 0–415–15450–2

1001356636

Contents

Contributors

Editors

Professor Colin Mackerras
Modern Asian Studies, Griffith University

Professor Donald H. McMillen
Asian Studies, University of Southern Queensland

Professor Andrew Watson
Asian Studies, University of Adelaide

Other Contributors

Professor Bill Brugger
Politics, Flinders University

Dr Anita Chan
China and Korea Centre, Australian National University

Dr Gerald Chan
Politics, Victoria University of Wellington

Professor Jae Ho Chung
International Relations, Seoul National University

Professor John F. Cleverley
Social and Policy Studies, University of Sydney

Dr Michael DeGolyer
Government and International Studies, Hong Kong Baptist University

Professor Lowell Dittmer
Political Science, University of California

Dr Michael Dutton
Political Science, University of Melbourne

Dr Christopher Findlay
Economics, University of Adelaide

Dr Keith Forster
Asian Studies, Southern Cross University

Professor David S. G. Goodman
International Studies, University of Technology, Sydney

Dr Jennifer Grant
Modern Languages, Macquarie University

Dr Lijian Hong
Asian Languages and Studies, Monash University

Professor Beverley Hooper
Asian Studies, University of Western Australia

Dr Paul Ivory
Business, Sunshine Coast University, Queensland

Professor J. Bruce Jacobs
Asian Languages and Studies, Monash University

Dr Beverley M. Kitching
Marketing and International Studies, Queensland University of Technology

Associate Professor Nick Knight
Modern Asian Studies, Griffith University

Dr Carlos W. H. Lo
Management, The Hong Kong Polytechnic University

Dr Sonny S. H. Lo
Politics and Public Administration, University of Hong Kong

Professor Richard Pomfret
Economics, University of Adelaide

Dr David Schak
Modern Asian Studies, Griffith University

Dr Warren Sun
Asian Languages and Studies, Monash University

Dr Pradeep Taneja
Business, Humanities and Social Science, Swinburne University of Technology

Professor Frederick C. Teiwes
Government, University of Sydney

Dr Jonathan Unger
Contemporary China Centre, Australian National University

Dr Dennis Woodward
Politics, Monash University

Professor Dali L. Yang
Political Science, University of Chicago

Dr Yen Ching-hwang
History, University of Adelaide

Dr You Ji
Political Science, University of New South Wales

Dr Yongnian Zheng
East Asia Institute, National University of Singapore

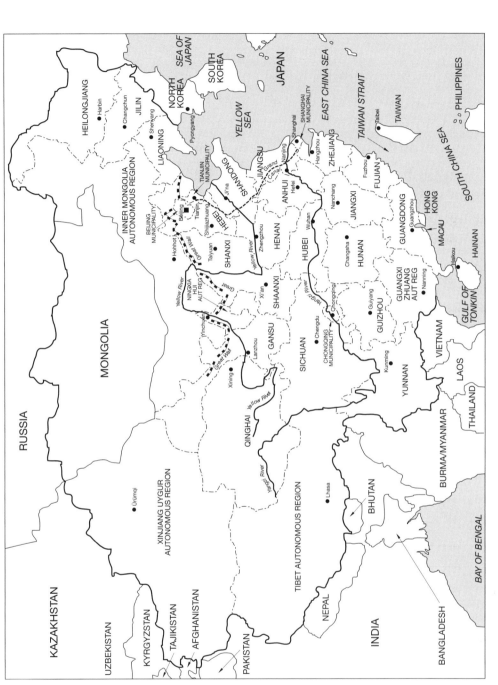

The People's Republic of China and its neighbours

Introduction

The People's Republic of China (PRC) is the most populous country in the world and one with an ancient political system and culture. It is gaining in political power both in the world at large and in its own region, and its economy is growing very rapidly. The idea of a dictionary of the PRC's politics hardly requires further justification.

The focus is those territories which are governed as part of the PRC at the time of publication. These include Hong Kong, a British Crown Colony until June 1997, but now a Special Administrative Region of the PRC. Others, such as Taiwan, Macau and the Overseas Chinese, are included only as relevant to the PRC. This is a dictionary, not an encyclopedia or a handbook. It aims to inform and to fill a gap in the current literature. Beyond being descriptive, the volume is concerned with assessing the dynamic nature of Chinese politics, especially in the reform period since 1978, the final cut-off point being the Fifteenth Party Congress of September 1997. Its focus is politics, but with particular reference to how the concept and nature of politics have been shaped by the political dimensions of the economy, society and international relations.

The dictionary is aimed mainly at students, government, media and business personnel, and non-specialist academics: people who need to know concrete and accessible information about the PRC, presented as objectively as possible. It takes account of recent trends in the study of a China experiencing dynamic change. Researchers of Asia and China, as well as students in the field, have a need to be able to put their hands on a compendium of reliable and useful information. In addition, such readers will need to know where else to find more relevant information on particular topics, hence the lists of further reading.

In line with the book's political focus, the introductory essays and general entries cover items in the following categories:

- major political processes and events; in general, major meetings are included appropriately under other headings;
- the main areas of domestic policy issues and processes;
- China's evolving foreign policy environment;
- main political personalities;
- major political institutions and groupings;
- sub-national units, including regions, provinces, cities and rural entities;
- a few of the most politically important nationalities; and
- important aspects of the legal system, including law and legal processes.

The dictionary does not aim to be totally comprehensive. Inevitably it is a matter of judgement whether a specific item is really 'important' enough to warrant inclusion. However, the criteria for selecting entries are:

- importance to the political culture;
- importance to the political economy;
- importance to China's external political relationships and activity or security;
- political importance for China's society; and
- importance for the political identity, aspirations and direction of the Chinese.

The system of romanization used is the *pinyin*. Adopted in the PRC for all publications in languages using the Roman alphabet at the beginning of 1979, it has since become nearly universal in scholarly and journalistic work on the PRC in such languages throughout the world. The only exceptions to the use of *pinyin* are a few names, such as Sun Yat-sen and Chiang Kai-shek, which have become fully standard in their non-*pinyin* forms.

We have normally avoided acronyms. Where they are used, they are explained the first time they occur within each individual essay or entry. Other than acronyms accepted as standard world-wide, such as US for United States, the only acronyms used herein without being consistently explained within each entry are:

CCP Chinese Communist Party; and

PRC People's Republic of China.

The editors would like to thank all those whose work has contributed to the compilation of this dictionary. In particular, the contributors have been models of cooperation and diligence, and without them the dictionary could not possibly have been completed.

Introductory Essays

1. Overview History of the People's Republic of China
Colin Mackerras

The aim of this introductory overview history of the People's Republic of China (PRC) is to provide some basic historical interconnections among the various individual items, which explain particular personal careers, events and trends in more detail. One way of achieving this aim is to periodize PRC history.

In any attempt at historical periodization, there are inevitably many overlaps among periods. Not everything changes just because we enter a new period. But the explanations will focus on the changes, rather than the continuities, because change is what justifies a new period. In all cases the overwhelming emphasis will be on the political economy, since that is the thrust of the present dictionary.

PRC history can be divided into two broad periods, each with subdivisions. These are:
- the period of left-wing revolution, 1949 to 1976; and
- the period of reform and modernization, from 1976.

The Period of Revolution, 1949 to 1976
The general characteristics of the period from the accession of the **Chinese Communist Party** (CCP) to power on 1 October 1949 to the fall of the **gang of four** in October 1976 are as follows:
- an emphasis on revolution, including revolutionary change, in politics, the economy, society and culture;
- the domination of Chinese politics, to a greater or lesser extent, by **Mao Zedong**;
- a consequent emphasis on mass-based campaigns as a mechanism of government, with resultant instability;
- frequent disagreement between the more radical and in theory mass-based revolution of **Mao Zedong**'s line and the more economically pragmatic and orderly revolution advocated by **Liu Shaoqi** and his supporters;

- an emphasis on economic growth, but strongly tempered during much of the period by the revolutionary aims of **Mao Zedong**, which tended to balance economic growth against social revolution and was at times prepared to sacrifice the former in the interests of the latter.

The Consolidation of Revolutionary Power, 1949 to 1952
Immediately after **Mao Zedong** announced the establishment of the PRC at a major demonstration in Tiananmen Square in the centre of Beijing, several campaigns were launched or intensified, all designed to implement revolutionary change and consolidate the revolutionary regime. The most important of these campaigns was the land reform (see **agriculture**), which by 1952 had effectively destroyed the landlord class and transferred land away from the richer classes and towards the poorer. Another was a comparable move in the cities aimed at destroying the comprador bourgeoisie, that is the big bourgeoisie with major attachments to foreign concerns. A third one was the issuing of the 1950 **Marriage Law**.

Although supported by the **Soviet Union**, Mao's new regime encountered strong opposition from the **United States**. The fact that China and the US fought on opposite sides in the **Korean War** (1950–3) increased tensions within China itself, where it became very easy to accuse an opponent of being not only a class enemy but also a spy working for the imperialists.

Stabilization and Economic Growth, 1953 to mid-1957
The years 1953 to 1957 were notable for the First Five-Year Plan (see **5. Politics and the Economy: Policy Patterns and Issues**). At the same time the process towards the socialization of the economy gained momentum, both in the cities and in the countryside, with the

growth of the **collective sector** and of **collective agriculture**.

Mass campaigns continued at intervals over this period, but the period is one of greater stability than the ones which preceded or followed it. It saw the holding of the First **National People's Congress** in September 1954, and the formal adoption of the PRC's first State **Constitution**. In September 1956 came the convening of the Eighth **National Party Congress**, the first since 1949. Mao's influence was slightly undermined at the Eighth Congress, which officially designated the ideology of the CCP as Marxism-Leninism, rather than Marxism-Leninism-**Mao Zedong Thought**. In April 1957, the CCP felt confident enough of its authority to call for criticism of its performance: the **Hundred Flowers Movement**.

The First Major Radical Phase, mid-1957 to 1959

This movement was soon succeeded by a large-scale attack on opponents called the Anti-Rightist Movement. In 1958 **Mao Zedong** decided to step up the socialization of the economy, especially through two mass-based movements. The first of these was the **Great Leap Forward**, the second the people's communes (see **collective agriculture**). The initial implication of the communes – that privately owned land would disappear – did not last long, with private plots reasserting themselves quite quickly.

Mao's radical policies aroused opposition among his own colleagues, resulting in a power struggle. In April 1959 Mao stepped down from the presidency. From the beginning of July until 1 August 1959 a series of meetings took place on Lushan, a mountain in Jiangxi province, culminating in the Eighth Plenum of the Eighth Central Committee, usually known simply as the Lushan Plenum. Minister for National Defence Peng Dehuai (1898–1974) wrote a 'letter of opinion' to Mao criticizing his **Great Leap Forward** policies as ultra-leftist. Mao counterattacked furiously, charging Peng with being capitalist. Very few dared come out in Peng Dehuai's support, although many sided with him secretly. Mao won the power struggle, and Peng Dehuai's career was finished. He was replaced as minister for national defence by Mao's supporter **Lin Biao**. At the same time, however, Mao was forced to allow a withdrawal from his most radical policies.

The Period of Recovery, 1960 to 1966

Just as Peng Dehuai had predicted, the overall impact of Mao's radical policies, combined with the withdrawal of **Soviet** experts in the summer of 1960 and bad weather, was a disastrous downturn in the economy. The most spectacular result was a famine so serious that population figures for 1960 and 1961 actually show an overall decline on the previous year. As the withdrawal from Mao's radical policies began to take effect, and the weather improved, the economy began to show a strong recovery, evident especially from 1962 on.

Politically Mao began to reassert his authority with frequent references to class struggle at the Tenth Plenum of the Eighth Central Committee in September 1962. He also began competing with **Liu Shaoqi** in attempts to influence patterns of development in the countryside, Mao favouring a mass-based approach and Liu a more orderly and rational method.

*The Second Major Radical Phase, the **Cultural Revolution** to the Fall of **Lin Biao**, August 1966 to September 1971*

The period from 1966 to 1976 saw a significant intensification of the revolution, substantial enough that many periodizations of PRC history place it in an entirely different category. In August 1966, at the Eleventh Plenary Session of the Eighth Central Committee, **Mao Zedong** decided to launch his second major attempt at radicalization of the Chinese revolution through a movement he called the Great Proletarian **Cultural Revolution**. It was in this period that his power reached its zenith, enabling him to force his policies through and destroying many careers and lives as he did so.

An intensely ideological movement, this

saw the height of Mao's obsession with class struggle, continuing revolution and mass mobilization (see **3. Ideology: Radicalism and Reform**). It also saw the suspension of normal government operations in many fields for several years, an example being the total closure of institutions of higher learning. Led by youthful groups called the Red Guards, the **Cultural Revolution** threw China into chaos for several years, the worst being 1968, when full-scale civil war briefly raged in Guangxi and Sichuan.

Mao's main enemy during the **Cultural Revolution** was **Liu Shaoqi**, whom he dubbed a revisionist and the number one person in the Party taking the capitalist road. In October 1968, Liu was condemned as a counter-revolutionary renegade.

The man who had been presented to the masses as Mao's greatest supporter for the **Cultural Revolution** was **Lin Biao**. The Ninth **National Party Congress** of April 1969 even described him as 'Chairman Mao's close comrade-in-arms and successor'. However, shortly after this accolade, Lin followed **Liu Shaoqi** into Mao's bad books and in September 1971 died in an air crash.

*The **Cultural Revolution** in Decline, From the Aftermath of the Fall of **Lin Biao** to the Death of **Zhou Enlai**, September 1971 to January 1976*

The fall of **Lin Biao** produced a major effect on the psychology of the Chinese people and dealt a blow to their faith in the values of the **Cultural Revolution**. In official propaganda, the man who had been touted as a hero great enough to be Mao's successor suddenly became a traitor who had tried to assassinate the chairman. At the same time, the government had invited the world's arch-imperialist, US President Richard Nixon, to visit China, which he did in February 1972, signalling a significant turn for the better in Sino-American relations.

In the mean time, Premier **Zhou Enlai**, one of the very few senior leaders who had not quarrelled with Mao, assumed greater influence in the government. It was Zhou who gave the Report at the Tenth **National Party Congress** in August 1973. He succeeded in keeping out of the incessant ideological campaigns which characterized this period and in keeping the government on a relatively even keel of operation.

The problem was that **Zhou Enlai** was suffering from cancer. On 8 January 1976 he succumbed to the disease.

*The Upheavals of 1976 to the Fall of the **Gang of Four** in October*

Zhou's death was followed by great and genuine public mourning. It introduced the most dramatic year in the history of the PRC so far.

Who would succeed **Zhou Enlai**? The obvious answer was **Deng Xiaoping**. But Mao still did not trust Deng, launching yet another ideological campaign against him and allowing the relatively unknown **Hua Guofeng** to take over as premier. In April the **Tiananmen Incident** took place in central Beijing, with enormous demonstrations in support of **Zhou Enlai** and, by implication, **Deng Xiaoping**. **Hua Guofeng** jumped in to support Mao's and the **gang of four**'s view that it was a 'counter-revolutionary political incident'.

On 28 July the coal-producing city of Tangshan was struck by an enormous earthquake, in terms of human casualties among the worst in history. The **gang of four** tried to use the disaster to press their own ideological case against Deng. By contrast, **Hua Guofeng** actually went to Tangshan.

On 9 September 1976, **Mao Zedong** died. Mourning took place, although it was neither as intense nor as sincere as that for Zhou. People revered Mao almost as a god, but many thought he was a tyrant too. Potential successors prepared to take over.

In the evening of 6 October 1976, the Politburo met to decide on a successor. Just before the meeting, on **Hua Guofeng**'s instructions, the four leading supporters of Mao's cultural revolutionary line were arrested in a quick surgical strike. The Politburo meeting went ahead without them, and early on 7 October appointed Hua as CCP chairman.

The Period of Reform and Modernization, from 1976

The general characteristics of the period of reform and modernization are as follows:

- the domination of the political economy by the needs of economic modernization and growth;
- an opening to the outside world, especially the West and Japan, as a way of promoting modernization;
- the domination of politics by the personality of **Deng Xiaoping** and his ideology entitled 'socialism with Chinese characteristics';
- a move away from **Mao Zedong**'s campaign style of politics to a more normal authoritarian style based on law and order, and hence a greater emphasis on stability;
- the insistence of the CCP that it remain in power, balanced by the growth of non-CCP and even anti-CCP influences within society;
- a stunningly successful growth in the economy overall, exemplified by spectacular rises in the standard of living for most citizens but also a substantial widening of inequalities; and
- a strong growth in those features tending to accompany modernization, such as consumerism, corruption and crime.

The Interregnum, October 1976 to December 1978

The fall of the **gang of four** stands like a great gulf in PRC history. It symbolized the end of the **Cultural Revolution** and its values and it led on to a period with a totally different texture. Already on 25 December 1976 **Hua Guofeng** made a speech pressing for the **Four Modernizations**. In July 1977, just before the Eleventh **National Party Congress** in August, **Deng Xiaoping** was restored to all his posts, preparing the way for his greater ascension later.

Yet the emphasis of this interregnum between the periods dominated by Mao and by Deng is on denunciation of the **gang of four**. The Chinese political system was not yet ready to condemn the **Cultural Revolution**.

The Early Stages of Reform, Between Third Plenums, December 1978 to October 1984

It was the **Third Plenum of the Eleventh Central Committee** that introduced the period of reform and consolidated the emphasis on modernization, as well as strengthening the leadership of **Deng Xiaoping**. Although it stopped short of criticizing **Mao Zedong** and his **Cultural Revolution**, it did open the way for a thorough-going criticism both of Mao and his brainchild at the **Sixth Plenum of the Eleventh Central Committee** in mid-1981. In the mean time, the authorities arranged for the **gang of four** to be put on trial, along with quite a few other leaders of the **Cultural Revolution**. Designed as a show-case trial to display China's progress towards a formal **legal system**, the verdicts were, as expected, very condemnatory of the four. In addition, the trial raised again the whole question of **Lin Biao** and his supposed attempt to assassinate Mao. Not surprisingly, the verdict against Lin was uncompromising and harsh.

Over this period, the **Cultural Revolution** was negated in a range of ways. These included the abolition of the communes and the **revolutionary committees**. In addition, traditions began to re-emerge. A religious revival began, with the traditional arts once again receiving attention.

The economy picked up greatly, especially in the countryside. The reform measures of the Third Plenum produced a dramatic effect on rural production. The Third Plenum of the Twelfth Central Committee, held on 20 October 1984, decided to include urban enterprises in the reform, to relax controls on prices and to give managers greater authority in their own enterprises, including in hiring and dismissing employees.

Acceleration of Reform and the Emergence of Student Movements, October 1984 to May 1989

The Third Plenum of the Twelfth Central Committee gave the necessary spur to the urban economy and the following years saw it re-establish priority over the countryside. The free enterprise economy began to take root, with the beginnings even of a stock exchange. The standard of living rose almost everywhere, although much faster in some places than in others. Inflation gathered momentum to become a very serious problem.

The years following the Third Plenum of the Twelfth Central Committee saw an acceleration in 'modern' lifestyle in the cities, such as more varied food and dress, and a taste for disco, karaoke and the Western pop idiom in music, Western television programmes and the rise of such consumer items as beauty parlours. Western, and especially North American, influence accelerated, especially among the youth. Increasing numbers of students went to study and work in the West and Japan, substantial numbers failing to return. Corruption gathered momentum, in part since the changes in the economy and society gave much more incentive to officials to embezzle or accept bribes. Although the traditional 'relationship (*guanxi*) networks' had never died, they regained strength to a major extent.

Student movements became an important political influence. At the end of 1986 large-scale student demonstrations led to the dismissal of CCP General Secretary **Hu Yaobang** in January 1987 as too sympathetic to student demands for greater reform and freedoms (see **protest movements**). It was Hu's death which sparked off much larger and more persistent demonstrations from April to early June 1989, costing his successor **Zhao Ziyang** his position.

*The **June 4 Incident** and its Aftermath, June 1989 to January 1992*
The student demonstrations were suppressed by the military on the night of 3–4 June 1989. A period of great tension followed, during which some feared that civil war would break out. The government took steps to control inflation, with a consequent slowing down of the economy, especially until the middle of 1990.

Politically, the man to benefit most from the **June 4 Incident** was **Jiang Zemin**, who became CCP general secretary later in June. An atmosphere of repression prevailed, with intellectuals afraid to speak out too strongly. Although sentences handed down in 1991 and 1992 on those leaders of the student demonstrations who had failed to escape to the West were generally rather lighter than expected, the credibility of the CCP and of **Deng Xiaoping** had clearly suffered a major blow.

Deng Xiaoping's Inspection Tour of the South to the Fifteenth Congress, Early 1992 to Late 1997
In January and February 1992, **Deng Xiaoping** made a much publicized inspection tour of the south, especially the oldest and most successful of the **special economic zones** Shenzhen. Rapid economic reform was the line confirmed at the Fourteenth **National Party Congress** late in 1992, pushing the market economy, economic growth and consumerism very strongly indeed.

The effect was to intensify the ethos of making money within a context of political stability. Socialism with Chinese characteristics became strikingly similar to capitalism with Confucian characteristics.

Traditional values associated with Confucianism, such as hierarchy, discipline, filial piety and obedience to authority, gathered momentum quite strongly, especially among the intelligentsia. The standard of living continued to grow at an astonishing rate overall, but it was very uneven, with concentrations along the eastern seaboard, especially the urban regions of the southeast, but much less spectacular growth in the inland and west.

Although the mid-1990s saw a revival of nationalism, there were still many people, especially among young intellectuals, who were keen to leave China for life in the West. Despite sincere efforts by such leaders as **Jiang Zemin** to control it, corruption remained an extremely serious problem. Another to gain considerable publicity was narcotics, high-profile executions of drug-pedlars failing to stop this evil worsening, especially in Yunnan Province.

Deng Xiaoping died in February 1997. In contrast to Mao, his body was not displayed or placed in a mausoleum; instead he was cremated and his ashes thrown into the sea. The Fifteenth **National Party Congress**, held from 12 to 18 September 1997, confirmed the main part of the leadership he had put in place, as well as his ideology. In particular, it saw **Jiang Zemin** strengthen his leadership over the Party to an extent which surprised most commentators. This included an acceptance of the blueprint contained in his report to the Congress. Among the major initiatives in the report were the restructuring of the state-owned enterprises, further reduction of the size of the army, strengthening of the **legal system** and increased attempts to curb corruption, as well as rejection of notions of Western democracy.

The mid-1990s also saw a rise in nationalism in China. On 1 July 1997, China regained sovereignty over **Hong Kong** in a dignified ceremony at which **Jiang Zemin** represented China and Prince Charles Britain. Although change in Hong Kong was initially both gradual and shallow, the event was of major importance to China, because it was the last of the territories lost to other powers as a result of nineteenth-century imperialism.

see also: 3. Ideology: Radicalism and Reform; 4. Political Personae: Biographical Profiles; 5. Politics and the Economy: Policy Patterns and Issues; agriculture; Chinese Communist Party; collective agriculture; collective sector; Constitutions; Cultural Revolution; Deng Xiaoping; Four Modernizations; gang of four; Great Leap Forward; Hong Kong; Hu Yaobang; Hua Guofeng; Hundred Flowers Movement; Jiang Zemin; June 4 Incident; Korean War; legal system; Lin Biao; Liu Shaoqi; Mao Zedong; Mao Zedong Thought; Marriage Laws; National Party Congress; National People's Congress; protest movements; revolutionary committees; Sixth Plenum of the Eleventh Central Committee; special economic zones; Third Plenum of the Eleventh Central Committee; Tiananmen Incident; Soviet Union, relations with; United States policy; Zhao Ziyang; Zhou Enlai.

2. Government and Institutions

Colin Mackerras

The aim of this essay is to give some idea of how China is governed, and to analyse the changes and continuities in government over the decades since 1949. It attempts to establish interrelationships among the main organizations and institutions involved in government, but not to establish details on these bodies themselves, these being covered in separate items.

In ascribing 'models' to Chinese politics, terms frequently used include 'totalitarian', 'developing country' and 'modernizing country'. However, most specialists see the totality of Chinese politics as unique, which would point to 'the Chinese model' as a better designation. Within certain continuities, change in the texture of Chinese politics has been so deep-seated and multifaceted that only a 'model' specifically about China can adequately describe the whole period from 1949 to the late 1990s.

There are two main organs involved in formal government in China. These are the CCP and the government structure. Other institutions with administrative power, however, include the **People's Liberation Army** (PLA), the **police force** and the **legal system**.

China has, in the CCP and government, two separate, although related, organs of administration. There are comparable bodies in the CCP and the government in many areas and at various levels. The highest body in each is a large-scale and, apart from the period from 1958 and 1973, regularly held congress: the **National Party Congress** and the **National People's Congress.** Both have comparable congresses at lower levels, for instance, provincial party committees and provincial people's congresses, with similar bodies at county and other lower levels.

The highest position in the CCP was formerly the chairman, a position held by **Mao Zedong** from 1943 until his death in 1976, and then by **Hua Guofeng** and **Hu Yaobang**. However, the Twelfth National CCP Congress of September 1982 abolished the position, since when the most senior Party position has been the general secretary.

The most senior individuals in the non-Party structure are the president and vice-president of the PRC, both elected by the **National People's Congress**. The state **Constitutions** of 1954 and 1982 endow the president with considerable powers, including those of appointing senior ministers and ratifying treaties and important agreements with foreign countries. Unless held by an exceptional leader, the position's powers are more formal than real.

From 1959 until 1968 the position of state president was held by **Liu Shaoqi**, Mao's rival and enemy during the **Cultural Revolution**. So deep was Mao's obsession with Liu's supposed counter-revolutionary behaviour that he even had the position abolished altogether. It was revived in the State Constitution of 1982 and filled, by **Li Xiannian**, in June 1983.

The most senior executive body of the government is the **State Council**, which consists of ministers, councillors and others, and is headed by the premier of the **State Council**, equivalent to a prime minister.

The Supreme People's Court and Supreme People's Procuratorate are responsible to the **National People's Congress**, which appoints the heads of both bodies. The **legal system** is heavily dependent on the government and, in political cases, is supposed to obey the leadership of the CCP. The Procuratorate was totally destroyed during the **Cultural Revolution**, and the rest of the legal system almost totally destroyed, but both have revived during the 1980s and 1990s.

A feature of administration particularly characteristic of Mao's rule but largely reversed by **Deng Xiaoping** is 'mass mobilization'. As early as June 1943 Mao had formulated the notion that 'correct leadership' proceeded 'from the masses, to the masses' and throughout the 1950s and 1960s he orchestrated many mass campaigns. During the most intense of them, the **Cultural Revolution**, Mao give his own creation, the Red Guards, enormous power as representatives of the masses, so great indeed that they could denounce and attack CCP members. One government structure which bore the signs of 'mass mobilization' was the **revolutionary committee**, with its 'three-way alliance', born in January 1967 as a result of Mao's **Cultural Revolution** policies but discontinued in the early 1980s. During the 1980s the whole idea of 'mass mobilization' waned and by the 1990s persisted only in anti-corruption drives, when the masses were asked to 'supervise' the CCP.

As an overall principle, the CCP leads and makes policy, whereas the government implements policy. Both **Mao Zedong** and **Deng Xiaoping** were very insistent on CCP leadership, this theory being a major point of continuity in the history of the CCP. At a talk he gave to the Third National Congress of the New Democratic Youth League of China on 25 May 1957 **Mao Zedong** declared that 'the CCP is the core of leadership of the whole Chinese people. Without this core, the cause of socialism cannot be victorious.' This is one of the points on which Mao and Deng agreed. In a major speech on 30 March 1979 at a forum on the principles for the CCP's theoretical work, Deng declared his 'four cardinal principles' as 'the basic prerequisite for achieving modernization', one of them being: 'we must uphold the leadership of the Communist Party'.

During the early stages of the PRC, the CCP was so paramount in terms of authority that, although they had separate structures and roles, it was almost possible to say that Party and government were one. During the **Cultural Revolution**, both the CCP and government suffered severely, enormous numbers of senior leaders being criticized as reactionary and bourgeois by Mao and exuberant Red Guards. Power shifted away from the CCP and the government to Mao as an individual and towards his supporters among the masses.

In the period of reform, the trend has been for the authority of the CCP to decline. Although in power terms it remains the single most important body in China, the degree of exclusiveness is much less than in the 1950s. In a speech at the Seventh Plenary Session of the Twelfth CCP Central Committee in October 1987, CCP General Secretary **Zhao Ziyang** called for political reform, involving pulling the CCP out of matters more proper to government than to a political party. He criticized 'the usurpation of government role by the Party' and called for a 'switch from centralized leadership to the separation of Party from government'. The CCP should continue to lead, for instance by formulating political principles and making major policy decisions, and to play a 'supervisory and guaranteeing role'. But it should not involve itself in matters such as administration, the implementation of policy, or in those where professional expertise is vitally important.

This trend was reversed in mid-1989, when **Deng Xiaoping** believed that the CCP was about to be overthrown unless resolute action was taken (see **June 4 Incident**). Since **Deng Xiaoping**'s 'inspection tour of the south' of early 1992, however, the trend has changed once again. Not only the government but also various community groups and even the law have gained in authority at the expense of the CCP.

Most commentators see in China the beginnings of 'the civil society', the key feature being social activity and processes which are autonomous of imposition or regulation by the state. One example illustrating the trend in the mid-1990s is the growing number of legal cases which have shown individuals challenging state authority and, on occasion, even winning against it. However, this process is still in its infancy. The state can clamp down in legal cases when it really wants to, as the case of Wei Jingsheng showed at the end of 1995 (see **dissidents**).

It is notable that there is extensive overlap between the Party and state leadership positions. **Mao Zedong** held the top positions both in the Party and government, chairman and president respectively, from October

1949 until April 1959. Since 1993, **Jiang Zemin** has been both Party general secretary and state president.

However, it should not be assumed from this that the overlap is total. Song Qingling, the widow of Sun Yat-sen, occupied several very senior state positions, including vice-president of the PRC, but was not even a member of the CCP until two weeks before her death on 29 May 1981 at the age of 90. At the grassroots level, the overlap becomes very much less pronounced than in the central leadership. In the 1990s only about 60 per cent of elected village heads are members of the CCP.

One of the features of the Chinese political system is the role individual leaders are able to play. Despite the overlap in Mao's positions from 1949 to 1959, in fact his authority throughout his whole reign was greater than his tenure of formal appointments would suggest, if anything actually increasing in his late years. **Zhou Enlai** retired as foreign minister in February 1958, but he continued to play the crucial role in foreign affairs right until his death in January 1976. **Deng Xiaoping** never held either the top CCP or government positions, but is nevertheless acknowledged by all commentators and Chinese as the chief architect of reform and modernization in China. Despite the continuing power of individuals, an important trend of the 1990s is the institutionalization of governance in China. With the death of **Deng Xiaoping** this process has begun to gather momentum. It means that, to a far greater extent than Deng, let alone Mao, **Jiang Zemin** and his colleagues have had to rely on the institutions of the party, government and state to exercise authority and get their way. The other side of the coin is that they are able far less to appeal to personal authority.

Mao Zedong's view on the role of the army in politics was, first, that it was a necessary bulwark of a political order, and second, that the Party should control the army, not the other way around. In practice, the PLA has been highly influential in Chinese administration throughout the history of the PRC,

and at times taken what amounts to a controlling role. After playing a major role in the establishment of the new order, it tended to withdraw after the end of the **Korean War** (1953). However, it came back from time to time from the late 1950s. It was held up as the model for implementing Mao's ideas, exemplified in the campaign to learn from the young soldier Lei Feng begun in March 1963.

The most important period of PLA dominance was the **Cultural Revolution**. Early in 1967, the PLA was actually instructed to intervene because of the breakdown of state law and order. The PLA was one arm of the 'three-way alliance' which made up the **revolutionary committees**, and usually the dominating one. Of the twenty-nine provincial revolutionary committees set up by September 1968, no fewer than twenty had chairmen with PLA affiliations.

PLA units played a crucial role on behalf of the state in the disturbances at the end of Mao's life, leading on to the overthrow of the **gang of four**. Although the PLA has been less overwhelming in politics during the period of reform than that of the **Cultural Revolution**, it has always been necessary for the leadership to ensure the support of the PLA. It was **Deng Xiaoping**'s position as chairman both of the CCP's and the State **Central Military Commission**s which made it possible for him to send in troops to suppress the demonstrations in Beijing in the **June 4 Incident**. Martial law was formally in operation from May 1989 to January 1990 in Beijing and from March 1989 to the end of April 1990 in Lhasa.

see also: Central Military Commission; Chinese Communist Party; Constitutions; Cultural Revolution; Deng Xiaoping; dissidents; gang of four; Hu Yaobang; Hua Guofeng; Jiang Zemin; June 4 Incident; Korean War; legal system; Li Xiannian; Liu Shaoqi; Mao Zedong; Mao Zedong Thought; National Party Congress; National People's Congress; People's Liberation Army; police force; revolutionary committees; State Council; Zhao Ziyang; Zhou Enlai.

3. Ideology: Radicalism and Reform
Bill Brugger

Party ideology, as a set of legitimizing ideas and programmatic goals, lays down the parameters within which policies may be formulated. It is particularly important as an integrative device in a situation where organizations are subject to rapid change and local leaders exercise a high degree of initiative.

Such was the situation in Yan'an in the early 1940s which saw the birth of the ideological system known as **Mao Zedong Thought**, an adaptation of Marxism-Leninism. Indeed, Leninism is itself an adaptation of the ideas of Karl Marx to economically 'backward' conditions in which it is necessary to formulate a revolutionary role for the peasants. **Mao Zedong Thought** in the 1940s constituted a further accommodation to what was seen as a temporary situation in which certain elements of capitalism could still be promoted.

In 1949, therefore, the **Chinese Communist Party** set policies in China within the framework of 'new democracy', aiming to achieve socialism some time in the future. According to the 'new democratic' formula, a 'four class bloc' of workers, peasants, petty bourgeoisie and national capitalists was to exercise 'people's democratic dictatorship', 'bureaucratic capitalists' and 'landlords' being designated as the 'enemy'. According to the CCP, capitalism thrived in such a situation, though constrained by state control over the commanding heights of the economy.

In 1955–6, however, the CCP undertook a rapid programme of socializing industry and commerce and accelerating agricultural cooperativization. But the CCP was wary of declaring in 1956 that China had basically achieved 'socialism'. It seemed unwilling to accept the implications of such a formulation for its 'united front' policy with the petty bourgeoisie and national capitalists. It was also wary of echoing Stalin's position of 1936, which had declared the 'basic achievement' of socialism, because the CCP initially went

along with Nikita Khrushchev's denunciation of Stalin at the Twentieth Congress of the Communist Party of the **Soviet Union** in early 1956. At the CCP's Eighth National Congress in 1956, therefore, it specified the basic contradiction in society not in terms of class struggle against the old enemies but in terms of the relationship between the 'advanced socialist system and the backward productive forces' (the industrial infrastructure, technology and the like). The idea that 'large-scale turbulent class struggle' had ended was a major theme in **Mao Zedong**'s speech 'On the correct handling of contradictions among the people' (1957).

After the launching of the Anti-Rightist Movement later that year, which saw the publication of a revised version of Mao's speech, however, the CCP reaffirmed class struggle against residues of the old society and soon lauded Stalin as a symbol of opposition both to peaceful coexistence with imperialism and to peaceful competition with the US. Despite the radicalism of the late 1950s, the **Great Leap Forward**'s 'uninterrupted revolution' notion, which saw all progress in terms of waves of imbalance punctuated by temporary balance, still rested within the framework of a model of socialism deriving from the Soviet Union. What had changed was the specifications of the model, in particular the relationship between the 'relations of production' and the 'productive forces'. Priority was now accorded to the transformation of both by political mobilization – a view which led to Mao's being accused of 'voluntarism' (an excessive non-Marxist reliance on the human will). This was a far cry from the economic determinism of Leon Trotsky whose 'permanent revolution' many have compared with Mao's uninterrupted revolution.

The basic change in official Chinese thinking on socialist transformation was not to occur until the 1960s. At that time it took the form of a re-formulation of socialism not as a model basically achieved but as a process of continually negating capitalism. That position was to result from Mao's pessimistic view of the prospects for rapid socialist transition, in the aftermath of the economic crisis associated with the **Great Leap Forward** and in the face of doubts about his policies by senior CCP members. It was also, in part, a reaction to the evolution of Khrushchev's theory about socialist transition – the theory of 'building communism' which he had put forward at the Twenty-Second Congress of the Communist Party of the **Soviet Union** (CPSU) (1961).

China's denunciation of the CPSU Twenty-Second Congress programme, 'On Khrushchev's phoney communism and its historical lessons' (1964), took the form of a demonstration of how the **Soviet** advance to communism had been made impossible by the restoration of 'capitalism' in the **Soviet Union**. The official Chinese technique in the 1960s was to present a catalogue of features of **Soviet** 'capitalism', suggesting that these features had become more serious since Stalin's time, and thus conclude that a restoration of capitalism was taking place in the **Soviet Union**. But Mao's analysis went much further than simple conclusions based on behaviour. What later became known as Mao's theory of 'continuous revolution under the dictatorship of the proletariat' did not rest on simple behavioural analysis and prescriptions to counter capitalist behaviour. Mao suggested that power and status differences, in a transitional society, might grow over into class differences defined in relation to the means of production; at one stage he even hinted that counter-revolution might begin in the weakest link of the system, namely in culture.

The resulting view, an extremely radical one, was that new classes could actually grow out of positions of power, particularly within the **Chinese Communist Party** itself; and if they did so, it was possible to sustain the revolutionary process only through a thorough purge of the CCP from without. Mao never presented these arguments in any

systematic form, even though they constituted the theoretical logic of the **Cultural Revolution** (1966–76). What dominated that movement was crude views of conspiracy and denunciations of conscious betrayal of the revolution. Wary of the view that it was possible to generate 'new classes', CCP leaders made recourse to the old theme that the retrogression of the revolution was the result of old enemies. Ideological confusion was such that in 1975 Zhang Chunqiao and Yao Wenyuan, two members of the **gang of four**, tried to develop the need for 'continuous revolution' out of their idiosyncratic reading of Marx's concept of 'bourgeois right': they maintained that an equal standard for evaluating work gives rise to inequality, and thus the only way to combat inequality was through an extreme form of positive discrimination. But many leaders feared the economic consequences of such a view and no sooner had **Mao Zedong** died in 1976 than the gang was arrested and its main ideas discredited.

In the period between the death of Mao and the crucial **Third Plenum of the Eleventh Central Committee** in 1978, **Hua Guofeng**, who held the posts of CCP chairman and premier of the **State Council**, strove to revive Mao's ideas on 'uninterrupted revolution' of the late 1950s referring to them, inaccurately, as 'continuing the revolution'. His aim was to give the appearance of continuity with Mao while distancing himself from the **Cultural Revolution**. Those ideas of Mao from the late 1950s fitted in with Hua's advocacy of a new great leap into modernity (known colloquially as the 'foreign leap' *yang yuejin*).

But, as in so many fields, 1978 saw the beginnings of major changes in the CCP's ideological position. The victory of **Deng Xiaoping**'s 'practice faction' at the **Third Plenum of the Eleventh Central Committee** took its cue from Mao's statement that 'practice is the sole criterion for evaluating truth', as opposed to the views of those who were supposed to have said that whatever Mao said or did was correct. The result was a collapse of the Marxist notion of 'praxis' (teleologically oriented towards a communist goal) into pragmatism. And since practice has meaning only according to some goal, the obvious candidate was 'liberating the productive forces' – or simple economic development regardless of the class consequences.

But the new leadership couched the argument in Marxist language, as they did the plea for 'observing objective economic laws', such as adherence to the 'law of value', meaning that people should exchange goods according to the socially necessary labour time they embodied. It was Stalin who had actually articulated those laws and at various times Mao had affirmed and criticized them. But after the Third Plenum of 1978 interpretations of those laws were more in accordance with orthodox neo-classical economics than with any revolutionary values such as those of the **Cultural Revolution**.

Politically, criticism emerged of China's feudal heritage and the mentality of the 'small peasant producer'. But the post-1978 leaders soon stamped on such criticism, among other reasons because the revived idea of the 'people's democratic dictatorship' accorded an important position to the peasants. Moreover, criticism soon extended from Stalin to Lenin, and more importantly to Mao. To maintain authority, **Deng Xiaoping**, at the end of an important ideology conference in 1979, declared that all discussion should take place within his 'four cardinal principles': maintenance of Marxism-Leninism **Mao Zedong Thought**, the socialist path, leadership of the Communist Party and the dictatorship of the proletariat.

But in the new situation, those four principles lacked clarity – particularly the first. In 1981, therefore, the Party came to a definitive assessment of Mao and his thought (see **Sixth Plenum of the Eleventh Central Committee**). The official 'Resolution on Party history' declared that Mao had been a great Marxist-Leninist who made serious mistakes in his later years. Apparently, Mao at that stage departed from '**Mao Zedong Thought**' which the Sixth Plenum depicted as the collective product of the Party. Attempts to restore the

line of the Eighth Party Congress, which had declared the main contradiction in society to be between the 'advanced socialist system' and the 'backward productive forces', failed in the light of the observation that the 'socialist system' was not all that advanced. There began to be talk of 'undeveloped socialism', dictated by the development of the productive forces, which implied that the changes in the mid-1950s were undertaken prematurely.

Undeveloped socialism provided a rationale for the decollectivization of agriculture but the CCP did not adopt that notion officially until 1987, calling it the 'primary stage of socialism', and only after disciplining its most eloquent exponent, Su Shaozhi, for 'bourgeois liberalization'. The above thinking reflected a mechanical Marxist theory of stages of development and the notion of socialism as a model (or series of sub-models), far from the thinking of Mao in his later years.

The loosely connected set of ideas which constituted ideology in the early 1980s contributed among some people to an 'emancipation of the mind'. Others, however, began to lose faith in official ideology. For some, chagrined by mechanical materialism, dressed up in Marxist guise, the call for a 'socialist spiritual civilization' could have offered a new socialist vision, while for others it was merely a dogmatic profession of content-less faith. Some socialists sought to infuse ideology with the richness of wider Marxist analysis, to combine it with other strands of theory and to utilize the early Marx to inform contemporary critique. But the repeated campaigns of the 1980s to combat 'spiritual pollution' or 'bourgeois liberalization' produced among most people a cynicism and, among a few, a spirit of resistance. Although it is resistance on which many Western commentators have focused, the cynicism is probably more important.

Such Western commentators might be confused by the sight of a CCP general secretary, **Zhao Ziyang**, extolling a form of neo-authoritarianism not unlike that of the modernizing Asian 'tigers', and at the same time opposing Marxist critics who affirmed democracy, only to find himself dismissed as a supporter of 'bourgeois democratic' turmoil. They might also be confused by the fact that the Fourteenth **National Party Congress** in 1992 seemed to adopt Zhao's neo-authoritarian programme without rehabilitating Zhao and even more so, in his continual eclipse, by the 1997 Fifteenth Congress reaffirming the 'primary stage of socialism' as a justification for corporatizing state-owned enterprises. A looser definition of 'public ownership' is now heralded as a cardinal element of 'Deng Xiaoping Theory' of 'building socialism with Chinese characteristics', enshrined in the 1997 Party Constitution.

The party is left in an ideological vacuum. When it faces ideological problems, the CCP can, and often does, invoke nationalism; but to be credible it needs to give concrete content to its various official formulations – such as 'a socialist commodity economy' or, more recently, a 'socialist market system', which deprives the word 'socialist' even of the strand of **planning** and makes it a synonym for authoritarianism. Marx was sufficiently an admirer of capitalism to provide enough ideological support for a 'socialist market economy'. It is easy to forget that he was also a supreme critic of ideology, by which he meant a system of ideas and practices which legitimize the interests of a dominant class.

see also: Chinese Communist Party; Constitutions; Cultural Revolution; Deng Xiaoping; gang of four; Great Leap Forward; Hua Guofeng; Mao Zedong; Mao Zedong Thought; National Party Congress; planning, economic; Sixth Plenum of the Eleventh Central Committee; Soviet Union, relations with; State Council; Third Plenum of the Eleventh Central Committee; Zhao Ziyang.

4. Political Personae: Biographical Profiles

Frederick C. Teiwes

Mao Zedong once referred to the '800 people who rule China', a statement emphasizing the enormous importance of political leadership in shaping PRC history. In fact, the fate of the Chinese people has for a long time rested in the hands of a small handful of individuals and, at crucial junctures, solely with Mao himself. The unusual degree of leadership dominance of society for the Maoist period in particular had both broad cultural and historical specific roots: a culture of obedience to strong leadership, and a revolutionary process producing unimaginable success which led the elite and public to believe **Chinese Communist Party** leaders had the right to rule and transform China. A corollary to this is the tremendous importance of relationships among the political personae occupying the highest positions in the Party, relationships which by the 1990s involved more than sixty years of interaction for various key figures. This interaction was by no means static; it underwent dramatic changes under Mao from a very stable leadership for most of the 1950s to a less secure but still relatively unchanged power structure in the pre-**Cultural Revolution** decade, to the internecine turmoil of the **Cultural Revolution** itself. Throughout this drama links to the revolutionary past were everpresent; political power usually derived more from revolutionary status than current performance. With the post-Mao period the importance of such status, which had been partially disrupted by the **Cultural Revolution**, was restored with the dominance of **Deng Xiaoping** whose decisions were obeyed largely because of his exceptional revolutionary prestige. But with Deng and his veteran colleagues ageing, policy formulation as well as administration, although initially not ultimate power, fell to a younger generation of leaders lacking comparable revolutionary credentials, with the result that in the 1990s the leadership group under **Jiang Zemin** engaged in a 'normal politics' where leaders were much more vulnerable to social forces and the relations among them reflected political bargaining rather than the obedience that had marked the rule of Mao and, to a lesser extent, Deng.

After early Party history where leaders were frequently changed at the behest of the Comintern, Mao Zedong began his rise to power during the Long March in 1935 as a result of the failures of factional rivals to forge a successful strategy against superior Nationalist (Guomindang) forces. It took nearly a decade for Mao to reshape the CCP around his own programme and attain unchallenged authority. These years to the Seventh Party Congress (1945) saw not only the systematization of Mao's strategy which maximized the CCP's position and the adoption of **Mao Zedong Thought** as official orthodoxy, but also the formation of a new leadership loyal to himself. Mao shaped a broad-based leadership rather than a clique of personal followers. **Liu Shaoqi**, who of all leaders had been most clear-sighted about past mistakes and consistent in his support of Mao but not personally close to him, became the designated successor, while **Zhou Enlai** became number three despite past differences with the new leader. This approach of unifying the 'mountaintops', i.e. all the separate groupings formed over the course of Party history, stood both the revolutionary cause and Mao's personal prestige well, but what was crucial was revolutionary success. When that was achieved in 1949, Mao's reputation and power soared to truly unprecedented heights.

From the founding of the PRC to the **Great Leap Forward** in 1958 the features of the preceding period continued to mark leadership practice:
- Mao's decisive authority;
- his willingness to listen to the advice of his colleagues and delegate authority;

- a broad consensus on direction (the **Soviet model**);
- relative tolerance of 'mistakes' by his colleagues; and
- a wide sharing-out of power among Party 'mountaintops'.

Most policies of this period were centrist and drew broad support, while the two occasions when Mao made individual decisions against the better judgement of his colleagues – entry into the **Korean War** and the speedup of agricultural cooperativization in 1955 (see **collective agriculture**) – were retrospectively viewed as correct and further proof of his special insight. Yet even after the cooperativization drive Mao continued to heed the advice of his colleagues, notably **Zhou Enlai** and **Chen Yun** on the need to curb the 'rash advance' resulting from the 'little leap forward' of 1956. The main leadership conflict in the period before the **Great Leap Forward** was the 1953–4 Gao Gang affair, a complex matter involving Mao's temporary dissatisfaction with **Liu Shaoqi** and **Zhou Enlai** and perceptions that military 'mountaintops' were about to be shortchanged in a reshuffled Party leadership. Politburo member Gao was removed from power by Mao for destabilizing Party unity, although the chairman was hardly blameless in the matter. Another consequence was the promotion of Mao's two favourite leaders and longtime supporters: **Lin Biao** and **Deng Xiaoping**.

The relationship among Party leaders changed dramatically with the Great Leap. The roots of the Leap and the changed intra-elite dynamics lay in an earlier episode launched by Mao, the spring 1957 **Hundred Flowers Movement**. Contrary to much scholarly argument, there was little high-level opposition to Mao's initiative nor any loss of power on his part as a result of its failure, but failure was not something Mao was used to or prepared to accept as his fault. While the Great Leap reflected a widespread desire for rapid growth and problems with existing policies, its political animus can be found in Mao's unwarranted conclusion that the 'rightists' of the **Hundred Flowers** period had gained encouragement from the 'mistaken' policies of 'opposing rash advance' in 1956–7. Mao alone determined the new policy direction, albeit with enthusiastic support from local leaders, but more significantly he turned it into a question of political line. At the January 1958 Nanning conference Mao launched an unprecedented scathing attack on **Zhou Enlai**, **Chen Yun** and others, creating an atmosphere where 'it was impossible to say anything different'. Nanning was thus a turning point in stifling intra-leadership debate even though no one was purged; the better known turning point at the Lushan conference in summer 1959 saw the process carried an additional step when Peng Dehuai's clumsy intervention to encourage Mao to go further in the effort to curb leftist excesses that the chairman had initiated the previous fall resulted in Mao's bitter reaction, the purge of Peng and others, and a new attempt to leap forward that resulted in tens of millions of deaths in the 1959–61 famine.

When Mao and the leadership as a whole finally faced up to the seriousness of the problem in 1960, a series of measures effectively dismantling the Great Leap were put into effect. Clearly **Liu Shaoqi**, **Deng Xiaoping** and others played critical parts in this process, but always with Mao's approval and his key role in the crucial agricultural area. Yet leaders remained wary of being too forthright, as seen in **Chen Yun**'s begging off from Mao's invitation to speak at the January 1962 7,000 cadres conference on the calculation that the chairman was still unwilling to face up to the full seriousness of the crisis. Chen was perceptive, for Mao silently resented **Liu Shaoqi**'s devastating summary of the situation even though he had urged Liu to make it, and touted **Lin Biao**'s observation to the same gathering that the problem was not following the chairman closely enough as a brilliant speech beyond the ability of others. Moreover, by summer 1962 Mao concluded the retreat had gone too far, shunted Chen aside, and initiated a limited turnaround under the slogan 'never forget class struggle'. The problem was that class struggle and work were 'two different kinds of problems', and 'our work must not be jeopardized just because of class struggle'. Dealing with this paradox was left to leaders on the 'first front', Liu, Deng, Zhou and their colleagues. Under discussion since 1952, the 'two fronts of leadership' was designed as a method whereby Mao would be freed for large issues on the 'second front' while Liu and the others would oversee daily work and in the process build up their prestige for an orderly succession. Now, however, with the country groping for new directions after the devastation of the famine, and Mao unable to offer clear guidelines but growing increasingly dissatisfied with the malaise in society and the performance of the 'first front', the 'two fronts' functioned as a parody of itself: those on the 'first front' would devise policies they believed both necessary and likely to win Mao's backing, and then take them to the chairman for approval or veto. While Mao usually approved the policies brought to him, his amorphous dissatisfaction only grew, merged with the feeling that he was somehow losing control, and increasingly focused on **Liu Shaoqi** as the leader of the 'first front', even though Liu had been the 'first front' figure most in tune with the chairman's 'leftist' impulses.

The result was the **Cultural Revolution**, a movement originating in a curious mixture of Mao's vendetta against Liu, a radical vision calling for a selfless society and participatory polity, and paranoid fears about an imaginary loss of power. The immediate result was the replacement of Liu by **Lin Biao** as successor in mid-1966, an event seen as credible even by Liu's supporters, despite Lin's poor health and lack of civilian experience, because of Lin's enormous revolutionary status as a military leader. Over the next three years of intense turmoil, established political leaders offered no direct resistance to Mao's orders even when their own careers and lives were at stake, suffered sharp attacks by previously fringe elite participants such as Mao's wife, Jiang Qing, and largely avoided attacks on one another except when Mao's views made such attacks mandatory – a phenomenon reflected in **Zhou Enlai**'s efforts to protect leaders under attack yet his willingness

to join the attacks in the harshest terms once Mao's opinion was clear. As for **Liu Shaoqi**, he died after three years of Mao-sanctioned physical abuse, in contrast to **Deng Xiaoping** who was protected by Mao despite his removal from office. Meanwhile, military officials moved into key posts due to the vacuum created by the disruption to civilian bodies, but **Lin Biao** adopted an essentially passive strategy, largely acting according to what he could fathom of Mao's intentions. The pathetic denouement came in 1970–1 when, as a result of tensions between members of **Lin Biao**'s group and Jiang Qing's civilian radicals, Lin's people raised the issue of Mao's 'genius', only to be confounded when the chairman rejected the notion. After a year of growing dissatisfaction – not because of policy issues or power plays but due to 'insufficient' self-criticisms of those concerned – Mao foreshadowed a showdown which led Lin to flee and perish in an air crash.

The period from **Lin Biao**'s demise to Mao's own death was marked by a bitter conflict between Jiang Qing's radicals, immortalized by the chairman's description as a **gang of four**, and the survivors of the pre-**Cultural Revolution** establishment led by **Zhou Enlai** and, following his rehabilitation in 1973 on Mao's initiative, **Deng Xiaoping**. Mao, whose health was in serious decline from 1972, was unwilling to choose between the two forces which he saw as representing fidelity to **Cultural Revolution** ideals and skilled leadership respectively, intermittently lashing out against the 'excesses' of each. In between were younger Politburo members such as **Hua Guofeng** who would never have achieved their standing without the **Cultural Revolution**, but who basically implemented Deng's policies. Finally, fearing Deng would 'reverse verdicts' on the **Cultural Revolution**, Mao endorsed criticism of Deng and denied him the succession to premier when Zhou died in January 1976. Mao's rejection of Deng was not total, however, and it was only the April **Tiananmen Incident** reflecting popular support of Deng and disgust with the radicals that led Mao to sanction Deng's removal from office (but not expulsion from the Party) and Hua's formal appointment as premier. With Mao terminally ill, both groups plotted for the succession but the dominant forces of the old guard led by **Ye Jianying** held their hand in respect for Mao until he passed away, then moving decisively to arrest the gang within a month of the chairman's death.

Hua Guofeng was quickly named Party chairman, but was in a vulnerable position given his lack of revolutionary status. While much analysis sees the next two years as a power struggle between Hua and Deng, this was not the case. Although Hua seemingly sought to delay Deng's return the only issues were timing and terms, and once back in office by mid-1977 Deng had an authoritative voice. The situation was complicated in that Hua had formal authority and much real power, but once Deng spoke Hua did not challenge him. Also, many of the initiatives commonly assigned to Deng in fact came from others like **Hu Yaobang** with little if any Deng involvement initially, while Deng's role was to intervene and provide political muscle to push such policies through. By the time of the **Third Plenum of the Eleventh Central Committee** at the end of 1978 the reform orientation associated with Deng was in place, Deng was unambiguously if informally the top leader, and Hua had suffered a reversal of fortunes that would continue until his removal as chairman in 1981.

Deng's acceptance as leader even without the formal office underlines the importance of revolutionary status. In addition to being the highest ranking veteran (with **Chen Yun**) of the Maoist era, Deng had enormous *military* prestige as one of the key figures in the civil war. Despite claims that Deng was limited by a struggle with Chen, once Deng made a decision it was usually obeyed without

argument, and Chen, as with Mao earlier, always accepted the authority of his leader notwithstanding substantive differences. During this period, the reform version of the 'two fronts' created great difficulties for the younger officials handling detailed policy formulation on the 'first front'. These officials had to deal not only with Deng and Chen, but also with a range of influential veteran leaders on the 'second front' with diverse ideas and important followers. Unlike these old cadres they could not invoke a sacred revolutionary prestige, but instead had to rely on a combination of performance and political alliances. The two 'first front' leaders removed in the 1980s, **Hu Yaobang** and **Zhao Ziyang**, ran afoul of conservative elders and unpredictable events in the student movements of 1986 and 1989 respectively, but they also failed as political leaders. In Hu's case it was the alienation of a broad range of key political constituencies, and in Zhao's a policy programme that proved unable to control inflation. The trend was set for the future leadership of **Jiang Zemin** as the influence of the revolutionary veterans inevitably faded: leaders drawn from diverse bureaucratic backgrounds without unusually long association or unchallengeable status now faced each other as political managers, with interests to be accommodated or fought over, and current performance rather than past heroics the key to political standing.

see also: Chen Yun; Chinese Communist Party; collective agriculture; Cultural Revolution; Deng Xiaoping; gang of four; Great Leap Forward; Hu Yaobang; Hua Guofeng; Hundred Flowers Movement; Jiang Zemin; Korean War; Lin Biao; Liu Shaoqi; Mao Zedong; Mao Zedong Thought; Soviet Union, relations with; Third Plenum of the Eleventh Central Committee; Tiananmen Incident (1976); Ye Jianying; Zhao Ziyang; Zhou Enlai.

5. Politics and the Economy: Policy Patterns and Issues
Andrew Watson

Debate over economic issues has been a central feature of the political process in China since 1949. The **Chinese Communist Party** came to power on the basis of a rural demand for economic justice and with a commitment to build China into a strong, independent, modern, industrial power. Its ideology was shaped by a view of society that gave priority to the economic base, consisting of the forces of production and the social relationships they embodied. The Party was determined to transform China into a socialist society, in which the role of private ownership and the market was to be curtailed and public ownership and planning were to shape economic development. **Mao Zedong** was also particularly concerned with the social relations to be created in the socialist state and with the underlying moral system. His focus was one of egalitarian development, self-reliance and self-sacrifice to the building of the new society.

The practical policies to achieve these broad goals, however, were constrained by problems of scarcity and uncertainty. Each phase in the evolution of economic policy was thus associated with profound debate over the ideological foundations, the social effects, the practical outcomes and the long-term goals.

As a result, the economic changes associated with economic rehabilitation (1949–52), collectivization (see **collective agriculture**) and the First Five-Year Plan (1953–7), the **Great Leap Forward** (1958–61), economic readjustment (1962–65), the **Cultural Revolution** (1966–76), the post-Mao transition (1976–8) and the reforms (1978 to the present) served as the defining issues for shifts in the political debate and leadership struggles. Political developments in China since 1949 must thus be defined in terms of the cycles of economic policies.

Economic rehabilitation was both a period of restoration of economic health and a process of transition. Initially it was linked to political ideas of a period of 'new democracy' in which there would be a mixed economy and a united front between the CCP and other social forces in order to generate a renaissance in economic growth. The period was also associated with land reform, which redistributed wealth in the countryside and created a more equal small peasant society. Within that process, however, there were debates about the extent to which the capitalist economy should be tolerated and the speed with which the process of socialist transformation should begin. Campaigns against bureaucracy, waste, corruption and economic malpractices aimed to re-educate officials and reduce the authority of private entrepreneurs. And land reform was introduced against the background of debate over the extent to which the rich peasants should be spared. Though a lenient position was adopted, some later accused certain CCP members of obstructing the depth of the reform. While this period was very successful in restoring the economy, the intensification of the Cold War and the increasing reliance on the **Soviet Union** heralded a rapid shift towards a planned economy.

The policies of collectivization and the First Five-Year Plan drew on both the experience of the CCP in rural cooperatives before 1949 and the model of the **Soviet Union**. In that process, **Chen Yun** played a leading role in shaping economic policy. The adoption of the plan system was associated with a rapid end to the mixed economy approach and the 'socialist transformation' of private **industry**. By 1956, the market and private enterprise had ceased to play any role in the industrial economy, and the state system monopolized economic activity.

Many gains were made in industrial output, but Mao became concerned that the centralized system was generating a new bureaucratic elite, which he saw as the source of revisionist political ideas. In the country-side the introduction of cooperatives and collectives was also used as a mechanism to abolish private ownership and to make agricultural production subordinate to state needs (see **agriculture**). Initially Mao had argued that cooperativization would take fifteen or more years. As the dependence of industrial growth on the supply of raw materials and resources from the rural sector became clear, however, there was increasing pressure to accelerate the process. Apart from the speed of transformation, questions of the size and scale of collectives, the role of small family plots and sidelines, and the freedoms for peasants to produce for small local markets were also subjects for debate.

Mao was optimistic about the gains to be made from large size and stressed the importance of collective incentives. Others argued that mechanization and technical development should precede rapid collectivization. Difficulties in implementation slowed the process late in 1956, and Mao called for open debate on party policies during the **Hundred Flowers Movement**. The wave of criticism he provoked led to a strong backlash. In the Anti-Rightist Movement of 1957, many of Mao's critics were denounced and sent for re-education. This laid the foundation for the **Great Leap Forward** in which Mao revived his push for greater levels of rural collectivization and also sought to correct the failings he saw in the **Soviet** model.

The **Great Leap Forward** was the quintessential expression of Mao's approach to economic policy. Mao stepped outside the formal structures of economic management and encouraged a major social movement to transform the economy. It was a period of great optimism in which technical controls and reliable figures were brushed aside in favour of a race to overtake advanced economies.

Opposition was seen as political resistance. In the countryside, the collectives were transformed into huge people's communes and labour was mobilized for both agricultural infrastructure such as canals and road build-ing and for industrial production. In **industry**, there was considerable decentralization of controls and a huge surge in local and central investment. The lack of controls and effective management, however, resulted in much waste. During 1959, the leap collapsed in the face of bad harvests, overheating and inefficient investment. The break with the **Soviet Union** also cut off China's main source of aid and technical inputs. It is estimated that some 30 million people died. The economy entered a period of decline and did not return to 1957 levels until 1965.

In the readjustment period that followed the **Great Leap Forward**, **Liu Shaoqi** and **Deng Xiaoping** became more prominent in managing the economy, and a series of pragmatic policies were introduced. The internal scale of the people's communes was reduced, and in some places forms of individual contracting were introduced.

Small-scale rural free markets reappeared. Labour drawn into the cities returned to the countryside, and many projects were abandoned. Efforts were also made to reassert central controls over economic management. Expertise regained emphasis in the 'red and expert' duality.

While these policies gradually nursed the economy back to health, they also generated the political debates which fuelled the struggles of the **Cultural Revolution**. Mao saw the retreats in policy as vindication of his view that the new state system was becoming revisionist and retreating from socialist goals. He blamed the failings of the leap on implementation rather than on the policies themselves. He also set out to regain central political power. In doing so, he created the framework in which factions within the CCP expressed struggle in ideological and economic terms. The initial stages of this process were expressed through Mao's critique of the **Soviet Union**. It was extended by rural campaigns to educate rural cadres and to reassert the collective model as represented by the **Dazhai** Brigade. The army and social models like Lei Feng were used to promote Mao's emphasis on self-reliance, self-sacrifice and egalitarian principles. Once again Mao stepped outside the administrative system to mobilize youth, who formed the Red Guards of the **Cultural Revolution**.

Though Mao and his supporters launched the **Cultural Revolution** in the ideological sphere, the essence of their attack focused on economic issues. Key elements included:

- denunciation of revisionist policies alleged to be leading to the regrowth of private ownership and market forces;
- reaffirmation of the egalitarian collective model for rural development;
- criticism of the role of economic and material incentives;
- assertion of the importance of physical labour in generating economic development;
- emphasis on 'redness' (political rectitude) over technical expertise; and
- attacks on the bureaucratic hierarchy for following the 'capitalist road'.

Much of the debate was expressed through discussion of policy initiatives in the 1940s and 1950s and through theories of the nature of socialist transformation and socialist society. The 'socialist' policy of payment for work done was thus seen as a continued expression of 'bourgeois right' since it failed to account for the unequal basis on which individuals engaged in production. Various factions linked such theoretical economic debates to the advancement of their political legitimacy, seeking evidence to demonstrate the economic revisionism of opponents.

The initial and most violent phase of the **Cultural Revolution** from 1966 to 1969 saw considerable disruption to the economy. After 1969, the restoration of order through the involvement of the military in administration brought about a gradual return to stable economic management. Within that framework, however, a range of experiments were implemented in the economic, administrative, educational and cultural spheres to try to realize the principles Mao was advocating. Mao's advancing years also encouraged increasing factional struggles beneath him The **Lin Biao** affair of 1971 represented a profound blow to Mao's position and began a process of retreat from the more radical polit-

ical positions. Changing external circumstances, primarily the military clashes with the **Soviet Union** in the late 1960s and the winding down of the Vietnam War, also changed the pressures on the Chinese economy. During the 1970s, therefore, political debate and changes in economic policy reflected the fluctuations in the positions of the various leadership factions. From the early 1970s China began to increase its interaction with western economies, experienced leaders such as **Deng Xiaoping** were rehabilitated, and in 1975 **Zhou Enlai** put forward the first call for China to achieve the **Four Modernizations**. Such efforts to switch the emphasis from class struggle to more technical and economically based development programmes, however, were always open to attack from the more radical Maoist position and led to another period out of office for **Deng Xiaoping**.

This uncertain phase did not come to an end until after Mao's death in September 1976 and the subsequent arrest of the **gang of four**. While political and economic debate remained couched within the discourse and language Mao had established, the period to late 1978 saw foundations laid for the shift away from both Mao's experiments and the system of **planning**. **Deng Xiaoping**, who still saw economic policy as dominated by the plan system, argued that primacy should be given to the role of 'objective economic laws' over social and economic development. The ideas of the reform economists of the early 1960s readjustment period were rehabilitated, and many of the officials denounced and removed during the **Cultural Revolution** were brought back to work. It was suggested that once the system of ownership had changed, class struggle was over and the focus should shift to economic growth. The political legitimacy of the CCP should thus depend on the realization of the **Four Modernizations** and the achievement of rapid economic development.

The reforms launched first in rural policy in December 1978 did not set out with a clear blueprint for change. Five general goals were identified:

- greater emphasis on improving consumption and living standards;
- greater economic efficiency;
- greater economic diversity in terms of ownership;
- acceptance of a role for the market; and
- greater openness to trade and the world economy.

Thereafter a series of experiments and pragmatic adjustments were made to achieve those aims. In many instances the experiments and demands from below exceeded the extent of official policy and forced further adjustment. In other cases, political leaders used economic experiments as a means of promoting their political standing. As they evolved, therefore, the reforms began to break out of the planned economy framework and built up their own momentum. Inevitably this also generated further political debate as established orthodoxy was undermined and new problems arose. The pragmatic nature of the process also led to internal inconsistencies and periods of hesitation and retreat. The political cycle thus came to reflect the economic cycle very closely.

A relaxation of planning policy and the introduction of more market-oriented reforms stimulated a phase of rapid growth. As the economy overheated, bottlenecks, friction between remaining plan and new market forces, and inflation began to threaten economic and social stability. This then led to a period of hesitation and the reassertion of authority. Given the lack of effective macroeconomic mechanisms for managing market forces, this invariably meant strong administrative intervention. The troughs in the cycle were associated with efforts by the 'conservative' left to reassert the principles of the socialist planned economy and changes in the central leadership, when leaders such as **Hu Yaobang** and **Zhao Ziyang** were criticized for failing to handle the crises they confronted. Meanwhile, many reform economists proposed increasingly fundamental changes to systems of ownership and reliance on markets as necessary to ensure efficient macroeconomic management and the reform of state enterprises.

The most severe of these cycles came in 1989, in the wake of the sharp austerity programme introduced in 1988 to cool down the economy. Students, intellectuals and workers, alarmed at rising prices, growing economic insecurity and burgeoning economic corruption, began to link economic reform to political reform and called for a transformation of the political system. Their massive demonstrations in most of China's major cities resulted in the brutal reassertion of CCP authority in the **June 4 Incident**. Although this led to an uncertain period in 1990 and 1991 when a retreat from the reforms appeared possible, the economic costs of the slowdown of 1990 threatened to undermine the entire process of growth and made such a retreat unworkable. Eventually, **Deng Xiaoping** made a much publicized tour of southern China early in 1992 and reasserted China's open economy policies and his reform programme. Thereafter a new reform cycle began and economic growth accelerated to high levels.

By the mid-1990s some seventeen years of reform had transformed the Chinese economy. Annual growth rates of around 9 to 10 per cent had quadrupled its size, China was deeply engaged in the world economy, and the entire energy of the political system was focused on economic and material growth. Nevertheless, the pragmatic nature of the reforms, the lack of a decisive shift to a full market system, and the remaining friction between plan and market forces had created a set of new economic issues which had come to dominate the political agenda. These included:

- regional disparities between the developed eastern coast and the more backward interior;
- conflict between the central government and provincial governments over resources and economic policies;
- a growing sense of crisis in the inefficient state-owned enterprises; and
- the need to implement financial, fiscal and pricing reforms which would create effective levers for economic management of a market economy.

Given the relative success of China's gradualist approach over the previous years, further pragmatic experiment was under way. The position adopted by **Jiang Zemin** at the Fifteenth Party Congress in September 1997 also heralded a further surge in state enterprise reform. The process of gradual reform was thus set to continue. This also implied, however, that the potential for further cycles of economic policy and growth remained strong, with inevitable implications for the politics of reform.

see also: 1. Overview History of the People's Republic of China; 3. Ideology: Radicalism and Reform; 8. China, the Region and the World; agriculture; Chen Yun; Chinese Communist Party; collective agriculture; Cultural Revolution; Dazhai; Deng Xiaoping; Four Modernizations; gang of four; Great Leap Forward; Hu Yaobang; Hundred Flowers Movement; industry; Jiang Zemin; June 4 Incident; Lin Biao; Liu Shaoqi; Mao Zedong; planning, economic; Soviet Union, relations with; Zhao Ziyang; Zhou Enlai.

6. Peoples of China
Colin Mackerras

Although the Chinese terms *min*, meaning a or the 'people', and *zu*, corresponding roughly to an 'ethnic group', have been in use since ancient times, the combination, or *minzu*, is not found until the 1880s. The word means 'nation' or 'nationality' and has been subject to various definitions and understandings. Official circles in the PRC have adopted a definition based closely on one propounded by Stalin in 1913, and although it is not universally accepted by any means, it is the one most commonly used by Chinese scholars and government workers. It states that a *minzu* is 'a historically constituted stable community of people, having a common language, a common territory, a common economic life and a common psychological makeup which expresses itself in a common culture'.

From this definition the Chinese state recognizes fifty-six nationalities in those territories ruled as of the mid-1990s as the PRC, that is not including Hong Kong or Macau. Of these, the most populous is the Han, while the remainder are termed **minority nationalities**.

The table shows the Han and total minority populations in the four PRC censuses, those of 1953, 1964, 1982 and 1990. The 1995 sample census showed that by 1 October that year the proportion of Han people had declined to 91.02 per cent, while that of the minorities had risen to 8.98 per cent.

Other than the people whom the four censuses classified as belonging to 'not yet identified nationalities', of whom there were 752,347 in 1990, everybody in China is registered as belonging to one of the fifty-six officially state-recognized nationalities. In cases where a person's parents are of different nationalities, it is normally the father's which is the determining one. Yet the issue of identification is often far from simple. The state's view of a person's or group's nationality is not always shared by the people themselves or by their neighbours.

The two main linguistic groups represented in the PRC are the Sino-Tibetan and Altaic. The overwhelming majority of the people of China speak a language belonging to the first of these groups, and within that group by far the most important and widespread language is Chinese.

The Han

Although all classified as belonging to a single nationality, the Han people demonstrate a great many linguistic, cultural and other variations. Mostly these are regionally based, but over history migration has resulted in substantial intermixing and intermarriage between peoples of different localities.

Despite the variations, there are many consistencies among the Han people. They are agricultural, not pastoral, their diet dominated by rice in the south or wheat-based products in the north, with pork a favourite

Year of census	Han	Minorities
1953 total	547,283,057	35,320,360
percentage	93.94	6.06
1964 total	651,296,368	39,923,736
percentage	94.22	5.78
1982 total	936,674,944	67,245,090
percentage	93.30	6.70
1990 total	1,039,187,548	91,323,090
percentage	91.92	8.08

form of meat. Their culture is based on Confucianism because of their history, with Confucian values retaining strong influence to this day, despite the insertion of Marxism-Leninism. In particular, the concept of loyalty to the family, which derives from Confucianism, is very strong among the vast majority of Han Chinese. Although Buddhism, Daoism and folk religions retain following among ordinary Chinese people, Han political culture has always been noted for its secularity, priests and clergy having never exercised great influence, let alone control, in government and political life.

The Chinese language shows some very strong consistencies everywhere. The Chinese written language, among the most ancient of surviving scripts, is understandable to all but a very few literate people in China, and certainly displays virtually no regional differences. The structure, vocabulary, syntax and grammar of the language is largely the same everywhere, despite some comparatively minor variations in lexicology and grammar. By far the most important difference is the pronunciation, which shows very strong regional variations.

The official language of China is called *putong hua*, meaning literally 'the common words'. In 1997 the State Language Work Committee announced a plan to adopt instead the name *tongyong yu*, literally 'commonly used language', one reason being the implication in the earlier title that non-official languages, such as those of the minorities, were somehow abnormal or 'uncommon'. The Nationalist Party (Guomindang) describes the language as *guoyu*, or 'national language', but this is a difference of name, not substance. The most formal English translation of the terms is 'Modern Standard Chinese', but many people refer to the language as Mandarin. This language is based on the pronunciation found in Beijing.

Although the term Mandarin is not universally accepted as valid to describe the official language of China, it is certainly legitimate to refer to the Mandarin dialects, which are the ones closest to Modern Standard Chinese. There are four main

groups of these on the Chinese mainland, as follows:

- Northern Mandarin dialects, spoken in Beijing and the northeastern provinces of China, as well as in several provinces south of Beijing;
- Northwestern Mandarin dialects, spoken in northwestern provinces such as Gansu and Shaanxi, as well as the Ningxia Hui Autonomous Region;
- Southwestern Mandarin dialects, spoken in Sichuan, Hubei and Yunnan provinces; and
- Eastern Mandarin dialects, spoken around Nanjing and part of the Lower Yangzi Valley.

In the mid-1980s, Leo Moser estimated the number of speakers of the Mandarin dialects at about 700 million. Of these it was the Northern Mandarin dialects which were most important, with some 330 million speakers.

In addition to these there are seven main distinct southern Chinese sub-languages. These are:

- Cantonese, or Yue, spoken in Guangdong and Guangxi;
- Shanghai dialect, or Wu, spoken in parts of Jiangsu Province and most of neighbouring Zhejiang;
- Hunanese, or Xiang, spoken in Hunan Province;
- Jiangxi dialect, or Gan, spoken in Jiangxi Province;
- Southern Fujian dialect, or Minnan, spoken in southern Fujian Province and by most in Hainan Province;
- Northern Fujian dialect, Minbei, spoken in northern Fujian Province; and
- Hakka, spoken by the Hakkas scattered throughout southern China.

Moser estimated the number of speakers of these sub-languages in the mid-1980s at about 300 million. The one with the largest number of speakers was the Shanghai dialect, spoken by some 85 million people, followed by Cantonese, with about 55 million.

Other than linguistic differences, regional variations are quite strong among the Han people. Some cultural phenomena which tend to follow linguistic variations are distinctive music and theatre, cuisine, festivals, clothing, marriage customs, village architecture and burial customs. The regional theatre styles, for instance, use not only the local dialect but also distinct musical instruments and, sometimes, melodies. Although some regions have their own stories, on the whole these do not vary widely from place to place.

Another area of consistency, accompanied by strong variations, is food. The northern Chinese place great emphasis on steamed wheat rolls and dumplings with or without filling and there are some world-famous dishes like Peking duck. Western China, and especially provinces such as Sichuan and Hunan, is noted for its spicy dishes. In the east, including the Lower Yangzi Valley, soups and stews are very popular, and there is an immense variety of fish and other seafood; heavy use is made of lard and peanut oil, with the result that eastern food is more oily than that of other regions. Cantonese and other southern food is noted for its very quick cooking and stir-frying at high temperatures, and in addition for its rich and filling sweet dishes.

Chinese people are convinced of the genuineness of regional variations in culture and even extend these to differences in behaviour and character. They frequently speak of other Chinese in a way similar to that by which Europeans brand other Europeans with 'national characteristics'. For instance, Cantonese have the reputation for being very good in business, while Hunanese are often described as hot-tempered.

One subgroup of the Han Chinese which has aroused particular interest both inside and outside China is the Hakka people, of whom there were estimated to be some 30 million world-wide in the early 1990s. The term *hakka* means 'guest families', possibly because the Hakka came originally from the north of China, but settled in the south, notably territory in the border areas of Guangdong, Fujian, Jiangxi, Hunan and Guangxi. The Hakkas were at the forefront of the Taiping rebellion of 1850 to 1866, their

leader Hong Xiuquan belonging to this subgroup.

One respect in which the Hakka distinguished themselves from other Han people was that their women never bound their feet. This has led to the suggestion that Hakka women are better treated and more independent than other Han women, as well as being very industrious farm labourers. In the nineteenth century Western observers noted that Hakka men, even rich ones, took concubines less frequently than other Han.

The Hakka have, in general, developed the reputation for being shrewd and industrious, but not very good at business. They are known as the most song-loving Han Chinese group, the content emphasizing stories about Hakka ancestors and heroic tales of past Hakka struggles. In the twentieth century, the Hakkas have been noted for their feelings of ethnic identity and consciousness. However, under the PRC all attempts to get them recognized as a nationality separate from the Han have met with total failure.

The Minority Nationalities

The fifty-five minorities fall into several distinct groups. Most are physically similar to the Han. The main exceptions are the Turkic peoples of Xinjiang, speaking Altaic languages, the most populous of which are the Uygurs. Other than Chinese, the Sino-Tibetan language family includes the Zhuang-Dong, Tibeto-Burman and Miao-Yao language groups, spoken by a wide range of minorities living throughout Southwest China, in **Tibet**, Yunnan, Guizhou, Guangxi and Hunan. The Koreans of Northeast China, who numbered 1,923,361 according to the 1990 census, are ethnically identical to their co-nationals in Korea. Two of the main minorities are now Chinese-speaking. These are the Hui, whose distinguishing feature is their adherence to Islam, and the Manchus, who absorbed Han Chinese features and came close to assimilation during the centuries they ruled China's Qing Dynasty (1644–1911).

Although the minorities are not numerous by comparison with the Han, they occupy about five-eighths of the total land area of

Minority	1953	1964	1982	1990
Zhuang	6,919,558	8,386,140	13,383,086	15,555,820
Manchus	2,418,931	2,695,675	4,304,981	9,846,776
Hui	3,559,350	4,473,147	7,228,398	8,612,001
Miao	2,511,339	2,782,088	5,021,175	7,383,622
Uygurs	3,640,125	3,996,311	5,963,491	7,207,024
Yi	3,254,269	3,380,960	5,453,564	6,578,524
Tujia	no data	524,755	2,836,814	5,725,049
Mongols	1,462,956	1,965,766	3,411,367	4,802,407
Tibetans	2,775,622	2,501,174	3,847,875	4,593,072
Buyi	1,247,883	1,348,055	2,119,345	2,548,294

China. The majority live fairly near China's borders, and in a few cases co-nationals run independent states on the other side, examples being the Koreans, Mongols, Kazaks, Kirgiz and Tajiks. There are also quite a few of the minorities of Southwestern China with co-nationals in one or more countries of Southeast Asia. There are, for instance, Miao communities in Vietnam, Thailand and Laos.

The population, according to the four PRC censuses, of the ten most populous minorities in 1990 is shown in the table.

Issues of registration are very important in interpreting these figures. The reason why the number of Manchus rose so fast between 1982 and 1990 was because many people formerly registered as Han changed their registration to Manchu in the intervening years. The same factor explains the lack of data for the Tujia in 1953 and the very rapid growth in the following censuses. However, the exemption from the one-child-per-couple policy also explains some of the growth between 1982 and 1990 (see **population policy**).

The minorities show various cultural traits, some of them very different from those of the Han. The religious mosaic of China is extremely broad. The Turkic minorities of Xinjiang are believers in Islam and, on the whole, still take their faith extremely seriously despite the inroads of Marxism-Leninism from the 1950s to the early 1980s. Although the Hui are very similar culturally to the Han, their Islamic faith marks them out as quite distinct, because of the rather easy-going attitude towards religion that most Han people hold. The Tibetans are strong believers in a form of Buddhism which pervades their entire lifestyle and culture. Many of the minorities believe in folk religions, most of them influenced to a greater or lesser degree by the Han. The Koreans, although traditionally Buddhist, show very little interest in religion nowadays. The small number of believers are as likely to be Christian as Buddhist.

The arts of the minorities also exhibit enormous variety. Some have music and dance traditions which are totally dissimilar from the Han. In such cultural terms, the Turkic peoples of Xinjiang are very much closer to other Turkic peoples further west, including the Turks themselves, than to the Han Chinese. One cultural phenomenon found among a great many of the minorities, but not the Han, is the epic poem, an oral tradition chanted for a folk audience, not written down for a reader. The longest epic poem in the world, not just in China, is the story of Prince Gesar of Gling, his adventures, enthronement and triumph over evil, which can take several years to chant out in a full version. The Gesar epic is Tibetan, dating back probably to the twelfth century or even earlier, but it has spread also to other minorities, especially the Mongols. While the number of artists who can perform the Gesar story is declining, and performances are fewer than they once were, PRC scholars have carried out an immense amount of research on the epic in order to prevent its dying out, including writing it down and publishing it.

Another area of immense variety among China's minorities is in family and gender relations. One commonality is that very few practised the Han custom of foot-binding among women. On the whole the Confucian and Islamic nationalities imposed tight constraints in family matters and on women. Among the southwestern nationalities, courtship was, and remains, less controlled by parents and society at large, than among the Han, and women held a higher status, although Confucian influence crept in among the Miao and others to the detriment of women. 'Walking marriages', in which a man visits a lover at night but returns to his own family by day, survive among communities of the Mosuo, a people with a population of about 40,000 in the mid-1990s living mainly in northwestern Yunnan province. However, although many Mosuo regard themselves as a separate nationality, the PRC continues to classify them as a branch of the Naxi.

In the 1980s ethnic identity feelings developed or revived among virtually all the minorities, with the strength of this consciousness varying very strongly indeed among the various minorities. Among the Zhuang, for example, it is comparatively weak and nobody pushes for secession. The Koreans have a strong sense of national consciousness, but without any strong feelings of hostility towards the Han. On the other hand, among many Uygurs and **Tibetans** feelings of ethnic pride and identity result in passionate hostility to the Han and a wish for an independent state and, on occasion, even secessionist rebellion.

see also: minority nationalities policy; population policy; Tibet Autonomous Region; Tibetans.

7. Regional China
Dali L. Yang and Yongnian Zheng

Occupying around 7 per cent of the earth's land area, China is an immensely varied subcontinent. It is marked by significant spatial disparities and is well known for the multitude of dialects, cuisines and ethnic groups in different locales. A major theme in Chinese history has been the gradual shift of the centre of human activity from the interior to the coast over the past millennium or so.

The wide range of spatial variations has led to the adoption of diverse schemes for regionalizing China. Scholars of regional change generally take two stances in defining their 'regions'. Some like Lewis Mumford and G. William Skinner have emphasized the resilience of natural regions. Skinner, in particular, has undertaken meticulous and fundamental research to uncover the details of Chinese macroregions. Most social scientists, however, have tended to use the term 'region' loosely. For them, the 'region' is merely a taxonomic category for dividing up the national space. There would be different types of regions depending on the criteria used. A region can be an area with distinct natural boundaries or simply an administrative unit such as a province or a county (see **provincial government**). Or it may be a broad geographical area containing a population whose members possess sufficient historical, cultural, economic and social homogeneity to distinguish them from others. In this essay, we use the term 'region' in a somewhat narrowly defined sense to refer to relations that span provincial boundaries in China.

Regions of China

The Maoist Era

Since the CCP came to power, state policy has played a major role in the regionalization of China. In the early 1950s, the CCP drew on its lineage of decentralized military base areas and set up six large regions – the Central-South, East China, the Northeast, the Southeast, North China and the Northeast (Inner Mongolia and **Tibet** were administered separately). These large regions, headed by an illustrious group that included generals such as **Lin Biao**, Liu Bocheng and Peng Dehuai, not only were a layer of government administration but also overlapped with Party regional bureaux and military regions. Regional leaders were allowed considerable scope for local experimentation and soon gained much leeway in governing their territories. The centre laid down policies in fairly general form and left it to the regions to determine the pace and means of policy implementation. Each region was supposed to attain self-sufficiency in the production of key minerals and industrial products so that it could survive independently in the event of foreign invasion, a scenario that was not far-fetched in light of the Sino-American confrontation on the Korean Peninsula (see **Korean War**).

The regional administrations were abolished in 1954 when central leaders perceived that some regional leaders were using their regional bases to further their personal political interests. Gao Gang of the Northeast and Rao Shushi of the East regions were purged partly for building 'independent kingdoms' and using these to support their bids for more political power. Even though they were formally abolished (they were briefly reinstated in 1960 as regional bureaux), the great administrative regions continue to find much currency in Chinese analyses of regional development and in the spatial organization of military power.

While the great administrative regions were partly designed to cope with the varied conditions across a large country, the Chinese government was also confronted with a long legacy of coast–interior disparities: over 70 per cent of China's industrial assets and output were concentrated in the coastal areas, especially **Shanghai**, Jiangsu and Liaoning, in the late 1940s. As it embarked on the road of **Soviet**-style industrialization, the Chinese leadership considered the coast–interior imbalance unacceptable for both economic and national security reasons. The industrial centres were not only located away from resource bases and the interior market but also easily exposed to foreign military power. In consequence, the Chinese leadership began to channel a disproportionately large share of state investment into the interior, which is often divided into the central and the western regions. During the First Five-Year Plan period (1953–7), for instance, nearly two-thirds of the major projects, including three-quarters of the projects built with **Soviet** aid, were located in the interior. Pre-existing industrial centres in the coastal region were neglected and even skimmed (see **industry**).

In the aftermath of the **Great Leap Forward** famine and the Sino-**Soviet** split, China's pro-interior stance was further reinforced, albeit not for economic reasons but by the Chinese leadership's perception of rising international security threats, since by then China was the enemy both of the **Soviet Union** and the US. In autumn 1964, **Mao Zedong** decided that China should concentrate its resources on building defence industries in the third-front areas to prepare for a protracted defensive war. While the coastal areas were considered to be the first front and strategically vulnerable, the third-front areas were mostly in the western region (**Sichuan**, Yunnan, Gansu, Shaanxi, Guizhou, Qinghai, **Xinjiang**), though Hubei, the hometown province of **Lin Biao** and **Li Xiannian**, and Hunan, the hometown province of Mao and several other top leaders, also became favourite investment destinations.

Between 1965 and 1972, the third-front areas received more than half of China's basic construction investment funds, compared with 21 per cent for 1953–7 and 37 per cent for 1958–62. **Local government**s, including those in the coastal region, launched their own 'small third-front' projects in an effort to achieve self-sufficiency. Most third-front projects were built in areas that lacked proper infrastructure and fully one-third of the total investment under the third-front programme was estimated to have been wasted. The third-front programme was halted in 1972 as the Sino-American rapprochement altered China's strategic environment. Yet, as the economist Barry Naughton pointed out, the legacy of the third-front programme lasted far beyond 1972 as inadequately funded projects were slowly brought to completion. During the reform era, the central government has had to expend substantial resources to relocate and reorganize many of the third-front entities that were established for security rather than economic considerations.

The Maoist era was thus marked by an emphasis on interior investment at the expense of the coastal region. Between 1952 and 1983, the interior's share of fixed assets, measured in their original value, rose from 28 per cent to nearly 57 per cent. Chinese geographers calculate that, from 1952 to 1971–5, China's centre of economic activity moved inland by 395 kilometres. In comparison, it took eight decades (1880–1960) for the centre of population of the United States to move a comparable distance.

The Post-Mao Era

In the reform era, Chinese policy makers have drawn painful lessons from the patterns of regional development that prevailed during the Maoist era. Instead of the pursuit of heavy industrial development in the interior, the post-Mao era has laid emphasis on comparative advantage and specialization. This concern with efficiency and growth led the leadership to give priority to the development of the more prosperous coastal region, which was to serve as the anchor and engine of the Chinese economy. As China's Sixth (1981–5) and Seventh (1986–90) Five-Year Plans stipulated explicitly, only after the coastal region becomes sufficiently developed, would the focus of regional development shift to the interior regions. While the coastal region was urged to transform traditional industries and move into

higher value-added industries, the central and western regions were asked to concentrate on producing energy and raw materials, certain machinery and electrical products, and **agriculture**.

In addition to more investment funds, the defining characteristic of the post-Mao regional policy regime has been the offering of preferential treatment for the coastal region, beginning with the establishment of four **special economic zones** (SEZs) in Guangdong and Fujian Provinces in 1979. The SEZs were followed by the designation of fourteen coastal open cities for foreign investment (1984) and of coastal economic development zones (1985). In 1988, Hainan, formerly part of Guangdong, became a separate province and China's largest SEZ. In 1990, Shanghai was given approval to launch the development of the Pudong (East Shanghai) new area. In addition, a wide variety of special development areas has come into existence since the mid-1980s, including free trade zones, economic and technological development zones, state tourist vacation zones, as well as open provincial capitals and border region open areas. Most of these development zones or areas enjoyed special authorities and tax privileges for attracting outside investment.

While development zones and special areas have proliferated across China since the mid-1980s, the coastal region continues to host most of them, making that region the primary beneficiary of preferential territorial treatment. While simple geography would have favoured the coast more than the interior in an era of opening and globalization, there is little doubt that the availability of preferential policies has served to enhance the coastal region's existing strengths, helping it attract 90 per cent of the foreign investment that has come into China as well as compound its lead in domestic investment.

The investment gap between coast and interior has in turn enlarged the economic inequalities between the two regions, even though the interior has also enjoyed rapid economic growth in the reform era. As of the mid-1990s, the vast majority of China's poor, officially estimated at the end of 1995 at 65 million, live in the interior and especially the western region. The issue of the east–west divide is further complicated by the fact that many of China's **minority nationalities** live in the western region. Rising regional economic disparities have served to accentuate ethnic identities and thus cleavages. There has been growing interior demand for a more balanced regional development policy.

Since the late 1980s, the Chinese leadership has sought to moderate the pro-coast slant in regional policy. The Ninth Five-Year Plan (1996–2000) explicitly called for slowing down the enlargement of coast–interior disparities. The central government has promised more state investment for the interior and has also promulgated policies to encourage foreign investment in the interior. In the mean time, the central government has decided to phase out preferential treatment for the **special economic zones** by the year 2000. Nevertheless, central leaders admit that these policies are not intended to reverse the trend in regional development.

Varieties of Regional Ties
The post-Mao period has also seen the flourishing of ties across provincial boundaries that were suppressed by the Maoist emphasis on self-sufficiency. The initiatives for this trend have come from both the central government and the local authorities.

In 1980, the **State Council** issued the first of a series of regulations on promoting such linkages as a strategy for overcoming local and departmental protectionism. The Shanxi Energy Base region, for example, was centred on Shanxi but linked to parts of Inner Mongolia, Hebei and Shaanxi. The Shanghai Economic Zone included **Shanghai** as well as the adjacent provinces of Jiangsu, Zhejiang, Fujian, Anhui and Jiangxi.

Many of the inter-provincial cooperation initiatives were started on an *ad hoc* basis by the parties involved and then evolved into more formal regional cooperative arrangements. In 1981, for example, five provincial units in northern China (**Beijing**, Hebei, Inner Mongolia, Shanxi and Tianjin) convened an economic and technological cooperation conference. Held annually, this conference became the North China Joint Conference of Governors, Mayors, and Chairmen in 1988.

By the early 1990s, over 100 regional economic cooperation organizations had come into being. These include more formal inter-provincial economic cooperation organizations such as the North China Joint Conference, the South-Central Region Joint Conference for Economic and Technological Cooperation (Guangdong, Hubei, Hunan, Henan and Guangxi), and the Southwest Economic Coordination Conference. Geographically, these regional conference organizations tend to resemble the regional bureaux of the 1950s and 1960s. Another mechanism for regional integration is the cooperative arrangements by adjacent prefectures and cities on the borders of several provincial units, such as the Nanjing Regional Economic Coordination Forum formed in 1986. This forum included eighteen prefectures and cities spanning Jiangsu, Anhui and Jiangxi provinces. Another example is the economic cooperation zone formed of sixteen adjacent prefectures and municipalities in the provinces of Fujian, Zhejiang, Jiangxi and Anhui, covering 250,000 square kilometres with 67 million people.

Finally, economic cooperation mechanisms centred around major railway lines, rivers, and bay areas have gained much prominence. For example, the Pearl River Delta and the Yangzi River Delta have become major economic powerhouses. The central government has made clear that the Yangzi River Valley region, starting with **Shanghai** to the east and Chongqing to the west, will become the pivot of China's economic development and is part of China's strategy to integrate balanced regional development across east and west. Between 1992 and 1995, at least five economic cooperation zones came into being along the Yangzi River. The Bohai Bay region is becoming the focus of development in north China.

Many of the regional cooperation arrangements were initially set up to cope with the bottlenecks in an economy caught between plan and market. Indeed, every province and major city in China has had an office for economic and technical cooperation to coordinate material supply and technical assistance across administrative boundaries. As the Chinese economy has become market-oriented, the various regional conferences have turned increasingly to the nurturance of regional markets and especially the coordination of industrial development strategy. Moreover, the regional cooperative arrangements have made it possible for some local authorities to win more attention and resources from the central government than would have been the case had each locality struck out on its own. The most prominent example, formed in 1984, is that of the Southwest Economic Coordination Region comprising the province-level units of **Sichuan**, Yunnan, Guizhou, Guangxi and **Tibet**, as well as Chengdu and Chongqing, the latter being promoted to provincial level in March 1997. By 1995, the region had set up eighty-three regional trade organizations. Parties to the region have made strenuous efforts to promote a common market by removing local protectionist restrictions and blockades and opening up regionwide markets. The region has also vigorously promoted **international trade**, especially border trade. Most important, regional cooperation appears to have sped up investment in infrastructure, with a major improvement in rail transport that leads not just to **Beijing** but to the Guangxi coast, making the region more oriented toward booming Southeast Asia. The region has also won central funding for an array of state key projects in communications, energy, metallurgy, building materials, and the chemical **industry**.

see also: 6. Peoples of China; agriculture; Beijing Municipality; Great Leap Forward; industry; international trade; Korean War; Li Xiannian; Lin Biao; local government/administration; Mao Zedong; minority nationalities policy; provincial government; Shanghai; Sichuan; Soviet Union, relations with; special economic zones; State Council; Tibet Autonomous Region; Xinjiang Uygur Autonomous Region.

8. China, the Region and the World
Donald H. McMillen

Any assessment of China's foreign policies and relations since 1949 must consider the complex interplay of several factors.

- China's legacy is one in which authoritarian rule, weakened by corruption and conservative Confucianist ideology, have combined with humiliation imposed by rapacious foreign powers, contributing to the rise of a revolutionary Chinese Marxist order under the **Chinese Communist Party**.
- China's huge population, with the Han at the core and **minority nationalities** at the periphery, has greatly increased the government's difficulties in controlling and providing for the people, while at the same time searching for a definition of national identity amidst shifting policies and rising expectations.
- Personalities, interest coalitions and bureaucracies have played significant roles in the shaping of the PRC's domestic and foreign policies, but particularly **Mao Zedong** and **Deng Xiaoping**, who came to symbolize quite different policy approaches.
- The PRC has functioned within a systemic geopolitical and geoeconomic context over which its control has been limited. At times China has attempted to reshape this context, regionally if not globally, at first as a largely 'denied', developing state actor but later as one courted by others and prompted by its own extended family for both strategic and economic reasons.

Given the increasingly transnational and interdependent character of China's recent foreign relations environment, the definition of 'China' itself demands consideration. What constitutes 'inner' (*nei*) and 'outer' (*wai*) has recently become confused in practice by the plethora of actors from the centre and from the regions operating across China's borders, despite Beijing's continuing emphasis on state (and particularly CCP)

sovereignty and a nationalism (and concept of 'nationality') ranging from affirmative to assertive to aggressive. China's foreign relations also operate in the party-to-party, state-to-state and people-to-people spheres and have been conditioned periodically by radical ideological formulae, the principle of national interest and regime integrity, and the pragmatics of 'techonomic' linkaging, and they have ranged from cooperation to conflict.

The first decade of PRC foreign relations was one of 'leaning to one side', as evidenced in the February 1950 signing of the Treaty of Friendship, Alliance and Mutual Assistance with the **Soviet Union**. Beijing's reluctant reliance on Moscow as the Cold War developed was partly based on broad ideological ties and on the necessity to obtain assistance in consolidating its domestic rule at a time when US-led forces isolated and threatened it politically and economically from global affairs as a 'pariah state'. This was underlined by China's involvement in the **Korean War** from late 1950 and by the establishment of a Western security system of bilateral and multilateral treaties in Asia directed against it. China's alliance with Moscow, however, came at the price of its virtual dependence on **Soviet** economic and technical assistance and subordination to the leadership of Joseph Stalin and, later, Nikita Khrushchev of the world communist movement.

When Khrushchev denounced Stalin's personality cult and outlined a policy of 'peaceful coexistence' with the West in 1956, Mao initiated his own path to socialism at home by launching the **Great Leap Forward** in 1958 and continued Chinese confrontation with the West. This was particularly notable in Beijing's continued attempts in 1958 to seek the reunification of Taiwan through military force, and in its cultivation of non-aligned **Third World** states based upon the 'five principles of peaceful coexistence'. It was **Zhou Enlai** who enunciated these principles at the Bandung Conference (1955), aiming initially at creating a united front against 'US imperialism'. By 1959–60, open Sino-**Soviet** polemics led to the withdrawal of **Soviet** aid and assistance and, effectively, the demise of the alliance.

During the 1960s, China's adopted 'dual adversary' foreign and defence policies aimed at countering the hegemonism of both the US- and **Soviet**-led camps. The Sino-**Soviet** (and Mao–Khrushchev) estrangement was reflected in more intense polemics within the world communist movement, leading to a 'polycentrism' which challenged the bipolar framework of East–West relations and contributed to challenges against **Soviet** predominance within its bloc along the lines of the Hungarian Uprising in 1956. Following the **Soviet** backdown in the Cuban Missile Crisis of 1962 and the signing of the 1963 US–USSR Limited Test-Ban Treaty, Beijing accused Moscow's 'new tsars' of launching armed clashes along their borders and fomenting trouble in China's minority nationality frontier regions. Thereafter, the Sino-**Soviet** borders were militarized and China developed its own nuclear weapons capacity (testing its first device in **Xinjiang** in 1964). In 1962, China launched a limited border war with India, one intention (beyond securing its claims to **Tibet**) being to damage Nehru's reputation in the non-aligned world by compelling him to seek **Soviet** support. China also proposed the establishment of an anti-American united front excluding Moscow at an Afro-Asian Conference in Algiers; this was to have taken place in 1965, but failed to do so.

During the height of the **Cultural Revolution** (1966–9), China basically turned in on itself, withdrawing all but one of its ambassadors from abroad. One of the central features of Mao's attempt to rebuild the CCP on renewed revolutionary vigour was the denunciation and removal of Party leaders perceived to be 'revisionist' and/or pro-**Soviet**. With the **Soviet** invasion of Czechoslovakia in 1968 and the earlier US build-up in Vietnam, Beijing faced immediate security threats on two fronts. In March and August of 1969 serious Sino-**Soviet** border clashes occurred in the northeast and far western sectors. The establishment of the **Association of Southeast Asian Nations** (ASEAN) in 1967, regionally inspired but dependent on great powers, and the Nixon administration's July 1969 'Guam Doctrine' (by which Vietnamese troops would take on the main fighting in Vietnam, allowing the US to withdraw), led to China's reappraisal of its domestic policies and its strategic stance. In this, influence in foreign policy decision-making shifted from the CCP Politburo and towards defence and foreign policy professionals in the CCP Secretariat who favoured an ordered and stable environment.

For the next decade, Beijing's foreign policy came to be based on a 'principal enemy' outlook focused on the USSR (and its allies). This followed diplomatic recognition by a number of countries led by Canada and Italy late in 1970, a rapprochement and 'normalization' of relations with states in the Western camp following the Kissinger and Nixon visits of July 1971 and February 1972 and the PRC's re-entry into the **United Nations** (1971). In the early days of this transition, China continued to hold up its anti-hegemonist credentials among developing and non-aligned states, with **Deng Xiaoping** enunciating Mao's 'three worlds theory' at the UN in April 1974. However, **Zhou Enlai**'s announcement of the **Four Modernizations** in 1975, Mao's death the next year, the overthrow of the **gang of four**, and the return of Deng to power all favoured the development of relations with the West (and Japan) over those with the **Third World**.

Under Deng's leadership, the pragmatics of Chinese economic development and linkaging into the global economy replaced Maoist revolutionary politics and ideology as the 'key link' in policy terms. As market mechanisms and other liberal policies took root in China, the economy experienced a boom and China not only attracted significant **international trade** and investment, but also experienced what Party conservatives con-

sidered to be anti-socialist 'spiritual pollution'. Trade and investment with **Japan**, for
instance, grew to the point where in 1985
there were demonstrations against a 'second
Japanese (economic) invasion' and protests
about Japanese textbooks which white-
washed Japanese wartime atrocities in China.

China's total **international trade** grew at
an annual rate of 12.9 per cent with the share
of foreign trade as a percentage of GNP rising
from less than 10 per cent to 38.5 per cent in
the 1979–92 period. According to purchasing-
power parity calculations by the International Monetary Fund, in 1992 China's
economy at US$1.7 trillion ranked it third
largest in the world after the US and **Japan**.
Given its population of 1.2 billion, however,
China was still one of the poorer countries in
the world and grappling with the consequences of its own rapid economic growth.

China made some progress from being an
international pariah to an international participant during this transformative decade,
but its path was encumbered by the perceived 'encirclement' by an emerging USSR–
Vietnam strategic partnership framed in
November 1978 when Hanoi signed a twenty-
five-year Treaty of Friendship and Cooperation with Moscow. Seven weeks later, and
only ten days after the announcement of
official **United States**–PRC diplomatic relations, Vietnam invaded and occupied Cambodia, then ruled by a Chinese-backed
Khmer Rouge regime under the notorious Pol
Pot. On 17 February 1979, China launched
a seventeen-day-long punitive attack on
northern Vietnam. This campaign resulted
in considerable economic and human costs,
showed the impotency of China's techno-
logically inferior **People's Liberation Army**,
and raised 'China fears' in the Asian region.
That China continued to back anti-
government insurgents in the Cambodian
conflict also contributed to the prolongation
of anxieties in the region, particularly with
Indonesia, which had cut relations with
Beijing after the failed pro-communist coup
of 1965. China's anti-**Soviet** stance was
further enhanced by Moscow's December
1979 invasion of Afghanistan, which drove

Beijing to abrogate its 1950 treaty with the
USSR.

When the USSR became bogged down in
Afghanistan and relations with the US were
strained by the passage through Congress of
the Taiwan Relations Act of 1979 and President Ronald Reagan's polices on **Taiwan**, the
way was again open for a shift in China's
superpower relations. Leonid Brezhnev's
Tashkent speech of March 1982 not only
acknowledged Chinese sovereignty over
Taiwan, but also proposed discussions to
remove the 'three obstacles' to Sino-**Soviet**
rapprochement outlined by **Deng Xiaoping**
in 1980 (see **Soviet Union, relations with**). In
late 1981, China had enunciated an
'independent', equidistant foreign policy,
and in September 1982 again attacked both
hegemonisms.

With Mikhail Gorbachev's ascent to
power in the USSR in 1985 and his subsequent introduction of liberal domestic economic and political reforms and his advocacy
of *glasnost* (openness) in **Soviet** foreign relations in Vladivostok in July 1986, dialogue in
the state-to-state sphere of relations became
firmly re-established. The **Soviet** resolution
to ensure that Vietnamese forces were
removed from Cambodia by late 1989 and its
support of the concurrent Paris talks to
resolve the conflict, the removal of **Soviet**
troops from its borders with China, and Moscow's withdrawal from Afghanistan (all of
which had been a huge drain on the budgets
and foreign policy flexibility of both states)
removed the 'three obstacles' to further
improvement in relations. Gorbachev's visit
to China in May 1989, during the student
demonstrations (see **June 4 Incident**), basically normalized party-to-party ties –
although both sides denied that relations
would ever duplicate those of the 1950s.

Chinese foreign policy was complicated by
the collapse of the USSR and the creation of
the Commonwealth of Independent States
(CIS) in December 1991. China found it
increasingly difficult to play the CIS against
US supremacy. Even after his removal from
power, as the architect of communism's
demise in Eastern Europe and the USSR,

Gorbachev's shadow hung heavily over most CCP leaders in the post-Cold War era. Yet with the visits of Russian President Boris Yeltsin in 1992 and 1996, a new non-military 'strategic partnership' of economic cooperation and good will was cemented. Beijing became concerned about the spill-over of ethno-nationalist (predominantly Islamic) activity into its **Xinjiang Uygur Autonomous Region**.

Sino-US relations soured after the **June 4 Incident** of 1989 due to a range of issues. Factors contributing to the downturn have included:

- US sanctions against China for its suppression of the protestors;
- US linkage of human rights and intellectual property disputes with the renewal of China's 'most-favoured nation' trading status;
- Beijing's favourable balance of trade with the US;
- Chinese arms dealings abroad;
- US concern over China's handling of **Hong Kong** issues (in the lead-up to the 1997 turn-over of sovereignty); and
- a reaffirmation of the US–Japan security alliance.

While US sanctions against China were largely abandoned during the Gulf War (early 1991), Chinese neo-authoritarianism and assertive nationalism have affected all dealings between the two states, making Chinese leaders claim that Washington has adopted a 'neo-containment policy' against the PRC.

In this regard, China has sought, with some success, to develop a constructive engagement with ASEAN over economic and security issues as one means of checking the perceived US strategy. The normalization of relations with Indonesia in August 1990 and Singapore in 1991 were instrumental in this process. China subsequently became an ASEAN dialogue partner, and joined the ASEAN Regional Forum to engage in discussion over mutual security issues and the **Asia-Pacific Economic Cooperation** mechanism to negotiate such issues as the lowering of trade barriers. These fora provide

China and the US with venues for leadership summits and dialogue. But, even though ASEAN member-states have recognized trade and investment opportunities in congenial relations with China, there has been considerable concern about growing Chinese economic and military power and assertive activities in support of claims to sovereignty over territories and resources in the **South China Sea**. As a result, regional organizations like ASEAN also represent a collective counterweight to growing Chinese power.

As of the mid-1990s, Chinese foreign policy decision-making has become complicated by the differing agenda and tactics of the various bureaucratic players in the process, including the CCP Secretariat, the Ministry of Foreign Affairs and the Ministry of Foreign Economic Relations and Trade, and the defence establishment. Leadership succession, nationalism and an 'adjusted' form of Chinese socialist ideology constitute ingredients in foreign policy processes and national unity. China's future stability and economic growth largely depend on the CCP's capacity to mediate domestic political, social and economic problems and manage an increasingly decentralized, pluralistic and transnational economy. In this context, while the emphasis will be on its immediate foreign policy region, there will be no single PRC foreign policy as such, and the outside world will have to deal with individual regions as well as the centre.

see also: 1. Overview History of the PRC; 4. Political Personae: Biographical Profiles; 6. Peoples of China; Asia-Pacific Economic Cooperation; Association of Southeast Asian Nations; Chinese Communist Party; Cultural Revolution; Deng Xiaoping; Four Modernizations; gang of four; Great Leap Forward; Hong Kong; international trade; Japan, relations with; June 4 Incident; Korean War; Mao Zedong; minority nationalities policy; People's Liberation Army; South China Sea; Soviet Union, relations with; Taiwan policy; Third World policy; Tibet Autonomous Region; Tibetans; United Nations policy; United States policy; Xinjiang Uygur Autonomous Region; Zhou Enlai.

9. Taiwan and the Overseas Chinese

Yen Ching-hwang

Due to its history, **Taiwan** has always been close to its Overseas subjects and its **Overseas Chinese policy** is shaped by its experiences before 1949. Indeed, the Nationalist government traces its origins back to the Revive China Society (*Xing Zhong hui*), founded in November 1894 by Sun Yat-sen in Hawaii. Sun obtained strong support from his Overseas compatriots to help overthrow the Manchu regime early in 1912. Despite ebbs and flows in the fortunes of the Nationalist Party (Guomindang), the Overseas Chinese gave it their support at various times after 1912.

The founding of the Nanjing government in 1927 under Chiang Kai-shek's leadership marked a new beginning for a cordial relationship with the Overseas Chinese. Prominent Overseas Chinese leaders were recruited into the Guomindang to reflect the needs and aspirations of the Overseas Chinese, while the government took steps to strengthen its relationship with them through diplomatic protection and Chinese education. During the Anti-Japanese War (1937–45), Overseas Chinese supported the Nationalists against the Japanese, including with huge financial contributions. However, the postwar era saw China politics spill over to the Overseas Chinese communities throughout the world, with deep divisions between pro-Nationalist and pro-CCP camps.

Taiwan's Overseas Chinese Policy, 1949–71

The loss of mainland China to the CCP compelled the Nationalist government in Taibei to look for strong support among Overseas Chinese. Its long-term aim during this period was to crush the communists and to recover the mainland by force. But even more urgent was the survival of the regime on the island against the military threat from the CCP, the socio-economic problems the regime faced in Taiwan itself, and Beijing's competition for influence among the Overseas Chinese. The

Overseas Chinese policy pursued by the Nationalists immediately after 1949 was to prevent defection of Overseas Chinese to the CCP, especially in Southeast Asia where the majority of the Overseas Chinese resided. The loss of influence over the Chinese in British Malaya (including Singapore) as a result of British recognition of the Beijing regime in January 1950 dealt a severe blow to the Nationalists. In the Southeast Asian countries where the Nationalists had diplomatic representation, such as the Philippines and Thailand, their diplomats were actively involved in maintaining influence among the local Chinese and their host governments. However, the CCP's victory and its aim to build a strong united China attracted young Overseas Chinese, some of whom went to China for study.

In April 1951, to prevent further defection of Overseas Chinese to the CCP and to strengthen its grip on the Overseas Chinese, the Nationalist government in Taibei laid down several principles for its new Overseas Chinese policy. These were:

- to unite the Overseas Chinese against the aggression of international communism;
- to restore the confidence of Overseas Chinese in the Nationalist government in Taibei;
- to foster national consciousness among Overseas Chinese through Chinese education; and
- to promote Overseas Chinese business activities.

To translate the new policy into action, the Nationalist government approved several practical measures in May 1952. These included:

- introducing new facilities for Overseas Chinese remittances;
- encouraging Overseas Chinese students to study in Taiwan;
- stepping up propaganda activities among the Overseas Chinese through cultural

institutions and private Chinese newspapers;

- encouraging of Overseas Chinese youth to participate in anti-communist and anti-**Soviet** activities; and
- promoting welfare activities among Overseas Chinese.

Among these measures, encouragement to study in Taiwan, the propaganda war, and the promotion of welfare programmes produced long-term effects on later policies.

But the most important step taken by the Nationalist government in its early years in Taiwan was the world convention of the Overseas Chinese in Taibei from 21 to 30 October 1952. The ten-day convention gathered 250 Overseas Chinese representatives from all over the world. President Chiang Kai-shek addressed the convention, summarizing Taiwan's aim to mobilize Overseas Chinese to combat communism through educational, cultural and economic means. He spelled out three important policy points:

- promotion of Overseas Chinese education so as to perpetuate traditional Chinese cultural values;
- economic sanctions against the communist regime in mainland China; and
- promotion of unity and organization among Overseas Chinese all over the world to fight against communism.

The rapid political change in the PRC in the early 1950s seemed to raise hope for the Nationalists to recover the mainland, with social revolutionary movements creating turbulence and alienating the national bourgeoisie and bureaucrats. In particular, the land reform turned Chinese rural society upside down, and many Overseas Chinese families in Guangdong and Fujian Provinces were greatly affected, providing fuel for agitation among Overseas Chinese against the CCP. At the same time, PRC involvement in the **Korean War** in 1950 and the American imposition of an embargo against it brought China and the **United States** to the brink of total war. The Nationalists were expected to capitalize on these developments by mobilizing the Overseas Chinese in the struggle against communist rule in China.

Despite adverse political conditions in the PRC throughout the late 1950s and 1960s, Taiwan failed to gain solid support among Overseas Chinese for its aims. This failure was mainly due to the changing political and economic conditions both abroad and in Taiwan. The changing political orientation of the Overseas Chinese from Chinese to local citizens, especially in Southeast Asia, meant that fewer Overseas Chinese were prepared to commit themselves politically either to Taiwan or the PRC. At the same time, political realism forced the Taibei government to shift its focus from recovering the mainland by force to economic reconstruction of the island. However, Taibei's policy of trying to attract Overseas Chinese to invest in the island scored some success in the 1960s, contributing to its early industrialization success.

Taiwan and the Overseas Chinese, 1972–86

Before the policy makers in Taibei had time to assess the success or failure of their Overseas Chinese policy in the 1960s, the Nationalist government suffered a severe setback from its loss of the China seat in the **United Nations** (UN) in October 1971, and consequent end of its political influence in this world body. More serious were the implications of its diplomatic status in the world community and its claim of legitimacy to represent China. Beijing's success in replacing Taibei in the UN was followed by US President Nixon's February 1972 visit to China. The bandwagon effect was felt throughout the world, many of the Western and Afro-Asian countries abandoning Taibei in favour of Beijing. US diplomatic recognition of Beijing in 1978 and the consequent severance of its official ties with Taibei further strengthened this trend.

The diplomatic setbacks of the 1970s tended to create a siege mentality among the populace. At the same time the 1970s saw the rise of a new leadership. Chiang Kai-shek died in 1975, but his son Chiang Ching-kuo had first become premier in 1972 and in 1978 president. Chiang Ching-kuo belonged to a younger generation of Nationalist politicians who understood the new political and international reality. Under his stewardship, Taiwan carried out political reforms and the process of localization in an attempt to unite the divided mainlanders and local Taiwanese of Chinese descent. This new policy gained increasing support and achieved unity and solidarity among the general populace, with a strong sense of purpose and sacrifice emerging as a result.

In accordance with the new political direction, Taiwan's **Overseas Chinese policy** in the 1970s and 1980s was based on three planks:

- continuous mobilization of Overseas Chinese political support for anti-communism;
- the encouragement of Overseas Chinese investment in Taiwan; and
- the perpetuation of Chinese culture and values through education and cultural activities.

With shrinking scope for its diplomatic activities, it may have been unrealistic for Taibei to continue down the track of anti-communist alliance. But what the regime could not afford was to abandon political struggle against the CCP among the Overseas Chinese, particularly at a time when Beijing had recently won diplomatic recognition. To check the downward trend, Taibei launched an attempt to win political support among Overseas Chinese. Pro-Nationalist social and cultural organizations in Overseas Chinese communities received various forms of aid, especially services and advice. At the same time, Taibei also tried to gain pledges of loyalty at world conventions of Overseas Chinese. For instance, the world Overseas Chinese representatives convention held in 1979 pledged its continuous stand against communism and its opposition to communist influence among Overseas Chinese.

But the main thrust of the new policy rested more on attracting Overseas Chinese investment in Taiwan, and on perpetuating Taibei's influence in the Overseas Chinese communities through education and cultural activities. Since its new focus on economic growth following its diplomatic failures of the early 1970s, Taibei viewed Overseas Chinese communities as markets and potential sources of capital. The wealth of the Overseas Chinese had long been known to the Nationalists, so what they now attempted was to utilize Overseas Chinese financial resources in the service of Taiwan's quest for economic great power status. In the 1970s, delegations from Taiwan were sent out to Overseas Chinese communities to solicit capital and to encourage tourism.

The policy had some notable success. One claim has it that by 1980 more than 1,000 Overseas Chinese enterprises were investing in manufacturing and other industries in Taiwan, with an estimated capital of over US$400 million. Another source claims that in the four decades from 1952 to 1992 Overseas Chinese enterprises ranked third in providing valuable foreign capital to Taiwan. Of an estimated US$16.5 billion of the foreign capital attracted to Taiwan during this period, Overseas Chinese capital accounted for about 15 per cent, behind only Japan (29 per cent) and the US (27 per cent).

Chiang Ching-kuo aimed to win the support not only of the current generation of Overseas Chinese, but the next one as well and the best means to achieving this end was Chinese education. But the drastic political change in Southeast Asia caused the decline of Chinese education there, undermining Taibei's efforts. By 1980, the number of Chinese schools had fallen sharply. In Indonesia and Burma, more than 1,500 Chinese schools were closed as result of the implementation of an anti-Chinese policy; while in Thailand and the Philippines, the number of Chinese schools fell, the remaining schools being subjected to stringent control.

Despite these failures, Taiwan's strengthening of its earlier policy of attracting Overseas Chinese students won notable success. Many Taiwanese universities offered concessions to Overseas Chinese students, attracting many, especially from poor families. Education in Taiwan made most of these students sympathetic to Taibei's cause. After returning to their home countries, they worked as teachers, cultural workers and professionals, and many of them were involved in business and politics. They became the vanguards of Taiwan's business penetration into Southeast Asian countries, and since the late 1980s have effectively served as a bridge for Taiwan's investment in the region.

Taiwan and the Overseas Chinese since 1987: the 'Go South' Policy and the Overseas Chinese

The ascendancy of Taiwan to the position of a new economic power in Asia in the 1980s increased its prestige and status in the world community, and provided it with immense confidence in the expansion of its economic influence throughout the globe. Southeast Asia, like the southern part of China, was viewed by Taibei as an attractive economic hinterland. Southeast Asia is rich in both human and material resources but poor in industries, providing excellent opportunities for Taiwanese investment and trade. In addition, the large number of the Overseas Chinese and their existing business networks gave the Taiwanese investors a competitive edge over other foreign investors in the region, including a better understanding of the language and culture of the main trading community, access to the existing marketing networks, and lower managerial costs.

Taiwan's 'go south' policy for its investors attempted to curb the outflow of Taiwanese capital to South China, thereby reducing Taiwan's economic reliance on the PRC. Before 1987, Taiwanese investment in major Southeast Asian countries such as Indonesia, Malaysia, Thailand and the Philippines was estimated at US$800 million between 1959 and 1986. But the pace was accelerated by the lifting of government control over foreign exchange in May 1987, together with rising domestic costs and appreciation in the value of Taiwan's currency. Between 1987 and 1993, Taiwanese investment in Southeast Asia rose to an estimated US$20 billion, a twenty-five-fold increase over the pre-1987 figure. Taiwan's investment in Southeast Asia had indirectly stimulated its trade expansion to

the region. Nationalist President Lee Teng-hui had observed that trade had closely followed investment, and two-way trade between Taiwan and Southeast Asia increased rapidly. A large volume of spare parts, machinery, and other industrial products was exported to Taiwanese-owned factories or affiliated companies in Southeast Asia. This trade expansion contributed significantly to the buoyancy of the domestic Taiwanese economy.

The increased expansion of investment and trade with Southeast Asian countries raises the image of Taiwan as a new economic power in Asia. More and more Overseas Chinese business people are seizing opportunities to develop closer business ties with Taiwan. Among the most active are the returned Taiwan graduates, some of whom hold a high profile in business and local politics. Taiwan's economic success has also changed Southeast Asian governments' attitudes towards it, and the fear of Taibei's political appeals and influence among their citizens of Chinese descent has been much alleviated. Modern Standard Chinese (Mandarin), the official language of both the PRC and Taiwan, has been transformed from a political into a business language, and more and more indigenous Southeast Asian children are learning it as a second language, some of them even going to Taiwan to pursue their higher studies.

As a result of these new developments, the relationship between the Overseas Chinese in Southeast Asia and Taiwan has moved to a healthier basis. Southeast Asian Chinese business people no longer fear that the local authorities will regard them as a tool serving Taiwan's political objectives and they can feel at ease in their role as Taiwan's business partners in a region of growing economic prosperity.

see also: 1. Overview History of the People's Republic of China; Korean War; Overseas Chinese policy; Soviet Union, relations with; Taiwan policy; United Nations policy; United States policy.

Dictionary

A

agriculture (policies, organizations, units)

Agricultural policy has been the focus of many of the defining moments in the PRC's political and economic development. Land reform, the formation of cooperatives and collectives, the people's communes and the introduction of the household responsibility system were all associated with key shifts in China's political climate. In part, this prominence reflected peasant predominance in the population. It also reflected **Mao Zedong**'s emphasis on the transformation of rural society as part of the process of socialist revolution.

Ironically, however, China's centrally planned economy gave priority to urban industry. Agriculture became a source of capital for industrial development, and peasant living standards were slow to improve. The economic reforms after 1978 thus saw a rejection of Mao's models and the reintroduction of household farming.

Land reform (1949–52) was the fulfilment of a long-standing commitment to the peasant supporters who had brought the CCP to power. The Land Reform Law, adopted in 1950, was implemented from north to south over several years. The landlords were the main target, rich peasants being to some extent protected. This practice was associated with Mao before 1949 but **Liu Shaoqi** was later criticized for its use during land reform. Communist work teams entered every village and mobilized the poorer peasants to denounce the local landlords. The process was both economic and political. It transferred ownership of the landlords' land, animals, and implements to poor peasants on a roughly equal basis. This major redistribution of wealth generated powerful incentives for peasants to increase production. Agriculture developed rapidly, and peasant living standards improved. At the same time, the reform destroyed the power of the landlord class,

many being executed, and classified peasant families into landless, poor, upper and lower middle, rich and landlord categories. This class status, for which distinct boundaries were often difficult to define in practice, lasted until 1979 and was significant in that it determined the peasants' political and social rights.

Almost before land reform was finished, fears that the small peasant economy would recreate the economic basis for rural social inequality led to the introduction of cooperative farming. At first Mao envisaged that the process might take fifteen to twenty years, but soon accelerated it to completion by 1956. The first stage was the formation of mutual aid teams, whereby groups of relatives and friends cooperated to share implements and animals and to work each member's land in turn. This enabled peasant families to combine their resources efficiently, while keeping their land and incomes separate. The Party then moved to organize the peasants into larger 'elementary' cooperatives of twenty to thirty households in which, although peasants maintained private land ownership, they pooled all land and resources to achieve economies of scale. Peasant income depended on a rent for their share of inputs and a return for the labour contributed. The CCP intended the process to be voluntary, promoted it through propaganda, by active mobilization from rural cadres, and by policies which distributed state support and inputs only to members of cooperatives.

The rural transformation was based on Mao's arguments that larger farming units offered economies of scale and that changes in the organization of production were a precondition for agricultural modernization. It was also believed that the erosion of private ownership would lead to a more egalitarian process of development, in which social change would provide the incentive for peasants to work hard. The dynamic for progress lay in the accumulation of resources by the cooperative rather than by individuals. A related factor was that the extension of planning and the rapid growth of industry was placing demands on the rural sector for food and raw materials, and it was argued that the formation of cooperatives would both accelerate agricultural growth and enable the state to obtain the materials it needed. At the same time, the formal **planning** apparatus for agriculture was strengthened, peasant mobility was restricted by the introduction of the **household registration** system, the marketing of agricultural products was controlled through unified purchases and sales quotas, and industrial inputs were allocated through the state commercial system. The effect was to create a dual economy, with strict separation between the urban and rural sectors, in which the trading relationship between the two was mediated through state regulation.

Against that background of policies and organizational change, the next phase of development was the 'high tide' of agricultural transformation in 1956. The formation of elementary cooperatives was overtaken by a push to create 'advanced' cooperatives which were larger in size (up to 350 families) and more firmly managed by the state administration. The key difference in this form of **collective agriculture** was that ownership of land, animals and all other means of production passed to the cooperative. By the end of 1956, some 90 per cent of peasant households were members. Many peasants, however, reacted negatively against the loss of private ownership and the tighter controls. Output of animals and special products fell, and the decline of opportunities for off-farm subsidiary work affected household incomes. The result was a retreat during the first half of 1957, which saw the size of many cooperatives reduced.

This retreat fed into the debates of the short-lived **Hundred Flowers Movement** in 1957, when there was considerable criticism of collective policies. The denunciation of the critics in the subsequent Anti-Rightist Movement, however, led to a strong reassertion of Mao's approach, which culminated in

the formation of people's communes during 1958 as part of the **Great Leap Forward**. Mao stepped outside formal procedures and encouraged a broad campaign from below to establish the communes, each of which absorbed large numbers of advanced cooperatives.

Communes were structured as comprehensive organizations uniting local government, economic management, social services and public security. The commune exercised ownership as a single entity, and, in many places, egalitarian systems of income distribution were introduced. One of the most distinctive experiments was the diversion of much agricultural labour to industrial and construction projects, including the 'backyard furnaces' which produced large amounts of poor quality steel.

Although 1958 saw a very large harvest, waste and poor management exacerbated the natural disasters of the following three years, with estimates that famine and malnutrition resulted in 20 million to 30 million deaths. In the face of this catastrophe, Mao was forced to withdraw from policy implementation. Ownership and management were decentralized to the team level, creating basic units much the same size as the elementary cooperatives. The recovery phase also saw the revival of small-scale rural markets and various forms of contracted individual farming, without abandoning the commune shell. These pragmatic policies led to a restoration of production, although output did not return to 1957 levels until 1965. Mao, however, saw the retreat as evidence of revisionism in the CCP.

Between 1962 and 1965, agricultural policy thus became a focus of political debate. Mao launched a 'socialist education movement' and a 'four clean-ups' campaign to correct errors in basic management, and called on the countryside to learn from the model commune **Dazhai** which he presented as the embodiment of the principle of egalitarian collective development based on self-reliance.

These efforts culminated in the **Cultural Revolution**, when Mao and his followers blamed the retreat on **Liu Shaoqi** and **Deng Xiaoping** and reaffirmed the commune model. The communes became entrenched as the basic organization in the countryside, albeit using the slightly more decentralized structure, with team ownership and accounting. From 1958 until 1978, therefore, China's agriculture was organized under collective management and ownership. Assigned quotas and targets regulated production, with production support organized through the Ministry of Agriculture. Marketing took place through the state grain bureaux and supply and marketing cooperatives. Communes had to deliver assigned quotas of produce at state determined prices. Inputs were distributed through the plan system, and major infrastructural investment was allocated through the state budget. Under the policy of self-reliance, communes were largely responsible for their own **education** and **welfare** systems. They relied on mobilizing peasant labour for basic investment in irrigation, land-levelling and roads. Over time there were also experiments with large-scale collective ownership.

The commune system did lead to considerable improvements in basic infrastructure and generated an annual growth rate in grain output of over 2 per cent (1957–80), slightly greater than the rate of population growth. Nevertheless, there was very limited improvement in agricultural output per labourer and in rural incomes and consumption. There were also low incentives and low productivity, which resulted in inefficient use of resources. In particular, the operation of the pricing system meant that the state bought agricultural products at low prices, selling industrial products to the peasants at high prices. Agriculture thus became the source of funds for urban industry. Agricultural development and living standards lagged far behind the city, resulting in considerable disillusionment with the communes among the peasants. This slow and inefficient growth of agriculture was thus a crucial problem facing the post-Mao leadership.

In 1978, China launched a programme of economic reform in the countryside. There were three main elements in the initial policies:

- the decentralization of farm management to the household level through a system of contracting which allocated land in return for guaranteed sales quotas and left the peasants free to use their resources as they wished;
- a large rise in state purchase prices which substantially increased the returns to farming; and
- the development of free markets for products after the delivery of quotas.

These changes dramatically transformed the incentive structure within agriculture.

Peasants became sharply aware of their opportunity costs and responded by increasing production and diverting resources to profitable off-farm activities. Within four years, the commune system had withered away and was replaced by a hierarchy of township government, village committees to manage the land and other collective assets, and independent household farming. Peasant farmers also became free to accumulate their own capital and to invest in private means of production. In addition, with the exception of grain, cotton and a small number of industrial raw materials, the distribution of agricultural products was gradually transferred to the market. The role of state institutions in directing agricultural production declined, and the barriers to urban–rural exchange began to erode.

Such changes signified a shift away from Mao's egalitarian, collective model, characterized by self-reliance, a rejection of private ownership and markets and a concentration on grain production. Organizational changes during the 1980s and 1990s moved towards acceptance of a more diversified system of production which took account of comparative advantage, allowed regional specialization and centred on efficient use of resources guided by market signals. While the state continued to intervene in respect of politically sensitive crops such as grain, the agricultural sector experienced profound deregulation. The result was a dramatic acceleration in the output of all crops, a rapid growth in peasant incomes, and a doubling of agricultural growth rates.

Among the most notable developments was the emergence of the **township and village enterprise** sector which rapidly became the engine of growth of the rural economy. As a result, although agriculture grew strongly, its relative position in the economy declined, in line with China's lack of agricultural comparative advantage.

Despite these economic gains, by the mid-1990s a number of new problems had become the focus of debate.

- Uneven development had resulted in growing regional disparities in peasant incomes.
- The interior lagged far behind the coastal regions, giving rise to political concerns.
- The nature of land contracting created considerable fragmentation of land, with the family farms of around two-thirds of a hectare commonly broken up into many small plots dotted around villages.
- Many saw uncertainty of family land tenure as an obstacle to long-term investment and to economies of scale.
- While the diversion of labour out of agriculture to off-farm employment was a solution to low incomes and rural development issues, the flow of migrant rural labour to cities and coastal provinces became a potential social problem.
- Continued state intervention in grain and a small number of other crops led to problems in production and the need for producer subsidies.
- Many local officials at township and village level were placing excessive burdens on peasant households to maintain their own benefits.

The next round of reform thus required renewed consideration of rural property rights, further separation of administrative and economic powers, and a deepening of market reforms to remove price distortions and to break down the remaining barriers between the urban and the rural economies.

see also: 1. Overview History of the People's Republic of China; 3. Ideology: Radicalism and Reform; 5. Politics and the Economy: Policy Patterns and Issues; collective agriculture; Cultural Revolution; Dazhai; Deng Xiaoping; education policy and system; Great Leap Forward; household registration; Hundred Flowers Movement; Liu Shaoqi; Mao Zedong; planning, economic; township and village enterprises; welfare policy.

Andrew Watson

Anti-Rightist Movement
See **Hundred Flowers Movement.**

Asia-Pacific Economic Cooperation (APEC)
This eighteen-member grouping was launched as an inter-governmental mechanism in Seoul in January 1989 by Australian Prime Minister Bob Hawke. China, along with **Hong Kong** and **Taiwan** as 'regional economies', joined APEC at its third ministerial meeting in Seoul in November 1991. The primary business of APEC is to enhance fair and free trade in the Asia-Pacific. In this regard, APEC can be described more as a forum-driven process to facilitate constructive dialogue on issues related primarily to trade liberalization than a structured set of institutions.

At its Bogor meeting in 1994, APEC set targets for free trade by the year 2010 for developed nations in the group (including the **United States**, Canada, **Japan** and **Australia**) and by the year 2020 for developing nations. According to these arrangements, each nation was to draft a free trade individual action plan. While these plans were re-endorsed at the Manila meeting in November 1996, most countries had made only modest advances toward their fulfilment, particularly the opening of domestic and agricultural markets (such as **Japan**) and the broader lowering of protective tariffs. China was quietly sympathetic with Malaysian Prime Minister Dr Mahathir's reservations that opening up the markets of the rich to the poor is meaningless if the poor have nothing to sell and that, therefore, direct foreign investments that can help enrich developing countries should precede market opening.

More recently, Beijing has been assertive over sovereignty and reunification issues relating to the **South China Sea** (where disputed territorial and maritime resource claims have heated up) and **Taiwan** (where democratic elections and continued sentiments for independence led China to demonstrate its willingness to use force, if necessary, to bring the island entity back into its embrace). Coupled with this, the widely publicized reports of China's rapid ascent towards 'economic superpower status' in the late 1990s have brought with them renewed regional fears about the growth of Chinese power. Beijing itself has claimed that some powers, particularly the US, are denying China its rightful place in both the region and in the global system through a neo-containment policy.

Over time, APEC's role expanded into a summit forum among regional leaders. At the Manila APEC meeting of late 1996, no issue dominated the regional economic and security agenda more than the growth (for some the 'threat') of Chinese power. In this light, one of APEC's true values, both for China and its regional counterparts, is that it provides an ongoing venue for quiet economic and strategic diplomacy of considerable weight and volume. Much of the behind-the-scenes diplomacy has aimed at finding concrete ways to reassure and engage China in constructive terms, such as bringing about its early entry into the **World Trade Organization**. Indeed, at that meeting, which was attended by Foreign Minister **Qian Qichen** and Economic Cooperation Minister Wu Yi, an agreement was reached for a summit between US President Bill Clinton and Chinese President **Jiang Zemin**, with the aim of easing the tension in Sino-US relations.

China's involvement in APEC not only underscores its policy of bilateral 'good neighbourly' relations with individual countries, but also enmeshes it in a significant broader multilateral and multifunctional framework.

see also: 8. China, the Region and the World;

Australia; Hong Kong; Japan, relations with; Jiang Zemin; Qian Qichen; South China Sea; Taiwan policy; United States policy; World Trade Organization.

Donald H. McMillen

Association of Southeast Asian Nations (ASEAN)

ASEAN was founded in 1967, largely as an initiative from within the region, to promote economic cooperation and development, national viability and regional peace and security, and combat domination by outside powers. Its member states included Indonesia, Singapore, Malaysia, Thailand and the Philippines, with Brunei and Vietnam joining in 1984 and 1995 respectively. As of 1997 it has fourteen 'dialogue partners', including **Japan**, the **United States**, China, Russia, India, **Australia** and the European Union. Geopolitical concerns, particularly the conflicts in Indochina, dominated the first two decades of the organization's life, but after the Cold War geoeconomic issues became equally important.

Sino-ASEAN relations have been shaped by historical factors and proximity, including former Chinese suzerainty over parts of the region (and attendant territorial claims), the presence in the region of numerous and economically influential people of Chinese ancestry, and China's post-1949 support for revolutionary movements in the region. In fact, Beijing's relations with ASEAN's leading member-state, Indonesia, were broken after the 1965 coup when Suharto's New Order regime condemned China for supporting communist elements attempting to capture power there. Events like the **Cultural Revolution**, Beijing's backing of the Pol Pot regime in Cambodia, its military confrontations with Vietnam, and its assertiveness in the **South China Sea** lent credence to this position.

China's reform and opening policies from the late 1970s, its normalization of relations with Western powers, and the resolution of the Cambodian conflict paved the way for improved Sino-ASEAN relations. ASEAN recognized the potential for trade with and investment in the dynamic Chinese economy, and the PRC became a 'new economic frontier'. By 1992, Sino-ASEAN trade had increased to US$8.4 billion, with a slight balance in China's favour. Singapore became the largest ASEAN investor in China, with about US$1 billion in 1992–3.

Premier **Zhao Ziyang**'s August 1981 visit to Malaysia and the Philippines and his downplaying of China's links with regional communist groups opened the way for a rapprochement in relations. The key step was the normalization of Sino-Indonesian relations in August 1990, with Singapore and Brunei following suit in October 1990 and October 1991.

From 1991, China participated in ASEAN foreign ministerial meetings and later became involved in the **Asia-Pacific Economic Cooperation** mechanism. Prime Minister Mahathir visited China with 300 Malaysian business people in June 1993 and declared that China's past was 'forgotten and irrelevant'. The following month, the ASEAN Regional Forum was established with China as one of the twenty-one member-states. The first ASEAN–PRC forum was held in Hangzhou in April 1995 to discuss trade issues, China's defence modernization and the **South China Sea** territorial dispute, ASEAN-sponsored workshops on which had started in July 1991. There was considerable ASEAN concern over China's 1995 occupation of Mischief Reef, its May 1996 declaration of sovereignty over maritime claims and resources, and its continued advocacy of bilateral rather than multilateral negotiations concerning the area.

As China obtained a greater regional presence, both fears and uncertainties as well as opportunities were recognized in the general ASEAN view favouring engagement over isolation. For example, Beijing shares a common view with ASEAN on the definition and handling of human rights and it supports ASEAN's objectives of regional peace and stability and the organization's function as a check against US predominance. While ASEAN has also assured Beijing that it is not a part of any US-backed anti-China coalition,

it generally welcomed Japanese Prime Minister Hashimoto's January 1997 proposal for 'regular bilateral summit meetings' between Tokyo and ASEAN leaders on regional security issues. Undoubtedly, China's rapid economic growth and opening, its military posturing, and its territorial ambitions (which some in ASEAN call 'creeping irredentism') will remain major factors in relations between the PRC and the ASEAN member-states.

see also: Asia-Pacific Economic Cooperation; Australia; Cultural Revolution; Japan, relations with; South China Sea; United States policy; Zhao Ziyang.

Donald H. McMillen

Australia

Being in the Pacific region, Australia has a certain importance for China as a non-threatening, prosperous country with an essentially Western culture and rich natural resources.

From 1949 until 1972, Australia refused to recognize the PRC, regarding it as a threat to regional and world peace. Australia sent troops to the **Korean War**, and in 1951 joined in the ANZUS (Australia, New Zealand and United States) alliance with the **United States**, the effect being to cut Australia off from any possibility of diplomatic relations for the indefinite future. This did not prevent the growth of a substantial wheat trade from the early 1960s.

In December 1972, the Australian Labor Party (ALP) gained office for the first time in twenty-three years, and one of its first actions was to establish diplomatic relations with the PRC. Prime Minister Gough Whitlam had already, when still leader of the Opposition, led a delegation to China in mid-1971, meeting Premier **Zhou Enlai**. Late in 1973 he revisited China, this time meeting CCP Chairman **Mao Zedong** as well. Whitlam and Zhou got on very well with each other, this being one factor in taking the broader Australia–China relationship from a state of fear (at least on Australia's side) to friendship.

When Malcolm Fraser's Liberal National

Party Coalition government replaced Whitlam's at the end of 1975 it changed many policies, but not that towards China. Indeed, because both countries were placing high priority on hostility to the **Soviet Union**, it became possible for them to form an entente even stronger than that which Whitlam had forged. Moreover, the fact that Mao died soon after Fraser came to power in Australia led on to a series of new policies in China which suited the more conservative and economically oriented Australia very well.

In March 1983, the ALP was re-elected, with Robert Hawke as prime minister. At first the Australia–China relationship did very well indeed under Hawke. Visits by senior leaders both ways expanded greatly, CCP General Secretary **Hu Yaobang** making an Australian tour in April 1985, Hawke returning to China in May 1986 and **Li Peng** going to Australia in November 1988.

Australia reacted harshly to the suppression of demonstrations at the **June 4 Incident** of 1989, downgrading its relationship with China. Hawke attended and spoke at a memorial rally denouncing the Chinese government action and cancelled a planned visit to China. Although the relationship began to improve in 1990 and continued to do so later in the 1990s, the Incident made the issue of human rights a far more important one for Australia than it had been before. Paul Keating, who became prime minister at the end of 1991, visited China in the middle of 1993 and his renewed thrust towards engagement with Asia exercised a beneficial effect on relations with China.

Both Hawke and Keating did their best to prevent Australia from becoming embroiled in the debate over **Taiwan** which has affected Sino-American relations so badly. At the same time, in the 1990s the tendency was for Australia to upgrade its unofficial relationship with **Taiwan**. In 1995, China began to show itself restive with Australia's expanding links with **Taiwan.**

The election of March 1996 saw Paul Keating defeated by John Howard's conservative Liberal Party. Initially, the relationship was disrupted over political differences on such matters as **Taiwan** and relations with the **United States**. In addition, the Dalai Lama visited Australia in September 1996 and met Howard, to China's intense annoyance. However, Howard soon visited China (28 March–1 April 1997), to a large extent repairing relations with China.

The economic side of the relationship is crucially important. Two-way trade and later investment have increased with time, trade surpassing A$8 billion (about US$6.3 billion) in value for the first time in 1996. Although wheat was once Australia's main export commodity to China, for various reasons this trade declined in the 1980s and 1990s. But meanwhile minerals and then wool established themselves as primary Australian exports to China.

Australia and China enjoy a good relationship, sharing many interests, especially in economic terms. However, the relationship continues to be volatile and could change if a major crisis were to erupt over **Taiwan**.

see also: Hu Yaobang; June 4 Incident; Korean War; Li Peng; Mao Zedong; Soviet Union, relations with; Taiwan policy; United States policy; Zhou Enlai.

Colin Mackerras

B

Beijing Municipality

PRC national capital and, as such, the focal point of its political life, Beijing first became China's national capital late in the thirteenth century and has remained so for most of the period since then, the most recent exception being from 1928 to 1949. On 27 September 1949, the **Chinese People's Political Consultative Conference** declared Beijing China's capital again and it was there, in Tiananmen Square, that the ceremony formally establishing the PRC took place on 1 October 1949.

At the end of 1995, Beijing Municipality had ten districts, which are the most densely populated urban areas, and eight counties, which are more rural, with mountains and far more agricultural land. With a total area of 16,806 square kilometres, it is one of four municipalities in China which has the status of a province. (The other three are **Shanghai**, Tianjin and Chongqing, the last achieving province-level status in March 1997.)

The PRC's four censuses of 1953, 1964, 1982 and 1990 showed Beijing's population, respectively, as 2,768,149, 7,568,495, 9,230,687 (males 50.6 per cent) and 10,819,407 (males 51.7 per cent). The 1990 census put the population of the ten urban districts at about 6.9 million or slightly less than two-thirds of the total. At the end of 1995, the total population of Beijing Municipality was 12.51 million. The natural growth rate was 2.8 per thousand, that being the lowest in the country at the time other than for **Shanghai** (−1.3 per thousand).

Although not the most important economic centre in China, Beijing boasts a range of modern heavy and light industries, including iron and steel, coal, machinery manufacture, petroleum, chemical and electronic. It is China's main tourist city, and in 1995 received 1.67 million foreign visitors. Beijing has, by Chinese standards, good transport facilities, as well as being a major communications and aviation centre. In November 1995, the Beijing–Kowloon railway line was completed, and on 21 January 1996 a formal opening took place for the enormous new Beijing West Railway Station to form the northern starting point of the line. The line was formally opened on 1 September 1996, the first passenger train leaving Beijing West Railway Station that day. Direct services between Beijing and Kowloon (and between Shanghai and Kowloon) began in May 1997.

Beijing can claim to be China's most important cultural and educational centre. Because of its history, it is the site of the magnificent Imperial Palaces, the residence of the emperors of the Ming and Qing dynasties, and the Temple of Heaven, among other sites. It is noted for carpets and traditional handicrafts such as cloisonné enamels, ivory and jade carvings. In addition, it is the place of origin of the Peking Opera and remains one of its major centres, being the site of the China Peking Opera Company, formally set up in January 1955. Many of China's most prestigious universities are located in Beijing, especially Beijing (Peking) University and Qinghua University, as well as the Academies of Sciences and Social Sciences of China.

Beijing is the site of the full sessions of the **National People's Congress** and, since 1949, of the **National Party Congress**es, as well as of most other national political meetings. The main building for China's central-level large-scale political meetings is the Great Hall of the People. Flanking Tiananmen Square in the centre of Beijing, it was completed at the end of August 1959.

In addition to central-level political activity, there is a Beijing Municipal **Chinese Communist Party** Committee and a Beijing government structure, headed by a people's congress and mayor. Beijing and Chinese national politics frequently become interwoven.

In the early days of the PRC, the most important political figure in Beijing politics was Peng Zhen. Already the municipal CCP secretary when the PRC was established, he was also appointed mayor on 28 February 1951, retaining both positions until the early phase of the **Cultural Revolution**. In November 1965, the supporters of the **Cultural Revolution** launched strong attacks on a Peking opera called *Hai Rui baguan* (*Hai Rui Dismissed from Office*) by Deputy Beijing Mayor and historian Wu Han, denouncing the play as an 'anti-Party poisonous weed' and an attack on **Mao Zedong**. In May 1966, a long extended meeting of the Politburo condemned Peng Zhen, among others, for a range of 'bourgeois revisionist' crimes and determined to dismiss him from all positions both inside and outside the CCP, making him among the first major victims of the **Cultural Revolution**. (He later reappeared as among the most important members of the old guard in the period of reform.) The politics of Beijing became closely bound up with the early stages of the **Cultural Revolution** as a whole.

The blurring of the distinction between Beijing and national politics is also exemplified in the career of Chen Xitong. Appointed mayor of Beijing in 1983, he was a dominant figure in the Beijing CCP and municipal organs for much of the 1980s and into the 1990s, becoming Beijing CCP Secretary in 1992. When the military crushed the student movement of 1989 in the **June 4 Incident** in Beijing, Chen Xitong was among the main advocates of the action. On 30 June 1989 he gave a 'report on checking the turmoil and quelling the counter-revolutionary rebellion', which included a detailed defence of the official account of events and trends over the preceding three months. In 1982 Chen joined the **CCP Central Committee** and in 1992 the Politburo.

Early in April 1995, Deputy Mayor of Beijing Wang Baosen committed suicide, because he was facing an investigation for corruption, large-scale embezzlement and other misdemeanours. Some of his crimes were found to involve Chen Xitong, who as a result was dismissed from his position as Beijing Municipal CCP Secretary. On 28 September, the **CCP Central Committee** also dismissed him both from the Politburo and Central Committee for seriously neglecting his duty, for involvement in Wang Baosen's crimes, for leading a dissolute life, abusing his power on behalf of relatives and accepting gifts. Just before the Fifteenth **National Party Congress** (1997) Chen was dismissed from the CCP itself and prosecuted. The implication of Chen's case is that Beijing politics has become a primary site for the struggle against corruption in the 1990s.

see also: Chinese Communist Party; Chinese Communist Party Central Committee and Politburo; Chinese People's Political Consultative Conference; Cultural Revolution; June 4 Incident; Mao Zedong; National Party Congress; National People's Congress; Shanghai.

Colin Mackerras

Bo Yibo

A senior leader in economic matters, Bo Yibo exercised an influence in CCP affairs over a long period that was not fully reflected in his formal status. He was a key economic official from 1949 until the **Cultural Revolution** although he never ranked higher than alternate member of the Politburo. Even more dramatically, in the post-Mao period his highest position was vice-premier and he was among the earliest of the old guard to retire, but he continued to exert great influence well into the 1990s.

Born in Shanxi in 1908, Bo joined the CCP in 1925 as a university student in **Beijing**. After a period in a Nationalist prison, he played an important role in developing a united front with the Shanxi warlord Yan Xishan in 1936–7 and later as a political and military leader in the Taihang-Taiyue area, and was elected to the **CCP Central Committee** in 1945. Bo was the leading Party figure in the North China region by the late 1940s, but with the founding of the PRC he became Minister of Finance. He was dismissed from that post in 1953 due to **Mao Zedong**'s anger over his tax policies which treated the public and private sectors equally, but was soon performing other key economic roles, notably as head of the State Economic Commission from 1956. In 1956 he also attained his alternate Politburo status, his 'mistake' in 1953 apparently costing him higher honours. Bo provided moderate or radical policy advice according to political circumstances, although his basic instincts were moderate. Bo was an early purge victim during the **Cultural Revolution**, probably due to historical ties to **Liu Shaoqi**, and he did not reappear until the end of 1978. In 1979 he became a vice-premier and Central Committee member, again having considerable influence in economic affairs. In 1982 he took the first steps toward retirement by giving up his vice-premiership and leaving the Central Committee for the new Central Advisory Committee. But his importance as one of the Party's leading elders was seen in his guiding role concerning the 1983–7 rectification campaign and by presiding over the 'Party life meeting' in early 1987 which marked the downfall of General Secretary **Hu Yaobang**. Moreover, Bo has played a key role well into his eighties on the body overseeing the writing of Party history, as well as writing the most valuable memoirs yet produced by a CCP leader.

see also: Beijing Municipality; Chinese Communist Party Central Committee and Politburo; Cultural Revolution; Hu Yaobang; Liu Shaoqi; Mao Zedong.

Frederick C. Teiwes

C

Canton
See **Guangzhou**.

capitalists/entrepreneurs
Big business people generally are referred to in post-Mao China as 'entrepreneurs', the term 'capitalist' being difficult to apply in a 'socialist' state.

Their social origins are of three types:

- the new capitalists who rose from among the ordinary populace;
- the 'bureaucratic capitalists' or 'nomenclature capitalists' who originated from the political elite, sometimes still holding official positions; and
- the 'red capitalists' from the old monied families.

The new capitalists often started off small in the 1980s as private vendors and petty manufacturers, attaining the official status of 'entrepreneurs' (*qiyejia*) with the acquisition of wealth. In the first half of the 1980s they were defensive about their success, feeling that government policies and corrupt local bureaucrats were discriminating against them. Their precarious status became evident after the **June 4 Incident** when the government began a campaign against them, ostensibly to wipe out corruption. But more recently, as their numbers and assets continued to increase, reaching 184,000 officially designated 'entrepreneurs' by mid-1993, they have been granted a more positive official image (see **new entrepreneurs**).

The 'nomenclature' capitalists are officials and their close kin, who have recently amassed wealth illicitly, through corruption, nepotism and inside deals, by transforming power and state resources into private wealth. Understandably their assets cannot be estimated.

The original 'red capitalists' came from prominent pre-1949 families of great wealth. They were used by the government under Mao Zedong in its contacts with **Overseas Chinese** and sometimes were given official positions. Under **Deng Xiaoping** they have been able to resume their business networks and in the 1990s are hailed for contributing to China's economic growth.

The most prominent 'red capitalist' is Rong Yiren who, from an extremely wealthy **Shanghai** family, was deputy minister of the Textile Industry from 1959 to 1966. Reportedly, **Deng Xiaoping** personally invited him to re-enter business to make big money for the country. In 1979–93, Rong headed the China International Trust and Investment Corporation (CITIC), the biggest of China's 'state' investment companies, with an outpost in **Hong Kong**. He was appointed vice-president of China in 1993.

To incorporate the interests of these three kinds of capitalists into the political structure, the All China Federation of Industry and Commerce (ACFIC, *Gongshanglian*) was revived at the beginning of the economic reforms with Rong as chairman. Reportedly, Rong and other former capitalists were reimbursed the interest owed to them by the government for the nationalization of their properties in the 1950s, and they contributed part of this sum to create a financial base for the revived ACFIC. It was granted a status equivalent to a sort of ninth **democratic party** (DP). Like these, the ACFIC has been placed under the supervision of the CCP's United Front Department, and state bureaucrats were sent to establish the ACFIC headquarters and provincial branches.

The ACFIC was to be another 'bridge' between the state and society, in this instance the country's new capitalists. Its ostensible function is to implement 'political education' among its members. However, within a few years the ACFIC was instead largely pursuing its own members' interests. Although enjoying the political status of a DP, it is actually quite different, in that it has a class-based constituency and an ideology, both of which are lacking among the DPs.

The ACFIC had 620,000 members as of the end of 1992, half of whom had been private entrepreneurs before 1949. This number is twice that of all eight DPs combined. The ACFIC can also afford to be financially independent, drawing from its investments and on the wealth of its membership.

see also: democratic parties; Deng Xiaoping; Hong Kong; June 4 Incident; Mao Zedong; new entrepreneurs; Overseas Chinese policy; private sector; Shanghai.

Anita Chan

Central Committee
See **Chinese Communist Party Central Committee and Politburo.**

Central Military Commission
The Central Military Commission (CMC) is the most powerful institution in China's political structure. As the highest military command, it exercises tight control over the Chinese armed forces: the **People's Liberation Army** (PLA) and the militia, which are the foundation and guardian of China's current political and social system. There are a Party and state central military commissions, the former being by far the more powerful and the one of concern here.

When the **Chinese Communist Party** came to power in 1949, it continued to share earlier vital political and economic interests with the PLA, granting it the highest possible social status and favourable treatment in the state budget in return for political support. Thanks to these shared common interests, the PLA twice saved the CCP: during the **Cultural Revolution** in the late 1960s and in mid-1989 (see **June 4 Incident**).

Both **Mao Zedong** and **Deng Xiaoping** owed their political power largely to control of the CMC. Mao assumed command of the Red Army at the Zunyi Conference in 1935, which led to his confirmation as CMC chairman in 1937. Until his death in 1976 he dominated China's political stage based on his firm control of the CMC. Although Deng never held the most senior post either in the

CCP or state, he remained as China's post-Mao leader because of his position as CMC chairman. CCP General Secretary **Jiang Zemin** became Party CMC chairman in 1989, but whether he succeeds Deng as national leader for a significant period depends on his acceptance by the PLA as indisputable CMC chairman.

The CMC chairman's authority rests on the leadership principle that the CMC exercises a commander's responsibility. In contrast to the Party's organizational principle of collective leadership for the civilian sector, the chairman of the CMC, as commander-in-chief, has ultimate personal power to appoint the top brass, to deploy troops, to control nuclear weapons and allocate the budget. Promotion of officers above the divisional level and the transfer of units at certain levels becomes valid only with the CMC chairman's signature. Such institutional mechanisms make it easy for him to consolidate his personal authority and build up his own following.

The CMC wields power fairly independently. Officially, it enjoys the same rank as the **State Council** and the Standing Committee of the **National People's Congress** and in the CCP's hierarchical pyramid, it is below the Politburo, actually operating largely outside the latter's reach. This has been a long tradition that can be traced to the reign of Mao, who deliberately separated the government and military systems. While the CMC, under Mao's personal control, was responsible only to him, civilian politicians tried to avoid unnecessary contact with PLA generals for fear of displeasing him. Mao remarked that 'the Politburo's realm is state affairs, the CMC's is military'.

To a large extent Deng inherited this tradition. The CMC reported only to him over the 1980s. Following his two predecessors, **Jiang Zemin** has tried to prevent his Politburo colleagues from involvement in CMC affairs. As a result the CMC enjoys the final say on matters ranging from personnel to legal, from commercial to cultural.

Since the late 1930s, the CMC has commanded the PLA through three general headquarters: the General Staff (which handles military affairs), the General Political Department (ideological, personnel, legal and disciplinary affairs) and the General Logistics Department (financial and budgetary affairs). Under these three general headquarters are the ground force, with seven military regions, namely Beijing, Shenyang, Ji'nan, Nanjing, Chengdu, Lanzhou and Guangzhou, the air force, the navy, the strategic missile force, the State Commission of Science, Technology and Industry for National Defence, the National Defence University and the PLA Military Science Academy. The General Staff is the CMC's most crucial organ, its general office being also that of the CMC itself and its security department being responsible also for the CMC's security.

The composition of the CMC is small and clear. At the top echelon are the CCP head (chairman) and a few senior PLA figures as deputies. As of late 1997, they included **Jiang Zemin**, **Zhang Wannian** and **Chi Haotian**. At the second echelon there are functional figures representing the three headquarters.

see also: Chi Haotian; Chinese Communist Party; Cultural Revolution; Deng Xiaoping; Jiang Zemin; June 4 Incident; Liu Huaqing; Mao Zedong; National People's Congress; People's Liberation Army; State Council; Zhang Wannian.

You Ji

Chen Boda

A senior leader until his fall in 1970, Chen Boda was one of the most important left intellectuals in the history of the **Chinese Communist Party**. He rose to prominence in the early 1940s as an interpreter of **Mao Zedong Thought** and a close collaborator of **Mao Zedong** in the development of that thought. He assumed high positions from that time and was a notable figure in such radical upsurges as the **Great Leap Forward** and the **Cultural Revolution**, only to fall dramatically in 1970 in a development linked to the **Lin Biao** affair.

Born in Fujian in 1904, Chen joined the Party in 1924, participated in the Northern Expedition, and studied in Moscow from 1927 to 1930. He then did propaganda work

in Fujian and the North China underground, but his significance dates from 1937 when he went to Yan'an, served as Mao's political secretary, and became a major contributor to the emerging Maoist orthodoxy at the time of the 1942–4 Party rectification. Chen's significance was recognized by his election as a **CCP Central Committee** alternate in 1945 and as an alternate Politburo member in 1956, but his key position was still as Mao's senior secretary. During the early PRC period Chen continued to publish authoritative interpretations of Mao's thought, and also to serve as troubleshooter in pushing forward Mao's favourite projects, notably agricultural cooperativization. He assumed a very high profile during the **Great Leap Forward** as editor of *Hongqi (Red Flag)*, and adopted radical positions such as the abolition of money that Mao soon rejected. Chen rose to even greater heights with the **Cultural Revolution**, becoming a member of the Standing Committee of the Politburo and, more significantly, head of the **Cultural Revolution** Group in 1966. While the latter position gave him a leading voice in pushing the movement forward, he soon developed bitter personal relations with other members, particularly Mao's wife, Jiang Qing, and junior members of the body. This led Chen to associate increasingly with those around **Lin Biao**, but this in no way meant any diminution of his intense loyalty to Mao. Ironically, Chen's fall was occasioned by his role in advocacy of Mao's genius by the **Lin Biao** group at the 1970 Lushan plenum, a view Mao rejected to the surprise of the meeting. Chen was sentenced to prison as a member of the **Lin Biao** clique in 1981 but was soon released on health grounds, dying in 1989.

see also: Chinese Community Party; Chinese Communist Party Central Committee and Politburo; Cultural Revolution; Great Leap Forward; *Hongqi (Red Flag)*; Lin Biao; Mao Zedong; Mao Zedong Thought.

Frederick C. Teiwes

Chen Yi

A native of **Sichuan**, Chen Yi was born in 1901 and died on 6 January 1972. He studied in France (1919–21), joining the Chinese Socialist Youth League and, after return to China, joined the CCP (1923). He participated in the Northern Expedition and the Nanchang Uprising (1927), after which he followed Zhu De to Jinggangshan and accompanied **Mao Zedong** to Jiangxi. Covering the retreat of the Red Army as it began the Long March, Chen was out of contact with the **CCP Central Committee** until 1937. He went to Yan'an in 1944, becoming a **CCP Central Committee** member the next year. He commanded the New 4th Army and then the East China Field Army in 1947–8, taking part in the Huaihai campaign and the capture of Nanjing and **Shanghai** in 1949.

Chen was chairman of the **Shanghai** Military Control Commission (with the rank of Marshal in 1955), mayor of **Shanghai** (1949–58), and first secretary of the **Shanghai** Municipal CCP Committee (1952–8). He was a CCP Politburo member (1956–69), vice-premier of the State Council (1954–68), and minister of Foreign Affairs (1958–72). He was also a vice-chairman of the CCP Central Committee's **Central Military Commission** (1961–72) and of the Fourth **Chinese People's Political Consultative Conference** Standing Committee (1965–72).

As foreign minister, Chen Yi travelled abroad extensively, particularly to **Third World** and Eastern Bloc states. In this capacity, he signed many friendship treaties, nationality and cultural accords, boundary agreements and international arrangements with states such as Burma, Pakistan, Afghanistan, Indonesia and Cambodia. From December 1963 to February 1964, he accompanied **Zhou Enlai** on a high-profile African tour during the height of China's courtship of the non-aligned, **Third World** states. It is significant that Chen Yi was minister for Foreign Affairs when the Sino-**Soviet** split occurred. In this context, his brief was to develop China's image among, and relations with, those states and movements outside the camps of the two superpowers, the **Soviet Union** and **United States**.

In 1967, Chen Yi was repeatedly attacked by wall posters in Beijing, and in March 1968

admitted to having committed mistakes. Although retaining **CCP Central Committee** membership in 1969, his name was not among those officially listed on the Politburo. Most likely, **Zhou Enlai**'s support for Chen prevented his further disgrace and possible removal at that time.

see also: 8. China, the Region and the World; Central Military Commission; Chinese Communist Party Central Committee and Politburo; Chinese People's Political Consultative Conference; Mao Zedong; Shanghai; Sichuan; Soviet Union, relations with; Third World policy; United States policy; Zhou Enlai.

Donald H. McMillen

Chen Yun

Chen Yun was one of the half dozen most significant figures in the history of Chinese communism. One of the least public of Chinese leaders, Chen played roles of great importance during the revolutionary struggle before 1949, the first decade of the PRC, and especially during the early post-Mao period up to about 1985.

Born near Shanghai in 1905, Chen was one of the few early communist leaders with a working-class background. He joined the **Chinese Communist Party** in 1925, rising to **CCP Central Committee** membership in 1931 and a seat on the Politburo in 1934. These two appointments came at meetings controlled by factional enemies of **Mao Zedong**, but they did not prevent Chen from siding with Mao at the watershed Zunyi conference in 1935, which was the crucial first step in establishing Mao's leadership. In late 1937 Chen gained further key posts including head of the Party's Organization Department, and he firmly sided with Mao in the revived factional struggle which raged throughout 1938. By the mid-1940s he was clearly one of Mao's closest supporters in organizational and ideological matters, and he had also become the chief economic expert among the top leadership. In 1945 Chen was named the Party's sixth-ranking leader at the Seventh Party Congress. Chen Yun's economic expertise became even more central to his career after

1949. Over the next eight years Chen was clearly the main economic policy maker, earning great prestige for overseeing economic recovery after decades of warfare, and then for guiding the transition to a **Soviet**-style planned economy. His position at the very top was confirmed at the Eighth **National Party Congress** in 1956, now as a Party vice-chairman and member of the Politburo Standing Committee. While Mao strongly supported Chen's economic stewardship during this period, by 1958 he became impatient for rapid growth and took control of the economy himself, launching the wildly ambitious **Great Leap Forward**. Chen's influence was sharply reduced, but he was given crucial roles by Mao briefly in 1959 and 1962 to deal with some of the Leap's gravest dislocations. Throughout the Great Leap saga, Chen never challenged Mao's leadership but his preference for caution and balance was clear, finally leading Mao to shunt him aside in 1962, commenting that 'this man has always been a rightist'. Yet in terms of Party politics Mao also observed that Chen 'has a strong sense of discipline' – that is, when finding himself in disagreement with an insistent Mao he would remain silent until Mao showed signs of changing his views.

After fifteen years of a minimal role, Chen Yun began to exert enormous influence following Mao's death. His first major step in early 1977 was to press for the return of **Deng Xiaoping**, ousted by Mao in 1976, to the top Party leadership. At the crucial meetings in late 1978 which launched the reform era and placed Deng unambiguously in control, Chen more than Deng raised the critical issues – the need to rehabilitate Party leaders who had suffered at Mao's hands, the economic mismanagement caused by excessively ambitious policies in 1977–8, and generally to undercut the position of Party Chairman **Hua Guofeng**. Chen's own position was enhanced at the meetings and he emerged in his former posts as Party vice-chairman and member of the Politburo Standing Committee. He now played a critical role in shaping the reform agenda. Chen was again the regime's economic architect, overseeing both the first

steps of reform through decentralization and increased reliance on the market, and readjustment measures to curb unsustainable growth. Chen also played key roles in other areas, notably the design of personnel reforms to promote younger, better educated and more professionally competent officials. By the mid-1980s, however, Chen's economic vision was overtaken by the momentum of economic reform. This was reflected in differences with Deng who, similar to Mao before him, was impatient for both rapid growth and further reforms. But also similar to the Mao period, Chen's influence reappeared with difficult economic circumstances, this time caused by sharp inflationary pressures in 1988 which produced a new round of readjustment lasting to early 1992. While Chen's role is not entirely clear given his semi-retirement since 1987, there can be no doubt of his significance in the process. This last period to his death in 1995, especially his grudging support of Deng's new reform push in 1992, underlined a further similarity to the Maoist period. Notwithstanding substantive differences with Deng, rather than being a hard-line rival of Deng's as often portrayed, at no point did Chen directly challenge him. Chen continued the 'disciplined' pattern of his earlier career in obeying the Party's leader once that leader had made his demands clear.
see also: Chinese Communist Party; Chinese Communist Party Central Committee and Politburo; Deng Xiaoping; Great Leap Forward; Hua Guofeng; Mao Zedong; National Party Congress; Soviet Union, relations with.

Frederick C. Teiwes

Chi Haotian

People's Liberation Army (PLA) general and core member of the **Central Military Commission** (CMC) from 1988. Chi was born in July 1929 in Zhaoyuan, **Shandong** Province. Among his many civilian and military portfolios, the most important are deputy chairman of the Party CMC and member of the Politburo, which he joined at the Fifteenth Party Congress (September 1997).

General Chi started his military service as

an infantry soldier in the 8th Route Army in 1944 and was awarded the title of East China people's hero in 1949 for distinguished services against the Japanese and Nationalist Party forces. General Chi participated in the **Korean War**, being promoted to battalion political instructor and commended by merit citation, first class. Graduating from the PLA Military Academy in 1960 he was promoted in 1970 to political commissar of 81 Division, 27th Army. Two years later he joined a special working group to take over the leadership of the *PLA Daily*, a crucial transfer giving him much needed access to the top PLA brass. Indeed, when **Mao Zedong** instructed the PLA to place younger officers in key command posts after the **Lin Biao** affair (1971), he was selected to become deputy commissar of **Beijing** Military Region in 1973, a three-step accelerated promotion.

General Chi has shown political skill throughout his career. A beneficiary of the **Cultural Revolution**, he was promoted to deputy chief of staff in 1977, just after it had ended. In 1987 he defeated a number of candidates to become chief of staff, a crucial step enabling him to climb the pyramid of PLA command. During the factional strife between old PLA veterans and the brothers **Yang Shangkun** and Yang Baibing, he stood firmly with the veterans, winning respect from many professionally minded officers. This paved the way for him to enter the CMC in 1992.

As of 1997, General Chi has been a member of the **CCP Central Committee** since 1982. As deputy chair of the CMC, he is in charge of political/organizational affairs, the PLA's relations with foreign armed forces, and the Ji'nan and Chengdu Military Regions. As minister of National Defence, he is also one of nine state councillors in the **State Council**, requiring him to take care of links between the CMC and the highest level of government. *see also:* Beijing Municipality; Central Military Commission; Chinese Communist Party Central Committee and Politburo; Cultural Revolution; Korean War; Lin Biao; Mao Zedong; People's Liberation Army; Shandong; State Council; Yang Shangkun.

You Ji

Chinese Communist Party

The ruling party and most important power-holding organization of the PRC. The CCP was founded in 1921 in **Shanghai**. Within two years it entered into an alliance with the Nationalist Party (Guomindang) which ended in the purge of Party members in 1927. Civil war between Nationalists and Communists ensued until a united front was concluded to resist Japan in 1936. The uneasy united front deteriorated in the early 1940s and civil war resumed in 1946, ending with the defeat of the Guomindang in 1949.

Seven **National Party Congress**es were held before the proclamation of the PRC and (as of late 1997) eight since. The **National Party Congress** is charged with the task of formulating the basic orientation of the Party for the next few years, though in 1953 the first 'general line' (*zong luxian*) of the Party after the foundation of the PRC was not the product of a Party congress. From 1958 to 1969, no congress was convened due to internal strife but a more regular procedure was adopted in the late 1970s. Since 1977 the party congress has met every fifth year. Formal Party history tends to be written not only in terms of decisions taken formally by Party congresses but also in terms of those ratified by plenary sessions of the **CCP Central Committee** (plenums), required to meet once a year. From the foundation of the PRC until late 1997, there had been fifty-three such plenums, those plenums being recorded by reference to the relevant Party congress, e.g. the **Third Plenum of the Eleventh Central Committee** (1978). Many of those plenums have been much more important in policy formulation than Party Congresses, primary examples being the **Third Plenum** and **Sixth Plenum of the Eleventh Central Committee**.

Party membership has fluctuated over the years due to purges, the most recent of which occurred in the 1980s when large numbers of Party members recruited in the **Cultural Revolution** were removed. Membership in late 1997 was 58 million. Party members are relatively senior in age and overwhelmingly male.

There have been many complaints about the relatively uneducated nature of most Party members, though in recent years attempts have been made to recruit those with educational qualifications. In 1995, less than 40 per cent had completed the equivalent of a higher secondary school **education**, though this is a considerable improvement on 1978, when the reforms began.

The formal structure of the Party mirrors the formal state structure. At the centre, the **National Party Congress** appoints the **CCP Central Committee**, under which there is a very powerful Politburo (with an even more powerful standing committee) and a number of other bodies. Of these the most important is the large Secretariat and the **Central Military Commission**. The relative importance of these bodies has changed over time. For example, the Secretariat, headed by a general secretary (originally **Deng Xiaoping**), played a major role in the late 1950s, was abolished in the **Cultural Revolution** and revived again in the reform period. With the abolition of the post of Party chairman in 1982 and the elevation of the post of general secretary (filled at that time by **Hu Yaobang**), an attempt was made to transfer some of the functions of the Politburo to the Secretariat, though that trend was reversed after 1989.

Similarly an attempt was made to transfer many of the functions of the **Central Military Commission** to a Military Commission within the formal state structure, though the Party body (seven members in 1997) remained powerful, reflecting the particularly close relationship between the Party and the **People's Liberation Army**.

While the formal organizational principle is appointment of small bodies by larger elected bodies (e.g. the **National Party Congress** appoints the Central Committee, the Central Committee appoints the Politburo and the Politburo appoints its standing committee), in practice the reverse seems usually to have been be the case. In fact, the informal structure is very different from the formal provisions. For most of the Party's history, policy initiatives have stemmed from a 'core leader' (notably **Mao Zedong** and **Deng**

Xiaoping) and some twenty-five to thirty-five leaders who have exercised considerable power regardless of formal position. Those leaders have maintained informal networks of power based on patron–client relations (subsumed under the general term *guanxi*, or relationships). The formal organizational chart, moreover, underestimates the importance of central work conferences, which in the past were often more important than Central Committee plenums, and in the 1980s of the Central Advisory Commission to which old leaders were removed but who continued to wield much power. It ignores the extraordinary influence of those leaders' personal secretaries (*mishu*), the role of guard units and the importance of networks (known colloquially as gateways [*kou*, functional areas] and systems [*xitong*]) which cut across formal organizational boundaries. The most important systems are Party Affairs, Organization and Personnel (which manages the *bianzhi* – a system of Party control over key posts – the equivalent of the **Soviet** Nomenklatura), Propaganda and Education, Political and Legal Affairs, Finance and Economics and Military (over which the Party exercises more direct control than the other systems).

Party fractions (or small groups, *dangzu*), performing an important controlling and policy formulation role, exist in all ministerial bodies and state organizations. The late 1980s saw formal proposals to separate Party and state functions – the former to be concerned with overall long-term policy and the latter with normal administration – resulting in demands to abolish these fractions.

While the Party controls government ministries, it has its own internal control structure, such as that maintained by the Central Disciplinary Inspection Commission. In the past, Party organs were regarded as above the formal **legal system**, under the rubric of 'rule by persons' (*renzhi*) rather than 'rule by law' (much less 'rule of law', both terms translated as *fazhi*) – a situation which led to much arbitrariness. Since 1982, however, Party members have been made subject to the formal legal structure; but the fact that the Party may impose its own sanctions on its members has impeded the institutionalizing of the formal **legal system**. Utilizing their long-held preference for the 'campaign' style of leadership, Party bodies have recently played a major role in mobilizing people to combat corruption to the detriment of formal legal procedures. In that endeavour, only a few senior leaders, believed by many to be corrupt, have been brought to task.

A structure similar to that of the centre exists at lower levels. There are Party committees at the provincial, county and township levels. Between province and county, prefectural levels usually exist and contain Party bodies. There are usually Party organizations at the lowest level – the *danwei* – or basic organizational **unit** (enterprise, school, residents' organization, etc.) (see **local government/administration**). There is also a Party network in the **People's Liberation Army**, extending a committee structure down to company level. In 1997 there were 3.4 million primary party organizations. Recently Party bodies at lower levels have exhibited an unprecedented degree of autonomy from the centre, though provincial leadership (often represented in the centre) has occasionally been brought to heel. In the past the Party secretary, at the **unit** level, exercised a considerable degree of power in controlling the daily life of its members (rations, transfer, political study, policing, etc.) but that level of Party secretary suffered considerably during the **Cultural Revolution**. The power of the **unit** Party secretary declined in the 1980s and 1990s (particularly in state economic enterprises, though Party secretaries have often been ingenious in mobilizing support against formal management).

In contrast to the former **Soviet Union**, Party control of lower levels has been characterized by what has been called the 'dual rule' nature of administration. Units at all levels are subject to control from above (by lines, *tiao*) and from local Party bodies (by localities (*kuai*). Authority relations, therefore, are fragmented while still remaining authoritarian. This has been a source of much administrative confusion but at times has exhibited greater flexibility than in the case of the former **Soviet Union**.

Party rule, therefore, is authoritarian but not totalitarian (in imposing rigid conformity from above). Within the Party the principle of 'democratic centralism' is still maintained whereby there is a broad canvassing of opinions before a decision is made, but the demand for rigid compliance thereafter. **Mao Zedong**, after 1959, violated that principle but efforts have been made to restore it. Nevertheless, the ideological cement which once held the Party together has weakened and the centre is no longer able to exercise the ideological sway it once did. When ideological integration fails, the Party has to stress strengthening organizational integration. When that fails, as it sometimes does, the Party structure is held together by little more than patron–client relations. These, however, are still strong.

see also: Central Military Commission; Chinese Communist Party Central Committee and Politburo; Cultural Revolution; Deng Xiaoping; education policy and system; Hu Yaobang; legal system; local government/administration; Mao Zedong; National Party Congress; People's Liberation Army; Shanghai; Sixth Plenum of the Eleventh Central Committee; Soviet Union, relations with; Third Plenum of the Eleventh Central Committee; unit.

Bill Brugger

Chinese Communist Party Central Committee and Politburo

Other than the **National Party Congress**, the top bodies of authority within the **Chinese Communist Party**.

The Central Committee of the CCP, which is empowered by the Party **Constitution** to enact policies and manage Party affairs when the **National Party Congress** is not in session, is formally selected by the **National Party Congress**, though in practice is largely chosen by top leaders and selected members of the outgoing Central Committee.

In the early days of the PRC the Central

Committee consisted of forty-four full members. The first Party Congress after 1949 (the Eighth in 1956) increased the number to ninety-seven. From the Ninth to the Twelfth Congresses, the number of members escalated and, as a result, measures were taken in the late 1980s to reduce the size of the Committee.

The Central Committee produced by the Fifteenth Congress in 1997, while smaller than some previous ones, had 190 full members and 151 alternates. The rapid growth of the Central Committee in the 1980s resulted from a desire to reward senior Party members for loyal service, recompense for their sufferings during the **Cultural Revolution** and an informal notion of functional representation. Considerations of functional representation in a changing political environment are reflected in very high **People's Liberation Army** (PLA) representation in the Ninth Central Committee (1969), less in the Tenth Central Committee (1973), falling to 17 per cent in the late 1980s but rising again to 25 per cent in the Fourteenth Central Committee (1992). Such considerations explain why representation of 'mass organizations' increased dramatically in the drive to revive radicalism in the early 1970s and declined in the more pragmatic climate thereafter; they explain why representation of veteran officials grew significantly after 1977 until considerations of forced retirement produced a significant change in 1985 and why representation of provinces increased in 1992.

Members of the Fourteenth Central Committee, produced in 1992, were better educated than their forebears: some 84 per cent had a college education (compared with 73 per cent in the previous committee). Their average age was 56, which is much the same as the previous Central Committee on election but younger than the one before that. Of particular note, when one considers the leadership, is the fact that many of the 'princeling faction' (thought by many to be corrupt) did not secure membership.

Since the late 1970s the Central Committee has met in plenary session once or twice annually in accordance with the CCP **Consti-** tution, though that was not always the case in the past, due to war or internal Party tension; no plenary sessions were held in 1951–3, 1960, 1963–5, 1967, 1971, 1974 or 1976. Some plenums have been celebrated as initiating radical policy shifts, though usually such plenums only ratify decisions taken at prior work conferences. Those work conferences are sometimes the site of vigorous policy debates and on occasions have blocked the initiatives of central leaders (for example concerning financial recentralization in 1989); such blockages have resulted in delay of a formal meeting by the Politburo, which is responsible for convening a plenum.

The greater power of the Central Committee since the late 1970s (albeit in forums other than the formal plenum) is also seen in the fact that only rarely has the core leader overridden its decisions taken at work conferences. Politburo deliberations, unlike in the days of **Mao Zedong**, are usually very sensitive to the reactions of the Central Committee. But there have been exceptions, for example in 1987 when a formal decision was taken to remove General Secretary **Hu Yaobang**, without Central Committee endorsement.

Sometimes meetings of the Central Committee have been stacked by the inclusion of non-members. A notable example occurred when Central Committee members were summoned to Beijing during the crisis of 1989 but disagreement resulted in a plenum being delayed until the removal of General Secretary **Zhao Ziyang** had been finalized. Eventually, to ensure agreement, the plenum which finally ratified the action was stacked by other leading personnel, resulting in a meeting of 557 participants. The autonomy of the Central Committee has also been limited by the use of national conferences of Party delegates. Ratifying action taken by such a body in 1985 to retire 18 per cent of members, the 1992 and 1997 Party **Constitutions** empowered a national conference of Party delegates to replace up to one-fifth of the total number of Central Committee members and alternates elected by the **National Party Congress** and to decide major issues (unspecified).

The Politburo exercises immense power over all important policies and the appointment of key personnel – a fact not captured in the bland statement in the Party **Constitution** (1997, Article 22) that it 'exercises the functions and powers of the Central Committee when a plenum is not in session'. The Politburo is formally elected by the Central Committee in plenary session though, during his lifetime, it was in practice selected by **Mao Zedong**. In the 1980s, **Deng Xiaoping** played a major role in selecting and dismissing members. Most notably, in 1985 he managed to secure the removal of ten Politburo members (40 per cent) and the appointment of some new ones, an action legitimized by the Conference of Party Delegates (rather than a formal plenum). Deng's power, however, was not as great as Mao's and selection of the Politburo has involved intense lobbying among top leaders. The Politburo grew from eleven members in 1949 to thirty in 1978, declining to twenty-two (plus two alternates) in 1997. Over a quarter of the 1997 Politburo are leaders who achieved power in various provinces and are identified with them.

Since 1956, the Politburo has maintained a Standing Committee which constitutes the formal apex of political power. Until 1982, when Party titles were changed, the Standing Committee of the Politburo consisted of the Party chairman, vice-chairmen and the general secretary. Both in 1992 and 1997, the Standing Committee comprised seven members, headed by General Secretary **Jiang Zemin**.

In the 1980s attempts were made to limit the enormous power exercised by the Politburo. Throughout the reform period measures have been taken to transfer some of its power to formal state bodies. As a result, the bulk of legislation passing through the Standing Committee of the **National People's Congress** now does not require prior Politburo ratification, as was shown in a 1991 Central Committee document. But the transfer of power has been limited, not least because the Politburo brings together the very top leaders of the government, the military and the security apparatus. The power of the seven-person Politburo Standing Committee is even greater. A Standing Committee member usually presides over the small 'leading group' which controls each of the functional areas and 'systems' (*xitong*) which cut across formal organizational boundaries and integrate Party and state functions.

The Politburo Standing Committee seems to meet weekly and the full Politburo, which contains several provincial leaders, less regularly. On important matters, such as the dismissal of **Hu Yaobang**, the Politburo or its Standing Committee might convene an enlarged meeting. Formally non-Politburo members who attend do not have voting rights.

The exercise of power at the centre does not depend on formal institutional position. **Deng Xiaoping** was notable for retaining the power to decide on all important issues after he had resigned from his formal posts. One post, however, which he retained until 1989, was chair of the Party's **Central Military Commission**. Maintenance of that position might have reflected the PLA's desire for direct access to the 'core leader' who could exercise potential power greater than that of people who formally held the top posts. More significantly, it reflects the central Party leadership's desire to maintain direct control over the PLA.

Informal power has also been exercised by veteran leaders other than **Deng Xiaoping**, who in 1990–1 were reported to have issued instructions to formal bodies. For a decade (1982–92) many of those veterans held official positions in a body known as the Central Advisory Commission (of some 175 members). Vice-chairmen of that Commission maintained the right to attend Politburo meetings (again formally as non-voting members), many more members of that Commission attended the stacked meeting of the Central Committee in 1989 referred to above and many attended **National Party Congresses** without being formally elected as delegates.

The routine work of the central Party apparatus is the responsibility of the Secretariat, presided over by the general secretary and seven secretaries. The power of that body has fluctuated over time. It played a major role in the mid- to late 1950s, disappeared in the **Cultural Revolution** but revived in the late 1970s. The Secretariat coordinates the work of several functional departments. These have varied over time in size and number but have usually been assigned separate responsibilities for organization, propaganda, the united front, international liaison, subordinate Party organs and state organs. There has also been a General Office and at various times a Policy Research Office.

Another important Party body at the centre is the Central Disciplinary Inspection Commission, which has 115 members. This body, created in 1977 under **Chen Yun**, was the successor of the Party Control Commission abolished in the **Cultural Revolution**. Its original function was to restore Party morale and discipline disrupted during the **Cultural Revolution**. Later, it became greatly concerned with the behaviour of Party organizations and investigating breaches of conduct among CCP members in a climate of increasing corruption. Some of its members attended the enlarged Politburo meeting which dismissed **Hu Yaobang**, the stacked plenum of 1989 which ratified the dismissal of **Zhao Ziyang** and served as voting members of Party congresses.
see also: Central Military Commission; Chen Yun; Chinese Communist Party; Constitutions; Cultural Revolution; Deng Xiaoping; Hu Yaobang; Jiang Zemin; Mao Zedong; National Party Congress; National People's Congress; People's Liberation Army; princelings; Zhao Ziyang.

Bill Brugger

Chinese People's Political Consultative Conference

A political organ representing the united front, the Chinese People's Political Consultative Conference (CPPCC) traces its origins back to the period when the Nationalist Party and the **Chinese Communist Party** formed a united front during the Anti-Japanese War (1937–45). It was the CPPCC, meeting in September 1949 and dominated by **Mao Zedong**, which formally designated **Beijing** as the PRC's capital, adopted its interim **Constitu**-

tion, called the Common Programme, and decided to declare the foundation of the PRC on 1 October 1949.

After their victory the CCP manipulated the CPPCC as a component part of the new state structure and as a forum to appeal to those non-communist democratic elements who favoured peace and the reconstruction of the country under a non-corrupt regime. At first the CPPCC proved effective in helping to woo back distinguished Chinese intellectuals living overseas, but the reality of communism for this stratum soon became apparent, and many lived to regret their optimism and patriotism.

Since 1949 the CPPCC has proved to be essentially a united front weapon for building legitimacy and influence among leading non-communist democratic parties and non-aligned intellectuals. It is also a transmission belt for conveying CCP principles and policies to these same groups. All along it has been led and controlled by the CCP, with its successive chairmen being party-state leaders such as **Zhou Enlai**, **Deng Xiaoping**, **Li Xiannian** and **Li Ruihuan**. This state of affairs is duplicated in the provinces. Many of its supposed non-communist activists have in fact proved to be long-term, secret members of the CCP.

The CPPCC consists of a national conference with authority delegated to a standing committee consisting of a chairman, numerous vice-chairmen and ordinary members. This structure is replicated at the provincial, municipal and county levels. The CPPCC holds congresses every five years, to coincide with congresses of the **National People's Congress**, together with yearly sessions (usually commencing and concluding a day earlier than people's congress meetings). A party group decides upon the composition and leadership of conferences at different administrative levels. Delegates are selected on the basis of their membership of various social and political groups, and CCP members can comprise a substantial minority.

For most of the period since 1949 the CPPCC has been, superficially at least, a tame organization, with those daring to voice opinions contrary to the leadership's suffering retribution when policy has shifted. For example, in the mid 1950s, during the **Hundred Flowers Movement**, **Mao Zedong** encouraged, almost cajoled, members to speak out about the shortcomings of the CCP. Those who did so found themselves under heavy criticism or even incarceration in labour camps when their comments were denounced during the Anti-Rightist Movement of 1957.

The CPPCC was among those organizations destroyed during the **Cultural Revolution**, and was not revived until the First Session of its Fifth National Committee met from 24 February to 8 March 1978, electing **Deng Xiaoping** as its chairman. While the political atmosphere is less threatening than it was under Mao, the CCP still exerts tight control over the organization and closely supervises its activities.

At the national sessions of 1988 and 1989, strong complaints were made concerning the lack of state funds for education. The brutal repression of the student movement in June 1989 (see **June 4 Incident**) quickly put an end to such outspoken criticism, however. Concern has been raised in recent years concerning the feasibility and environmental consequences of building the enormous **Three Gorges Dam** on the Yangzi River, but this did not prevent it from starting construction.

The CPPCC runs newspapers and compiles and publishes a series of cultural and historical materials recording the deeds of patriotic intellectuals and local identities. As of 1997, these materials have concentrated on the pre-1949 period. It also carries out other public relations duties to put a gloss on the often rough image of the PRC. The CPPCC derives its funding from **local government**, and therefore its activities are constrained by the generosity, goodwill and solvency of these local authorities. Under the socialist market economy the CPPCC has access to rather few funds but is asked to carry out a wide range of activities.

The CPPCC has never really thrown off the appearance and behaviour of a club of faithful, obedient retainers who go through the motions of debate knowing well that their role is limited to providing a façade of discussion and consultation for decisions made elsewhere. If major changes occur to China's political system it is unlikely that the CPPCC will be a key instigator of such reform.

see also: Beijing Municipality; Chinese Communist Party; Constitutions; Cultural Revolution; Deng Xiaoping; Hundred Flowers Movement; June 4 Incident; Li Ruihuan; Li Xiannian; local government/ administration; Mao Zedong; National People's Congress; Three Gorges Dam; Zhou Enlai.

Keith Forster

collective agriculture

Agricultural production in China was organized collectively from the establishment of the advanced cooperatives during 1956 until the demise of the people's communes in 1983. It persists in those villages in the richer coastal areas where local communities have found it more economic to continue farming collectively (see **agriculture**). In addition, **township and village enterprises** (TVEs) remain under collective ownership.

Collective agriculture was a system in which peasants pooled all their land, animals and large pieces of equipment into common ownership, and a cooperative committee managed production in accordance with production and sales quotas issued by the government. Supplies of inputs were allocated through state marketing cooperatives. Peasants could maintain small private plots, managing them as they wished, but priority was given to collective farming and the production of grain, oil crops and raw materials required for urban industry. At year's end, after deductions for production, management and welfare costs, tax and investment, the balance was distributed among the community according to each member's labour contribution. The work done by each peasant for the collective was recorded as work points. The value of each work point was determined by dividing total distributed income by total work points, and individual peasants received a share according to the number of points they had accumulated. The system assumed:

- that collectives provided economies of scale compared with individual farms;
- that they enabled efficient management of resources;
- that they were more easily controlled through state planning; and
- that they created a more equal social basis for rural development.

The advanced cooperatives, which consisted of around 300 families, were introduced rapidly during 1956. Many peasants reacted against them at first, and output of animal and special products declined. Studies by Chinese economists found that while production of major crops improved and the income of the poorer peasants rose, the abolition of private sidelines had an adverse effect on many incomes. As a result, the pace of collectivization slowed in early 1957 and some advanced cooperatives disbanded.

The issue then became the subject of intense political debate. **Mao Zedong** argued that collectivization was a necessary precondition for agricultural modernization. Collectivization would allow the mobilization of labour which could prime the pump for development. In contrast, opponents argued that prior improvements in technology and output were necessary for collectivization.

Mao's opponents were condemned as 'rightists' in 1957, and in 1958, during the **Great Leap Forward**, collectives were reasserted through the establishment of the people's communes. The communes then formed the basic institution for agricultural organization until 1983.

At first, communes were very large, consisting of up to 60,000 households and incorporating many natural villages. Three levels of management were established: the commune, the brigade and the team. The commune was the level of ownership and accounting. All the assets of the community, apart from their homes and individual implements, were owned collectively, and income was shared among all commune members. The view was that the larger the size and the more collective the structure, the more efficient and socialist the commune would be. The brigades had around 300 to 400 families and managed large equipment. The teams consisted of 30 to 40 households, and actually farmed the land.

Apart from agriculture, the communes also absorbed the lowest level of administration, the township, and acted as an integrated structure for government, production, welfare, education and public security. In line with Mao's ideas, there was a strong emphasis on egalitarian sharing of income and on the diversion of labour to non-agricultural work in order to boost economic growth. The symbol was the 'backyard furnace' which attempted to produce steel using local resources in order to boost China's total output to world levels. Many communes introduced communal mess halls, issued food freely, drew **women** into the labour force, and provided collective services for the very young and the very old.

There was a substantial boost in output in 1958, aided by fine weather, but poor management and considerable waste meant that much was lost. The communes then faced three years of natural disasters which resulted in as many as 30 million deaths from famine and malnutrition and in a drop in output to below 1957 levels. The response was to decentralize management within the commune and to make the team the unit of ownership and accounting. The peasants' rights to private plots were re-emphasized. During the recovery period up to 1964, there were also experiments with free markets and contracting farming to individuals. The commune structure remained, however, and its position as the key rural institution was reaffirmed during the **Cultural Revolution** as exemplified by the **Dazhai** model.

Over the period from 1965 to 1978, the commune system delivered modest agricultural growth of around 2.7 per cent per year. Considerable labour was invested in land management, irrigation and basic infrastructure, and the state channelled technical inputs into the communes, such as new seeds, fertilizers and equipment. Communes also developed a range of collectively owned sidelines and industrial enterprises, primarily aimed at supporting agricultural development, and a number of social services including paramedics known as 'barefoot doctors' (see **health system**) and local teachers. Nevertheless, output per labourer did not improve, peasant living standards languished far behind urban levels, and rationing of grain, vegetable oils and cotton was required in urban areas.

One of the subsequent criticisms of the commune system was its failure to provide incentives for peasants. The work point system required complex records and management. Norms had to be developed for different types of work and for different types of labourers. **Women**, for example, were typically recorded at half the rate of men. During the **Cultural Revolution**, political attitude was also seen as part of the assessment. In many places there were very small variations between the points awarded to people. The system thus created a significant 'free rider' problem. Peasants were unwilling to work harder since, although their effort might increase total output, they received no commensurate reward while the less industrious got more than their fair share. Problems of this kind were also created by attempts to raise the level of accounting to the brigade. In effect, this meant sharing income across separate teams, with similar free rider risks.

Apart from these incentive problems, the operation of the **household registration** system and low agricultural prices, which acted as a mechanism to extract surplus for industrialization, also undermined peasant support, so when production contracting was introduced in 1978, peasants responded positively. The communes were formally abolished in 1983 and replaced with a new three-tiered structure of rural organization consisting of the township (the basic level of government), the village (the owner of land and any remaining collective assets) and the household (farming the land under contract from the village and free to develop production as it liked after meeting its obligations). Thereafter, the key things remaining under collective ownership were

the TVEs and the land. By the mid-1990s, issues related to the efficiency of the TVEs and of land use were leading to reconsideration of the definition and role of collective property rights to enable a role for market forces to develop.

see also: 5. Politics and the Economy: Policy Patterns and Issues; agriculture; Cultural Revolution; Dazhai; Great Leap Forward; health system; household registration; Mao Zedong; township and village enterprises; women.

Andrew Watson

collective sector (non-agricultural)

China's non-agricultural collectives can be found across the full range of economic activities, including **industry**, construction, **transport**, commerce, restaurants and many other services. Although in theory owned collectively by their employees rather than by the state, they have always been defined as a 'major component part of the socialist publicly owned economy'. Their origins lay in the cooperatives of urban handicraft workers established in the early 1950s. Like their rural counterparts, these urban cooperatives underwent a process of collectivization during the mid-1950s whereby the workers lost any rights of individual ownership, and the collectives were brought under the leadership of local state agencies. They were not part of the centralized **planning** system but were subordinate to **local government** controls. After payment of taxes and other charges, net income was divided within the collective, with some used for reinvestment and some used for dividends and bonuses for collective members. As a result, wage levels varied between collectives, depending on their levels of profitability, and there were lower **housing** and **welfare** benefits compared to those for workers in state enterprises. At the beginning of the **Cultural Revolution**, dividend payments to collective workers were abolished.

By the late 1970s, there were three main types of collectives:
• 'big collectives';
• 'small collectives'; and

- collectives established within state-owned **units**.

The 'big collectives' were larger-scale enterprises with fairly good levels of technology. They were administered by the appropriate industrial department in the **local government**. Ownership and management rights were exercised by the controlling department, which also allocated profits after payment of taxes and other levies. Although subject to separate accounting, these collectives functioned in roughly the same way as state enterprises under the department concerned. By 1978 they employed about half the collective workforce and produced over half the output of urban collective industry.

The 'small collectives' were small-scale 'street industries' run by residential committees in urban areas. They provided employment for housewives, retired people and unemployed youths. They lacked capital and equipment and could not rely on state support. Many were formed during the **Cultural Revolution** period as examples of self-reliant development mobilizing local resources. They came under the administrative wing of the local district office. Given their lack of resources, their products were usually crude and low quality. In 1978 they employed about 25 per cent of the workforce but produced only about 14 per cent of total collective output.

The third category of collectives was those established within state-owned **units**. These collectives might be engaged in work entirely different from that of their parent organization, such as a garment collective in a steel factory or a shop run by a hospital. In many cases, they were developed to provide employment for the dependants of the state enterprise workers. While quite distinct from the parent enterprise itself, they clearly depended on their host for support and inputs.

The economic reforms after 1978 have given broad support for the growth of the urban collective sector. In 1981 regulations were issued to allow available urban land and buildings to be leased for collective use. A major **State Council** policy document of 14 April 1983 called for a revival of an independent collective sector and laid out the parameters for employment, taxation and management. In addition it further encouraged the growth of properly constituted collectives within state enterprises. Renewed emphasis was also given to the relative independence of collectives from the state, and they were encouraged to develop in line with market demand. Given the Marxist orthodoxy of the plan period, backing the collective system required minimal ideological adjustment.

While the urban collective sector maintained its relative importance within the urban industrial system during the 1980s and 1990s, its significance within the whole collective sector failed to increase, due to the dramatic growth of **township and village enterprises**. Between 1991 and 1995, the state enterprise share of total industrial output value dropped from 56 to 34 per cent, and the urban collective share also fell from 13 to 8 per cent. The balance was largely accounted for by the growth of the township and village sector.

One collective category which did experience substantial development during the reform period, however, was that within state enterprises. Many large state enterprises continued to establish collectives as internal subunits. These not only employed dependants but also made use of the state enterprise's assets to generate additional income. Educational institutions, government departments and so forth commonly set up restaurants, shops and service departments which were either run as collectives or sub-leased to managers. By the mid-1990s, when further reform of state enterprises required a stocktaking of state assets, the status of these internal 'collectives' created difficulties in determining the ownership of assets and the relationship of these collectives to the state system. It was also common for private entrepreneurs to disguise their private ownership by registering as a collective. Over the long term, the growing diversity of forms of ownership in the Chinese economy was also beginning to blur the significance of the urban collective sector as a distinct category, and the statistical system was recording all collective industry (urban or rural) as part of the same basic industrial type.

see also: Cultural Revolution; housing; industry; local government/administration; planning, economic; State Council; township and village enterprises; transport and telecommunications; unit; welfare policy.

Andrew Watson

Commonwealth of Independent States, relations with

See **Soviet Union, relations with.**

Constitutions (State and Party)

The first interim Constitution governing the PRC consisted of three laws promulgated by the **Chinese People's Political Consultative Conference** in 1949. These were the 'Common Programme', the 'Organic Law of the Central People's Government of the People's Republic of China' and the 'Organic Law of the Chinese People's Political Consultative Conference'. In 1954, the newly convened **National People's Congress** ratified a Constitution, based on that of the **Soviet Union** adopted in 1936. The 1954 Constitution, consisting of 106 articles, dealt with government organization, the judicial system and their guiding principles. In line with the formal policy of separating Party and state functions, it mentioned the **Chinese Communist Party** only in its preamble and then only with reference to its leadership before 1949.

That Constitution, which was seen to privilege 'bourgeois law', though still in force for two decades, did not find favour in the radical period after 1957. During the **Cultural Revolution**, a draft Constitution, nominating **Mao Zedong** explicitly as head of state and **Lin Biao** as his successor, was circulated but rejected by Mao and never promulgated.

Following the **Cultural Revolution**, a new State Constitution was adopted in 1975. That Constitution consisted only of thirty articles. The twelve articles covering the judicial system in the 1954 Constitution were reduced to only one and many of the rights enshrined in the earlier document were removed. In **Cultural Revolution** vein, however, it added the right to strike (see also **labour policy and sys-**

tem), to engage in mass debates and to put up big-character posters. The new Constitution, which deleted even programmatic reference to judicial independence, affirmed the primacy of class struggle and implied direct Party control over the judiciary. What was left of the judiciary was reduced to a bare minimum and the people's procuratorate was abolished (see **legal system**).

After Mao's death (1976), attempts were made to restore many of the provisions of the 1954 Constitution. The result was a document, ratified in March 1978, which restored the people's procuratorate, but that document still fell short of the wishes of those who wanted to entrench the rule of law. Following the reintroduction of legislation, held in cold storage since the Anti-Rightist Movement of 1957, and the Party's official verdict on Mao in 1981, the **National People's Congress** approved a new 138-article document in December 1982.

The 1982 Constitution defined the state as 'a socialist state under the people's democratic dictatorship' – a much softer term than the previous 'socialist state of the dictatorship of the proletariat' and one which could legitimize 'national capitalist' business. While adhering to **Deng Xiaoping**'s 'four cardinal principles', which affirmed Party leadership, it explicitly placed Party members under the law. In united front spirit, it went on to restore more of the rights of the 1954 Constitution but abolished some of the **Cultural Revolution** innovations such as the right to strike. The 1982 Constitution, however, still adhered to the 1954 Constitution's view that rights were programmatic and the gift of the state. Any advance on a positivistic view of rights had to wait until a **State Council** white paper of 1991.

The programmatic, rather than protective, nature of the Constitution needs emphasis. After a statement of rights, the Constitution usually inserts the words 'according to law', implying that law makes rights rather than rights shaping the law and that there might be laws superior to the Constitution. Statements about rights, moreover, are usually accompanied by statements about duties and one is not sure of their legal force. As a programmatic document, moreover, the Constitution has been amended several times to reflect political exigencies and a rapidly changing economic situation, in particular over ownership rights. As a result, there has been some demand in recent years for a new state Constitution.

Party Constitutions have appeared more frequently than state Constitutions; in fact each **National Party Congress** ratifies a new one or makes significant amendments. Since the formation of the PRC there have been eight such Constitutions. Far more than state Constitutions, Party constitutions reflect the exigencies of a particular situation and perhaps should more properly be referred to as 'Party rules'. The 1956 Constitution (with some sixty articles) specified current principles, membership criteria and the structure and functions of various levels of organization. Occurring at a time when the 'cult of personality' was criticized, it removed reference to **Mao Zedong Thought**, which had figured prominently in the 1945 Constitution. It also stressed that the basic contradiction in society was between the 'advanced socialist system and the backward productive forces' – a classical Marxist productivist view not in keeping with the radical mood of the late 1950s. The ensuing radical period ensured that the following Party Constitutions extolled a more voluntarist rendering of **Mao Zedong Thought**. The first few were brief and said only a little about Party organization.

The 1969 Constitution extolled **Lin Biao** as Mao's successor while the 1973 Constitution, a document similar in structure, removed that provision. The 1977 document, appearing in the midst of a trauma within the Party concerning moving away from the politics of the **Cultural Revolution**, stressed Party unity and the need to revive the Party's organizational principle of 'democratic centralism'. The amended documents of 1982, 1987 and 1997 continued that trend as the Party restructured to meet the challenges of economic reform and the demands for professionalism. The fifty-article document adopted by the Fifteenth Party Congress (1997) extols **Mao Zedong Thought** (purged

of Mao's later ideas and with a specific repudiation of the 'cult of personality') and **Deng Xiaoping** Theory of 'building socialism with Chinese characteristics' and advocates the general principle of creating a 'socialist market economy'.

see also: 3. Ideology: Radicalism and Reform; Chinese Communist Party; Chinese People's Political Consultative Conference; Cultural Revolution; Deng Xiaoping; labour policy and system; legal system; Lin Biao; Mao Zedong; Mao Zedong Thought; National Party Congress; National People's Congress; Soviet Union, relations with; State Council.

Bill Brugger

cultural policy

Since the **Chinese Communist Party** sees a strong link between politics and literature and the arts, its most consistent policy has been to control 'cultural workers' to serve its own interests.

Even before the CCP won victory in 1949, **Mao Zedong** and others had put forward views on culture, especially in Mao's 'Talks at the Yan'an Forum on Literature and Art' of 1942. Mao's views included the following notions:

- the unity of politics and art, that is high perfection of artistic form combined with content consistent with CCP policy;
- all culture represents the interests of a class or classes, Chinese revolutionary culture those of the workers, peasants and soldiers; and
- traditional Chinese and foreign cultures should be 'critically assimilated', their 'democratic essence' retained but their 'feudal dross' rejected.

In July 1949, the First National Congress of Literature and Art Workers took place in Beijing, setting up the All-China Federation of Literature and Art Circles. Once the PRC was established, the government set up a further range of bodies aimed at sponsoring, reforming and controlling the various branches of the arts and sought distinguished artists as directors. The selection criteria were political reliability, high artistic standards and class stand, meaning representing the interests of the poor. Two notable examples were the Peking Opera Company of China, set up in January 1955 with Mei Lanfang (1894–1961) at its head, and the Beijing Chinese Art Academy opened in May 1957 with Qi Baishi (1864–1957) as its President. Mei and Qi were respectively twentieth-century China's most famous actor and traditional-style painter and their administrative tasks were partly formal. Qi was extremely old and died only a few months after taking up the position.

Other than pushing pride in China's national cultural heritage, obvious in the above examples, the CCP developed several other cultural policies, including the following:

- to submit the traditional arts to reform to make them conform to the CCP's social and political standards, with many items considered incorrect or inappropriate being banned;
- to encourage works reflecting contemporary times, provided they advocated the CCP's political viewpoint;
- to support a limited number of foreign artists and works, as long as they were politically appropriate; and
- to sponsor training programmes to foster a new generation of artists and writers who would be loyal to the CCP and its policies on the arts, such recruits to include **women** and members of the **minority nationalities**.

During the **Cultural Revolution**, Mao's 'Talks at the Yan'an Forum' were reinterpreted to place total emphasis on class struggle and the need to use art as propaganda. Mao's wife Jiang Qing (see **gang of four**) was given almost total control of the arts. A former film starlet, she developed an obsession with revolutionizing the Peking Opera and other arts, and banned a wide range of artistic forms, including virtually all traditional and foreign works. In February 1966 she convened the Forum on the Work in Literature and Art in the Armed Forces, which adopted a range of radical ideas, among them handing over authority in all artistic works to the CCP and the proletariat.

With the fall of the **gang of four** in October 1976, cultural policy soon changed to discredit the stereotyped ideas of the **Cultural Revolution**. Traditional works, including paintings, novels, poems, dramas, music and dances, quickly revived. On 30 October 1979, **Deng Xiaoping** gave a 'Speech Greeting the Fourth Congress of Chinese Writers and Artists' which set out the basics of policy for the period of reform. His main points were:

- the CCP's line on literature and art before 1966 was 'in the main correct' and the works produced at that time good;
- the basic standard for judging all cultural work is whether it helps or hinders modernization;
- culture should belong to the people and portray and help foster 'the new socialist man';
- traditional and foreign culture are basically good and China's cultural workers 'should draw on and learn from all that is progressive and advanced' in them;
- writers and artists should study Marxism-Leninism and **Mao Zedong Thought** and constantly improve their professional skills; and
- writers and artists should be able to follow their own creative spirit, including being allowed to choose their own topics without 'arbitrary meddling'.

The overall trend since then has been in the direction of greater variety and freedom in culture. There has been cultural flowering in some areas, especially film.

However, censorship and restrictions remain. Despite Deng's insistence that cultural workers study Marxist ideology, there has been a constant tug between them and the CCP, with the former estimating how far they can use their own initiative and the latter remaining suspicious of departures from its ideological line. The result has been occasional crackdowns on artistic and literary deviance.

By far the most serious of these was in 1989 after the **June 4 Incident**. In 1988, a television series entitled *Heshang* (*River Elegy*) portrayed Chinese traditional culture in a negative light, pleasing many student leaders and young intellectuals, but alarming the CCP and cultural officials. The CCP saw the series as an example of a general drift away from patriotism and belief in Marxism-Leninism.

Although **Deng Xiaoping**'s policies have remained in place, the thrust of policy in the 1990s has shifted towards cultural nationalism. Two principal advocates of this trend have been CCP General Secretary **Jiang Zemin** and Politburo Standing Committee member **Li Ruihuan**. One expression of cultural nationalism has been an attempt to revive traditional drama forms, especially the Peking Opera.

In a major speech at a national conference on cultural and art work in January 1990, **Li Ruihuan** emphasized the greatness of China's cultural heritage. He condemned cultural figures who had belittled Chinese culture as backward, especially those who had 'fled abroad' after the **June 4 Incident** 'to take the road from national nihilism to national betrayal'. Although Li favoured foreign culture, he was keen for China to absorb it critically. One must guard, he said, against those who would take advantage of China's opening to the outside world to bring in 'a flood of bourgeois liberal materials'.

see also: Chinese Communist Party; Cultural Revolution; Deng Xiaoping; gang of four; Jiang Zemin; June 4 Incident; Li Ruihuan; Mao Zedong; Mao Zedong Thought; minority nationalities policy; women.

Colin Mackerras

Cultural Revolution

The largest and most important of **Mao Zedong**'s ideological campaigns, with the full name Great Proletarian Cultural Revolution. Commentators have given different boundary dates, the **Sixth Plenum of the Eleventh Central Committee** of the Communist Party (1981) declaring them to be from May 1966 to October 1976.

Mao Zedong opposed the moderate economic policies initiated in the wake of the economic failure of the **Great Leap Forward**, and the growing elitism and bureaucratization of the Party. He regarded the CCP as displaying the characteristics of a new ruling class, one whose power rested not on ownership but on control of the means of production. He perceived these economic policies and political tendencies as a manifestation of a line within the Party which, if left unchecked, would result in a 'capitalist restoration'.

The Cultural Revolution was thus a struggle for power between Mao and his radical supporters on the one hand and the Party hierarchy led by **Liu Shaoqi** and **Deng Xiaoping** on the other. For Mao, the Cultural Revolution was also a struggle over fundamental questions of policy that would determine the direction China would take (see **Mao Zedong Thought**). He believed in the need for an increasing socialization of China's economy and society and for continual revitalization of the revolution through a campaign style of politics which both mobilized the masses and prevented the Party and its cadres from becoming elitist. **Liu Shaoqi**, on the other hand, perceived the need for careful economic **planning** premised on CCP control. He also believed a retreat from the radical economic policies of the **Great Leap Forward** was necessary, and reintroduced measures, such as private plots for the peasants and rural markets, which encouraged production through material incentives. Mao believed Liu's policies facilitated the emergence of a new bourgeoisie, and it was consequently those 'persons in authority taking the capitalist road' such as Liu and his supporters who were to become the main target of attack during the Cultural Revolution.

Increasingly isolated from the Party leadership, Mao turned to China's students and the **People's Liberation Army** under the control of **Lin Biao** for support in his struggle against the 'capitalist roaders' within the CCP. Frustrated by attempts by the mayor of **Beijing**, Peng Zhen (initially placed in charge of implementing the Cultural Revolution) to limit its scope to strictly cultural affairs, Mao had Peng purged and a Cultural Revolution Group established under the control of Jiang Qing (later a member of the **gang of four**) and **Chen Boda**, which encouraged and directed much of the radical activity over the next few years. In late May 1966, secondary and university students began to organize themselves into groups called Red Guards and, encouraged by Mao's support in August when he reviewed a mass rally of Red Guards in Tiananmen Square, these organizations spread across China and beyond the confines of the **education system**. The Red Guards subjected university and school teachers to often violent criticism and effectively closed down the **education system**. They frequently spearheaded the attack against the 'capitalist roaders' within the CCP, ransacking Party offices, parading cadres through the streets wearing dunce's hats and subjecting them to humiliating criticism sessions which often ended in violence. The ideological orientation of the Red Guard organizations was very variable, and in the hothouse atmosphere of the Cultural Revolution fuelled by the cult of personality surrounding Mao, these ideological differences often ended in pitched battles between rival Red Guards, resulting in numerous casualties.

The first official Party document on the Cultural Revolution was the sixteen-point 'Decision' adopted by the Eleventh Plenum of the Eighth Central Committee held in August 1966, presided over by Mao himself. The 'Decision' emphasized the need to struggle against and overthrow those in authority taking the capitalist road and endorsed the struggle in education against 'bourgeois' academic authorities. The 'Decision' did, however, caution against using violent struggle or force to resolve contradictions amongst the people. It was the failure of the Red Guards to observe this injunction, and the heightened radicalism and violence of late 1966 and early 1967, which led the **People's Liberation Army** to extend its control to many civilian institutions in the attempt to restore order, and the military became a prominent presence in many of the newly formed **revolutionary committees**. However, a resurgence in mid-1967 of radical Red Guard activity, particularly from the ultra-left wing of that movement, culminated in violent conflict between Red Guards and the military in several areas. Mao consequently moved to end the chaos caused by Red Guard factionalism and the tensions between mili-

tary and Red Guards by sending many Red Guards to the countryside.

The Ninth Party Congress held in April 1969 drew to a close the most important phase of the Cultural Revolution, and stressed unity and the need to rebuild the Party. The years from the Ninth Party Congress to Mao's death were characterized by a retreat from the radicalism of the early years of the Cultural Revolution, as the Party rebuilt itself along Leninist lines and reasserted its authority. A series of bitter struggles between supporters and opponents of the Cultural Revolution marked the final years of the Maoist era, struggles which resulted in the political destruction of radicals such as **Chen Boda**, and the physical demise of **Lin Biao** himself. It also resulted in the political re-emergence of **Deng Xiaoping**, one of the Cultural Revolution's most prominent victims whose ultimate ascension to power was a major factor in the eventual total repudiation of the Cultural Revolution.

According to the 'Resolution' of the 1981 **Sixth Plenum of the Eleventh Central Committee,** the arrest of the **gang of four** in October 1976 signalled the end of the Cultural Revolution. The 'Resolution' roundly condemned the Cultural Revolution. It had 'led to domestic turmoil and brought catastrophe to the Party, the state and the whole people'. Despite the authoritative tone of the 1981 'Resolution', there are numerous divergent views, from both Western scholars and Chinese commentators, of the causes, course and consequences, and even the dates, of the Cultural Revolution. Controversy about it is likely to continue indefinitely.

see also: 1. Overview History of the People's Republic of China; 3. Ideology: Radicalism and Reform; Beijing Municipality; Chen Boda; Chinese Communist Party; Deng Xiaoping; education policy and system; gang of four; Great Leap Forward; Lin Biao; Liu Shaoqi; Mao Zedong; Mao Zedong Thought; People's Liberation Army; planning, economic; revolutionary committees; Sixth Plenum of the Eleventh Central Committee.

Nick Knight

D

Daqing

A major oil field in Heilongjiang province in Northeast China. Before 1949, it was commonly assumed that China was poorly endowed with oil, but the discovery of Daqing in the late 1950s made it basically self-sufficient. In 1964 **Mao Zedong** called on Chinese **industry** to learn from Daqing because it exemplified the values of self-reliance, improvisation and the struggle to conquer nature which he believed essential to develop the Chinese economy and socialist values in China's population. Daqing also pioneered innovative management techniques which combined politics and production through cadre participation in labour.

Daqing attracted further attention in 1966 when Mao praised its efforts to integrate **industry** and **agriculture**. A number of communities had been established close to the oil field which combined farming, light **industry**, education and administration with work on the oil field. The workers of Daqing and their families had attempted to achieve self-sufficiency and to eliminate the differences between **industry** and **agriculture**.

Among the first oil workers at Daqing were the 1205 drilling team and its leader Wang Jinxi, later dubbed the 'iron man' for his bravery and persistent efforts to open the Daqing oil field in the face of the extreme hardships of cold, isolation and the lack of basic equipment. He became famous for these achievements and in September 1964 was elected deputy to the Third **National People's Congress**, and in January 1967 to the Standing Committee of the Heilongjiang Provincial **Revolutionary Committee**. He was attacked and physically mistreated by Red Guards in 1968 and denounced as a 'traitor worker'. Nevertheless, he was elected a full member of the **CCP Central Committee** at the Ninth **National Party Congress** in April 1969. However, his political career was cut short by gastric cancer and he died in Beijing in November 1970 at the age of 47.

After Mao's death, the significance of Daqing changed and it was promoted, not for its Maoist virtues of self-reliance, but for its importance to the development of China's productive forces and for its efficient enterprise management. It remains one of China's most important oil fields.

see also: 5. Politics and the Economy: Policy Patterns and Issues; agriculture; Chinese Communist Party; Central Committee and Politburo; industry; Mao Zedong; National Party Congress; National People's Congress; revolutionary committees.

Nick Knight

Dazhai

A production brigade in Xiyang County, northeast Shanxi Province. The brigade members of Dazhai were reputed to have transformed, through their own arduous labour, their steep and deeply eroded loess farming land by levelling and terracing. Refusing all state aid and taking self-reliance as their motto, they overcame many natural disasters and dramatically increased grain production. The production brigade was made famous in 1964 when **Mao Zedong** called on Chinese **agriculture** to learn from Dazhai. Mao believed that the Dazhai experience – hard work, simple living, self-reliance, collectivism and egalitarianism – if adopted by all other agricultural **units**, would lead to a substantial increase in agricultural production with little investment by the state in the agricultural sector. Dazhai consequently became the model which other agricultural **units** emulated, and it became the focus of a nationwide campaign. It was visited by a vast number of people from all over China, one estimate being 4.5 million people between 1964 and 1971.

Chen Yonggui, the CCP secretary who had

led Dazhai since 1947 and who exemplified the qualities admired by Mao of hard work, self-reliance, and persistence in the face of adversity, rose to national prominence as a result of Mao's call for Chinese agriculture to learn from Dazhai. Chen was elected to the Third **National People's Congress** in 1964, and a full member of the **CCP Central Committee** at the Ninth **National Party Congress** in April 1969. He was elected to the Politburo of the Party's Central Committee at its Tenth Congress in August 1973, and at the Fourth **National People's Congress** in January 1975 was appointed a vice-premier of the **State Council**.

The 'Learn from Dazhai' campaign went through several stages. Initially promoted as a model for radical rural social change, Dazhai became, with the relative deradicalization of the **Cultural Revolution** in the early 1970s, a model for improvement of production techniques. In 1975, the Dazhai campaign was revived in the context of the sharpening political struggle prior to Mao's death. In September 1975, the first national congress on Dazhai was held at Dazhai, and at this congress **Hua Guofeng** restated the significance of the Dazhai experience for Chinese **agriculture**. He was to reiterate this message following Mao's death, although in terms of agricultural policy, the practical significance of Dazhai declined, and following the **Third Plenum of the Eleventh Central Committee** in December 1978, Dazhai was denounced for its part in the leftist line which had prevailed in Chinese **agriculture** during the **Cultural Revolution**. Dazhai's experiences were repudiated as spurious and concocted, and Chen Yonggui purged from the Central Committee in February 1980.

see also: 5. Politics and the Economy: Policy Patterns and Issues; agriculture; Chinese Communist Party Central Committee and Politburo; Cultural Revolution; Hua Guofeng; Mao Zedong; National Party Congress; National People's Congress; State Council; Third Plenum of the Eleventh Central Committee; unit.

Nick Knight

Democracy Wall

The name given to one or more walls, mainly in **Beijing**, on which various contending opinions were written, especially late in 1978 and early in 1979.

The term 'Democracy Wall' was used during the **Hundred Flowers Movement**. In May 1957 students stuck up posters at **Beijing** (Peking) University putting forward their views. The posters took many forms, including essays, poems and cartoons. They covered topics ranging from attacks on CCP policy towards intellectuals, to excessive emphasis on politics in university courses, and fawning on **Soviet** educational models. The liberal phase, when it was possible to put forward such views, proved very short-lived.

Another period of free expression of views occurred at the Democracy Wall over a few months from November 1978. It was associated with a political struggle between **Deng Xiaoping** and **Hua Guofeng**, and with the former's attempt to discredit the **Cultural Revolution** which had ended in 1976. The great blow inflicted on the prestige of the CCP by such events as the **Cultural Revolution** resulted in the public airing of views questioning the Party's monopoly over truth and challenging the authoritarian nature of the political system.

Despite the context, it was perhaps inevitable that the manner in which views were presented and the environment in which the ideas were discussed found their roots partly in the political style of the **Cultural Revolution** itself. It is ironic then that Democracy Wall occurred in the lead-up to and aftermath of the most important political meeting convened in post-Mao China – the **Third Plenum of the Eleventh Central Committee** of the CCP. Fuel was added to the charged political environment when, on the eve of the plenum, the CCP announced a reversal of the verdict on the mass movement of April 1976, the **Tiananmen Incident**, when mourners for the late Premier **Zhou Enlai** had been driven from Tiananmen Square by baton-wielding worker militia and later condemned as incited by **Deng Xiaoping** himself. Thus, Democracy Wall and the **Third Plenum** represented in sum the confluence and inter-action of elite inner-party political struggle and the popular movement for a more responsive, humane, rational and even repre-sentative polity. Both strands fed off and, to a certain degree, played themselves out against each other.

Democracy Wall itself witnessed an out-burst of poetry, prose and political commen-tary reflecting this volatile political and social climate. The first batch of posters came in mid-November 1978, when citizens pasted numerous posters on Democracy Wall at Xidan in central Beijing, expressing many dif-ferent points of view. One such poster, of fourteen pages, accused **Mao Zedong** of sup-porting the **gang of four** and of responsibility for **Deng Xiaoping**'s fall in 1976. The best-known examples of Democracy Wall litera-ture appeared in China's capital, and most politically aware city, **Beijing** (although simi-lar activities occurred in other Chinese cities), and the writings were pasted up on city walls in the form of big-character posters (*dazibao*) which had proliferated during the **Cultural Revolution** and which had often been used to make anonymous and vicious attacks on individuals and groups for all kinds of reasons. The right to post *dazibao* had been guaranteed in the radical state **Constitution** of 1975.

A variety of groups and individuals par-ticipated in Democracy Wall, each with their different agendas which were pushed in various directions by the dynamic political environment. The anti-leftist party group led by Deng undoubtedly leaked sensitive information to discredit supporters of **Hua Guofeng** such as **Beijing**'s Party Secretary Wu De. But the movement was not confined to the parameters defined by the ruling party, and, when writings on Democracy Wall offended Deng's life-long Leninist organisa-tional principles, he suppressed them in the name of stability and unity. Moreover, on 16 October 1979 one of the most prominent **dis-sidents** and contributors to the debate on Democracy Wall, Wei Jingsheng, was sen-tenced to fifteen years' imprisonment, allegedly for passing on military intelligence

to a foreign journalist and carrying out coun-ter-revolutionary agitation, but in reality for proposing democracy as the 'fifth' modern-ization (see also **Four Modernizations**).

After it had outlived its usefulness for the victorious Deng reform group and had turned into an embarrassment, Democracy Wall was shifted from Xidan to a more remote location outside the city centre, and in 1980 the **National People's Congress** removed the article in the Chinese constitution guarantee-ing the right of Chinese citizens to post *dazibao*.

see also: Beijing Municipality; Constitutions; Cultural Revolution; Deng Xiaoping; dis-sidents; Four Modernizations; gang of four; Hua Guofeng; Hundred Flowers Movement; Mao Zedong; National People's Congress; Soviet Union, relations with; Third Plenum of the Eleventh Cen-tral Committee; Tiananmen Incident; Zhou Enlai.

Keith Forster

democratic parties

Before 1949, while the CCP on the left and the Nationalist Party on the right contested for power, groups of well-known intellectuals did not join forces with either. Historians characterize them as a third force, though they did not truly contend for power. After 1949, their associations were co-opted into the new polity, and the CCP's United Front Department reorganized them into eight 'democratic parties' (DPs) each of which was assigned to recruit its members from one particular grouping:

- two were reserved for high-level academ-ics in the social and natural sciences (the China Democratic League [*Minmeng*] and the September Third Study Society [*Jiusan xueshe*]);
- two were reserved for professionals such as doctors, educators and journalists (the Chinese Peasants' and Workers' Demo-cratic Party [*Zhongguo nonggong minzhu dang*] and the China Association for Pro-moting Democracy [*Zhongguo minzhu cujin hui*]);
- one was to incorporate business people

(the China National Construction Associ-ation [*Zhongguo minzu jianguo hui*]); and

- three were specifically for people with Nationalist Party, **Taiwan** and **Overseas Chinese** connections (respectively the Revolutionary Guomindang [*Guomindang geming weiyuanhui*], the Taiwan Demo-cratic Self-Government League [*Taiwan minzhu zizhi tongmeng*], and the Party for Public Interest [*Zhi gong dang*]).

The CCP imposed strict limitations on the breadth and numbers of their membership, not allowing them to recruit from small towns or villages, from among peasants, workers or minority nationalities.

Within a few years the DPs had acquired a reputation for being 'flower vases' of the CCP. But when the **Hundred Flowers Movement** erupted in 1956–7, they spoke out immediately, criticizing the Party. The CCP's crackdown on the DPs was quick and thor-ough. A substantial number of the most out-spoken DP members were sent to labour camps, the DPs being silenced for the next twenty years.

Among **Deng Xiaoping**'s liberalization pol-icies was one to revive the DPs under the slo-gan 'institute multiparty cooperation under the leadership of the CCP'. Up to 1989, with the permission of the CCP, all the DPs rapidly recruited new members and doubled or even trebled in size. The largest and most pres-tigious of them, the Democratic League, expanded from 16,000 to 99,000 between 1983 and 1989. Some top CCP leaders like **Hu Yaobang** and **Zhao Ziyang** were known to be supportive of the DPs. Just before the 1989 **protest movement**, Zhao was in the process of drafting a document to expand the role of the DPs in the government, judiciary and legislature.

Large numbers of DP members partici-pated at the fringes of the 1989 **protest movement**. But after it was crushed, the CCP decided that opening up wider chan-nels for the frustrated intellectual elite would help ward off further major disturb-ances in China. Thus, late in 1989, the CCP issued a major document promising to pro-mote the influence of the DPs. Henceforth

they were to be referred to as 'parties par-ticipating in government affairs' (*canzheng dang*).

According to this document, although the DPs should not regard themselves as 'oppos-ition' parties with a possible chance to take government, there should be more consult-ation between the CCP and DPs, more im-portant government posts would be opened to DP members, and more DP members would sit in such bodies as the **National People's Congress**. In 1993 the roles of the DPs were enshrined in the **Constitution**.

The three DPs that are reserved for edu-cational, medical/scientific and journalistic personnel function more like professional associations. Much of their energy is directed to advancing their own professional interests and providing better social services for their assigned constituencies. On occasion they tender their expert professional advice to the government on policy matters within their professional spheres.

The two most politically assertive DPs are the China Democratic League (high-level intellectuals) and the China National Con-struction Association (people involved in economic matters). The Democratic League had a membership of about 150,000 in 1994, by far the largest of the eight. The China National Construction Association is com-posed today of economists, business people and government specialists involved in over-seeing the economy. Since reforming the economy has become the priority of the gov-ernment, the prestige and influence of some of its leading members have increased.

see also: Chinese Communist Party; Constitu-tions; Deng Xiaoping; Hu Yaobang; Hun-dred Flowers Movement; National People's Congress; Overseas Chinese pol-icy; protest movements; Taiwan policy; Zhao Ziyang.

Anita Chan

Deng Xiaoping

The 'paramount leader' of the **Chinese Communist Party** during the 1980s and the person most responsible for overturning the politics of the **Cultural Revolution** and leading China into rapid economic modernization and growth.

Born in 1904 in **Sichuan** Province, Deng went as a worker-student to France at the age of 16 where he was socialized into what rapidly became the leadership circles of the CCP. From then on a long and varied career in its service saw him develop the political connections and relationships that ensured both survival and continued influence. He trained as a political activist in Moscow in 1926 and later worked closely with **Zhou Enlai** in **Shanghai**. After difficulties working as a peasant organizer in Southwest China, in 1931 he moved with the CCP's central offices to the Central China Soviet, where he was severely disciplined for his support of **Mao Zedong**. Thereafter until the **Cultural Revolution** Mao relied heavily on Deng as the ablest and most reliable of his lieutenants.

Deng Xiaoping served in the military from 1938 until 1952 and was so successful that he ever after became almost universally regarded as the communist military's favourite political cadre and the CCP's favourite soldier. Together with another Sichuanese (Liu Bocheng) he led the CCP's forces in the southern part of the Taihang Mountains, into what later became the **People's Liberation Army**'s 2nd Field Army first against Japan and then in the civil war against the Nationalist Party forces. With Deng in a leading role these forces participated in the decisive Huaihai Campaign, then crossed the Yangzi River at Nanjing and went on to establish CCP rule in Southwest China from late 1949 on.

After 1949 Deng's commitment led to high office – in 1952 he moved to **Beijing** and became vice-premier, occupying a number of roles including minister of Finance, and the leader of the committee responsible for drafting the nascent PRC's electoral laws and regulations. In the mid-1950s he was appointed to the CCP's Politburo and to be its general secretary. Deng occupied this central position in China's politics until the mid-1960s and his persecution and vilification in the **Cultural Revolution**. In 1966, he was dismissed and castigated as China's 'number two person in authority taking the capitalist

road' – the second most important 'capitalist roader' after **Liu Shaoqi** in opposition to Mao.

Deng was recalled to office in 1973. Although his earlier relationship with Mao no doubt provided part of the explanation, it cannot have been irrelevant that the then Politburo contained a substantial number of members who had been Deng's subordinates during the Anti-Japanese War. Deng's relationship with Mao this time was not what it had been, and Deng rapidly moved (with the support of other senior leaders including **Zhou Enlai**) to campaign for the ideas later associated with the reform era.

Confrontation was always on the cards, and in 1976 during Mao's last days and when severely attacked by the **gang of four**, Deng Xiaoping was again criticized and removed from the leadership. On this occasion he was cushioned from the worst effects of dismissal through support and assistance provided by supporters. As when he had been disciplined in 1933, Deng accepted the need for Party discipline to be maintained through the process of criticism and self-criticism – though not necessarily the conclusions of that criticism. He accepted Party discipline as stoically as possible and waited for the opportunity to re-present his case. With Mao's death and the arrest of the **gang of four** in 1976 the opportunity on this occasion was not slow in coming, and was assisted by the degree of support for Deng and his position within the leadership.

Deng Xiaoping's policy position of the mid-1970s was nothing new. He had always been a committed modernizer and nationalist, determined to make China both economically strong and politically powerful in international terms. In that endeavour he was intensely pragmatic, though not a pragmatist; on the contrary, he was a committed revolutionary throughout his political career, attempting to ensure that the CCP achieved power and China's modernization. For Deng Xiaoping communism was an organizational as much if not more than an intellectual response to the problems China faced in the twentieth century. What was required was a united China, strong leadership, and the energy of the Chinese people, all of which could only be provided, in Deng's opinion, by the CCP.

It was these beliefs that led him in his mid-seventies, together with the main architect of economic reform **Chen Yun**, to overhaul the social, political and economic institutions of the PRC. Despite the importance of collective leadership Deng's own role was not negligible. After the mid-1980s, when the coalition that had launched the reform era started to drift apart, it was often his personal intervention that maintained both the pace and direction of reform. This was most notable in early 1992. An economic crisis in 1988 and 1989, when the economy overheated and there was serious inflation, led to a deliberate government-induced recession for the best part of two years. For largely political reasons, some in the leadership were unwilling to allow economic growth to accelerate once again. Deng forestalled objections by making a much publicized 'inspection tour of the south' (*nanxun*) where he visited the Shenzhen **Special Economic Zone** and other areas famous for being in the vanguard of economic growth. Putting his personal authority behind such developments ensured an almost immediate policy change.

Deng retired as chairman of the CCP's **Central Military Commission** in November 1989 and from his last major position, chairman of the State Central Military Commission, in March 1990. Although officially described as 'a Chinese citizen holding no leading posts', he remained very influential, as evident from his inspection tour of early 1992. He died on 19 February 1997.

see also: Beijing Municipality; Central Military Commission; Chen Yun; Chinese Communist Party; Cultural Revolution; gang of four; Liu Shaoqi; Mao Zedong; People's Liberation Army; Shanghai; Sichuan; special economic zones; Zhou Enlai.

David S. G. Goodman

dissidents

China's dissidents (*chi bu tong zhengjianzhe*) are a disparate collection of individuals and groups who often share little in common

except opposition, in varying degrees of intensity and for different reasons, to the CCP. The term dissident derives from the former socialist societies of Eastern Europe which China continues to resemble in that the ruling party attempts to close most channels through which meaningful political debate can be conducted.

Dissidents utilize a variety of means, many of necessity semi-clandestine, to express their political opinions. These include the publication of pamphlets and journals outside the boundaries of the controlled official media, petitions and open letters to state and Party leaders and institutions, one example being the 1996 open letters to the **National People's Congress** from concerned prominent citizens raising such issues as the questionable legality of China's reform-through-labour system. More direct forms of action include marches and demonstrations and even, as in the case of the **Tibet** and **Xinjiang Uygur Autonomous Regions**, attacks upon state institutions and officials.

The goals of dissidents can vary from demands for minor or major changes to the *modus operandi* of the political system, to calls for the overthrow of the system and its leaders. The concerns of dissidents range across religious, ethnic, moral, historical and political issues.

All four Chinese state **Constitutions** since 1949 (1954, 1975, 1978 and 1982) guarantee political and civil freedoms. However, the Party has always seen these freedoms as conditional on not disturbing political 'stability and unity' and, more importantly, on involving no challenge to the leadership of the CCP.

Laws concerning the definition of political dissent are vague and all-embracing. In particular, the state can, and often does, invoke the crime of 'counter-revolution' in circumstances when it feels itself under threat or wishes to cower its opponents into silence and despair. Dissidents are treated severely, often cruelly, and in many instances emerge with their health and spirits broken by the ordeal of prolonged incarceration (see **prison system**).

A particularly well known example of a

dissident is Wei Jingsheng. Having been released on parole in September 1993 from a fifteen-year sentence imposed in 1979 (see **Democracy Wall**), he was illegally detained in April 1994, being sentenced to a further fourteen years' imprisonment and three years' deprivation of political rights in December 1995 for 'attempting to overthrow the government'. The Chinese government took no notice of the international protest which greeted the sentence.

In recent years the Chinese government has resorted to the virtual deportation of troublesome and influential critics, and has even refused entry to Chinese citizens wishing to re-enter their motherland.

The protection of the legal and human rights of China's dissidents has become of concern to many governments, most importantly the **United States** and other Western countries, who have expressed alarm at the gross disparity between the flimsiness of the evidence and the brutal judgments of the courts, clearly directed in their sentences by CCP masters. During the **Cultural Revolution** any sign of political non-conformity was treated arbitrarily and harshly, with public execution being frequent. The situation has improved under **Deng Xiaoping** (see **legal system**). There are at least trials, and it is common for public statements to be made by or on behalf of dissidents to the Western media, unimaginable during the **Cultural Revolution**. Nevertheless, it remains extremely difficult and dangerous for dissi-dents under Deng and his successors, with the threat of arrest and imprisonment everpresent.

As of 1997 the dissident movement in China has seemingly been broken by a sustained attack from the authorities, and there is little evidence of any organized underground movement in China, except perhaps among minority nationality groups such as **Tibetans** and the Uygurs of **Xinjiang**. **Overseas Chinese** dissident organizations are rent by disunity, and weakened by isolation from their social milieu. Reasons for the feeble state of Chinese dissidence include the power of the Chinese police state, the pessimism and lethargy which emerged in the wake of the massive defeat of 1989, and the dynamic state of China's economy which has induced many former political activists into business.

There remains, however, an acute tension between market capitalism and social liberalism on the one hand, and political authoritarianism on the other. No matter how severely the authorities treat dissidents, it is doubtful that they can sweep such people from the landscape altogether.

see also: Constitutions; Cultural Revolution; Democracy Wall; Deng Xiaoping; legal system; National People's Congress; Overseas Chinese; prison system; Tibet Autonomous Region; Tibetans; United States policy; Xinjiang Uygur Autonomous Region.

Keith Forster

E

economic planning
See **planning, economic**.

education policy and system
Politics and education have been indissolubly linked in China's history. In all periods the state has sought to control and direct the education sector. The CCP and its professional educators must take account of deep seated attitudes and decisions, past and present. The educational heritage of China stretches back to its prehistory. Modern education was introduced from the West in the nineteenth century and, in the early twentieth, both the Nationalist Party and CCP sought to establish their own school systems.

After 1949 education developed under a mix of policies: **Soviet** advice; the indigenous **Great Leap Forward** movement; conventional readjustment; and the dislocations of the **Cultural Revolution**. Under **Deng Xiaoping**, Chinese education developed further at home and began to draw on overseas practice again.

China's modern education has been unashamedly instrumental in outlook and directed at economic growth. Education is viewed as an engine of development. While the government of the reform period has broadened subject offerings, giving some priority to law and the social sciences, the latter have been directed to functional subjects like trade, commerce and management. The sector's objective is the production of trained personnel.

China manages the world's largest education system with a total of 226 million students at various levels in 1996. Plans to develop it further cover quantitative and qualitative expansion. Total enrolments are expected to peak in the year 2000.

Educational Precedents
The Chinese empire attempted a meritocracy, utilizing the imperial civil service examinations as a means of selecting members of the bureaucracy. The aim was a moral and stable Confucian society led by the emperor and managed by the worthy and the able. Contemporary China carries this heritage.

Modern education came to China with the Western impact, with British, Japanese and later North American influence shaping China's early efforts. The dying Qing Dynasty founded a Ministry of Education (1905), opened several girls' schools, and foreshadowed plans for universal elementary schooling. Later the Nationalist Party attacked American mission influence, which had already laid down a basic structure: primary (grades 1–6), junior middle (7–9) and senior middle (10–12). In 1928–37, Chiang Kai-shek's government adopted laws and regulations to run national schools and curb foreign influence.

On gaining power in 1949, the **Chinese Communist Party** already had twenty years' experience in managing an education system. As a Marxist party, it supported low-fee, non-sectarian, compulsory schooling, and productive labour for all students. In its Yan'an years the CCP had abandoned conventional education in favour of a decentralized and self-sufficient model, based on essential literacy and numeracy, and cadre preparation.

First, the CCP leadership reformed the Nationalist Party's school system. Its Decision on Schooling and System Reform (1951) modified the length of schooling, recognized a wider range of school types, and introduced accelerated schooling for older people. Private schools were turned into public ones, the number of comprehensive universities was cut and specialized ones increased, and foreign and religious control of educational institutions was disallowed. **Soviet** educational influence reached a peak from 1954 to 1956 when China–**Soviet** exchanges, cooperative ventures, and expert visitations were common. However, this association ended in 1960.

Chinese solutions to Chinese educational problems took centre stage in the late 1950s. The Anti-Rightist Movement (see **Hundred Flowers Movement**) fell hard on teachers, tens of thousands of whom were worked to death or gaoled for allegedly expressing pro-foreign sentiment. In 1958, **Mao Zedong** launched the **Great Leap Forward**. In one year, it was claimed, enrolments in primary education had increased by 25 per cent, secondary numbers had doubled, and higher education enrolments risen by half.

Educational standards were reimposed in the early 1960s. The Ministry of Education drafted Provisional Working Regulations of Higher Education Schools Directly Under the State Council (1961). Similar Articles were issued for primary and middle schools. Prominent CCP leaders made speeches reassuring intellectuals of their worth.

The disruption of the **Cultural Revolution** caused most educational institutions to suspend operations for five years as students left the classroom to join the Red Guards. The Ministries of Education and Higher Education were replaced by a Science and Education Group. The Decision of the **CCP Central Committee** Concerning the Great Proletarian Cultural Revolution (1966), which outlined the direction of the educational reforms to come, required that education serve politics and be combined with productive labour.

Educational institutions set up **revolutionary committees** comprising representatives from workers, peasants, army units and teaching staff. Courses were highly politicized and study times shortened. Entry to university was subject to political criteria. Workers from factories known as **Mao Zedong Thought** propaganda teams entered the larger schools and college campuses to provide mass leadership, and graduates were expected to return to their home commune or **unit**. Counterattacks from conventional educators in the period 1975–6 were put down by the radical leadership.

Education in the Period of Reform
Deng Xiaoping, a supporter of conventional education, took charge of the education sector in the summer of 1977. Moves to improve the quality of education began almost immediately. National unified examinations were reintroduced in December 1977; the 'key' schools concept reappeared; and, on 18 February 1978, a list of ninety-seven 'key' universities was published. On 18 March 1978, the National Conference on Science approved an urgent upgrading for **science and technology**. The Fifth Educational Work Conference the same year re-evaluated the work of teachers.

The Decision of the **CCP Central Committee** on the Reform of the Educational Structure (May 1985) declared nine years' schooling (primary and junior middle) as the target across China. Furthermore, academic general education would be cut back to 50 per cent of the senior middle sector, the balance being technical/vocational. The Law of the PRC on Compulsory Education (April 1986) laid down a timetable for its achievement.

The socialist market-place has permitted a private education sector. Fee-paying primary and middle schools opened in the mid-1980s, some being ambitious projects, well equipped with grounds and facilities and with correspondingly high fees. Private colleges were also established, usually in association with existing institutions. In some cases joint ventures with foreigners commenced. These are governed under the Interim Provisions for Chinese–Foreign Cooperation in Running Schools. Such ventures are expected to be non-profit; schools operated by religious groups are specifically banned.

Modernization calls for educational interchange across national boundaries. According to Chinese official figures, since the beginning of the reform policy in the late 1970s, 250,000 Chinese students have gone to 103 countries, of whom more than 80,000 had returned home by 1995. In the same period, China hosted 173,000 students from 150 countries. In the 1980s, nine World Bank projects were taken up, early efforts going into university upgrading.

China followed international example by paying more attention to the education of atypical children. Plans enacted in the 1980s permitted gifted children to skip grades and enter university early. China also began to host international conferences on educational and **health policy** issues; and new programmes were introduced for the treatment of juvenile delinquents. Regulations issued in 1988 asserted the rights of disabled people to educational services.

Early political liberalization under Deng brought the diminution of the authority of the CCP in the senior management of universities and schools, where greater responsibility was given to academic leaders. There were sporadic disturbances on campuses on local issues which led into a broader movement for democracy. Mourning for the death of **Hu Yaobang** led on to a massive student movement in **Beijing** and other cities in April–June 1989.

After the **June 4 Incident** authorities combed the education sector for pro-democracy supporters. Academic leaders considered too lenient towards students' aspirations were dismissed and demoted; political ideology was re-emphasized; academic and Party leadership must work together; and military training was re-introduced on some campuses. Many international university links and cooperation schemes closed down. The events encouraged Chinese students studying abroad to take up economic opportunities and remain.

Real progress is evident in Chinese education despite stops and starts since 1949. According to official figures, in 1995, the sector held 226 million students in formal education (plus 67 million in adult education). Gross enrolment rates counted 98.5 per cent in primary education, 78.4 per cent in junior middle, and 33.6 per cent in senior middle. Kindergarten enrolments stood at 27.1 million. Enrolments in special education classes reached 295,600. More than 15.8 million students were enrolled in minority regions, including 13,000 **Tibetan** students.

In 1995, higher education institutions numbered 1,054, with 2.9 million students;

there were 1,200 private colleges, and 1,156 adult higher education institutions. All universities are required to find additional monies from their business ventures and commercial enterprises. About 100 higher education institutions are recognized as of world standard deserving of national funding.

Deng Xiaoping established the State Education Commission (SEdC) in 1985 as the senior bureaucratic organ. Its provincial, municipal, prefecture and county level educational bureaux provide feedback and execute secondary policy. The government heads of these bureaux work parallel to the heads of the appropriate level CCP committee.

Educational rights and responsibilities are defined under the Education Law of the PRC (1995) which pledges commitment to communist ideology and socialist economics. Supporting laws and regulations have followed. Future planning directions were released in 1996 in the Ninth Five-Year Plan for Educational Development and the Long-Range Development Programme Toward the Year 2010.

This Development Programme encourages the self-placement of graduates. It has the following aims:

- to coordinate national and local schooling better;
- to obtain more private and local funds for education;
- to improve teachers' qualifications;
- to expand vocational and technical education;
- to engage with the information era;
- to have basic nine-year education cover 95 per cent of the school age population by 2010;
- to have 50 per cent of the age cohort graduate from senior middle school by 2010; and
- to have higher education institutions reach 700 per 100,000 of the population by the same year.

Plans are easier to promulgate than execute. China's record in educational funding has not been good, with the percentage of GNP falling from 2.62 in 1994 to 2.4 in 1995. The aim is to reach 4 per cent by 2000. Even so China is unable to meet an insatiable public and private demand for improved educational services. The problem should not be seen just as a Chinese one. That nation educates 20 per cent of the world population, yet public expenditure is less than 2 per cent of the world total.

see also: Beijing Municipality; Chinese Communist Party; Chinese Communist Party Central Committee and Politburo; Cultural Revolution; Deng Xiaoping; Great Leap Forward; health policy; Hu Yaobang; Hundred Flowers Movement; June 4 Incident; Mao Zedong; Mao Zedong Thought; revolutionary committees; science and technology; Soviet Union, relations with; Tibetans; unit.

John F. Cleverley

electoral laws

There have been two electoral laws of the PRC, those of 1953 and 1979. The Electoral Law of the PRC for the **National People's Congress** (NPC) and the Local People's Congresses of All Levels was adopted by the Central People's Government Council on 11 February 1953 and promulgated by President **Mao Zedong** the following 1 March. It provided that 'all citizens of the PRC who have reached the age of 18 shall have the right to elect and be elected, irrespective of race, sex, occupation, social origin, religion, education, property status, or residence', but excluded from voting or being elected a few groups, notably unreformed landlords, counter-revolutionaries, and lunatics.

The 1953 Electoral Law laid down a hierarchy of elections, but not national general elections. The population voted directly for candidates at the lowest levels, notably urban and rural townships (*zhen* and *xiang*). It was the people's congresses of these low administrative levels which elected the representatives of people's congresses at higher levels. However, these elections did not necessarily all take place simultaneously, but might vary in time from place to place. Delegates to township people's congresses were expected

to range in number from 15 to 35, depending on population, with provincial people's congresses ranging from 100 to 500 delegates and the NPC having about 1,200. A drawback to the Electoral Law of 1953 was that there was nothing to prevent **Chinese Communist Party** members from sifting through nominees and allowing only those they wanted to stand, and only the same number as were required for election, meaning that in effect the CCP members and not the electors chose the successful candidates.

The subsequent Electoral Law for the NPC and the Local People's Congresses of the PRC was adopted by the Fifth NPC on 1 July 1979 and came into effect on 1 January 1980. In proposing the law to the Congress, Director Peng Zhen of the Commission for Legal Affairs of the NPC Standing Committee stated that the right to elect and recall their deputies was 'an important guarantee of the people's management of state affairs as masters of the country, and an essential prerequisite for practising democracy'. Three main features distinguished the 1979 Law from that of 1953.

- It stipulated the possibility of nominating more candidates than the number of deputies to be elected.
- It specified that the nomination of candidates should be made by repeated discussions from the bottom up and from top down. The CCP may make nominations, but so may the various democratic parties, people's organizations or any elector or deputy. The final list of candidates must be determined after repeated deliberation and discussion.
- The 1979 Law laid down that direct election of deputies to people's congresses be extended to the county level, which is higher than the township levels specified in the 1953 Law (see **local government/administration**).

Polling is by work **units**, not wards. In 1980 students, who had been among the groups seeking election in their own universities, fought strong campaigns in **Beijing** and Changsha to secure election to local congresses. However, the CCP, which has tried to keep control of the nomination of candidates, insisted on its own proposed slates. The manipulation of elections by CCP members was one of the main issues which provoked the student demonstrations of December 1986 (see **protest movements**). Students in the Anhui capital Hefei demonstrated demanding that elections give real democracy, with further demonstrations following in **Shanghai**, **Beijing** and elsewhere. The term democracy was central to these demonstrations, students arguing that elections held under the 1979 Law were frequently mockeries of a valid political notion.

Despite these important shortcomings, the 1979 Electoral Law indeed produced some effect, and above all at the lower levels. Especially since the late 1980s, younger people have become active in politics by seeking election to local people's congresses in parties other than the CCP (see **democratic parties**). It is even possible in the 1990s for a person whose nomination the local CCP branch resisted strongly to stand for and win election to a local people's congress. Election results are written on large sheets of paper and placed on public walls. They show the list of people who have stood for election, including the number of votes secured by each one and the consequent victors.

In November 1987 the NPC adopted the Organic Law on Village Committees of the PRC. This held that 'the control over village cadres by farmers and the level of villagers' self-government will be improved through the direct election of the directors, deputy directors and members of the villagers' committees'. Village heads seek and obtain election whether or not they belong to the CCP.

However, the likelihood that enough people hostile to CCP rule could actually use the electoral system to bring about the overthrow of the CCP is most unlikely in the near to medium term.

see also: Beijing Municipality; Chinese Communist Party; democratic parties; local government/administration; Mao Zedong; National People's Congress; protest movements; Shanghai; units.

Colin Mackerras

energy policy

To achieve the 9 per cent gross domestic product (GDP) growth target set in the Ninth Five-Year Plan (1996–2000) the energy sector must address three ongoing problems to avoid becoming a bottleneck. These are:

- continued ecological degradation from rural overuse of biomass;
- severe air and water pollution; and
- the loss of industrial output from deficient and unreliable supplies of commercial energy.

As of 1995, primary energy production was about 1.85 to 1.95 billion tons standard coal equivalent: 25–30 per cent from biomass and 70–5 from commercial sources. Of commercial energy, coal contributed 77.7 per cent; oil, 3.0 per cent; natural gas, 2.0 per cent and hydro, 2.0 per cent. One trillion kwh of electricity output were generated: hydro, 19.6 per cent, and thermal, 80.6 per cent (including 1 per cent from two nuclear plants). Targets for 2000 are coal, 1.45 billion tons (50 million for export); crude oil, 155 million tons; power, 1.4 trillion kwh. Compared to other developing countries, four features, all requiring amelioration, stand out in China's energy picture:

- high per capita energy use;
- low GDP per kilogramme of fuel;
- high ratio of coal in the energy budget; and
- high per capita CO emissions.

Central planning used rationing to repress household demand. While money prices were low, private automobiles and electric appliances were few, streets and buildings were ill lit, and space heating and air conditioning were forbidden in places where seasonal extremes justified both. Yet, simultaneously, **industry** flagrantly wasted energy. Low coal prices encouraged output-maximizing state-owned enterprises (in any event not cost sensitive) to overuse it, though this kept the coal mines unprofitable, many requiring continuous fiscal subsidies. Meanwhile, notorious energy tigers (e.g. hundreds of suboptimal scale nitrogenous fertilizer plants built under the Five Small Industries plan of the 1970s) abounded. Output composition reinforced this tendency. In the name of national self-sufficiency, energy saving, light industry export products were shunned for energy intensive import replacements like steel and machinery. Buoyed by new oil production, GDP rose 88 per cent in the 1970–8 period, while energy production rose 95 per cent. Reform after 1979, by correcting the most irrational technologies and introducing export-led development, saw GDP rise by 90 per cent from 1978 to 1984, while energy rose only 24 per cent.

Thereafter energy use reaccelerated. Easy productivity gains had been exhausted while urban consumers demanded more energy-using appliances and vehicles (washing machines, refrigerators, television sets, motorcycles, even cars). Renewed agricultural stagnation and environmental deterioration made it clear that sustaining output growth required serious rural electrification. Most energy prices are too low, but the situation of coal is worst. Since its price (and of the rail services needed to move it) have not kept up with inflation, daily production costs are barely covered, despite skimping on safety. Economically rational pricing, however, poses immediate and palpable risks:

• it adds a cost-push inflationary component to persistent excess demand pressures;
• it raises costs for the shaky state-owned enterprises; and
• it reduces the real incomes of the poor.

Local governments diverted coal shipments, leading to shortages downstream. This required administrative stopgaps (rotating power blackouts) to ration deficient power supplies, forcing people to adopt inefficient, power wasting expedients (e.g. restaurants use tiny gasoline powered generators for illumination and to keep refrigerators running). Furthermore, coal's unprofitability has made domestic, and especially foreign, capital hard to attract. Undercapitalization, in turn, meant that most coal was shipped unwashed. Overburdened railways must move millions of tons of rock, combustion efficiency is reduced, and air pollution worsened.

Large injections of capital and technology must be attracted to address outstanding supply-side deficiencies. A Power Industry Law was adopted in 1996 that turned the Ministry of Power into a national power corporation which should be readier to see that energy users are charged full production costs – and perhaps even some external costs (CO_2, acid rain). Rationalizing electricity production and distribution will require replacing small, outdated generators with large, new ones equipped with pollution controls, linking fragmented grids, and installing infrastructures to monitor consumption (metres, billing systems). In coal production, the present patchwork of central, provincial and local mines must be integrated, well planned operations able to reduce both costs and tragically high accident rates. New financial arrangements are on offer but whether they can overcome foreign lenders' dissatisfaction over low rates of return and deficient sovereign guarantees is unclear

Reducing air pollution, acid rain, and greenhouse gases implies less reliance on coal and increased use of natural gas and other alternatives (solar, geothermal, wind, and nuclear) (see **environment policy**). Reducing biomass use implies moving commercial power to the countryside. Nuclear power may generate 3 per cent of electricity by 2010, but capital costs and long gestation will prevent production from rising by 2000. Wind power's development is impeded by high tariffs. Hydroelectricity, typified by the massive **Three Gorges Dam** project, is expanding rapidly, despite criticisms on economic, ecological and safety grounds.

see also: environment policy; industry; local government/administration; Three Gorges Dam.

Paul Ivory

entrepreneurs

See **capitalists / entrepreneurs; new entrepreneurs.**

environment policy

With the rapid growth in the country's economy since the launch of the economic reform programme in 1978, Chinese authorities have had to contend with a multiplicity of environmental problems. These range from acid rain to deforestation and soil degradation. Water pollution is another area of grave concern, with nearly a quarter of all fresh water being polluted. Since the early 1970s, the Chinese government has begun to pay attention to the environment, but it is often the demands of economic growth, rather than environmental concerns, which influence government decisions. While the government has become more conscious of these problems, the high rate of growth throughout the 1980s and 1990s has left little time or resources to address the ever worsening environmental conditions (see **energy policy**).

After 1949 the CCP placed heavy emphasis on economic development, which meant that the environmental problems flowing from agricultural and industrial growth were ignored. **Soviet** machinery, which provided the technology for new China's economic progress during the early years, was not designed to be friendly to the natural environment. Moreover, at the time few people globally were aware of the environmental consequences of industrial development.

Although industrial waste was, where possible, recycled for economic reasons, the measures adopted and the regulations enacted to deal with the numerous health problems caused by industrial pollution were wholly inadequate. The provision of clean running water to the cities was given a high priority and a concept of 'environmental hygiene' was promoted. On the whole, however, environmental safety was not a major concern for the country's economic planners.

The irrational policies of the **Great Leap Forward** (GLF) led to further erosion of environmental safety standards. Small-scale industrial units paid hardly any attention to environmental factors in their headlong rush to outdo each other by producing substandard and often useless industrial products. There were other ill-conceived ideas of the Chinese leadership which also created serious environmental problems during the

GLF. **Mao Zedong**, who had sworn 'to do away with all pests' in one of his poems, likened sparrows to pests during a visit to the countryside in 1958, thus effectively including the bird in a nationwide campaign to exterminate all pests including rats, flies and mosquitoes. When he was finally persuaded by Chinese scientists that the damage caused to **agriculture** by sparrows was small compared to the good they did by feeding on caterpillars, Mao grudgingly called for the campaign to be halted in April 1960.

Such fallacious undertakings caused immeasurable damage not only to the ecological balance but also to the national economy. The serious drop in grain production and food shortages that led to the devastating famine during and after the GLF, can be partly attributed to such human-made environmental catastrophes. Following the end of the GLF campaign and the restoration of administrative economic **planning**, new environmental regulations were issued, setting maximum legal limits for some types of industrial emissions (see **industry**). But progress in this area was short-lived. When the **Cultural Revolution** was launched in 1966, environmental concerns took a back seat behind the radical socio-economic policies of the period.

It was in the early 1970s, still under Mao, that the Chinese authorities began to look at environmental problems fairly seriously, possibly influenced by the growing awareness of the subject internationally. An official Chinese delegation attended the United Nations-sponsored Stockholm Conference on Human Environment in 1972, which led to the creation of the United Nations Environment Programme. The term 'environmental protection', suggesting a linkage between ecology and development, began to appear in the Chinese media and official documents. The first National Environment Protection Conference was also held in **Beijing** in 1973 to decide on strategies for environmental protection.

After 1978, the new leadership, under the effective control of **Deng Xiaoping**, encouraged foreign investment and decentralized control over state-owned industrial enter-prises. As well as increasing industrial output and creating diverse forms of ownership in the economy, these measures contributed to greater environmental pollution owing to a rapid increase in the number of industrial units and the state's reduced ability to exer-cise control over them. The shift from **collective agriculture** to private farming also resulted in the decline of environmental standards in the countryside. The institutional basis for many of the previously successful land improvement programmes has thus been eroded by the privatization of farming, with family as the basic unit of production.

The challenge of environmental pollution is such that it threatens to restrict economic growth if appropriate solutions are not found quickly. The CCP leadership is undoubtedly aware of this challenge, but its capacity to solve the problems is limited by several factors.

- The technology to reduce environmental pollution is not readily available in China, and the cost of importing foreign technol-ogy is high.
- The decentralization of decision making powers to the provincial authorities and enterprise managers has meant that they attach more importance to increasing agricultural and industrial production than to controlling pollution.
- The majority of factories and mines are still state-owned and under intense pres-sure to generate profits, so the managers see no reason to increase their costs by installing expensive anti-pollution equipment.

Nevertheless, the government has estab-lished an institutional and legal framework for environmental protection. The Environ-mental Protection Commission under the **State Council**, established in 1984, coordin-ates the work of pollution control. The National Environmental Protection Agency, a sub-ministerial authority, shares the responsibility for the enforcement of environmental laws with the environmental protection bureaux at provincial, city and county levels.

In 1979 the **National People's Congress** adopted the Environmental Protection Law and Article 26 of the 1982 State **Constitution** commits the state to 'protect and improve . . . the ecological environment'. Since the late 1970s central, provincial and local govern-ments have enacted a raft of new laws and regulations. In addition, the government has also repeatedly emphasized the need for rais-ing public awareness of environmental issues. However, fearful of any group or organization which could threaten its author-ity or undermine its image in the eyes of the public, the CCP leadership has shown no tol-erance for independent environmental movements in the country.

see also: 5. Politics and the Economy: Policy Patterns and Issues; agriculture; Beijing Municipality; collective agriculture; Con-stitutions; Cultural Revolution; Deng Xiaoping; energy policy; Great Leap For-ward; industry; Mao Zedong; National People's Congress; planning, economic; Soviet Union, relations with; State Council.

Pradeep Taneja

F

financial policy

Under the system of economic **planning**, the primary role of financial policy in China was to ensure the supply of capital for planned investment and to cover government expenditure. The main sources of capital were the state budget and bank deposits. Financial and fiscal policy were thus closely integrated.

Financial policy was developed through the **State Council** and the **CCP Central Committee** and implemented through the Ministry of Finance and the **People's Bank of China** (PBC). The ministry was responsible for the budget, the collection of revenue and supervision of government accounts, while the 'monobank' PBC provided the channel through which budget allocations were disbursed, issued the currency, managed government accounts, and looked after China's gold reserves.

The state determined the allocation of capital between the different economic sectors in accordance with the plan, and the bank implemented the policy. The bank was thus a passive instrument, and it did not have an active role in shaping the allocation of resources. Moreover, capital grants to state enterprises were interest-free, with the result that the bank did not impose financial discipline on enterprises.

Within that framework, specialized banks were established under the PBC for specific purposes. The Bank of China managed foreign exchange deposits and international settlements. A Joint State-Private Bank was set up in the 1950s to oversee the demise of private banking. The Agricultural Bank of China operated for short periods in the 1950s and 1960s and again after 1979 to manage agricultural funds and the rural credit cooperative. In addition, the Construction Bank, which disbursed industrial investment and managed extra-budgetary funds, and the People's Insurance Company operated under the Ministry of Finance. Two foreign banks

were also allowed to maintain offices in China to handle international business. The frequent changes in the structure and inter-relationship of these banks reflected the changing demands made on the financial system over time. In addition, the impact of the **Cultural Revolution** led to decentralization in the operation of the banks and the growth of extra-budgetary funds controlled by local governments and enterprises. These developments did not, however, change the 'monobank' nature of the financial system. Central planning decisions on the allocation of capital continued to dominate.

The evolution of the reforms after 1978 demanded changes to financial policy. The new emphasis on the efficiency of resource utilization, on enterprise autonomy, on market exchange and on the role of **international trade** required greater financial discipline in capital management and greater diversification in the banking system. During the 1980s and 1990s, therefore, financial policy moved towards separating the **planning** and commercial role of banks, using interest rates as an active mechanism for guiding the allocation of capital, and diversifying the range of financial instruments through the use of government bonds, experiments with stock markets, and the emergence of non-bank financial institutions. While these developments created much more vitality, underlying issues related to continued plan intervention in capital allocation, problems with price distortions left over from the plan system, and lack of fiscal discipline caused by decentralization in the tax system all combined to hinder the formation of a strong banking system.

The first changes came in the international area. The China International Trust and Investment Corporation was established in 1979 to mobilize foreign capital, and China joined the International Monetary Fund, the World Bank and the Asian Development Bank in 1980. Major changes to the domestic financial system did not begin until 1984, when a tax and profit system was introduced for state enterprises and it was decided to change state grants of capital into loans through the bank. By that time, fiscal contracting between different levels of government had also created a strong sense of local economic identity and increasing capacity for local governments at provincial level and below to develop their own investment plans. In addition, savings rose along with incomes. In 1983, therefore, it was decided that the PBC should act solely as a central bank to manage the currency, credit policy, exchange rates and reserves, and in 1984, the Industrial and Commercial Bank was established to take over its 'commercial' role. After 1984 there was a proliferation of other financial institutions such as local trust companies, rural and urban credit cooperatives, and informal loans. New types of financial instruments also developed, such as government and industry bonds, indexed deposit accounts and equity shares. China's financial system thus became more open, and financial policy had to take account of market forces.

Despite these changes, the 1980s also saw continued problems in financial management. Inflationary outbursts associated with surges in investment, particularly by local governments, political pressures on local branches of banks to exceed central credit limits and fluctuations in the economic cycle led to hesitations in reform and strong administrative interventions in credit supply. State enterprises were also protected from firm financial discipline by subsidies which had to be carried by the banks as bad debts. Eventually in 1994, a further round of reforms was launched in fiscal, banking and foreign currency management to address these problems. The most successful of these were the foreign currency changes which paved the way for full convertibility of the *renminbi* (people's currency). The tax reforms also began to claw back fiscal authority to the central government. The banking reforms were aimed at separating plan and commercial functions by setting up three 'policy'

banks to manage planned financial dealings (the State Development Bank, the Import and Export Bank and the China Agricultural Development Bank) and leaving the remaining banks as commercial operations. Foreign banks were also given greater access to do business in China. Nevertheless, these reforms were vitiated by bargaining between levels of administration, and major problems remained in how to handle poorly performing state enterprises with large debts and how to achieve the final separation of party and government from the direct management of the banking system. The non-bank sector also required closer monitoring and regulation.

see also: Chinese Communist Party Central Committee and Politburo; Cultural Revolution; international trade; People's Bank of China; planning, economic; State Council.

Andrew Watson

Four Modernizations

The modernization of **agriculture**, **industry**, national defence, and **science and technology**. At the Third **National People's Congress** in December 1964 **Zhou Enlai** first proposed the socialist construction of a 'modernized **agriculture**, **industry**, national defence, and **science and technology**' within the fairly near future. The onset of the **Cultural Revolution** prevented any further development of this theme until the Fourth **National People's Congress** in January 1975. In his last speech to a national congress **Zhou Enlai** renewed his call for a policy to bring about an 'independent and relatively comprehensive industrial and economic system' by 1980 and 'accomplish the comprehensive modernization of **agriculture**, **industry**, national defence and **science and technology** before the end of the century'.

The Congress endorsed his call and **Deng Xiaoping**, who travelled widely throughout China in 1975 speaking on modernization, gave his strong support. In the autumn Deng drafted three important documents on this theme, but the **gang of four** labelled them 'three poisonous weeds', condemning modernization as the 'road to capitalist restoration'. With **Zhou Enlai**'s death in January 1976 and the removal of Deng from all posts in April after the **Tiananmen Incident**, nothing more happened until after **Mao Zedong** died and the **gang of four** fell in 1976.

The first indication of the new policy line came in a joint *People's Daily*, *Hongqi* (**Red Flag**) and *Liberation Army Daily* editorial on 25 October 1976. **Zhou Enlai**'s strategic plan to bring about the 'comprehensive modernization of **agriculture**, **industry**, national defence and **science and technology**' was revived by CCP Chairman **Hua Guofeng**. At a national conference in May 1977 Party economist Yu Qiuli announced that by 1985 a comparatively complete independent industrial system covering the entire country would be in place. In his closing address to the Eleventh Party Congress in August 1977 **Deng Xiaoping** stressed the importance of modernization, the Four Modernizations being written into the Party **Constitution**.

At the Fifth **National People's Congress** in February 1978 **Hua Guofeng** announced a ten-year plan to achieve the Four Modernizations, which were also written into the State **Constitution**. The goals for **industry** included setting the annual industrial growth rate at 10 per cent with an estimated US$400 billion in investment for capital construction. There were to be a hundred and twenty major projects, including seven major trunk railways and five harbours. The goal for steel production was set at 60 million tons by 1985 and 180 million tons by 1999. Ten new oil and gas fields were to be constructed. Coal production was to reach 900 million tons a year with eight new mines opened. Electricity was to increase by 6 to 8 million kilowatts per year with thirty new power plants to be constructed, insufficient even to support the target of 10 per cent annual industrial growth, let alone any domestic consumption increase.

Goals in **agriculture** included an annual production increase of 4–5 per cent, mechanization of 85 per cent of major farming tasks, expansion of irrigation and the establishment of twelve commodity and food base areas. The cost of agricultural modernization was estimated at US$33 billion with a further US$50 billion needed to relocate and find jobs for the labour released by mechanization.

Modernization of defence was recognized as a very expensive goal unlikely to be realized in the short term. The urgent need to update obsolete equipment was recognized but the goal in long-term planning was to keep Chinese control of production capabilities, so only selective purchases of high-technology systems and weapons was planned.

Among the Four Modernizations, the late 1970s leadership saw **science and technology** as the key element, emphasizing that scientific research must lead economic construction. It was hoped that by 1985 China would be only ten years behind the most advanced nations and the goal was to catch up with or surpass them by the year 2000.

The goals of the Four Modernizations were far too ambitious. During 1978 around 100,000 construction projects were launched costing US$40 billion. When orders to foreign suppliers and military and scientific purchases were added, the investment for 1978 came to 36 per cent of China's national income. This level could not be sustained, the Four Modernizations had to be scaled down and during the late 1980s the term faded from use.

see also: agriculture; Constitutions; Cultural Revolution; Deng Xiaoping; gang of four; *Hongqi* (*Red Flag*); Hua Guofeng; industry; Mao Zedong; National People's Congress; *People's Daily*; science and technology; Tiananmen Incident; Zhou Enlai.

Beverley M. Kitching

G

gang of four

The designation given to four influential supporters of the **Cultural Revolution**: Jiang Qing, Zhang Chunqiao, Yao Wenyuan and Wang Hongwen, overthrown in October 1976.

Under **Chen Boda**, Jiang Qing was the first deputy head of the Cultural Revolution Group, set up in 1966 to guide the progress of the **Cultural Revolution**, and took **cultural policy**, political and other initiatives in her own right, especially that of designing and helping create the 'model revolutionary operas'. As **Mao Zedong**'s wife she also took the lead in 'carrying out his instructions'. Yao Wenyuan was the author of the article, published on 10 November 1965 in **Shanghai**, regarded at the time as the first salvo of the **Cultural Revolution**. Zhang Chunqiao became the Chairman of the **Shanghai** Municipal **Revolutionary Committee** in February 1967, **Shanghai** remaining a major focus of the gang's activities.

All four except Wang Hongwen were appointed to the Politburo on 28 April 1969 by the First Plenum of the CCP's Ninth Central Committee. On 30 August 1973 the First Plenum of the Tenth Central Committee appointed Wang Hongwen as one of the Deputy Chairmen of the CCP, all four to the Politburo, and Wang and Zhang to its Standing Committee.

The term 'gang of four' was used publicly only after they had fallen, specifically by **Beijing** Municipal CCP First Secretary Wu De in his speech of 24 October 1976 to some 1 million people assembled in Tiananmen Square in the centre of **Beijing**. Wu claimed that, on 17 July 1974, **Mao Zedong** had warned them against becoming 'a small faction of four'. Wu also said that at a meeting of the Politburo on 3 May 1975 Mao had warned them: 'Don't function as a gang of four'.

In his speech to the Eleventh **National Party Congress** on 12 August 1977, Party Chairman **Hua Guofeng** listed numerous examples showing that Mao had criticized the four for practising factionalism and stirring up trouble within the CCP leadership. He had criticized Wang Hongwen to his face on 24 December 1974: 'stop carrying on with your gang of four'. Wu claimed that on 11 September 1976, two days after Mao died, the four had required the provinces to report to them alone. Worse still, early in October 1976, they distributed arms and ammunition in **Shanghai** to carry out an armed rebellion to seize power.

On 6 October Wang Dongxing and his elite military force Unit 8341 arrested the four, on orders from **Hua Guofeng**. Wang, who had joined the revolution in 1933 and was enormously loyal to **Mao Zedong**, had developed Unit 8341 after 1949 in order to protect the top leadership. Obviously he had come to accept that Mao's heir as CCP Chairman was **Hua Guofeng**, not Jiang Qing.

Following their arrest, the gang of four were accused of a great variety of crimes and virtually all the excesses of the **Cultural Revolution** were blamed on them. Other than factionalism and plotting rebellion, their crimes included tampering with the **education** system, disrupting industrial and agricultural production, sabotaging **international trade**, opposing Marxism, and persecuting good government workers. On 21 July 1977, the Third Plenum of the Tenth Central Committee adopted a communiqué which formally expelled all four from the CCP as 'bourgeois careerists, conspirators and counter-revolutionary double-dealers' and 'dismissed [them] from all posts both inside and outside the Party'. The decision of the **Third Plenum of the Eleventh Central Committee** of December 1978 to discontinue the campaign against the gang of four caused the obsessive denunciations against them to wane, but not to disappear altogether.

In November and December 1980, a special

court tried the gang of four and six other living persons of various and numerous crimes (see **legal system**). Those against the gang fell mainly into three categories:
- framing and persecuting CCP and state leaders;
- persecuting and suppressing large numbers of cadres and masses; and
- plotting armed rebellion in **Shanghai** just before their overthrow.

All four were convicted, the sentences being handed down on 25 January 1981. Jiang Qing and Zhang Chunqiao were sentenced to death with two-year reprieves, Yao Wenyuan to twenty years' imprisonment, and Wang Hongwen to life imprisonment. In the event neither Jiang nor Zhang was executed, Jiang Qing committing suicide in prison in May 1991.

It was obvious at the time that, despite Mao's criticisms of some of their activities, they could not have seized as much power as they in fact enjoyed without support from him. To counter the possible suggestion that Mao might have been part of a 'gang of five', *People's Daily* published an article on 22 December 1980 stating that, while Mao had indeed made mistakes in his last years, he was certainly not a criminal.

see also: 1. Overview History of the People's Republic of China; Beijing Municipality; Chen Boda; Chinese Communist Party Central Committee and Politburo; cultural policy; Cultural Revolution; education policy and system; Hua Guofeng; international trade; legal system; Mao Zedong; National Party Congress; *People's Daily*; revolutionary committees; Shanghai; Third Plenum of the Eleventh Central Committee.

Colin Mackerras

gender equality

Gender equality has been a continuing official objective of the PRC government. It was proclaimed in the 1949 Common Programme and endorsed in the **Constitution**. Significant advances were made towards equality, particularly under **Mao Zedong**, but there have been continuing inequalities in both the domestic and public spheres. The economic reforms of the post-Mao era have led to a revival of some pre-revolutionary inequalities, including the sale of **women** and female infanticide.

In 1949 the new Chinese government proclaimed gender equality as an integral part of its official policy. The 1950 **Marriage Law** formally abolished the 'feudal' marriage system and the 1954 **Constitution** stated that **women** were to 'enjoy equal rights with men in all spheres of life'. These rights were endorsed in subsequent regulations and laws. In 1992 the government reaffirmed its commitment to gender equality in its Law on the Protection of the Rights and Interests of Women which spelt out **women**'s rights in politics, culture, **education**, work, property, person and family life.

Reality does not fully reflect legal requirements. In politics, the workforce and **education**, female participation declines as one goes up the ladder. In the mid-1990s, **women** comprised some 21 per cent of members of the **National People's Congress**, but only 12 per cent of its Standing Committee. Less than 8 per cent of the CCP Central Committee was female. In the workforce, according to 1995 figures, women comprised 46.6 per cent of primary school teachers but only 32.9 per cent of university teachers and about 10 per cent of professors. Although **women** participate in most occupations, they continue to be clustered in low status, lower paid and gender-specific jobs. For example, over 60 per cent of textile workers and clerical workers are female. In **education**, females comprised 47.3 per cent of primary school students in 1995 but just over 35.4 per cent of university students. In the mid-1990s some 70 per cent of the nation's illiterates were female; over 20 per cent of all urban women and 50 per cent of rural women were still illiterate.

Domestically, women have continued to bear the major responsibility for household labour, despite their general participation in the workforce. A **Beijing** survey of the mid-1980s revealed that, on average, women devoted 1.5 hours a day more than men to housework, while a rural survey in **Sichuan** and Fujian Provinces revealed that, while women spent 1.5 hours a day less than their husbands in the paid workforce, they spent four hours a day more on housework.

The economic reforms of the post-**Mao Zedong** era have increased gender inequality in some areas. Discrimination against women in the workforce has intensified, with higher unemployment rates for women (approximately 70 per cent of all unemployment) and frequent suggestions that married women should 'return home'. In rural areas there has been a growing gender division of labour, including a trend towards the feminization of **agriculture** as men have taken up jobs in industrial enterprises. The privatization of the economy has led to rising school dropout rates, with girls accounting for up to 90 per cent of all dropouts.

There has also been a revival of some pre-revolutionary practices. Since the early 1980s a rising level of domestic violence has led to a number of official campaigns for the protection of **women**. The kidnapping or buying of women, and their subsequent sale as wives in poorer provinces, became a national scandal in the early 1990s. The one-child family policy led to instances of female infanticide because of the continuing preference for sons (see **population policy**). Reports from **women's organizations** of growing gender imbalances in birth registrations led to a partial retreat to a 'two-child' policy, at least in the countryside, in the mid-1980s.

see also: agriculture; Beijing Municipality; Constitutions; Mao Zedong; Marriage Laws; National People's Congress; population policy; Sichuan; women.

Beverley Hooper

government
See **local government**; **provincial government**; **State Council**.

Great Leap Forward
The Great Leap Forward (GLF) was an attempt by **Mao Zedong** and other leftists to remedy perceived defects in centralized **planning**, but produced one of history's great catastrophes. Despite rapid growth, the

Soviet-style First Five-Year Plan (1953–7) revealed **agriculture**'s inability to guarantee exportable surpluses to finance **Soviet** aid projects and feed a growing urban workforce. The right concluded that China's labour-intensive farming system was unsuited to collectivization and that industrially based inputs were indispensable. The left concluded that the social energies of the village poor released by land reform could be channelled into labour-intensive capital construction and farming practices, able to guarantee surpluses without diverting capital from **industry**, provided that their enthusiasm were not blocked by centralizing technocrats in Beijing ignorant of class struggle.

The technical basis of the GLF was Mao's optimistic Draft Plan for Agricultural Development (1956–67). A melange of wildly optimistic schemes, it was supported by some top scientists like the aeronautical designer Qian Xuesen. Made national policy in October 1957 it initiated a massive mobilization of peasants for irrigation projects during the 1957–8 winter season , which in turn motivated the amalgamation of collectives into communes in 1958 (see **collective agriculture**). Meanwhile the central ministries lost their ability even to monitor events, as authority over statistical collection and planning authority was shifted to provincial and lower units swollen by mass promotions of untrained rural cadres. The latter, unconstrained by control from above, were encouraged to engage in competitive production drives, outbidding each other to report over-fulfilled targets. Meanwhile new project loans, requiring more agricultural exports, were secured from the **Soviet Union**.

Non-existent surpluses procured by state organs were either exported or used to feed millions of new urban dwellers, and vast amounts of labour were squandered on futile projects like backyard furnaces. The result was unprecedented subsistence crisis in the countryside. Mao was severely criticized for this in a string of Party conferences from 1959, from which an elaborate – but as the **Cultural Revolution** showed, unstable – political compromise emerged. Much of his authority passed to **Liu Shaoqi** and **Deng Xiaoping**. The worst follies (mess halls in over-large communes) were redressed quickly, but others (unprecedentedly high savings rates in 1959), lasted, unaccountably, right into the 'three difficult years (1959–61). A demographic deficit (deaths plus lost births) of between 20 million and 40 million accumulated by 1992 made the GLF the main cause of possibly the worst famine in recorded history. In badly affected provinces (**Sichuan**, Anhui), whole areas were depopulated.

Hong Kongers queuing to mail food to desperate relatives knew a famine was occurring, but careful information management regarding rural conditions concealed its magnitude from them and others at home and abroad. Social order collapsed in some villages, but the cities survived relatively unscathed through strict rationing, emergency production, grain imports and by sending home all new migrants. Party prestige may even have risen, face being preserved by scrupulously repaying **Soviet** loans, even after aid had been unilaterally suspended in 1960. International assistance was shunned. A downward spiral was averted by **Liu Shaoqi** and **Chen Yun**, who controlled inflation, partially decollectivized farming, and introduced more modern fertilizers. Although surviving the GLF was a huge achievement, the lesson was lost. Mao blamed the disaster on half-hearted implementation rather than flawed social and technical assumptions, and his **Cultural Revolution** was to some extent designed as a successor movement to the failed GLF.

see also: 1. Overview History of the People's Republic of China; 5. Politics and the Economy: Policy Patterns and Issues; agriculture; Chen Yun; collective agriculture; Cultural Revolution; Deng Xiaoping; industry; Liu Shaoqi; Mao Zedong; planning, economic; Sichuan; Soviet Union, relations with.

Paul Ivory

Guangzhou

Situated in the Pearl River Delta on the southeast coast of China, Guangzhou is the seat of the Guangdong provincial government and, with **Hong Kong**, the hub of economic activity in southern China. Since the beginning of the economic reform programme in the late 1970s, Guangzhou has earned a reputation for being a business-friendly and forward-looking city. Also known in the Western world as Canton, another Chinese name for the city is Yangcheng. The 1990 census put the population of Guangzhou Municipality at 6,299,989. Among these people 3,935,195 were in the main urban districts and the remainder in surrounding counties, while males numbered 3,248,747 and females 3,051,242. The total population at the end of 1995 was estimated at 6.47 million.

Guangzhou was the first Chinese city encountered by foreign maritime traders and became known around the world as the main port on the Silk Road of the Sea. Between 1757 and 1842, before the unequal treaties opened many cities, it was the only Chinese city where European merchants were allowed to work and live, albeit under strict rules and outside the city walls.

After 1949, the fact that a large percentage of Guangzhou's population maintained family ties with the **Overseas Chinese** communities in many parts of the world made them suspect in the eyes of the CCP leaders. However, once those with 'bad' backgrounds (i.e. capitalists, landlords, Guomindang supporters, etc.) had been identified and re-educated or punished, the families of **Overseas Chinese** were allowed to live and work like most other citizens. They were also told to encourage their relatives living abroad to return to China to live or witness the changes taking place in the country. During the **Cultural Revolution**, however, Red Guards attacked thousands of Guangzhou residents with **Overseas Chinese** connections for their alleged decadent lifestyles. Such people were forced to advise their **Overseas Chinese** relatives to refrain from contacting them or sending them money lest it should attract the wrath of the Red Guards. Yet, throughout the **Cultural Revolution** period, the city continued to host the Chinese Export Commodities Fair (the Canton trade fair), held twice a year since 1957. Attendance at the fair was by invitation only.

The period of reform has given Guangzhou a key role in the modernization of China. The city has attracted billions of dollars in **Overseas Chinese** and foreign investments. Along with Shenzhen and the other **special economic zones**, Guangzhou is now home to thousands of big and small foreign-invested factories, shops and hotels. Its reputation as a trading centre has been further enhanced by the liberal economic policies implemented by the central and provincial governments, although the Canton trade fair is no longer as important as it once was when only the state monopolies were allowed to import or export. **Hong Kong** Chinese investors account for the bulk of the foreign capital invested in Guangzhou (and in Guangdong Province as a whole). Their ability to speak Cantonese and a wide relationship (*guanxi*) network in the province and the country give them a strong competitive advantage over others vying for a share of the local market.

There is no doubt that the central government has accorded particularly favourable treatment to Guangzhou (and the other cities and towns in the Pearl River Delta). Whereas some powers were officially granted to Guangzhou in order to make it more attractive to **Overseas Chinese** and foreign investors, the city's leaders have also managed to enlarge these powers by passing additional local laws and regulations. Far from the watchful eyes of some of its critics in **Beijing** and so close to **Hong Kong**, Guangzhou has quietly but steadily created enough political space to surge ahead without much hindrance. Its greatest supporter was **Deng Xiaoping**, who was most impressed by the activist attitude of Guangdong leaders, and who, in 1992, entrusted them the task of joining the ranks of the Asian tiger economies within twenty years.

Guangzhou's economic power does not necessarily give it commensurate political influence in **Beijing**. **Yang Shangkun**, a strong advocate for the province, was sidelined in 1992. **Deng Xiaoping**'s death in 1997 left it with the need to find alternative political patronage in **Beijing**.

see also: 9. Taiwan and the Overseas Chinese; Beijing Municipality; Cultural Revolution; Deng Xiaoping; Hong Kong; Overseas Chinese policy; special economic zones; Yang Shangkun.

Pradeep Taneja

H

health policy

In 1949 the CCP inherited an inadequate number of medical personnel to cope with a war-torn population suffering from pervasive infection, malnutrition, poor hygiene and inadequate **education**. The first vice-minister of Health was Dr He Cheng, who had been instrumental in developing the CCP's medical system between 1929 and 1949. Dr He exerted a strong influence on health policy until his dismissal in 1955.

The new regime announced its policies at the First National Health Conference in August 1950. They were

- access to health care for all;
- prevention before cure; and
- integration of traditional and modern medicine.

Medical education was to be expanded greatly to produce large numbers of health workers quickly but high quality should be maintained. The Beijing Union Medical College (BUMC) retained its rigorous entry standards. Expertise was stressed both by the Western-trained doctors in the Medical Education Bureau of the Ministry of Health and the newly appointed **Soviet**-trained personnel.

In the area of medical research the three policy decision-making bodies were the Scientific Committee on Medical Science in the Ministry of Health, the Chinese Academy of Science and the Chinese Academy of Medical Science. In all three, professionals and doctors had substantial influence. Graduates and faculty from the BUMC were dominant members of the new elite and the pre-1949 research trends continued well into the 1950s.

In the late 1950s the Party began to assert more control by appointing non-medical personnel like Xu Yunbei as vice-ministers. Doctors were invited to join the CCP. Certain areas were removed from Ministry of Health control and in these areas policy-making systems were developed in which professional

medics had little control. **Mao Zedong**'s main concern was to redistribute health services to rural areas, while Lu Dingyi and **Zhou Enlai** tried to protect the interests of the Ministry of Health. The **Great Leap Forward** saw enrolment in higher level medical schools increase from 9,000 to 25,000 by 1960, with an emphasis on 'red rather than expert', but the agricultural failures resulted in retrenchment and by 1963 the number of medical colleges had fallen from 142 to 98.

The early 1960s saw an increased emphasis on expertise. The Ministry of Health increased the length of all courses in medical schools to six years and raised entry standards. The number of medical conferences reached record levels; so did the number of delegations to and from China. The *Chinese Medical Journal* published increasing numbers of pure research articles.

In 1965 **Mao Zedong** made a strong attack on the Ministry of Health saying it was dominated by elite doctors concerned with running the urban hospital-based **health system**. He claimed that three years' training for higher primary school graduates would be sufficient and they would then learn 'on the job'. The immediate impact of the **Cultural Revolution** was to transfer major policy-making authority from the Ministry of Health to a small political elite led by Mao. There was a major shift in emphasis from urban to rural health care, from material to moral incentives and from disdain to approval of manual work. The main policy focus centred on the problems of the effective delivery of mass health services. Traditional Chinese medicine and Western medicine were to be combined and there was to be mass participation in medicine. The 'barefoot doctor' programme was developed initially with a basic training of only six months. Medical insurance programmes were introduced in the countryside.

While central policy in the early 1970s was

still pushing for shorter training programmes for doctors and less emphasis on expertise, the grassroots demand became increasingly one for longer training for barefoot doctors, with greater emphasis on acquiring expert knowledge.

Health policy in the 1980s and 1990s has seen both continuity and change. There has been continuing preference for preventive medicine and a simultaneous emphasis on both traditional and modern medicine. Policies on large-scale immunization have continued. Change in policy is seen in a greater stress on individuals, resulting in a trend to privatization in health care delivery. Universal free health care is no longer a major aim.

Both the barefoot doctor scheme and the rural collective insurance system have disappeared. Government expenditure on health, however, has increased since 1984 in areas such as building hospitals, technology acquisition, medical education and research. Inequalities between urban and rural communities and between rich and poor have emerged during the 1990s with health care delivery almost non-existent for the rural poor in remoter areas. New areas for health policy include industrial diseases and the adverse effects of environmental pollution.

see also: Cultural Revolution; education; policy and system; Great Leap Forward; health system; Mao Zedong; Soviet Union, relations with; Zhou Enlai.

Beverley M. Kitching

health system

One of the problems confronting the new government in 1949 was how to integrate the three inherited elements – Western-style medicine, the system of the CCP's base areas, and traditional medicine – into a new workable system.

The Western-style medical system served mainly urban Chinese. It included a Ministry of Health, over 500 hospitals, 33 medical schools and about 20,000 Western-style doctors, three-quarters of whom were based in the main ports of the six coastal provinces. The CCP's base areas had had experience in public health work, including setting up a

public health school; this element featured an emphasis on preventive medicine, the use of paramedics with little formal training, mass movements and integration with traditional Chinese medicine. The third element came from traditional Chinese medicine, which also stressed prevention as well as cure.

By 1955 a national system was in place in which the Ministry of Health was predominant. Under the control of the ministry were national-level units dealing with the administration of matters such as medical education, mass campaigns, drugs, finance, contagious diseases, maternal and child health care, treatment and prevention of diseases, and traditional medicine. There were also affiliated agencies such as the People's Health Press and the Academy of Medical Sciences. Attached to the latter were various hospitals and research institutes. The Bureau of Traditional Medicine was at this time attached to the Ministry of Commerce. Much medical research was carried out in institutes of the Chinese Academy of Sciences.

At the provincial level were provincial health bureaux to which were attached county health departments and, in the cities, municipal health bureaux with responsibility for hospitals, pharmaceutical controls and anti-epidemic stations. These stations dealt with sanitation, environmental problems, food hygiene, school hygiene and industrial health matters, and were responsible for running laboratories and gathering statistics.

In the late 1950s several changes were made in the organization of the health system. The CCP began to assert more control by appointing non-medical personnel like Xu Yunbei to vice-ministerial portfolios, removing some units from control by the Ministry of Health and setting up new independent units such as the Subcommittee on Schistosomiasis. In 1957 the Bureau of Traditional Medicine was moved from the Ministry of Commerce into the Ministry of Health. **Mao Zedong** was pushing the need to extend health services in the countryside and educate medical personnel politically. The failure of the **Great Leap Forward** brought a renewed emphasis on professionalism. High priority was given to the treatment of severe burns, causes of cancer and brain and open heart surgery.

In 1965 Mao made a strong attack on the Ministry of Health and during the **Cultural Revolution** there was a major shift in emphasis from urban to rural health care. The main focus was on effective delivery of mass health services and the enormous and urgent demand for personnel that this required. College courses were shortened, traditional practitioners were recruited and the barefoot doctor service inaugurated. By the end of 1975 more than 100,000 urban health workers and more than 1.1 million personnel from urban and **People's Liberation Army** public health units had settled in the countryside. One-third of all urban doctors had been relocated in rural areas and 70 per cent of all medical and pharmacological graduates had been assigned to rural posts. The concentration of policy-making power in the hands of a small political elite and the decentralization of the health system resulted in bureaucratic immobility, the alienation of professionals and uncertainty at the local level.

The best known aspect of the mass medical system was the barefoot doctor programme. By 1973 there were about 1 million barefoot doctors. Their duties varied from region to region and included health education, prevention and cure of illness, immunization, supervision of sanitary facilities, family planning and first aid. Although they provided a fairly effective basic health network, lack of faith in their competence led to greater demands for referral to higher levels of health care which resulted in overcrowding of city hospitals. Starting around 1973 there were increasing trends towards a greater emphasis on expertise and longer training for doctors (see **health policy**).

These trends accelerated after 1976. Hospitals and research institutes returned to full-scale Western medical practices. The Ministry of Health resumed its primary role. The health care system during the 1980s and 1990s has tended towards privatization and has swung back to favouring urban areas, while the barefoot doctors have disappeared.

see also: Cultural Revolution; Great Leap Forward; health policy; Mao Zedong; People's Liberation Army.

Beverley M. Kitching

Hong Kong

Hong Kong's 1,078 square kilometres of land is divided into three main areas, Hong Kong Island, Kowloon, and the New Territories and Outlying Islands. Its population in 1996 was about 6.3 million, 96 per cent being Chinese and predominantly Cantonese-speaking.

Hong Kong was ceded to Great Britain in the Treaty of Nanjing (ratified in 1843), after the First Opium War. The Kowloon Peninsula and Stonecutter's Island passed to British control in the 1860 Convention of Beijing, and under the Beijing Convention of 1898 London obtained a ninety-nine-year lease of the New Territories. The PRC did not recognize these treaties, but claimed what amounted to residual sovereignty under British administration. For its first century under British rule, the colony (territory) thrived as a business entrepôt and a redoubt for refugees from mainland political and economic troubles. From December 1941 to August 1945, Hong Kong was occupied by the Japanese.

Although the population fell under Japanese occupation, over 1 million refugees fled to Hong Kong just after the Civil War (1946–9). This placed enormous pressures on the British authorities to house and sustain the population, interrupted Hong Kong's entrepôt role with China and short-circuited democratization proposals by Governor Sir Mark Young. This period also saw the emergence of a powerful local Chinese elite increasingly able to compete with and challenge British merchants and officials in all spheres of public life. During the 1950s and early 1960s, the territory responded to these changed circumstances by becoming a manufacturing centre in its own right. This boom faltered when communist-inspired riots broke out in Hong Kong in 1967 from the **Cultural Revolution**, which, again, inspired an influx of refugees from the mainland.

Around 1972, a turning point in Hong

Kong's evolution came with the waning of the Vietnam War, the normalization of Sino-Western relations, the slow shift to a policy of reform and opening in China, and the appointment of Sir Murray MacLehose as governor. Hong Kong once again became an entrepôt fuelling China's modernization drive. The Independent Commission against Corruption was established in 1974, and 'new towns' were built in the New Territories to accommodate the ever increasing population (which by 1990 stood at 5.8 million). Massive infrastructural development was undertaken with the construction of two underwater transportation tunnels, the Mass Transit Railway, the Kowloon–Canton Railway and the Light Rail Transit, and tunnels connecting Kowloon and the New Territories. In 1989 the British authorities announced plans for the massive US$21 billion Port and Airport Development Scheme.

Hong Kong became famous for its prosperity, stability, rule of law and human rights. By 1995, it ranked eighth among the world's trading economies, with a GDP of US$336.9 billion and an annual economic growth rate of over 5 per cent. Moreover, China now imported goods directly from Hong Kong as well as buying re-exports from the rest of the world. The US$1.6 million worth of direct imports from Hong Kong in 1980 had grown to US$15 billion by 1985.

China became Hong Kong's biggest trading partner, accounting for about one-quarter of the territory's total trade. Hong Kong also became China's leading investor, and much of its manufacturing capacity was transferred into the Chinese hinterlands, with over 3 million workers employed in territory-owned or joint-venture enterprises. About two-thirds of Hong Kong trade with China was related to the outward processing or the re-export of goods, increasing in value from US$7.15 billion in 1983 to US$121.5 billion in 1994 (an average annual growth rate of 29 per cent). Imports to Hong Kong grew from US$25.6 billion in 1984 to US$160.3 billion in 1994, while domestic exports fell annually in the decade to 1994, when they were valued at US$28.5 billion. Besides indicating a high

level of economic integration between the territory and China, these figures reflected a shift in Hong Kong's economy to services (including tourism), which, in the mid-1990s, accounted for four-fifths of the territory's GDP, or double that of a decade before. Concurrently, the territory established itself as a major world financial centre and a source of advanced technology, with high living standards (its 1994 per capita GDP of US$21,560 being second in Asia only to Japan).

In September 1982, British Prime Minister Margaret Thatcher visited Beijing for talks with **Deng Xiaoping**, who made it clear that the resumption of Chinese sovereignty over the territory on 1 July 1997 was non-negotiable. Deng enunciated his **'one country, two systems'** formula to allay fears in Hong Kong about the reversion to Chinese rule. The Sino-British Joint Declaration of December 1984 promised the territory autonomy and a continuation of its laws for fifty years as a 'special administrative region' (SAR) of China, with Beijing taking control only over its foreign and defence policies. In April 1990, the Basic Law of the HKSAR was promulgated, with final interpretation resting in the hands of the Standing Committee of China's **National People's Congress** (NPC).

At the time, the territory operated a three-tier, executive-led system of government composed of a meritocratic civil service and an elected Legislative Council (LegCo) at the central level having the powers to enact laws and to approve taxation and public expenditure (although the chief executive could veto bills and dissolve the body in some circumstances), two municipal councils at the regional level, and nineteen district boards at the grassroots level. An appointed Executive Council also served the governor in an advisory capacity. Direct elections to a proportion of seats on the district boards and the LegCo became a feature of the system in 1985 and 1991, respectively, and the formation of political parties and campaign activity introduced some scrutiny over the administration, heightening the importance of public opinion

in decision making. Political groupings advocating greater democracy in the territory's
administration dominated direct elections,
especially after the **June 4 Incident** in China.
However, China's condemnation of the June
1991 Hong Kong Bill of Rights Ordinance, on
the grounds that it substantially changed the
legal system, and the government's support
for a diluted Court of Final Appeal left many
territorians extremely uneasy about their
future legal protection and about the rise of
corruption and crime, fuelling an exodus of
migrants overseas (some 62,000 in 1994).

   With Governor Chris Patten's appointment
in July 1992, however, Sino-British cooperation under the '1997 through train' arrangements rapidly eroded. Despite Beijing's
objections, the LegCo passed his political
reform package aimed at broadening political
choice in June 1994. Patten's defiance of
Beijing was especially irritating given the
erosion of the centre's administrative and
financial control in the regions, and the linkage which the **United States** required
between China's human rights record and the
renewal of its 'most-favoured nation' status
(the loss of which would have cost Hong
Kong's economy some US$8 billion).

   On 1 September 1994, the NPC Standing
Committee legislated that all political structures thereafter established by Britain in
Hong Kong would be abolished on 1 July
1997. A fortnight later, direct elections took
place for the district boards. Only 33.1 per
cent of voters turned out, overwhelmingly
electing candidates whom Beijing opposed.
The same happened in the 17 September 1995
LegCo direct elections.

   In December 1995 China announced the
Preparatory Committee for the HKSAR, 94
from Hong Kong among the 150 members,
most of them business people and conservatives. Later Beijing established a 400-member
Selection Committee which on 11 December
1996 chose business tycoon **Tung Chee-hwa**
as the first HKSAR chief executive. Ten days
later it selected 60 (out of 130 approved candidates) for the Provisional Legislature which
would sit in Shenzhen until 1 July 1997 and
thereafter in the territory until the election of

the first HKSAR legislative body under
Beijing-determined processes in 1998.
see also: 8. China, the Region and the World;
   Cultural Revolution; Deng Xiaoping; June
   4 Incident; National People's Congress;
   one country, two systems; Tung Chee-
   hwa; United States policy.

Donald H. McMillen

Hongqi (*Red Flag*)

Theoretical journal of the **CCP Central
Committee**, established in May 1958 under
the editorship of **Chen Boda**, to provide a justification for the radical policies of the **Great
Leap Forward**. In an article in *Hongqi* on 1
July 1958, **Chen Boda** first used the term
'commune' to describe the large collective
units formed from the merger of agricultural
cooperatives (see **collective agriculture**).
Under Chen's editorship, *Hongqi* became a
radical journal devoted to supporting **Mao
Zedong** and **Mao Zedong Thought**. It played
an active part in the ideological feud between
the CCP and the Communist Party of the
Soviet Union during the early 1960s, and
denounced the **Soviet** Party for its revision of
the universal truths of Marxism-Leninism.
Hongqi expressed the radical line of the **Cultural Revolution** until November 1967, when
its publication was suspended due to the
move away from the violent tactics of the Red
Guards and towards the re-establishment of
order. **Chen Boda** was himself purged in 1970
for his 'ultra-left' activities during the **Cultural Revolution**, removed as editor of *Hongqi* (replaced by Hu Sheng), and denounced at
the Tenth **National Party Congress** in 1973 as
an 'anti-communist Guomindang element,
enemy agent and revisionist'.

   In the early 1970s, *Hongqi* articulated the
need for the rebuilding of the CCP following
the first phase of the **Cultural Revolution**. It
played an active part in the anti-**Lin Biao**
campaign, and voiced some muted criticisms
of certain features of the **Cultural Revolution**
with which **Lin Biao** was implicated, such as
the compilation of *Quotations from Chairman
Mao*, the 'little red book' which had been the
talisman of the Red Guards. *Hongqi* nevertheless continued to support a leftist position,

and defended the **Cultural Revolution** against moves to downgrade its importance. It continued this line following **Mao Zedong**'s death in 1976, and resisted attempts to reopen the verdicts on those purged during the **Cultural Revolution**. *Hongqi* also declined, during the autumn of 1978, to participate in the campaign, endorsed by **Deng Xiaoping**, to promote the view that practice is the sole criterion of truth (see **3. Ideology: Radicalism and Reform**). However, in September 1979 it was compelled to issue an apology for not participating in the 'criterion of truth' campaign, and it subsequently became a strong supporter of the significance of practice for evaluating the success of economic policies.

Throughout the early 1980s, *Hongqi* continued as the CCP's most important theoretical journal, publishing numerous articles justifying, in Marxist terms, the economic reforms instituted under **Deng Xiaoping** since 1978. It argued, in line with the official view, that development of the productive forces, rather than class struggle, was the key to the successful achievement of socialist transition in China. It participated in campaigns against 'spiritual pollution' and 'abstract humanism' in 1983 and 1984, and resisted the more radical pro-market reforms of **Zhao Ziyang**, insisting on the continued relevance of Marxist theory and ideology to China's problems. *Hongqi*'s views often contrasted with those expressed by *People's Daily*, the more reform-oriented newspaper of the CCP (see **media issues and policy**).

In September 1987, the editor of *Hongqi*, Xiong Fu, was removed from office, and rumours circulated on the impending closure of the journal. In May 1988 the **New China News Agency** confirmed that *Hongqi* would close, and in June 1988, it was replaced by a new journal, *Qiushi* (*Seek Truth*), which was intended to be more lively and to reflect more faithfully the move away from the leftist policies of the Maoist era with which *Hongqi* was associated.

see also: 3. Ideology: Radicalism and Reform; Chen Boda; Chinese Communist Party Central Committee and Politburo; collect-

ive agriculture; Cultural Revolution; Deng Xiaoping; Great Leap Forward; Lin Biao; Mao Zedong; Mao Zedong Thought; media issues and policy; National Party Congress; New China News Agency; *People's Daily*; Soviet Union, relations with; Zhao Ziyang.

Nick Knight

household registration (*hukou*)

An identity system, by which ordinary Chinese become the object of governmental determination. Also like an internal passport, it functions as the device through which citizens are given **welfare** rights.

Identity is based on the household, rather than the individual, because the household has traditionally been the basis of all state calculation. In dynastic times, household registers were used to levy corvée labour and exact taxes from the people. In socialist China, the function of the register has broadened greatly. Through the register, the state obtains a snapshot of the population which is helpful both to state economic **planning** officials and national defence strategists. For the public security forces (the **police**), the register long constituted the pillar upon which their system of a static community policing was built.

Under the CCP, China became not only the land of the register but, through it, the place where inequalities in wealth and resources were set in concrete. A hierarchy, with the peasants at the bottom, was kept in place throughout the pre-reform years by this system of household registration that not only registered one's abode, but also made it virtually impossible to move anywhere else. Such demographic policing became possible through the fact that the register was the basis of access to the **welfare** provisions.

Underpinning the entire system was a fear of peasant migration into the cities. Thus, until 1978, this fear of a 'blind flight' of peasants into the cities led to tight restrictions on movement between rural and urban centres. In November 1977, for example, the Ministry of Public Security issued a regulation stating that 'outsiders' from rural regions were to account for no more than 0.15 per cent of any urban workforce.

The registration system was first advanced as a priority in contemporary China in 1950 at the First National Public Security Administrative Work Conference. By 1953, the Public Security Ministry had issued temporary regulations on registration, following which a national, unified system of registration began to develop. Trials began to take place in certain cities and, by 1955, the **State Council** notice on household registration effectively spread the system into the countryside. By 1958, the system was complete and national household registration regulations came into effect.

The registration system is managed by the public security forces. In most places, registration work is the task of the local **police** station and it is the station that divides up their jurisdictional areas into household registration zones. Generally, between 500 and 7,000 households make up a zone. Each zone is the responsibility of one **police** officer who is assisted in checking and policing the register by the local neighbourhood or village committee.

Economic reform, with its demand for labour, for business and for trade between rural and urban areas made the restrictive registration laws something of an anachronism. Moreover, the existence of private markets, business and trade meant that the state no longer had a monopoly on the conditions of life. A slow trickle of peasants into the cities to trade, to work and to do business, began to signal the demise of the household register as the all powerful device by which the nation could be demographically policed. Indeed, by the end of the 1980s, this trickle had turned into a flood. The size of the 'floating population', as migrants are called, became so large that even the **police** could not accurately establish the numbers, but in the mid-1990s estimates varied between 60 million and 100 million peasants in transit at any given time.

Reform was clearly needed to the household registration system and this came in 1984 in the form of a resident identity card system. This card was heralded as the first major reform of the household registration system since 1949. While the card was not able, nor designed, to halt population flows, it could at least offer the **police** a new nationwide and unified means by which to establish the identity of the card bearer. For the police, long reliant on the register to implement their community policing methods, such reform was long overdue.

see also: planning, economic; police force; State Council; welfare policy.

Michael Dutton

housing

The provision of housing in China is diverse in technology, ownership, management and social significance, with sharp differences persisting between town and country. In the period 1996–2000 China plans to build 230 new cities and 5,000 towns, requiring 1.2 billion square metres of urban, 3 billion square metres of rural housing, and 2.9 billion square metres of refurbishment. Coping with ongoing rises in **population**, urbanization and income in the face of acute shortages of land will make this one of the most dynamic sectors for the foreseeable future.

The demand for housing was repressed under economic **planning** in keeping with revolutionary economic priorities and socialist conceptual distinctions. Under the Soviets' Net Material Product (NMP) notion housing, as a service, was defined as non-productive, devaluing investment in it for planners and officials who measured economic performance by NMP growth. Any deficits in housing and urban infrastructure were to be filled by revolutionary asceticism, with the heroic oil workers who endured the Manchurian winters in tents serving as models for the nation. Living space for urban and rural residents in 1978 was, respectively, 3.8 and 8.1 square metres per capita, resulting in severe overcrowding. Urban public authorities and large investors spent 1.05 trillion *yuan* (Chinese dollars *renminbi*) on housing from 1979 to 1996, raising the figure to 8.4 square metres; in the countryside, where housing is financed and built privately, the figure reached 21.7 square metres in 1996.

Rural construction technologies were always dictated by the immediate availability of building materials – rammed earth in the North China Plain, bamboo and rattan in the southwestern sub-tropics. Because structural timber was costly, single storeys predominated. Among **minority nationalities**, Han influences competed with local traditions, with large variations in style and techniques due to the peoples' diverse geographic, economic and cultural circumstances. Major stylistic and technical changes in domestic styles began in the Treaty Ports. The new bourgeoisies, native and foreign, copied contemporary European housing styles with abandon.

The 1950s land reform divided the landlords' excess housing among the poor. Though still a social and economic unit, the family's property rights were repeatedly challenged under collectivization. Early communes sometimes replaced family dwellings with dormitories and mess halls, and later houses were defined to include only the area under the dripline, with courtyards, where family production might distract peasants from the collective, confiscated (see **collective agriculture**). All villages became more crowded to prevent the conversion of cultivated land to housing and in **Dazhai** everyone lived under one roof. After 1978 the two- or three-storey brick or concrete farmhouses built without planning on sprawling lots in the big city suburbs contributed heavily to a sharp decline in the cultivated area. Compact, well-designed villages are now encouraged, but remain exceptional.

After 1949 all urban land became state property, but non-rental housing was allowed as private property. New housing was built as needed by local governments and **units** charging nominal rents, insufficient even for upkeep. The low priority assigned to new building from 1957 to 1976 produced a housing and infrastructure crisis, with overcrowding only slightly eased by illegal extensions and outbuildings. Though housing was ugly, overcrowded, unzoned, and crumbling from neglect, it was fiercely sought after, because it conferred rights to live in a city. Peremptory seizures of dwellings during the **Cultural Revolution** greatly confused ownership rights.

The post-reform housing boom has revolutionized Chinese urban landscapes. Forests of new high-rise apartment buildings sprang up, plus many new forms: hotels, villas, housing estates at every level of quality from five-star down. Scores of millions of poor and semi-legal itinerant workers are meanwhile being accommodated in sheds or basements, often paying exploitative rentals for substandard facilities.

A real estate market is evolving. Starting from spontaneous apartment exchanges to eliminate mismatches between workplaces and residences, **Hong Kong**-style land use auctions are now held in Shenzhen and **Shanghai** and apartments are increasingly fully transferable. Ancillary real estate institutions (valuation, mortgage lenders, sales agencies) and transparency are still lacking, leading to much shady dealing by officials, but land use efficiency and **labour** mobility are improving. Foreign investment is now vigorously sought as the authorities try to upgrade often low standards of construction, planning and energy efficiency.

Housing continues to bear heavy and conflicting ideological messages. The film *Raise High the Red Lantern* was politically sensitive because the architecture of a conservative merchant's mansion was strongly reminiscent of the **Beijing** palaces where the Party leadership still lives. In the countryside superstitions linking a family's fate to how its residence sits in the local topography (*fengshui*) are reviving, while in the cities vast anonymous apartment complexes epitomize globalized mass consumerism.

see also: Beijing Municipality; collective agriculture; Cultural Revolution; Dazhai; Hong Kong; labour policy and system; minority nationalities policy; planning, economic; population policy; Shanghai; unit.

Paul Ivory

Hu Jintao

Major CCP leader and, when appointed to the Politburo Standing Committee by the First Plenum of the Fourteenth Central

Committee on 19 October 1992, the youngest ever member of that extremely powerful body. Born in 1942, Hu's rise was very similar to **Hu Qili**'s in that his constituency lay in the Party's **youth organizations**, being promoted in 1984 as first secretary of the Communist Youth League.

During a drive to recruit young members Hu was elevated to full membership of the **CCP Central Committee** in 1985, and appointed Party secretary of Guizhou (1985–8) and, although often away due to his inability to cope with high altitudes, of **Tibet** (1988–92).

Hu is a graduate of the prestigious Qinghua University, and seen as a member of the increasingly powerful 'Qinghua faction' in the Party's top echelon; led by **Zhu Rongji** the faction represents the rise of technocrats. Hu's rapid rise is probably due also to support from the three former Party organization chiefs: **Hu Yaobang**, **Qiao Shi**, and especially **Song Ping**, who also served as director of cadre screening for the Fourteenth Congress with Hu Jintao as his deputy. Immediately after the Fourteenth Congress Hu was appointed to head the Party Reconstruction Group, with **Li Lanqing** and **Wei Jianxing** as deputies, and in 1993 succeeded **Qiao Shi** as president of the Central Party School, the CCP's main training-ground for potential leaders. Hu is mainly responsible for Party and organizational work and continues to carry these responsibilities after the Fifteenth Party Congress of September 1997, when he was elevated to the fifth position in the supreme Politburo Standing Committee, making him the undisputed leader of the youngest 'fourth generation' of Chinese leadership and a potential successor to **Jiang Zemin** as Party general secretary.

see also: Chinese Communist Party Central Committee and Politburo; Deng Xiaoping; Hu Qili; Hu Yaobang; Jiang Zemin; Li Lanqing; Qiao Shi; Song Ping; Tibet Autonomous Region; Wei Jianxing; youth policy and organizations; Zhu Rongji.

Warren Sun

Hu Qili

Minister of the Electronics Industry under the State Council from 1993. Nurtured by **Hu Yaobang** and **Deng Xiaoping** as a future general secretary, his career suffered a fatal blow when he failed to support **Deng Xiaoping** during the **protest movement** of 1989 which climaxed in the **June 4 Incident**.

Born in 1929, Hu Qili studied at Beijing (Peking) University and built up his reputation largely on the basis of his lengthy involvement in the Party's **youth organizations**, especially the Chinese Communist Youth League. In 1978 Hu's experience in youth work was recognized when he became the League Central Committee's secretary in charge of daily work. Two years later he was appointed mayor of Tianjin, a major stepping-stone appointment.

With **Hu Yaobang** in charge of CCP activities on the 'first front', Hu Qili rose in April 1982 to head the CCP's General Office, a crucial position in terms of the actual running of the **CCP Central Committee**. When in September 1985 a CCP National Conference decided to abolish life tenure and encourage younger leaders, Hu Qili was among those chosen to join the Politburo on 24 September. He also assisted General Secretary **Hu Yaobang** in dealing with propaganda, **education** and ideological work. Shortly after, it was reported that **Deng Xiaoping**, increasingly unhappy over **Hu Yaobang**'s tolerance of liberal intellectuals, was thinking of creating the new position of deputy secretary-general for Hu Qili.

Despite his association with **Hu Yaobang**, Hu Qili survived when the former was dismissed in January 1987, reportedly by delivering a serious self-criticism at the crucial meeting. The Thirteenth Central Committee's First Plenum, held on 2 November 1987, even named him to the Politburo's powerful Standing Committee, **Zhao Ziyang** being the new general secretary.

During the student movement of April to June 1989, Hu allowed uncensored journalism while embarking on political restructuring and then, together with **Zhao Ziyang**, opposed the 20 May declaration of martial law and **Deng Xiaoping**'s confrontational policy toward the student movement.

As a result, Hu Qili was immediately deprived of political power. Yet, unlike Zhao, he did retain full membership of the Central Committee, simply because **Deng Xiaoping** regarded his fault as in a different category from Zhao's. Probably for the same reason Hu was able, in 1991, to re-emerge as a vice-minister in the Machinery and Electronics Industry. The First Session of the Eighth **National People's Congress** (March 1993) put him in charge of the newly established Ministry of the Electronics Industry. Yet, frustrated by the lack of real progress towards political reform, for which he had pushed since early 1989, Hu tendered his request for resignation in July 1996.

see also: Chinese Communist Party Central Committee and Politburo; Deng Xiaoping; education policy and system; Hu Yaobang; June 4 Incident; National People's Congress; protest movements; State Council; youth policy and organizations; Zhao Ziyang.

Warren Sun

Hu Yaobang

A younger revolutionary, Hu Yaobang held important but secondary positions during the Maoist period before becoming one of the leading figures in the post-Mao reforms. Hu played a key role in breaking with the past in 1977–8, and was soon rewarded with the posts of Party general secretary (February 1980) and, from June 1981 to September 1982, CCP chairman. But his push for rapid reform alienated a broad range of leaders eventually including **Deng Xiaoping**, and Hu was forced to resign as general secretary in January 1987. His death in 1989 became the immediate cause of the **protest movement** which culminated in the **June 4 Incident**.

Born in Hunan in 1915 to a poor peasant family, Hu participated in the 1927 Autumn Harvest Uprising at a young age and subsequently engaged in **youth** work in the Jiangxi Soviet, taking part in the epic Long March. At the end of the Long March Hu was head of the Communist **Youth** League's Organization Department, and he subsequently became a political officer with various armies and during the civil war was director of the Organization Department of the Revolutionary Military Council. At the end of the civil war Hu participated in the conquest of **Sichuan** as a political department head in the 2nd Field Army led by Liu Bocheng and **Deng Xiaoping**. Hu then became the leading figure in north **Sichuan** under the Southwest region headed by Deng. Although the political links between Hu and Deng have been exaggerated, Hu did move to Beijing in 1952 about the same time as Deng to become leading secretary of the **Youth** League, a position paralleling that of Party general secretary which Deng assumed in 1956. Hu continued in this role until the **Cultural Revolution**, although he had several brief postings in the provinces including one in Hunan, where he established cordial relations with **Hua Guofeng**. Although ousted early in the **Cultural Revolution**, Hu reappeared by 1972 and played an especially significant role in Deng's efforts to promote the **Four Modernizations** in 1975, but he was eclipsed along with Deng in 1976.

The most significant part of Hu's career began following the death of **Mao Zedong**. Hu returned to office even before Deng, appointed to head the Central Party School apparently by **Hua Guofeng**. In this role Hu became a major force for overturning the ideological orientation of the **Cultural Revolution** in 1977–8, notably through the 'criterion of truth' debate (see **3. Ideology: Radicalism and Reform**). In this he paralleled the views of Deng, but often with greater initiative and not as part of an anti-Hua manoeuvre as often claimed. Hu also obtained key positions as head of first the Central Organization and then Propaganda Departments, while at the **Third Plenum of the Eleventh Central Committee** at the end of 1978 he was named to the Politburo. With the decline of Hua's position Hu assumed his Party role first in practice as general secretary, then formally as chairman before that post was abolished in 1982, but ultimate authority remained with Deng and the older generation of revolutionaries. Hu's leading position on the 'first front' of leaders directly responsible for day-to-day affairs not only was due to his backing of Deng's reform programme, but also reflected his acceptability to military leaders because of his pre-1949 career. But soon Hu's enthusiasm for reform led to conflict with a wide range of leaders. His efforts to push economic reform were regarded as unwelcome interference not only by relatively conservative planners such as **Yao Yilin**, but also by reformers, most notably Premier **Zhao Ziyang**. Meanwhile many of the older generation resented Hu's pursuit of corruption among their offspring, while the powerful **Chen Yun** was critical of his lack of careful study of actual conditions. Most importantly, Deng finally withdrew his support, particularly because Hu's more liberal political attitude exceeded that which Deng thought desirable. The true nature of power relations within the CCP was revealed by the active role of the older generation of revolutionaries at the early 1987 meetings that forced Hu's resignation as general secretary and set off the campaign against 'bourgeois liberalization' (see **3. Ideology: Radicalism and Reform**). While Hu remained on the Politburo he lacked concrete responsibilities, but his past support of political reform made him a symbol to many for even bolder reform. Thus his death on 15 April 1989 became the catalyst for proposals for democratic change far beyond Hu's own advocacy, and for a direct confrontation with the regime that surely would have been abhorrent to Hu.

see also: 3. Ideology: Radicalism and Reform; Chen Yun; Cultural Revolution; Deng Xiaoping; Four Modernizations; Hua Guofeng; June 4 Incident; Mao Zedong; protest movements; Sichuan; Third Plenum of the Eleventh Central Committee; Yao Yilin; youth policy and organizations; Zhao Ziyang.

Frederick C. Teiwes

Hua Guofeng

Hua Guofeng succeeded **Mao Zedong** as leader of the CCP in October 1976 at the relatively young age of 56. On paper Hua was even more powerful than Mao, assuming Mao's posts as chairman of the Party and its **Central Military Commission** as well as already holding the position of premier. While formally heading the three pillars of official power, the Party, government and army, in fact Hua was a transitional figure whose influence gradually declined until he was reduced to a ceremonial role at the end of 1980.

Born in Shanxi in 1921, Hua joined the Red Army in 1936. After 1949 he was posted to Hunan where he was promoted quickly, becoming a vice-governor and provincial Party secretary in 1958–9. When local 'power-holders' in Hunan came under criticism during the **Cultural Revolution**, Hua was also attacked, but he was deemed a 'revolutionary cadre' and named to leading provincial positions over the 1967–71 period and to the **CCP Central Committee** in 1969. In 1971 he moved to Beijing where he played a major role in investigating the **Lin Biao** affair, and he was elected to the Politburo in 1973. In 1975 Hua was named a vice-premier and worked smoothly with **Deng Xiaoping** in developing the **Four Modernizations**, but when Mao turned against Deng at the end of 1975, it was Hua and not the dismissed Deng who succeeded **Zhou Enlai** as premier. With Mao's death Hua played a key role in the arrest of the **gang of four** but was immediately faced with pressure for Deng's return to office. While conventional accounts claim Hua resisted Deng's return and then engaged in an unsuccessful power struggle against him, the actual situation was more complicated. As a member of a much less prestigious revolutionary generation Hua tried to accommodate Deng's power and policies, but as a product of the **Cultural Revolution** he was increasingly marginalized as the CCP renounced the movement and launched its reform programme. The 1978 **Third Plenum of the Eleventh Central Committee** saw a significant undermining of his position, in 1980 he was replaced by **Zhao Ziyang** as premier, and at the end of 1980 his Party and military functions were informally assumed by **Hu Yaobang** and Deng. Hua was officially removed as chairman in June 1981.

see also: Central Military Commission; Chinese Communist Party Central Committee and Politburo; Cultural Revolution; Deng Xiaoping; Four Modernizations; gang of four; Hu Yaobang; Lin Biao; Mao Zedong; Third Plenum of the Eleventh Central Committee; Zhao Ziyang; Zhou Enlai.

Frederick C. Teiwes

Hundred Flowers Movement

A movement in 1956–7 featuring both unusual freedom of discussion and thought, as well as unprecedented acceptance of criticism of the CCP, but followed by the diametrically opposite Anti-Rightist Movement, with its defence of the CCP and attacks on intellectuals.

There were three main stages, the last being by far the most important. The first began with a speech by **Mao Zedong**, on 2 May 1956, calling for greater intellectual and artistic freedom with the slogan 'let a hundred flowers bloom, let a hundred schools of thought contend', a reference to an adage of ancient times. This slogan was the origin of the term Hundred Flowers Movement, as well as of the phrase 'blooming and contending', or free exchange of ideas and criticism of the CCP. Intellectuals and artists were generally wary, fearing that they risked punishment later on if they spoke out too freely.

On 27 February 1957 Mao tried to reinvigorate the campaign with a speech called 'On the Correct Handling of Contradictions among the People'. He divided contradictions into antagonistic, those 'between ourselves and the enemy', and nonantagonistic, those 'among the people', arguing that only the former should be treated harshly. He thus offered a theoretical justification for greater intellectual freedom and tolerance of criticism of the CCP.

Again there was hesitation, and only late in April did the press and other media move in favour of 'blooming and contending'. In May and early June there followed a torrent of free intellectual and artistic ideas and of criticism of the CCP (see **media issues and policy**).

Many people expressed resentment of the CCP's monopoly on political power and its management of the economy. Others were extremely critical of the lack of freedoms, despite their being specifically laid down in the **Constitution** of 1954. A former friend of the great literary figure Lu Xun expostulated that more freedom had existed for writers in the wartime capital Chongqing under the Nationalist regime than in contemporary **Beijing**. The famous anthropologist Fei Xiaotong, reporting on a visit he had made to a remote area of Jiangsu, wrote an article suggesting that conditions were no better than they had been in the mid-1930s and that the **collective agriculture** policies were simply wrong.

On 19 May 1957, students at Beijing (Peking) University began putting up posters on a campus wall, soon known as '**Democracy Wall**', expressing divergent points of view, many of them strongly critical of the CCP and its policies. In addition to freely published debate, there were strikes, demonstrations and even riots. In many parts of China, students beat up cadres, ransacked files and urged other students to join them in sympathy strikes. What China was witnessing was the biggest public cultural and political outcry for many years.

The leadership was alarmed at the extent of the criticism, and began to suppress the **protest movement**. On 8 June, *People's Daily* published an editorial arguing that 'rightists' were using the movement to try and overthrow the CCP. This and similar articles over following days signalled the end of 'blooming and contending' and the beginning of a severe attack on anybody accused of being a rightist: the Anti-Rightist Movement. The initial wariness had proved well founded.

By the end of 1957 some 300,000 intellectuals had been labelled 'rightists'. Among them was Fei Xiaotong who was forbidden to teach or publish, and made a public confession of his errors. Many were sent to the countryside, labour camps or prison, while some committed suicide because of the pressure of intense public criticism sessions.

see also: Beijing Municipality; collective agriculture; Constitutions; Democracy Wall; Mao Zedong; media issues and policy; *People's Daily*; protest movements.

Colin Mackerras

I

industry

After 1949, industrial growth became the primary focus of China's economic policy. Heavy industrial development was seen as strategic for building national independence, the goal emphasized by humiliation from imperialist intervention and the failures of earlier industrial development. Priority went to the production of capital goods, far above light industry and consumer goods. The plan system was structured to deliver resources for investment in industry (see **planning, economic**), and the prices of raw materials and energy were kept low in order to reduce industrial costs. In addition, a focus on import substitution and relatively autarchic development reflected China's isolation, especially during the **Cultural Revolution** and the Vietnam War.

Overall, industrial growth was characterized by 'investment hunger' whereby growth was maintained by inputs of new resources and capital, rather than by improvements in efficiency and productivity. Industrial enterprises met physical output targets using planned allocations of inputs, and markets played no role in shaping production structure. It was not until the reform period that China's industrial structure began to change, policy placing greater emphasis on improving efficiency, meeting consumer demands and allocating resources according to market signals. There was also a shift towards labour-intensive manufacturing and greater diversity in ownership, with the introduction of private enterprises and foreign investment.

Industrial development policy after 1949 passed through four main phases:

- rehabilitation and transformation, 1949–56;
- the introduction of central planning, 1953–7;
- experiments with Mao's innovations, 1958–76; and
- reform, 1977 to present.

Each change was associated with political debate over China's development trajectory. The adoption of centralized **planning** signalled the shift towards the **Soviet** model. **Mao Zedong**'s innovations were a response to the problems generated by that model, and the debates of the **Cultural Revolution** reflected the internal conflict over Mao's ideas. The reform process involved the rejection of both the plan model and Mao's experiments in favour of a market economy.

In the first phase, the aim was to rehabilitate an economy disrupted by the Anti-Japanese War and hyperinflation, to nationalize industry owned by foreign capital and Nationalist Party leaders, and to promote a mixed economy by endorsing the persistence of industry owned by patriotic capitalists. Around 60 per cent of industrial output came under state ownership, and at the same time new laws for labour and union activity were introduced. Under this policy, industry recovered rapidly and by 1952 output levels had returned to their pre-Second World War peak.

In the second phase, a process leading through joint state–private ownership to full state ownership brought remaining private industry under state control. Simultaneously, centralized material balance planning was adopted as a direct copy of the **Soviet** model. **Soviet** experts stayed in China to design and install industrial enterprises using **Soviet** equipment. Chinese managers and engineers were trained in the **Soviet Union**. **Soviet** state economic structures and basic systems of industrial accounting and management procedures were replicated. The **Soviet Union** provided large amounts of aid, loans and technical inputs. The result was a period of rapid and successful industrial growth, especially in basic infrastructure and heavy industry. Total industrial output grew at around 18 per cent per year, from around 35 per cent of total national output in 1952 to 44 per cent in 1957. In particular 156 key industrial projects built with **Soviet** aid in sectors such as iron and steel, chemical industry, mining, machine-building and transport equipment laid the foundation for a large proportion of China's modern industrial output. One other significant policy of this period was the effort to redistribute industry towards the interior provinces.

Despite this success, Mao and other leaders became increasingly concerned at some of the social and political consequences of the **Soviet** model. As relations with the **Soviet Union** soured towards the end of the 1950s, Mao argued that the hierarchical controls of the plan system were creating a new technocratic elite, that the emphasis on capital-intensive technology was ignoring China's resources of labour, and that the centralized system was stifling local initiative. Since Mao still rejected a role for markets, he opted for decentralization of controls within the administrative hierarchy. He also promoted a mix of technologies and experimented with forms of industrial democracy to give greater authority to workers. His emphasis was on moral incentives rather than bonuses and material rewards, and he rejected reliance on **international trade** and technology imports. His concern with the threat of foreign intervention also led him to direct more industrial investment towards the interior under the 'third front' strategy. Many of these ideas reached their apogee during the **Great Leap Forward** and the **Cultural Revolution**, and as a result, locally controlled industrial systems began to expand. Nevertheless, Mao maintained a focus on heavy industry and import substitution, and the **planning** system basically persisted, though relatively decentralized.

By the late 1970s, industrial growth had continued around 10 per cent but with many problems. Enterprises used resources inefficiently and returns to capital declined. They carried large stockpiles of unwanted goods, yet consumer products were in short supply. There was a large proportion of incomplete investment projects. Decentralization had created a confused situation, compounded by

the political factionalism of the **Cultural Revolution**, in which enterprises were subject to a mixture of controls from local and central levels. The dispersion of industry to the interior had also added to transport costs and sacrificed economies of agglomeration. Meanwhile, despite the growth in gross output, there were continual shortages of key products such as energy and iron and steel. Employment growth was also increasingly unable to keep up with the growth of labour supply, with the result that large numbers of people were assigned to enterprises that did not need them.

In the face of these problems, the post-Mao leadership under **Deng Xiaoping** initiated a reform programme to stimulate greater efficiency and technological modernization. At first, this was conceived within the plan framework, and there was no clear blueprint for change. As the reforms evolved, however, they developed a momentum of their own which resulted in substantial changes in China's industrial structure and operation.

The reforms had five main components:

- an emphasis on economic efficiency and technical change;
- a shift towards satisfying consumer needs;
- greater openness to the world economy;
- acceptance of mixed forms of ownership; and
- a growing recognition of the role of markets in allocating resources.

As a result of these factors, China's industrial system experienced a significant structural transformation. By the mid-1990s market prices dominated both industrial prices and retail sales. State industry had shrunk from around 80 per cent of production to under 40 per cent. The **collective sector**, including the **township and village enterprises**, had risen to around 40 per cent, and private enterprise and foreign industry were approaching 20 per cent. The consumer market had a plentiful supply of new and up-to-date products. **International trade** had become an engine of industrial growth, and the change in industrial structure was reflected by the increase in exports of labour-intensive manufactures from just under 30 per cent of all exports in 1980 to nearly 54 per cent in 1994. Industrial output had also grown substantially at rates of around 15 per cent per year, and industrial efficiency improved. The emergence of competitive non-state sectors was important in this change, but the state sector also made some gains.

Despite these developments, a number of problems also emerged. The coastal bias in government policies of the 1980s together with the surge of foreign investment in coastal special economic zones meant that coastal development was rapid, while industrial development in the interior languished. The impact of foreign technology also led to rapid obsolescence in the inland state industries built up under the plan system. State-owned enterprises continued to face major problems, for while the introduction of profit retention and new tax regimes in the 1980s had increased their efficiency, the trend was diluted by the absence of thorough-going reform to the financial system and remaining distortions in prices, which meant that they lacked firm financial discipline. The fact that they continued to have large numbers of underemployed workers and substantial social **welfare**, **housing** provision and pension payment burdens undermined their profitability in a market context. The power of local governments to intervene to protect local enterprises or to stimulate investment also meant that investment hunger remained an important factor in sustaining growth. By the mid-1990s, around half all state enterprises were reported operating at a loss. Given that these still accounted for a substantial proportion of industrial output and employment, their condition represented a critical issue for further reform and development. The government had to provide large subsidies but hesitated to impose strict bankruptcy laws, since large-scale closures would produce major **welfare** and political problems. Furthermore, there were no clear mechanisms for transforming ownership and transferring resources and labour to alternative activities. The next stage of industrial reform thus required further reforms to the

financial and **welfare** systems. Nevertheless, the prospects for further industrial growth driven by structural change and continued involvement in world markets appeared strong. These trends were confirmed at the Fifteenth Party Conference of September 1997, which endorsed a programme either of converting medium and small state enterprises into shareholding companies and shareholding cooperatives, or of leasing them out, or of auctioning them to new owners.

see also: 5. Politics and the Economy: Policy Patterns and Issues; collective sector; Cultural Revolution; Deng Xiaoping; Great Leap Forward; housing; international trade; Mao Zedong; planning, economic; township and village enterprises; Soviet Union, relations with; welfare policy.

Andrew Watson

international trade

International transactions were a last resort in the period of the **planning** system. Imports filled gaps, with other items exported to pay for imports. Producers were isolated from world markets, lacking signals from those markets to which they could respond. The foreign exchange earned as a consequence of exporting was bottled up in the **planning** system. Goods exported were mainly primary products. Imports were mainly capital equipment, including whole plants. Trade over this period accounted for a very small proportion of national output. International transactions imposed a fiscal burden on the government where domestic prices of importables were lower than world prices.

Economic growth from the 1950s to the 1970s was based on the accumulation of inputs into the production process, but the productivity for which they were used declined over the same period. Raising productivity and therefore income growth were factors pushing for reform. Trade and foreign investment were key components of that reform package.

The process of reform can be divided into two steps. The first, which was partial, involved reform from within the bureaucratic system. It included the continued use of administrative methods and variation between regions and administrations, making the scope for discretion and favouritism wide at both central and local levels. These features created opportunities for gain for key actors in the previous **planning** system who might otherwise have opposed the reforms. The second step, much more thorough, involved a far greater degree of marketization in both foreign exchange and goods and services. The forces for continued opening up included pressure from outside China, from foreign firms setting up in China and from foreign governments. In addition, there were internal forces, some of them related to fiscal burdens associated with the reforms, others associated with export oriented interests who saw even greater gains from a more open economy. These forces met domestic resistance in the debate over the strategy for entry into the **World Trade Organization**, the context being the leadership's wish for China to take its place in world institutions.

Over the 1980s, the key elements in the trade reforms were:
- the decentralization of international transactions;
- the introduction of both import and export licensing in place of traditional planning mechanisms; and
- a more market-oriented foreign exchange policy.

Decentralization at first meant that authority to trade was transferred to ministry and provincial government level. By the end of the 1980s, the number of companies allowed to trade had increased from a dozen (in the **planning** period) to many thousands. In the new system companies acted as agents for local firms, rather than trading on their own account, so local firms became more aware of world prices.

Foreign exchange reform proceeded in a number of steps. In the first, exporters were allowed to retain a share of foreign exchange earnings. The next step was to permit domestic firms to trade foreign exchange, which led to a dual exchange rate system (one the market rate, one the official rate used

for the foreign exchange that was handed to government). The exchange rate was unified at the swap market rate in 1994 and the new rate was effectively fixed.

An important form of trade was export processing in which items were imported specifically for the purpose of re-export in a more processed form. Another was compensation trade in which a foreign firm supplied technology or equipment and received payment in the form of some of the goods produced. The development of these forms of trade was complemented by the changes in foreign investment law and the development of the **special economic zones**. By 1996, processing trade accounted for over 50 per cent of exports.

Enterprises which involved some foreign funding accounted for nearly two-thirds of all processed exports. Special advantages for these forms of trade were the duty reductions on items imported for processing and the tariff free entry for capital goods imported by foreign funded enterprises. Some argue that these policies created a dualistic foreign sector within the Chinese economy, since local enterprises did not have access to these preferential policies. Both policies were dropped in 1996, coinciding with a dramatic decline in export growth.

In the 1990s, the opening continued, eventually reaching convertibility of the *yuan* for current account transactions and substantial reductions in tariffs. By 1995, the proportion of trade (in value terms) subject to licensing was 25.3 per cent (43.5 per cent in 1992). Non-tariff barriers applied to over 26 per cent of imports (trade weighted) in 1993. China's tariff rate (unweighted) in 1996 was 23 per cent and China (in the **Asia-Pacific Economic Cooperation** process) has committed to reduce this to 15 per cent by 2000.

These rates are quite high among the East Asian economies but the reductions in rates are relatively rapid. Also the tariff data refer to official rates whereas actual rates may be much lower. The rate of collection of tariffs on imports has been low (the ratio of tariff revenue to import values was only 4 per cent in

1994, falling from just under 10 per cent in 1986). These low collection rates also reflect that discretion (with a consequent lack of transparency) that is a feature of the trading system.

The effect of these reforms on China's trade pattern has been dramatic. Exports in 1996 were US$152 billion, compared to US$28 billion in 1985, an average annual growth rate of nearly 17 per cent. Trade has grown faster than output and the trade share of GDP has risen. China has caught up again to a position of openness consistent with its size. Its share of world trade has also risen to over 2 per cent. The composition of trade has also changed and the share of labour intensive products in exports has increased dramatically. As of 1997, the share of primary products is relatively small.

see also: 5. Politics and the Economy: Policy Patterns and Issues; 7. Regional China; 8. China, the Region and the World; Asia-Pacific Economic Cooperation; planning, economic; special economic zones; World Trade Organization.

Christopher Findlay

J

Japan, relations with

China's post-1949 relations with Japan have been rife with contradictions, ranging from hatred, bitterness and fear due to wartime aggression and subsequent security alliance with the **United States** to admiration as an economic model and attraction as a source of aid, investment, technology and trade.

Early relations were virtually frozen in a Cold War environment (epitomized by the **Korean War**), precluding independent Chinese or Japanese initiatives to rebuild them. The souring of Sino-**Soviet** relations in the late 1950s allowed a slow thaw in the Sino-Japanese relationship with a memorandum on trade signed in November 1962 (China represented by **Liao Chengzhi**) and the establishment of a China–Japan Friendship Association the following year.

In the following decade Japan's economy boomed while China's stagnated largely due to internal unrest and external threats or conflicts. As the two superpowers became bogged down in a debilitating rivalry for supremacy, the stage was set for a transformation in the global strategic and economic scenes. After Henry Kissinger's secret visit to China in mid-1971, there was a rapid move towards normalization in Sino-Japanese relations and the enhancement of direct economic ties. In September 1972 Japanese Prime Minister Tanaka Kakuei visited Beijing and formalized diplomatic relations, on the basis that Japan recognized one China and respected China's claim to Taiwan. In 1978, China and Japan signed a Treaty of Peace and Friendship.

During the 1980s, Japan's economic relations with China developed rapidly, with trade and investment increasing to the point where, by 1985–6, some conservatives in the Chinese leadership worried about a 'second Japanese (neo-imperialist economic) invasion'. In 1985, anti-Japanese student demonstrations erupted, causes including perceived Japanese textbook 'whitewashing' of Japa-

nese atrocities in China (especially the Nanjing Massacre beginning mid-December 1937) and a growing trade imbalance. Moreover, in 1986–7 Sino-Japanese relations became a vehicle for factional debates over leadership and policy between conservatives and those supporting greater reform and opening within the CCP itself.

However, because the two economies were complementary and increasingly interdependent, Sino-Japanese trade reached over US$39 billion by 1993–4. The PRC came to account for about 5 per cent of Japan's total trade, and Japan nearly one-quarter of China's. A temporary setback occurred in 1989 when Japan acted in concert with the Western powers over the **June 4 Incident** to suspend loans, credit facilities and projects. Japan, however, largely refrained from moralizing and warned instead of the long-term dangers of isolating China. Moreover, Tokyo used its influence to moderate the **United States**' position on such matters as 'most-favoured nation' conditions, human rights and China's entry to the **World Trade Organization**. Two-way 1992 visits by **Jiang Zemin** to Japan in April and Emperor Akihito to Beijing in October helped improve relations.

A number of issues have continued to colour Sino-Japanese relations. These include:

- China's assertiveness against **Taiwan** and in the **South China Sea**, which causes unease in Tokyo, as well as in regional capitals, where it is seen as a factor which could enhance Japan's military presence;
- Japan's reaffirmed alliance with the **United States**;
- Chinese anxieties about neo-containment and Japanese remilitarization;
- the territorial dispute over the Diaoyutai (Senkaku) Islands, which Beijing has been keen to mute because of its fears over negative repercussions on Sino-Japanese economic ties and a reluctance to

encourage anti-Japanese demonstrations which could turn against the CCP itself;

- Japan's support (although lukewarm) for the principle of universal human rights;
- China's nuclear testing;
- Chinese coal pollution, which affects Japan's environment; and
- a continuing trade imbalance favouring Japan.

Certainly Japan will remain a major pre-occupation of Chinese policy. While the complexities of the relationship inhibit any solid predictions, both Tokyo and Beijing are likely to retain a desire for a peaceful and stable environment to enhance their respective development strategies.

see also: 8. China, the Region and the World; June 4 Incident; Jiang Zemin; Korean War; Liao Chengzhi; South China Sea; Soviet Union, relations with; Taiwan policy; United States policy; World Trade Organization.

Donald H. McMillen

Jiang Chunyun

Senior CCP and state leader, appointed vice-premier in March 1995, associated especially with **Shandong** Province. Jiang Chunyun was born in April 1930 in Laixi, **Shandong**. He joined the CCP in 1947 and fulfilled increasingly senior Party and state functions in **Shandong** from the 1950s to the 1980s, including during the **Cultural Revolution**. In 1988 he assumed the most senior Party and state positions in Shandong, that is the Secretary of the Shandong Provincial CCP Committee and Governor of Shandong, although he did not remain long in the latter post.

Meanwhile Jiang Chunyun had become a member of the Central Committee of the CCP at the Thirteenth **National Party Congress** of 1987 and just after the Fourteenth Congress of 1992 he was elected to the Politburo. The Fourth Plenum of the Fourteenth **CCP Central Committee** of September 1994 added Jiang Chunyun to the Central Committee's Secretariat. The Fifteenth Congress (1997) retained him on the Politburo.

Jiang was appointed one of six vice-premiers at the March 1995 Third Session of the Eighth **National People's Congress**, with the principal task of taking charge of **agriculture**. His election was remarkable for the fact that, although he was elected with a substantial majority, over one-third of the more than 2,700-strong Congress either abstained or voted against him. He had been nominated by **Jiang Zemin** and the extent of the negative vote was unprecedented in PRC history, where it was taken for granted that the general secretary and president's nominee would be elected without opposition. It is possible that one of the reasons for the opposition was that his power focus **Shandong** had been wracked by a serious corruption scandal in the city of Taian. But the vote was most certainly a sign of the growing desire of the **National People's Congress** to behave independently of central authority.

see also: agriculture; Chinese Communist Party Central Committee and Politburo; Cultural Revolution; Jiang Zemin; National Party Congress; National People's Congress; Shandong.

Colin Mackerras

Jiang Qing

See **gang of four**.

Jiang Zemin

General secretary of the **Chinese Communist Party** from 1989 and president of the PRC from 1993, and declared by **Deng Xiaoping** to be the third-generation 'core' of leadership of the PRC following **Mao Zedong** and himself.

Jiang Zemin was born in August 1926, coming from Yangzhou in Jiangsu Province. He joined the CCP in 1946 and the next year graduated from the Department of Electric Motors, Communications University in **Shanghai**, assuming senior industrial and government positions in that city in the first years after 1949. In 1955 he went to Moscow to study for a year, and on return continued in government positions connected with the economy in various parts of the country. From 1974 to 1979 he was deputy director and then director of the Foreign Affairs Bureau of the First Ministry of the Machine-Building Industry.

In the new period following the **Third Plenum of the Eleventh Central Committee** (1978), Jiang took over ever more senior positions in the CCP and government. From 1982 to 1985 he was Minister of the Electronics Industry and the CCP secretary of the ministry. In 1985 he was appointed mayor of China's largest city, **Shanghai**.

In the 1980s, Jiang assumed more and more senior CCP positions. At the Twelfth National Congress in September 1982, Jiang was appointed to the **CCP Central Committee**, and then, at the First Plenum of the Thirteenth Central Committee on 2 November 1987, to the Politburo. Meanwhile, in 1987 he also became general secretary of the CCP in **Shanghai**.

During the student demonstrations in 1989, Jiang showed himself more canny than the leaders in **Beijing**. Just after the **June 4 Incident**, and when a similar massacre threatened in **Shanghai**, Jiang was able to defuse the situation by persuading the students to withdraw. It is likely that it was on account of his ability to settle the issue peacefully in China's largest city that he was appointed general secretary of the CCP when the Fourth Plenum of the Thirteenth Central Committee met in **Beijing** on 23–4 June 1989 and chose a replacement for **Zhao Ziyang** who, having sided with the students during the crisis, was now in disgrace and in no position to occupy the CCP's most senior position. When **Deng Xiaoping** formally retired as chairman both of the CCP's **Central Military Commission** in November 1989 and the state counterpart the following March, Jiang was appointed to replace him in both positions.

In March 1993 the First Session of the Eighth **National People's Congress** appointed Jiang Zemin to replace **Yang Shangkun** as state president. Already in a very favourable position to exert his leadership in the Party and military organs of China, his appointment as state president added the state dimension to his powers.

When Jiang first became general secretary of the CCP there was a great deal of scepticism both inside China and abroad over whether he had the necessary charisma and ability to form the 'core' of leadership of a country in the throes of radical modernization and change, where strong centrifugal forces appeared to have the potential to weaken the central government. As of 1997, although it remains impossible to predict how long he will retain the country's top positions, he appears to a large extent to have consolidated, and still to be strengthening his leadership. The Fifteenth Party Congress (September 1997) saw him very much in control and able to edge out rivals, notably **Qiao Shi**.

Several factors are running in his favour. In the first place he has good family connections, having been adopted by the CCP 'martyr' Jiang Shangqing, an associate of **Li Xiannian**, president of China from 1983 to 1988.

Second, unlike **Li Peng** and several other possible contenders for leadership in the post-Deng era, Jiang Zemin is not tainted with involvement in the tragedy of the **June 4 Incident**.

Third, he has succeeded in establishing and strengthening his own power faction. One of many examples was his ability to have allies **Wu Bangguo** and **Jiang Chunyun** promoted to the Politburo in October 1992.

Fourth, in the mid-1990s, Jiang has pushed anti-corruption measures and shown a decisive attitude in dismissing and punishing corrupt officials, however senior. Perhaps the best example of these was **Beijing** Mayor Chen Xitong, who had taken the lead in defending the crackdown in **Beijing** in June 1989 and even written the official account. Jiang Zemin had him dismissed from the Central Committee and Politburo late in September 1995 at the Fifth Plenum of the Fourteenth Central Committee for leading 'a dissolute, extravagant life' and for abuse of power. At the same time, Jiang has earned himself the reputation of knowing where to stop, not pushing things so far as to make himself an undue number of powerful enemies.

Finally, in the mid-1990s, Jiang Zemin has gone out of his way to make his mark on policy by making major speeches on as many occasions as he can and by making his presence felt in foreign policy matters. For example, he made a long speech at the Fifth Plenum on 28 September 1995 in which he outlined twelve relationships relevant to modernization, rather in the style of Mao's ten relationships of 1956. He has taken care to attend the meetings of the **Asia-Pacific Economic Cooperation**; as far as possible on these occasions and at a summit in New York on 24 October 1995, Jiang has held high-profile meetings with US President Bill Clinton as a way of trying to smooth over the serious problems involved in the very important Sino-American relationship in the 1990s. At the memorial meeting for **Deng Xiaoping**, held on 25 February 1997, it was Jiang who delivered the long and emotional eulogy.

Ideologically speaking, Jiang is very much in the **Deng Xiaoping** mould in two major respects:

- he is very committed to economic reform, but less so to political; and
- he is totally dedicated to the preservation of CCP rule in China.

Jiang's continuation in the top CCP position due to the Fifteenth Party Congress placed him in a good position to persist in exerting influence over post-Deng China. Although most unlikely to rival either **Mao Zedong** or **Deng Xiaoping** in impact, Jiang's tenure had already lasted over eight years, a reasonable period for a top national job by world standards.

see also: Asia-Pacific Economic Cooperation; Beijing Municipality; Central Military Commission; Chinese Communist Party; Chinese Communist Party Central Committee and Politburo; Deng Xiaoping; Jiang Chunyun; June 4 Incident; Li Peng; Li Xiannian; Mao Zedong; National People's Congress; Qiao Shi; Shanghai; Third Plenum of the Eleventh Central Committee; Wu Bangguo; Yang Shangkun; Zhao Ziyang.

Colin Mackerras

joint ventures

The June 1979 Equity Joint Venture Law permitted foreign investment in the PRC for the first time. The text of the law was very brief, leaving open many operational issues, but it was significant as a major component of the open door policy. Both the environment for foreign investment and the response by foreign investors have evolved since 1979, but the general trend has been in the direction of decentralization and liberalization of regulations and increased foreign investment. By 1993 China had become the major developing country destination for direct foreign investment.

The official categorization of direct foreign investment has varied over time. Initially most Chinese sources distinguished between equity joint ventures operating under the 1979 law, cooperative ventures, processing and assembly, and joint oil projects. In practice the first three categories could be difficult to distinguish, with cooperative ventures sometimes involving large joint ventures which failed to meet the requirements for an equity joint venture in some minor way and equity joint ventures which were often little more than processing operations between domestic and **Hong Kong** partners.

Between 1979 and 1983 the value of approved joint ventures was small and there were frequent disputes as joint ventures became operational. Many points of dispute were clarified by precedent and by the publication of guidelines, especially in 1983. The first foreign investment boom occurred in 1984–5. The distribution of projects was bipolar with most projects capitalized under US$1 million (and mainly **Hong Kong** partnered), but with large, mostly North American, European and Japanese partnered projects accounting for a majority of the value of pledged capital. The boom was in part driven by rising wages and an appreciating **Hong Kong** currency, which encouraged entrepreneurs to seek new locations in the Pearl River Delta for their manufacturing operations.

Contractionary policies were associated with the boom's end in the second half of 1985. Many foreign investors also became frustrated by the continuing obstacles to their operations in China. The main issue concerned access to foreign exchange for imported inputs and for repatriating profits. The government responded with the October 1986 regulations, which improved the operating environment for foreign investors, especially with respect to access to foreign exchange and a more liberal attitude towards majority foreign ownership, and also signalled more active promotion of foreign investment.

The second foreign investment boom followed these measures and lasted until spring 1989. This boom was characterized by the same bipolar distribution of projects as in 1984–5. The geographical distribution of projects became more diverse as the share of the Pears River Delta declined and that of other coastal locations increased.

The **June 4 Incident** and ensuing uncertainty about the economic environment accentuated a slowdown in foreign investment. However, the growth of foreign investment resumed in the early 1990s and far exceeded 1980s levels. Total direct foreign investment had been US$2 billion in value in 1985, but the figures for the first half of the 1990s were US$3.8 billion (1990), US$4.7 billion (1991), US$11.3 billion (1992), US$27.5 billion (1993), US$33.8 billion (1994), and US$37.7 billion (1995).

Several previously restricted areas were opened to foreign investors (e.g. retailing and construction, banking and insurance), and some of the 1992–4 boom was speculative investment in construction projects (reflected in a wide gap between pledged and actual investment). Actual foreign investment continued to be primarily in manufacturing, fuelled by rapidly growing investment from the newly industrialized Asian economies. It continued to be heavily concentrated in the coastal provinces.

Measures taken in the mid-1990s aimed to create a level playing field between foreign-invested ventures and domestic enterprises and to increase transparency. The 1993 tax and financial reform package unified corporate tax rates by reducing the domestic rate from 55 to 33 per cent, the standard rate on foreign-invested ventures, and also brought foreign firms in line with domestic by ending the former's exemption from duty on imported capital imports. In June 1995 the State Planning Commission, State Commission on Economy and Trade, and the Ministry of Foreign Trade jointly promulgated Temporary Provisions on Foreign Investment and a *Catalogue of Industries for Foreign Investment*, intended to signal a shift from micro assessment of the returns to large projects or other quantitative performance targets to publicizing broad guidelines. In this respect the 1995 measures are a step towards greater transparency, which is an improvement over the situation during the first half of the 1990s when new areas were opened to foreign investors and then restricted by administrative action, leaving potential investors unsure where they stood. Some directives concerning foreign investment, however, remain unpublished.

Joint ventures have played a critical role in China's outward-oriented growth strategy since the mid-1980s. Exports by foreign-invested ventures grew from US$320 million in 1985 to US$46.9 billion in 1995, when these ventures accounted for two-fifths of China's **international trade**. Most of the export-oriented ventures were based on China's low-cost labour and had partners from newly industrialized Asian economies which were able to supply key missing inputs related to knowledge of overseas markets and quality standards.

In the 1990s the scope of foreign investment is broadening to other sectors. In financial markets and retailing, foreign investors are stimulating improved practices and better service. Infrastructure projects are attracting foreign investment in a variety of institutional forms. Limited experiments in allowing foreign investors to participate in the restructuring of China's large state enterprises have also been tried.

The position of foreign investors in China has evolved, and improved, significantly since the 1979 Joint Venture Law. The process has been characterized by substantial decentralization of decision making, so that

the situation facing foreign investors varies substantially from one part of China to another. Overall, the high levels of foreign investment in China during the 1990s are the clearest sign that the open door policy has been successful in transforming the economy.
see also: 5. Politics and the Economy: Policy Patterns and Issues; Hong Kong; international trade; June 4 Incident.

Richard Pomfret

June 4 Incident

The name given in China in the 1990s to the military crackdown against anti-government behaviour on the night of 3–4 June 1989. In the West, the incident is more often known as the Tiananmen Massacre or the Beijing Massacre.

The death of **Hu Yaobang** on 15 April 1989 sparked off massive and long-lasting student demonstrations in **Beijing** and many other Chinese cities. The issues were complex but in essence the students wanted more freedom and democracy, including freedom of the press (see **media issues and policy**), and opposed official corruption and inflation, both of them very serious problems. On 26 April, *People's Daily* carried an editorial on the student movement, declaring that it constituted a 'turmoil' and a challenge to the CCP and state. The editorial represented the views of **Deng Xiaoping** and many others in the leadership. However, the student **protest movement** ignited a serious power struggle within the leadership, with CCP General Secretary **Zhao Ziyang** being the main supporter of the students and also eventual loser.

On 13 May the students actually occupied Tiananmen Square, in the centre of **Beijing**, and announced their intention of staying there until their demands were met. The action aroused a great deal of interest around the world, especially since many representatives of the world's press were already in **Beijing** to cover the visit of **Soviet** leader Mikhail Gorbachev from 15 to 18 May aimed at normalizing Sino-**Soviet** relations. As it turned out, many reporters, especially those from the West, found the student demonstrations much more interesting than Gor-

bachev's visit, and some of them even took an active part in the movement.

With Gorbachev's departure, Chinese Premier **Li Peng** immediately declared martial law in parts of **Beijing**. Troops of the 38th Army of the **People's Liberation Army** (PLA) began to move into Tiananmen Square to force the students to leave. However, the students put up barricades and many tried to persuade the troops to their side. Nobody was injured in the fight and the Square remained under student occupation.

At the end of May students of the Central Arts Academy erected the Goddess of Democracy, a statue strikingly similar to the Statue of Liberty in New York. The effect of this action was to give the leadership the argument it needed that the movement was inspired by the **United States**.

On the night of 3–4 June 1989, troops of the PLA's 27th Army moved to Tiananmen Square with tanks and armoured vehicles to enforce martial law. There was again resistance, but this time it was crushed. When the troops actually got into the Square a deal was negotiated with the students there allowing them to escape unharmed. Although there were casualties, most were not actually in the Square itself but in the Chang'an Boulevard leading towards and into it. By dawn the PLA was in total control of the Square and the students defeated.

The precise number of deaths remains unclear. The government stated that only about 200 civilians were killed, including 36 students. However, this figure is certainly an understatement. In August 1989, Amnesty International released an account, claiming that deaths amounted to at least 1,000.

On 9 June **Deng Xiaoping** reappeared to congratulate the PLA for 'quelling a counter-revolutionary rebellion'. Without this action, he claimed, the CCP would have been overthrown and replaced by a 'bourgeois republic'. Fears that the country would collapse into civil war proved unfounded, with a modicum of stability returning somewhat more quickly than most in the West expected. Martial law was lifted in January 1990.

The evidence is not compelling that the

anti-government forces enjoyed leadership coherent enough or had arms in sufficient quantities to make their movement a real 'counter-revolutionary rebellion'. The Chinese government used the actual overthrow of almost all Marxist-Leninist parties in Eastern and Central Europe later in 1989 to support its claim that a similar fate would have befallen itself without the military action. While this is an argument difficult to counter, calls for the overthrow of the CCP were conspicuous by their absence until the night of the massacre. Moreover, non-lethal weapons such as tear gas and water cannon, which are readily available to governments in this day and age, could no doubt have produced the same result without the need for deaths.

The person mainly responsible for the June 4 Incident was **Deng Xiaoping**. He was the chairman of both the state and the CCP's **Central Military Commissions**. Moreover, everybody acknowledged his supreme authority at that time, even though he had already retired from the **CCP Central Committee**. A military action right in the middle of the nation's capital without his direct intervention would have been quite impossible.

In terms of power struggle, the CCP definitely won and remains in power in China as of 1997. **Zhao Ziyang** lost his position as general secretary of the CCP because of his support for the students and was replaced by **Jiang Zemin**. PRC President **Yang Shangkun**, who had actively supported the military intervention, remained in office until 1992, being replaced the next year by **Jiang Zemin**. **Li Peng**, who as premier was so hostile to the students and supportive of **Deng Xiaoping**, survived in the position until 1998, thus carrying out the two full terms allowed him under the state **Constitution**.

The overall effect of the June 4 Incident was harmful to China. In domestic terms, although it kept the CCP in power, it cost it support from many of the intelligentsia and dealt a blow to its credibility. However, it was in the field of foreign affairs that the damage was greatest. The Western powers, especially the **United States**, raised human rights issues nearer to the top of their priority in relations with China. In addition, Western images of China in general suffered an extremely serious setback.

see also: 1. Overview History of the People's Republic of China; Beijing Municipality; Central Military Commission; Chinese Communist Party Central Committee and Politburo; Constitutions; Deng Xiaoping; dissidents; Hu Yaobang; Jiang Zemin; Li Peng; media issues and policy; *People's Daily*; People's Liberation Army; protest movements; Soviet Union, relations with; United States policy; Yang Shangkun; Zhao Ziyang.

Colin Mackerras

K

Kang Sheng

Senior leader associated especially with the radical policies of the **Cultural Revolution**. Kang Sheng (real name Zhang Wang) was born to a landlord's family in Jiao county in **Shandong** Province in 1898, dying in **Beijing** on 16 December 1975 at the age of 77. At his death Kang, as a vice-chairman of the **CCP Central Committee**, was one of the most senior Party leaders.

Kang joined the **Chinese Communist Party** in 1925. The official obituary honoured him as a proletarian revolutionary, Marxist theorist, and glorious anti-revisionist fighter. These words were later revoked, and Kang has become the focus of several studies, both in Chinese and in English, which have depicted him as the representative of terror and evil within the CCP movement.

In the 1920s Kang was a leader of the CCP secret service, and in the 1930s, living in Moscow, he was a supporter of the Party leader Wang Ming, being responsible for the elimination of Trotskyists within the CCP. Kang returned to China after the retreat of the revolution to its base at Yan'an in northwest China and was placed in charge of the 'salvation' (*qiangjiu*) movement during **Mao Zedong**'s first rectification campaign. The excesses of the movement, which supposedly unearthed a number of traitors and spies within the Party, resulted in Kang's disgrace.

Just after 1949 Kang kept a low profile but resurfaced in the 1960s. He organized the leftist attack on orthodox Marxist philosophy as represented by Yang Xianzhen and, during the **Cultural Revolution**, acted as adviser to its leading group, the **Cultural Revolution** Group, headed by **Chen Boda** and Jiang Qing (see **gang of four**). This small group, reporting directly to Mao, organized or incited attacks on leading Party cadres, among other extreme activities. With his pencil moustache and thick spectacles, Kang appeared as a shadowy figure at many of the rallies held during those years.

While it is true that Kang played a major role in China's secret service organization after 1949, he was certainly not alone in his willingness to persecute opponents, flatter leaders and cultivate lackeys. Kang was interested in Marxist ideology, and contributed to the polemics which China exchanged with the **Soviet Union** during the early and mid-1960s, as well as publicizing the deeds of peasants who, armed with **Mao Zedong Thought**, reaped harvests of unlikely dimensions.

see also: Beijing Municipality; Chen Boda; Chinese Communist Party; Chinese Communist Party Central Committee and Politburo; Cultural Revolution; gang of four; Mao Zedong; Mao Zedong Thought; Shandong; Soviet Union, relations with.

Keith Forster

Korea, policy on

Over history, China mostly regarded Korea as a vassal state within its tributary system, while Korea sought to maintain autonomy over internal affairs while fulfilling largely symbolic tributary obligations.

With the civil war in China and the division of the Korean Peninsula in the 1940s, Sino-Korean relations bifurcated into two pairs of alignments: the PRC with the northern Democratic People's Republic of Korea (DPRK) and **Taiwan** with the southern Republic of Korea (ROK), both Korean states established in 1948. In this structure, China's policy toward two Korean states was determined mostly by the strategic and ideological considerations of the Cold War.

Despite fluctuations, especially during the early years of the **Cultural Revolution**, Beijing's relations with the DPRK remained friendly, due to their common fight during the **Korean War**. China's policy toward the

DPRK remained fairly consistent through the 1970s.

On the other hand, China had neither any plans nor intentions to deal with the ROK. Beijing did not respond even to rare ROK overtures toward Beijing in the 1970s for joint exploration of petroleum and the continental shelf in the Yellow Sea.

With China's eye set on development from the late 1970s, Beijing sought to transform its strategic environment. In 1980, both **Hu Yaobang** and **Zhao Ziyang** stated that the ROK's developmental experiences would provide a useful model for China. With such a prelude, China gradually moved from 'non-policy' to 'separating economics from politics'.

The new position meant that Beijing would expand economic relations with the ROK while maintaining its political affinity toward the DPRK. Despite obstacles set by China due to its relations with the DPRK, Sino-ROK trade rose from US$19 million in 1979 to US$134 million in 1983 and US$3.087 billion in 1988. The last was the year of the Seoul Olympic Games, which themselves helped to improve Sino-ROK relations since China sent a team to Seoul.

Happy with the fruits of bilateral economic relations, Beijing became more active in expanding its dealings with Seoul, even at the expense of infuriating Pyongyang. China became permissive of capital inflow from the ROK, with its first direct investment materializing in 1988. Such expanded economic contacts produced an acute need for an institutional mechanism to monitor and oversee the ever expanding relations. Consequently, trade offices were established in 1991 when bilateral trade reached US$5.8 billion and ROK investment in China totalled US$425 million over sixty-nine projects. Following the signature of agreements on trade, tariffs and investment guarantees early in 1992, China and the ROK agreed to normalize diplomatic relations on 24 August 1992. In 1995, with the total trade amounting to US$16.9 billion, China was the ROK's third largest trade partner, while the ROK was China's fifth.

China's policy toward two Koreas manifests a mixed rationale. Economically, it presses relations with Seoul forward. Politically, however, Beijing has been fairly consistently protective of Pyongyang. Whether out of ideological affinity or of the strategic calculus of the DPRK as a key buffer state, China has been very careful to minimize the sense of betrayal which Pyongyang might feel about Beijing. In so doing, however, Beijing has developed a formula whereby it strives to maintain neutrality or non-interference with regard to the issues that may affect both Korean states. Such a position may work to China's advantage by allowing it to play one Korea against the other.

see also: Cultural Revolution; Hu Yaobang; Korean War; Taiwan policy; Zhao Ziyang.

Jae Ho Chung

Korean War

The PRC's first major military involvement outside China's borders, having far-reaching implications for China's foreign relations. **Korea** was divided at the end of the Second World War at the 38th parallel, with the anti-communist southern Republic of **Korea** (ROK) and the communist northern Democratic People's Republic of **Korea** (DPRK) both being established in 1948. War erupted in June 1950, and the DPRK conquered almost all the south. This prompted **United Nations** intervention under US leadership and the command of US General Douglas MacArthur, which pushed the DPRK forces back north of the 38th parallel. MacArthur pressed on, intending to destroy the DPRK and reunify the peninsula.

Already late in August 1950 Chinese Premier **Zhou Enlai** had denounced the **United States** for intrusions by its military aircraft into China's air space and for bombing territory near the border with **Korea**. As MacArthur's intentions became clearer the Chinese leadership issued statements expressing increasing alarm and warning that UN troops near their border would be unacceptable.

In the middle of October 1950 China began secret military intervention. On 24 October MacArthur issued final instructions for the conquest of all north **Korea**, and the very next day a clash occurred between Chinese and ROK troops. On 2 November Chinese and US troops fought against each other for the first time. The Chinese official name for its troops was the Chinese People's Volunteers (CPV) and their commander-in-chief was Peng Dehuai (1898–1974).

On 24 November 1950, MacArthur announced his final offensive to retake all **Korea**, and declared that US troops would be home by Christmas. He still believed the number of Chinese troops in **Korea** to be quite small, a maximum of 71,000. In fact the number was more than four times that figure, and US reconnaissance had failed to discover the extensive Chinese troop movements. On the night of 25–26 November, the CPV launched their own major offensive, which succeeded in driving back MacArthur's troops south of the 38th parallel by mid-December.

CPV and DPRK troops then made another attempt to reunify the whole of **Korea**, seizing Seoul on 4 January 1951, but strong and quick UN reaction, especially aerial bombardments, forced them to evacuate the capital in mid-March. Meanwhile, on 2 February, following a US Senate resolution nine days earlier, the UN General Assembly declared China as aggressor in **Korea**.

MacArthur and US President Truman were in deep disagreement over policy towards China; in particular, MacArthur wanted to bomb China's Manchurian bases but Truman refused permission. The eventual result was that Truman dismissed MacArthur as UN commander on 11 April 1951, replacing him with General Matthew Ridgway.

The last major Chinese offensive in **Korea** occurred the same month, but like the one before it faltered. By June it was obvious that neither side could gain a total military victory and soon afterwards truce talks began in Kaesong just south of the 38th parallel, mov-ing in October to Panmunjong a few kilometres to the south. Although sporadic and intense fighting flared from time to time, it was all in the region of the 38th parallel and there were no major offensives of the sort which had characterized the first year of the war. The issue to require the most negotiations and time was that of prisoners-of-war.

Republican Dwight D. Eisenhower, who had announced his determination to end the Korean War and to roll back communism, became US president in January 1953. He let it be known that the US was prepared to use nuclear weapons and push the war into China itself if an agreement was not reached. The ROK's Syngman Rhee still wanted to reconquer the whole of **Korea**. In the end a truce was reached on 27 July 1953, by which the point of division was moved slightly south of the 38th parallel in the west, to include Kaesong in the DPRK, but to the north further east. About 6,700 Chinese prisoners-of-war elected to return home, while some 14,700 decided against repatriation. No comprehensive peace agreement was reached. Both the UN and China withdrew troops from **Korea**, the Chinese completing their withdrawal in October 1958. (As of late 1997, a US contingent still remains in the south.)

Although there was no clear victor, casualties in the Korean War were enormous, nearly 1 million for the Chinese according to official UN figures. The event solidified the Cold War in Asia and greatly intensified US opposition to communism in Asia. Despite the lack of declared war, the bitterness was so deep for Sino-American relations that they did not recover until the early 1970s. The Korean War also worsened the situation in China itself by intensifying spy-consciousness and justifying hostility to the US for its anti-China activities.
see also: Korea, policy on; United Nations policy; United States policy; Zhou Enlai.

Colin Mackerras

L

labour policy and system

In describing China's labour policy and system the parameters of the discussion have to be narrowed to manageable proportions by concentrating on urban state employees who, until recently, were covered by a range of benefits which accompanied their lifetime jobs. Recent reforms have made the system much more diverse and complex, and the following sketch can only highlight some of the more outstanding examples of policy change which have in effect put an end to universal tenured employment in this sector of the workforce, and gradually and hesitatingly introduced a labour market to the country.

The Maoist Period

The labour system in force during the Maoist period (1949–76) was enshrined in a series of laws passed in the mid-1950s, which remained essentially in force until the 1980s. Borrowed heavily from the **Soviet Union**, the system embraced a package of measures which included the workers' share of social output in the form of the distribution of wages, bonuses, allowances and subsidies (in the form of both cash and merchandise), as well as the allocation of subsidized **housing**, the provision of health and social **welfare** benefits, and the preferential supply of coupons to purchase consumer goods in an economy of chronic scarcity.

Both state cadres (white-collar employees, including professional and generalist officials) as well as blue-collar workers in **industry** had their own graduated wage and salary scales, based on seniority, qualifications and personal contribution to the Chinese revolution. The principle behind the wage system was the Marxist formulation of 'from each according to his ability, to each according to his work', which was supposed to limit wage disparities as well as avoiding egalitarianism in income distribution. State cadres enjoyed

the right to various benefits including cars, home telephones, servants and so on once they reached a certain grade in this system. Certain posts had wage-scale requirements attached, and the structure reached down from the central administration in **Beijing** to the provinces, municipalities and counties below.

Labour was recruited by the state on the basis of annual quotas. These were met by state labour departments which allotted school and college graduates to government offices, enterprises and public utilities in the educational, **health** and **cultural** fields on the basis of both their needs and those of society. It was virtually impossible to change jobs, and then it required the exertion of a great deal of time, effort and the assistance of a person of influence. With virtually no inflation for the greater part of the Maoist period, wage rates were rarely adjusted, and increased family incomes derived from promotion along the wage scale as well as resulting from a higher participation rate of family members in the workforce. **Housing** rents, utility charges and consumer prices remained basically fixed. State employees received pharmaceuticals free of charge and paid a minimum registration fee to see a doctor. Hospitalization expenses were also covered by the provisions of the labour insurance scheme (*laobao*) which was paid for by the individual's work **unit**.

The working week consisted of six days, each of eight hours, but in effect office time could be consumed by cups of tea, cigarettes and newspapers. Because the CCP claimed to represent the interests of the working classes there was no concept of a conflict of interest between the state, management and the workforce. The official trade union body, the All-China Federation of Trade Unions (ACFTU), protected workers' rights in the context of this principle, and any manifestation of trade union syndicalism was condemned and punished by the CCP. Trade unions acted as transmission belts (using Leninist terminology) for conveying CCP principles and policy to the working class, and unions, which were workplace based, worked harder to contain working-class activism than to promote it.

The two main criticisms levelled at the labour system under the planned economy were that it instituted the 'iron rice bowl' (*tie fanwan*) of lifetime employment and encouraged 'eating from the same big pot' (*da guo fan*) or egalitarianism in distribution. This meant that it was virtually impossible for management to fire their staff, and no financial incentive was provided for effective and efficient work. The system was rigid in that it did not always match talented and qualified people with suitable employment, and it was also repressive in that a breakdown in relations between an employee and work superior could result in a whole series of discriminatory measures being imposed upon the former.

The Period of Reform
Since the 1980s reforms to the labour system have been introduced at a slow pace, with the authorities hesitant to deprive state employees of rights and privileges which they have enjoyed for many years, for fear of the reaction and social tension which such steps may provoke. Nevertheless, the tenured employment system for blue-collar state workers has been eroded by the introduction in the early 1980s of labour contracts. By the 1990s about 25 per cent of the workforce of state-owned enterprises were employed on contract. The state's monopoly over the allocation of labour has been weakened by the opening of labour service companies and exchanges where employers advertise for suitable staff. Such notices specify age, gender and educational or work experience requirements, as well as wages offered and whether the employer will provide **housing** (which is often the case and indicates that many of those seeking such jobs are peasants from out of town). University graduates can now seek employment themselves and hope to obtain a job commensurate with their skills and training.

In 1995 and 1996 Chinese state employees moved to a reduced working week of a five-day, forty-hour system (this means that many Chinese workers enjoy shorter working hours than their Japanese counterparts). State cadres were the first to enjoy the benefits of this reform, while many factories have yet to apply the new regime to their employees. Newspapers carry articles discussing how citizens can use their new-found leisure of a two-day weekend to best advantage. It is clear to any outsider that many Chinese workplaces are grossly overstaffed, as exemplified by the boredom written over the faces of many office workers. On the other hand, a great number of state cadres are busy with their mouths, rather than their minds, cultivating clients and contacts over lengthy and extravagant lunches which stretch into the late afternoon. For many, this is a fitting end to a day at the office.

The labour insurance system has imposed a heavy burden on state enterprises and institutions. These work **units** have to make allowance in their monthly payroll not only for retirement pensions but also for **health** and **welfare** benefits to former employees. In an attempt to contain skyrocketing costs for the lavish and unrestricted use of pharmaceuticals from a population of seeming hypochondriacs, patients are now required to contribute 10 per cent to the cost of prescribed drugs, and the burden of the social **welfare** system is gradually being shifted from the workplace to **local governments** which are introducing a range of benefits including unemployment and retirement pensions. Creations of the reform period such as privately run and **joint venture** enterprises do not provide such benefits which have almost bankrupted many state enterprises and have also placed them in a very difficult situation when competing in the market economy. The absence of the most basic **welfare** provisions or labour rights for the employees of many **township and village enterprises**, for example, has only strengthened the impression that the primitive accumulation of capital in China comes at the expense of the health and livelihood of its people.

Article 28 of the 1975 **Constitution** included the freedom to strike, but there is no such right specified in either the 1982 Constitution or in the Trade Union Law of 1992. The 1992 Law also affirms the ACFTU as the sole legal trade union organization in the country, presumably in reaction to the formation of 'illegal' trade unions during the 1989 student movement, a development against which the CCP responded with vigour and ferocity. In 1989 the authorities carried out intensive propaganda among workers to prevent them from joining the student struggle, threatening wage deductions for those who joined the students and giving material rewards to those who remained at their posts.

As of 1997, China's labour system and policies are in a state of flux. The government must tread cautiously if it does not want to alienate a key constituency whose defection or resistance would cause it, and the economy it helps push along at rapid growth rates, serious difficulty.

see also: Beijing Municipality; Constitutions; cultural policy; health policy; housing; industry; joint ventures; local government/administration; Soviet Union, relations with; township and village enterprises; unit; welfare policy.

Keith Forster

law, socialist theory of

The socialist theory of law owes its origin to the **Soviet** lawyer A. Y. Vyshinsky (1883–1954), thanks to Stalin's endorsement of the notion of socialist law by rejecting the ideas about incompatibility between law and socialism embedded in the critical theory of the commodity exchange school. It was strictly formulated to legitimize law under socialism by bending elements of Marxist critical theory to serve an ideological purpose. The socialist theory affirms the positive value of law in the socialist transition, with the focus on differentiating the nature of socialist law from bourgeois notion of law. Accordingly, socialist law is not a further development of bourgeois law, but a new type of law that has

grown out of the socialist revolution of the proletariat (see **legal system**).

Socialist theory was formulated on the basis of Stalin's instrumental notion of law. It was held that law in the socialist society was the instrument of the socialist state for the elimination of all capitalist traits, for the defence and the development of the socialist economy, as well as for the realization of communism. Its normative trend was also constituted, since law in socialist society was defined as a system of norms established by the state in accordance with the socialist mode of production relationships. Hence, all subsequent theories of socialist law were instrumental theories as laid down by Vyshinsky that law is a political category.

The socialist theory is Marxist in the sense that it stresses the indissoluble link between the state and law, both historically and functionally. Law is viewed from a state-determined approach instead of the former economic perspective. Socialist theory is, therefore, positivistic, seeing law as being laid down by the state and geared to serve the interests of the state until communism sees the state transcended.

But socialist legal theory is ridden with problems and these are exacerbated by the unbridgeable gap between positivistic socialist law and Marxism. The acceptance of socialist law creates uncertainties which figure in the debate about the future of the state and law in Marxist ideology. Most serious here was the failure to resolve satisfactorily the paradox of class law in a classless society posed by the **Soviet** communists themselves. The recent challenge to formulating legal norms by economic materialists has shaken the very foundation of the socialist theory of law, since this demands a new definition of law which goes beyond positivism. In short, the poverty of socialist theory rests on the communists' fundamentalist approach of taking law as a force external to human society. The theories of socialist law which emerged after the Stalinist era have been widely regarded as pseudo-Marxist in that the nature of the Marxist theory of law has degenerated from a critical approach to that of an apology for the communist regime.

Progressive Chinese jurists in the reform era, such as Zhang Zhonghou, Wu Shihuan and Wan Bin, understood these theoretical shortcomings in their critical re-examination of the Vyshinsky-type instrumental theories adopted from the **Soviet Union** in the 1950s. They rejected the Maoist thesis that law was a pure instrument for class struggle and demanded a new theory of socialist law, going beyond class reductionism and accommodating law's regulative function. The purely instrumentalist theory of law was eventually discarded in favour of a Chinese socialist theory capable both of expounding legal phenomena and guiding legal reform in the primary stage of socialism (see **3. Ideology: Radicalism and Reform**). The demise of the **Soviet Union** has further pushed Chinese jurists away from the **Soviet** tradition in search of a new theoretical scheme for building a long-term socialist legal order.

see also: 3. Ideology: Radicalism and Reform; legal system; Soviet Union, relations with.

Carlos W. H. Lo

legal system (administrative, criminal, economic)

The Chinese legal system is basically an adaptation of the **Soviet** model. From the very beginning of its rule, the CCP denied the Western conception of a legal system which is based on the rule of law. But from the late 1950s, the Sino-**Soviet** rift drove China away from the **Soviet** model in its quest for socialist legality. Since the late 1970s the reform policies have implied a socialist legal system with Chinese characteristics (see **law, socialist theory of**).

Although **Liu Shaoqi** was heavily involved in introducing a **Soviet**-style legal system, it was **Mao Zedong** and **Deng Xiaoping**, during their respective leadership periods, who dictated the development course of the Chinese legal system. Mao's dislike of formal justice heavily circumscribed Liu's attempt to introduce an institutionalized legal system, while his theory of uninterrupted revolution negated the value of law.

During the **Cultural Revolution** all formal legal structures were destroyed and revolutionary justice was practised. In contrast to Mao, Deng accorded law a positive value in socialist construction. He restored a formal legal system to maintain social order for socialist modernization and to protect people's democratic rights. His legal principles have provided practical guidelines for institutionalizing the socialist legal system. These include:

- that there must be laws for people to follow;
- the law must be observed;
- law-breakers must be punished; and
- all are equal before the law.

Institutionally, the legal system in Deng's era is a continuation of Liu's **Soviet**-style framework. It consists of three vertical structures, extending from the central to local levels – the public security network, the people's procuratorate and the people's courts. There is a formal division of labour among them in investigation, prosecution and adjudication. The Ministry of Justice supports the legal system, taking charge of legal education and training for legal personnel, supervising the legal practice of professional lawyers, and raising popular legal consciousness. Law has increasingly served as a channel for economic modernization and as the sole means of resolving conflict and regulating social order. Beginning legal reform by introducing a highly institutionalized criminal justice system in 1980, China had, by the mid-1990s, consolidated a basic framework for a legal order covering almost every aspect of social life.

The Administrative Legal System

After about three decades of administration by policies and decrees, China turned to legislation to improve its administration, giving rise to the idea of administration by law and hence the proliferation of administrative laws. Under the communist positive notion of the state, government by law is a concept more related to efficient administration than the promotion of individual democratic rights. Administrative law serves the teleological social development of a Marxist vision which overrides any democratic considerations where efficiency clashes with individual rights.

Chinese jurists of the reform period regard the aim of administrative law as the elimination of arbitrary rule. Under this conception of administrative law, efficient and stable administration is the theme, whereas the strict observance of law is the central concern.

There are four aspects of administration by law.

- Administrative legislation. The 1982 **Constitution** and the Organic Law of Local Government formally recognized the practice of delegated legislation, which empowered the state's administrative authorities from central to municipal level to enact administrative regulations in respect to their jurisdiction under the **Constitution** and law. The promulgation of the Provisional Regulations on the Procedure of Enacting Administrative Regulations of the State Council in 1987 was a milestone in institutionalizing an administrative legislation system in China.
- The implementation of administrative law. This requires state administrative authorities to conduct their activities and to exercise their powers in accordance with relevant administrative laws and regulations. Although government agencies are not yet used to administering in accordance with law, the transition from administration by policy to that by law is clear from the fact that laws and regulations have been made and announced in virtually all aspects of public administration.
- Administrative justice. With the adoption of the Administrative Procedure Law in 1989, which enables citizens to sue the government for maladministration, and the establishment of administrative tribunals in the courts since 1990, the administrative justice system has gradually taken shape.
- The supervision of administration by law. The Ministry of Supervision and adminis-

trative supervisory bodies at all levels aim to ensure administration according to law on the part of the state administrative bodies.

Basically, China has entered the threshold of a legal order characterized by administration by law. However, problems arise if legality and efficiency conflict with each other. Moreover, the process of legalization of administration is at risk under the current practice of administration by both policy and law, since the proclaimed harmony between the two is illusory. The CCP must reconsider the current conception to grant a supreme status to law and to strike a balance between the positive as well as the negative effects of Chinese administrative law. Until then, lawful administration in China is still remote.

The Criminal Justice System

Mao's conception of revolutionary justice prevented his regime from institutionalizing a criminal justice system. Accordingly, criminal justice was an instrument of class struggle in the elimination of the enemies of the revolution. Such politicized criminal justice had to be dispensed strictly according to Party policy.

However, Deng's regime has reversed this trend to establish a formal criminal justice system. With the promulgation of a Criminal Code and a Code of Criminal Procedure in 1979, Mao's revolutionary justice gave way to procedural justice. Depoliticization of criminal justice was evident in the fact that appeals were no longer made to populist concerns, class justice nor to Mao's distinction between 'antagonistic' and 'nonantagonistic' contradictions (see **Mao Zedong Thought**). The proclaimed linkage between law and democracy seemed very different from the old image that criminal law was simply a repressive instrument of the Party. The new image made much of the notion that 'all are equal before the law'. Much also was made of the trials of Wei Jingsheng in 1979 (see **dissidents**) and the **gang of four** in 1980 as demonstrations that the judiciary was capable of dispensing justice according to principles of due process.

Commitment to 'socialist legality' and the renunciation of political arbitrariness were evident in the provisions for judicial independence laid down in the 1982 **Constitution**; and, throughout the 1980s, one saw the gradual consolidation of the criminal justice system. A legal institutional system was established which, to some extent, reached down to grassroots level. The process was enhanced by the rapid growth of a system which provided professional lawyers, who played an expanding role in criminal justice and the spread of legal education (with examinations and on-the-job-training) for judges, procurators and administrative personnel in the legal system.

To prevent miscarriages of justice, the presumption of guilt was replaced by 'taking facts as the basis and laws as the criteria'. Procedural credibility was enhanced by a commitment to conducting open trials, according to prescribed procedures, replacing the former practice of holding secret or irregular mass trials. The rights of the accused to defence council and to appeal were guaranteed.

However, despite legislated provisions, the Chinese criminal justice system is far from fulfilling international human rights standards. There is still no independent judiciary which is supreme in matters of law. Thus criminal proceedings are easily bent in the direction of administrative or political expedience. Inadequacies in the scope, coverage and clarity of criminal law have provided ample room for arbitrary interpretation by government. Taking the maintenance of political stability and public order as the overriding consideration has confined judges to the role of enforcers of the law rather than adjudicators. This has turned many trials into mere formalities in which defendants have not been able to exercise their legal rights. A confusion of functions has allowed violation of the principle that the same magistrate may not act both as prosecutor and judge in the same proceedings. On the whole, China's crime control approach has exhibited the priority of administrative concerns over formal justice, simple and rushed court proceedings,

and a lack of debate and cross-examination of witnesses in court.

In an attempt to accord greater protection to the rights of the defendant, the regime amended the two criminal codes to rationalize the criminal justice system. The recodified criminal law, which came into effect on 1 October 1997, made some major improvements, apart from adding another 260 articles to provide a clearer and more concrete yardstick for adjudication. These included the abandonment of the notorious principle of crime by analogy, the replacement of 'counter-revolutionary crimes' by 'crimes endangering state security', and the redefinition of criminal economic activities to put the criminal law within the context of a socialist market economy.

As for the amended Criminal Procedure Law, which went into effect on 1 January 1997, it stipulated that no one should be regarded as guilty until convicted by a court. It gave defence council an early involvement in criminal procedures with an improved status. It reformed the hitherto prosecution-dominated trial procedure to grant judges the exclusive rights of adjudication. It reorganized procedures to facilitate the cross-examination of witnesses. Most significant of all, it terminated the practice of shelter and examination (*shourong shencha*), through which the public security organs could detain a suspect for investigation indefinitely, even though the procuratorate had to give permission if the period was extended.

The general trend seems to be that crime and punishment have become more substantively defined than formerly and the criminal process has been made more judge-led and adjudicative than formerly. Overall one detects greater moves toward legality and a greater attention to procedural rights. However, in the absence of an independent judiciary and legal profession, one should be cautious about any promise of the achievement of due process.

Economic Law
Economic law emerged as an important topic in China with the beginning of economic

reform in 1979, with the government relying increasingly on legal, rather than administrative, means to manage the national economy. The introduction of a planned commodity economy into Chinese socialism under Party General Secretary **Zhao Ziyang** has broadened the horizon of economic law to regulate both the planned and market sectors. Under a state-centred conception, economic law was defined as the totality of legal norms enacted by the state in the management of the national economy for regulating economic relationships within a certain domain.

The institution of a socialist market economy, following Deng's visit to South China in 1992 (see **1. Overview History of the People's Republic of China**), has revived the liberal economy reform choked by the 1989 student movement and government reaction to it. Economic laws adopted in this period have four main functions.

- Government regulation and control of the market. Such laws include those enabling the government to carry out fiscal and monetary policies, like the Budget Law, the Auditing Law, and the Law on the **People's Bank of China**.
- Establishment of the boundaries of the market economy. This includes laws which define the state–market relation, such as the Urban Real Estate Management Law, the State Compensation Law and the Arbitration Law.
- The operation of the free market. Most such laws are financial and commercial, including the Advertisement Law, the Corporation Law and the Law on Commercial Banks, and the Insurance Law.
- The attraction of foreign investment and facilitation of foreign trade. Laws in this category include the Law on the Protection of Taiwan Investment and the Foreign Trade Law.

Due to the rapid growth of economic activities, the number of economic courts has risen greatly and by 1995 each of the nation's 3,488 people's courts had already established an economic court.

The inauguration of a socialist market economy has activated economic activities

and generated a large volume of economic cases in need of judicial adjudication. The total number of cases that the people's courts handled in 1995 was 1.27 million, twice that of 1990. Settling disputes over economic contracts has been by far the most important function of the courts in handling economic cases. As China's economy has become more market-driven, special attention has been given to cases related to finance and banking (see **financial policy**), including disputes over loan contracts and those concerning the raising of capital. In particular, the cases on the bankruptcy of enterprises have received the largest share of public attention, the adoption of the Law of Bankruptcy being a milestone event in China's economic reform. There has been a rapid increase in the number of state enterprise bankruptcy cases since 1993, with a total of 904 cases recorded in 1993–4. Settling disputes over intellectual property rights, although still small in number, has emerged as one of the courts' most urgent tasks, under external pressure for an effective protection of foreign trademarks, patents and copyrights in China. Finally, economic activities in the rural areas have also been brought under the legal umbrella and resolving economic disputes among rural enterprises, mostly concerning production contracts, is the chief responsibility of basic-level courts.

see also: 1. Overview History of the People's Republic of China; Constitutions; Cultural Revolution; Deng Xiaoping; dissidents; financial policy; gang of four; law, socialist theory of; Liu Shaoqi; Mao Zedong; Mao Zedong Thought; People's Bank of China; Soviet Union, relations with; Zhao Ziyang.

Carlos W. H. Lo

Li Lanqing

Vice-premier of the **State Council** from March 1993. An erstwhile graduate of business management from Fudan University in **Shanghai**, Li emerged as the rising political star at the Fourteenth **National Party Congress** (1992). Elected a full member of the **CCP Central Committee** for the first time, he nevertheless rose straight to full membership of the Politburo, the First Plenum of the Fifteenth Central Committee (September 1997) electing him to the Politburo Standing Committee. This extraordinary promotion reflected not only the ascendancy of technocrats in the CCP's policy-making process but also China's policy shift towards an export-oriented market economy.

Born in 1932, Li distinguished himself as a student leader and joined the CCP in 1952. Upon graduation he was assigned to work in an automobile manufacturing plant in Changchun under the directorship of Rao Bin, who would be a significant patron in Li's early successes. Rao's promotion to **Beijing** was instrumental in Li's appointment to a senior post in the State Economic Commission in 1961 and his consequent connection with **Bo Yibo**.

Although Li Lanqing suffered humiliation during the **Cultural Revolution**, he was rehabilitated when the reform period began in 1978. The patronage offered by **Bo Yibo** proved crucial to Li in the years following 1978, when Bo was extremely influential in economic policy and personnel matters. Li was first called upon to work in the foreign trade area, then in April 1983 appointed deputy mayor of Tianjin assisting **Li Ruihuan**. Three years later he returned to the central government, reportedly at the behest of Premier **Zhao Ziyang**, taking up the post of vice-minister of Foreign Economic Relations and Trade. In December 1990 he rose to be minister of Foreign Economic Relations and Trade.

Li Lanqing is hardly a shrewd innovative politician, yet his bold moves to encourage foreign investment and to have the Chinese currency floated have marked him out as a true reformer. From May 1992 on he collaborated closely with **Zhu Rongji** in the running of the newly established Office of Economics and Trade under the **State Council**. The establishment of this body, which was in line with **Bo Yibo**'s ideas and endorsed by **Deng Xiaoping**, appears to have been designed to promote **Zhu Rongji** as China's main chief in the economy by undermining the influence of the State Planning Commission, long con-

trolled by **Chen Yun**'s men. Yet over the years tensions have also arisen between Li and Zhu, and some see Li's 1997 promotion to the Politburo Standing Committee as a move by **Jiang Zemin** to balance **Zhu Rongji**'s grip on power in the **State Council**.

see also: Beijing Municipality; Bo Yibo; Chen Yun; Chinese Communist Party Central Committee and Politburo; Deng Xiaoping; Jiang Zemin; Li Ruihuan; National Party Congress; Shanghai; State Council; Zhao Ziyang; Zhu Rongji.

Warren Sun

Li Peng

Senior Chinese leader and, in particular, premier of the **State Council** from 1988 to 1998 and CCP Politburo Standing Committee member from 1987.

A **Sichuan** native, Li Peng was born in 1928 and reputedly became the adopted son of **Zhou Enlai**. Admitted to the Yan'an Institute of Natural Sciences and the Zhangjiakou School of Industry in 1941, Li joined the CCP in 1945. A technician in the power industry, he was sent to study at the Moscow Power Institute 1948–54, and served as the Chairman of the Chinese Students Association in the **Soviet Union**. After his return in 1955, he was an engineer in the northeast and came to be director and Party secretary of the **Beijing** Electric Power Administration during the years 1966–80. He then worked successively as vice-minister and minister of Power Industry and first vice-minister of Water Conservancy and Power (1982–3). From 1983 to 1987, Li was concurrently vice-premier of the **State Council** and minister in charge of the State Education Commission. After 1987, he served as acting premier and premier, as well as minister in charge of the State Commission for Restructuring the Economy. He was appointed a member of the CCP Secretariat and Politburo in 1985, and a member of the Politburo Standing Committee in 1987.

While he has no experience in nor substantial ties with the military sector, he has been staunchly conservative in the economic reform and opening period since the late 1970s, and particularly so in respect to political and internal security affairs. His high-profile role in the **June 4 Incident** in 1989 subsequently generated strong opposition and condemnation of him both domestically and internationally. A target of much of the students' wrath, Li imposed martial law in **Beijing** on 20 May and helped muster **People's Liberation Army** troops from outside the **Beijing** area to enter the city. He adamantly refused dialogue with the protestors in Tiananmen Square.

His heart attack in 1993 caused him to lose ground to Senior Vice-Premier **Zhu Rongji**, who championed faster and more decentralized economic reform than Li, especially following **Deng Xiaoping**'s famous early 1992 'inspection tour of the south', during which Deng pushed for an even more dramatic acceleration in China's economic growth. When Li made his government work report to the **National People's Congress** that year, he was compelled to make over seventy changes to bring it in line with Deng's preferences. Li's wife, Zhu Lin, is reported to be a deputy manager in 'a large firm in the south of China'.

Li Peng's role in China's post-1989 diplomacy has included the following:
- a late 1991 state visit to India, which was part of the process leading to the landmark Sino-Indian 'peace and tranquillity' agreement of September 1993;
- a high-profile involvement at the UN Earth Summit in Rio de Janeiro in June 1992;
- a trip to Vietnam in November 1992, where he promised his hosts that China would not seek hegemony in the **South China Sea** region;
- a four-nation, ten-day Central Asian tour in April 1994 prompted by trade and economic interests and, indeed, by concerns about the potential spread of ethnic and religious instability from that region into China's **Xinjiang Uygur Autonomous Region**; and
- a 1995 visit to Moscow.

Despite his ten-year premiership of the **State Council**, Li never succeeded in totally dominating it. Moreover, his influence appears to

have eroded with the death of **Chen Yun** in 1995, who had long been a major force backing him. In March 1996 he was named head of the National Leading Group for China's Science and Technology, suggesting that for some Party members there are advantages of having a firm-handed technocrat like Li at the forefront of the administration as China pursues its modernization objectives.

At the September 1997 Fifteenth CCP Congress, he retained his ranking in second place in the Politburo Standing Committee. For constitutional reasons he must vacate the post of premier in March 1998, but is a likely replacement for **Qiao Shi** as chairman of the **National People's Congress** Standing Committee, with **Zhu Rongji** succeeding him as premier.

see also: 1. Overview History of the People's Republic of China; Beijing Municipality; Chen Yun; Chinese Communist Party Central Committee and Politburo; Deng Xiaoping; June 4 Incident; Li Ruihuan; National People's Congress; People's Liberation Army; Qiao Shi; Sichuan; South China Sea; Soviet Union, relations with; State Council; Xinjiang Uygur Autonomous Region; Zhou Enlai; Zhu Rongji.

Donald H. McMillen

Li Ruihuan

Senior CCP leader, in particular member of the Standing Committee of the Politburo, with special authority in cultural and ideological matters.

Li Ruihuan was born in September 1934, being a native of Tianjin. He joined the CCP in 1959 and in 1963 graduated from the **Beijing** Spare-time Civil Engineering Institute. He was active in building **industry** and the trade unions, including holding senior positions in the **Beijing** and national trade unions in the 1970s. In 1981, he returned to his native Tianjin. In 1984 he became mayor of Tianjin and deputy secretary of the Tianjin Municipal CCP Committee, in 1987 rising to become secretary and remaining mayor. His tenure of power in Tianjin resulted in drastic reform in governmental work, as well as improvement in urban **housing** and traffic facilities there.

He had meanwhile joined the Twelfth Central Committee in 1982, being promoted to the Politburo at the First Plenum of the Thirteenth Central Committee on 2 November 1987. At the Fourth Plenum of the Thirteenth Central Committee of 24 June 1989, which followed the **June 4 Incident** and saw **Jiang Zemin**'s replacement of **Zhao Ziyang** as Party general secretary, Li Ruihuan was promoted to the Standing Committee of the Politburo. He was confirmed on that Committee by the First Plenums of the Fourteenth and Fifteenth Central Committees (respectively 19 October 1992 and 19 September 1997). In addition, Li was elected deputy to the Sixth, Seventh and Eighth **National People's Congresses**, which met first in 1983, 1988 and 1993 respectively, and in 1993 was elected chairman of the Eighth National Committee of the **Chinese People's Political Consultative Conference**.

Li is considered as a moderate politically. In the cultural field he has advocated the creation of a new Chinese culture 'which combines the form of our nation with socialist content'. He has also been involved in pushing cultural nationalism and the notion of the magnificence of China's national culture (see **cultural policy**). For example, he has been active in an attempt to revive Peking Opera since the second centenary of its birth was marked in 1990. On 17 November 1995 he attended and gave a short speech at the opening gala performance of the week-long First Peking Opera Art Festival held in Tianjin.

see also: Beijing Municipality; Chinese Communist Party Central Committee and Politburo; Chinese People's Political Consultative Conference; cultural policy; housing; industry; Jiang Zemin; June 4 Incident; National People's Congress; Zhao Ziyang.

Colin Mackerras

Li Tieying

Senior CCP and government leader. As of 1997, Li Tieying has been a Politburo member since the Thirteenth **National Party Congress** in 1987 and a senior member of the **State Council** since 1988. Given the **education** portfolio in 1988, since 1993 he has been responsible for the crucial area of economic restructuring.

Born in 1936, Li's father, Li Weihan (1896–1984), was head of the CCP's central United Front Department from 1948 to 1964. Probably due to his family background he was able to pursue tertiary studies overseas graduating in physics from Charles University, Prague, in 1961. From his return to China until 1980 he worked largely in the national defence industry. In the first half of the 1980s he followed the usual pattern for promising Party cadres of serving at the provincial level before quick promotion to the Party Centre, appointments including executive deputy secretary of the Shenyang Municipal Party Committee (1981–3) and secretary of the Liaoning Provincial Party Committee (1983–4).

By 1985, the year which saw the advancement of many younger 'third echelon' leaders, Li was already minister of the Electronics Industry as well as a full member of the CCP's Central Committee. In 1987 he briefly succeeded **Zhao Ziyang** in charge of the State Economic Restructuring Commission, followed by elevation to full Politburo membership at the Thirteenth Party Congress.

In the period leading up to the **June 4 Incident** (1989) Li is reported to have enthusiastically endorsed the severe policy that **Deng Xiaoping** adopted against the **protest movement**. At the Eighth **National People's Congress** in 1993 he suffered extraordinary humiliation when over one-third of the delegates failed to support his reappointment to the **State Council**. Yet not only did he retain his position on the Council but came back as director of the State Economic Restructuring Commission. Unconfirmed reports claimed that, following the Sixth Plenum of the Fourteenth Central Committee (October 1996), Li Tieying, as well as **Li Lanqing** and **Wei Jianxing**, would be allowed to attend meetings of the Politburo's extremely powerful Standing Committee. However, unlike the other two, Li Tieying failed to join the Standing Committee at the time of the Fifteenth Congress (1997).

see also: Chinese Communist Party Central Committee and Politburo; Deng Xiaoping; education policy and system; June 4 Incident; Li Lanqing; Li Peng; National Party Congress; National People's Congress; protest movements; State Council; Wei Jianxing; Zhao Ziyang.

Warren Sun

Li Xiannian

Li Xiannian was an important member of the older generation of revolutionaries whose initial elevation to Politburo status in the 1950s was something of a surprise, but who then held this rank continuously through succeeding turbulent events including the **Cultural Revolution**. Li's most prominent role came after the death of **Mao Zedong** when he became a member of the Politburo Standing Committee and, from 1983 to 1988, served as president of the PRC.

Born in Hubei in 1909, Li joined the CCP in 1927 following the split with the Nationalists. He became a significant guerrilla leader in the Hubei-Henan-Anhui Soviet and served in the 4th Front Army led by Zhang Guotao, who was to become one of Mao's main opponents. During the division of forces in 1935 and subsequently Li remained with Zhang and suffered major military losses, but he continued his guerrilla activities in Central China following Zhang's defection from the CCP. Li was elected to the Central Committee in 1945, and during the civil war served under both **Deng Xiaoping** and **Lin Biao**.

After 1949 he initially served in the Central-South region until he was transferred to **Beijing** in 1954 as minister of Finance. Li's elevation to the Politburo in 1956 over others of equal or superior credentials was probably a gesture to veterans of the 4th Front Army, and in any case he continued to perform key economic roles into the 1980s. Under Mao he was able to navigate both the cautious opposition to rash advance in 1956–7 and the radical **Great Leap Forward**, and he also played a role in economic policy making during the **Cultural Revolution**. But undoubtedly his greatest individual influence came with the rapid growth policies adopted in 1977–8 following Mao's death, although blame for the failures of these policies was placed on **Hua Guofeng**. Subsequently Li continued to play a major role in economic **planning** but now, as in the 1950s, under the leadership of **Chen Yun**. By the early 1980s Li's role became more ceremonial when he assumed the state presidency, but his continuing influence even after his formal retirement in 1988 was seen in his role as one of the old revolutionaries who endorsed Deng's crackdown during the **June 4 Incident** in 1989. Li died in 1992.

see also: Beijing Municipality; Chen Yun; Chinese Communist Party Central Committee and Politburo; Cultural Revolution; Deng Xiaoping; Great Leap Forward; Hua Guofeng; June 4 Incident; Lin Biao; Mao Zedong; planning, economic.

Frederick C. Teiwes

Liao Chengzhi

A key actor in the Chinese revolution and in the PRC government. When he died in 1983, Liao was a Politburo member and a vice-chairman of the Standing Committee of the **National People's Congress**, his political life having epitomized the inclusivist, united front version of CCP politics.

Liao's family was from Guangdong, but his grandfather had achieved wealth in the gold rush in California, where his son Liao Zhongkai, Liao Chengzhi's father, was born. Zhongkai met his wife, the brilliant, socially prominent and rebellious He Xiangning by advertising in **Hong Kong** for a bride with unbound feet. The couple were living as exiles with Sun Yat-sen in Tokyo when Liao Chengzhi was born in 1908. (Educated in Japanese, Liao thought in it rather than Chinese throughout his life.) Liao Zhongkai, who advocated the Nationalist–Communist united front, was Nationalist political commissar at the Whampoa Military Academy alongside **Zhou Enlai** when assassinated by rightist Nationalists in 1925. His death, which portended the **Shanghai** Massacre of 1927, made him a martyr to united front politics.

Liao Chengzhi joined the clandestine CCP in **Shanghai** in 1928 and was sent to Germany for four years to do trade union work. Returning to **Shanghai** he was arrested, tried and then fled to the Sichuan-Shaanxi Soviet, completing the Long March with Zhang Guotao's 4th Front Army. (Zhang nearly executed him as a Nationalist Party secret agent.) Sent from Yan'an back to Guangdong, he organized anti-Japanese resistance, working in **Hong Kong** and, after its occupation, in northern Guangdong.

After 1949 his speciality was united front work, in both its internal and international senses. His connections to the Nationalist Party left made him a natural ambassador to third-force Chinese (the **democratic parties**, **Overseas Chinese**, and **Hong Kong–Macau** brethren), while his cosmopolitanism and linguistic skills made him a natural patron for the peace-and-friendship societies in Africa, Asia (especially **Japan**) through which China conducted its foreign relations during the US diplomatic boycott. The **Cultural Revolution** left, seeing united fronts as antithetical to uncompromising class struggle, attacked Liao fiercely. He survived to help plan the coup against the **gang of four** and become an outstanding advocate of reform, including opening the Shenzhen **Special Economic Zone**.

see also: Cultural Revolution; democratic parties; gang of four; Hong Kong; Japan, relations with; Macau; National People's Congress; Overseas Chinese policy; Shanghai; special economic zones; Zhou Enlai.

Paul Ivory

Lin Biao

Once the CCP's sole vice-chairman and the most revered figure in China other than **Mao Zedong**, Lin Biao was Mao's designated successor from 1966 until 13 September 1971, when his flight crashed in the Mongolian People's Republic, Lin allegedly trying to defect to the **Soviet Union**. Since then Lin Biao has been posthumously and consistently accused of attempting to assassinate Mao and stage a military coup. Contrary to claims in the West that Mao had Lin killed in **Beijing**, forensic evidence has confirmed beyond doubt that Lin did perish in the plane crash. Yet the circumstances of the whole affair remain obscure and it is now clear that, during **Hua Guofeng**'s interregnum, many of the

most sensitive and important materials were secretly destroyed with Politburo approval, including telephone records, meeting minutes, conversation notes, and desk diaries concerning Lin Biao and other top leaders such as Mao, **Zhou Enlai**, Jiang Qing and Wang Dongxing. Although the full truth of the Lin Biao affair may never be revealed, enough new evidence has already surfaced to indicate this was basically a spectacular example, showing the precarious nature of elite politics at Mao's court, of Lin's being forced to ride a tiger that would devour him.

Lin Biao the man is also very much an enigma made up of apparent contradictions. He was extremely shy and introverted, but also a most accomplished general who earned the admiration and even awe of other military men and Party leaders generally. Always cool-headed in battle, in private life Lin composed passionate poems for his wife, Ye Qun. A young communist rebel, in many respects he was deeply Confucian, especially on matters concerning the relationship between ruler (Mao) and subject (himself). Unlike Mao, who enjoyed women and food, Lin lived a simple life that could only be described as stoic.

Born in 1907, Lin's career began as a cadet at the Whampoa (Huangpu) Academy in **Guangzhou** during the first Guomindang–Communist united front in the 1920s, a situation in which he served under both Chiang Kai-shek and **Zhou Enlai**. Although the Lin–Zhou relationship was not close, subsequent history was marked by a lack of conflict between the two, despite Western analysis to the contrary during the **Cultural Revolution** period.

When the united front collapsed in 1927, Lin was among the Whampoa cadets who joined the new Red Army, and he began a long-term relationship with Mao in the Jiangxi Soviet and on the Long March. Lin was clearly subservient to Mao as reflected in the disparities in their age and Party status, and a kind of Confucian student–teacher relationship developed. Whatever the precise dynamics of that relationship, it is clear that Lin became one of Mao's closest supporters and, in turn, along with **Deng Xiaoping**, one of the future chairman's two most favoured Party leaders. But at this and later stages of his career it was Lin's military prowess which brought him to the attention of the CCP. Despite being seriously wounded in 1938 and absent for a time from the battlefield, Lin's reputation was such that he was elected the sixth-ranking Central Committee member at the Seventh Party Congress (1945). Although plagued by serious ill health, Lin led communist forces in the Northeast after the Japanese surrender, becoming responsible for winning two of the three major military campaigns which were pivotal in overthrowing the Guomindang in 1949. Lin was youngest among the ten marshals named in 1955, a sign of his enormous military reputation.

Still plagued by ill health, Lin chose an inactive political career after 1949. Again his revolutionary status saw him named to some of the highest posts in the country, including Politburo member in 1955 and Party vice-chairman in 1958, but throughout most of the 1950s he was content with an honoured position that carried few responsibilities. This changed in 1959 due to Mao's dismissal of Peng Dehuai for criticizing the **Great Leap Forward** (see **1. Overview History of the People's Republic of China**). Despite Lin's reluctance, Mao insisted that Lin succeed Peng as minister of National Defence. Lin performed the role, exercising the final say in military matters other than Mao himself, but passed on much of the responsibility to Chief of Staff Luo Ruiqing and **Central Military Commission** Vice-Chairman He Long. Lin won Mao's approval for advocating 'politics in command' in the military: a key factor in Mao's decision to name Lin the new successor, replacing **Liu Shaoqi** in 1966. Lin once again tried unsuccessfully to avoid promotion.

Despite official accounts portraying him as an ambitious politician, Lin Biao was at best an acute observer but always a reluctant player. Essentially he was a soldier who had little interest in politics and avoided exalted positions. While there were instances where Lin must be held responsible, such as the promotion of Mao's personality cult, his performance during the **Cultural Revolution** was largely passive, and his few personal initiatives were on the side of moderation. He was extremely unhappy over the **Cultural Revolution** and essentially a victim of circumstances, trapped above all by Mao's whims, by the shifting currents of an unpredictable political situation and by the manipulations of his wife Ye Qun and son Lin Liguo. The strange events leading to his death in the plane crash resulted not from any military coup plot or even normal political manoeuvre, but rather from miscalculation: that it was natural as successor for him to persist in the extreme personality cult of Mao, even though Mao had inexplicably turned against such posturing at the 1970 Lushan Plenum. Growing pressure against Lin and his close associates for these 'mistakes' over the next year led to the fatal decision to flee.

Lin Biao was survived by two daughters. One of them, Lin Liheng (Doudou), was herself a victim of the tragic Lin Biao affair, over the past decades suffering humiliation and hardship in an unsuccessful attempt to have her father's name cleared.

see also: 1. Overview History of the People's Republic of China; Beijing Municipality; Central Military Commission; Cultural Revolution; Deng Xiaoping; Great Leap Forward; Guangzhou; Hua Guofeng; Liu Shaoqi; Mao Zedong; Soviet Union, relations with; Zhou Enlai.

Warren Sun

Liu Huaqing

A top **People's Liberation Army** (PLA) general and naval commander, as well as senior CCP leader, especially influential in the 1990s, sometimes called 'the father of the PLA navy'.

Liu Huaqing was born in October 1916 to a poor peasant family in Dawu, Hubei Province. He joined the Red Army in December 1930 and was active in the communist military in the 1930s, taking part in the Long March in 1934 and joining the CCP in 1935. He took leading positions in the CCP's military during the Anti-Japanese War and the civil war of 1946–9 which brought the CCP to power.

In the 1950s, Liu Huaqing did a great deal of work towards establishing a Chinese navy. He became a rear admiral in 1955. In the mid-1950s he studied in the **Soviet Union**, graduating from Leningrad's Voroshilov Naval Academy in 1958. Although he did not escape criticism entirely during the **Cultural Revolution** decade of 1966 to 1976, he generally did well at that time, becoming a member of the PLA Cultural Revolution Group in 1967 and, more importantly, deputy chief of staff of the PLA's navy from 1970 to 1975.

It was in the following period that Liu ascended to the peaks of power. In 1982 he became commander of the PLA navy urging, in a 1984 interview, that China must modernize its navy to assert sovereignty over, and protect, its maritime resources. In 1987 and 1988 Liu joined the CCP and PRC State **Central Military Commissions**, becoming vice-chairman of the former on **Deng Xiaoping**'s retirement as Commission chairman in November 1989. In 1988 Liu was given the rank of general. He served as PLA deputy in the Seventh and Eighth **National People's Congress**es, which met first in 1988 and 1993 respectively.

In 1982 Liu Huaqing joined the Twelfth **CCP Central Committee**; but resigned in 1985 to serve on the Central Advisory Commission. At the Fourteenth National Congress of the CCP in October 1992, he rejoined the Central Committee, and on 19 October, at the First Plenum of the Fourteenth Central Committee, was appointed to the Standing Committee of the Politburo, the only military member. However, he retired from the Central Committee and the Politburo Standing Committee at the time of the Fifteenth Party Congress of September 1997.

Since the late 1970s, Liu has travelled overseas many times, visiting European countries, the **United States**, Egypt and Sudan, Bangladesh and Pakistan, mainly as head of PLA delegations.

At a conference on the peaceful use of defence technology in 1995, Liu called on the defence industry to press forward the decade-long trend of serving not only military but also civil production, urging it to step up the conversion drive through reorganizing management and reallocating personnel and material resources.

As a military man in the Standing Committee of the Politburo, Liu Huaqing was at the forefront of attempts to get CCP policy accepted within the PLA. Early in 1996 *People's Daily* quoted him as urging his soldiers to continue 'resisting the temptations to worship money and hedonism'. He further demanded that the army give priority to politics. In the second half of 1995 he also took a lead in opposing the 'China threat' theory, and accused 'some Westerners', meaning mainly the **United States**, of 'fabricating' this idea for 'ulterior motives'.

see also: Central Military Commission; Chinese Communist Party Central Committee and Politburo; Cultural Revolution; Deng Xiaoping; National People's Congress; *People's Daily*; People's Liberation Army; Soviet Union, relations with; United States policy.

Colin Mackerras

Liu Shaoqi

Senior **Chinese Communist Party** leader under **Mao Zedong**, president of China from 1959 to 1968 and Mao's chief rival during the **Cultural Revolution**.

Liu was born in Ningxiang County, Hunan Province, in 1898, the son of a primary school teacher and youngest in a family of nine. After attending local schools at lower level, he went to study in Moscow, where he joined the CCP in 1921. Upon his return he plunged into the organization of urban trade unions, becoming director of the CCP Labour Department (at the Sixth Congress in Moscow, 1928) and chairman of the All-China Labour Federation in Shanghai (in 1931). Upon completing the Long March, Liu became the leading organizer of the underground Communist base areas behind Japanese lines, where he succeeded, by August 1945, in promoting a major expansion of CCP influence in some of the most populous and economically advanced regions of China.

When the PRC was established, Liu became second in command.

Although Mao and Liu gravitated into opposing ideological camps, they still cooperated and Mao named Liu his heir apparent in 1959. Yet during the **Cultural Revolution**, Mao blamed Liu for a systematically misconceived approach to policy questions, naming it the 'bourgeois reactionary line'. Liu was intensively criticized, culminating in his purge from all leadership positions and from the CCP itself at the Twelfth Plenum of the Eighth Central Committee in October 1968. He died miserably in Kaifeng, Henan, on 12 November 1969. However, his posthumous rehabilitation in February 1980, after a year's investigation by a special investigatory commission, ensured the survival of his political legacy and personal reputation.

Before 1966, most considered Liu a grey and faceless administrator, but few suspected policy differences between him and Mao. During the **Cultural Revolution**, he became the archetype of Maoist revisionism, 'China's Khrushchev', who threatened to lead the nation down the 'capitalist road'. Following his rehabilitation in 1980 he was reconstructed in a sort of synthesis of these two versions of his historical identity, an admixture of ideological orthodoxy and economic pragmatism, reflecting **Deng Xiaoping**'s agenda.

Before 1966, Liu's greatest contributions were to CCP organization theory. In a series of articles summarizing his experience as a labour leader in the 1920s and 1930s he emphasized the importance of using legal as well as clandestine tactics, material as well as idealist incentives, and not only riding the revolutionary flood tide but also weaving a net that would sustain momentum during its ebb. In the 1940s he shifted to Party organization, and in Yan'an, he wrote a number of articles that have since become classics, including 'How to Be a Good Communist' and 'On Inner Party Struggle'. The former included a conflation of Marxist-Leninist ideology with indigenous belief systems, dovetailing neatly with Mao's simultaneous attempts to adapt Marxism to Chinese conditions. From Confucianism Liu borrowed the notion of 'self-cultivation' to define the ethical self-realization of the model Party member. Finally, in his November 1948 essay endorsing Stalin's excommunication of Tito, 'On Internationalism and Nationalism', Liu made a pioneering contribution to the conceptualization of the 'capitalist road' that would ultimately become his own epitaph.

During the **Cultural Revolution**, Liu Shaoqi was redefined in dramatic juxtaposition to **Mao Zedong**, serving as the touchstone of Maoist 'revisionism'. In policy terms revisionism reflected the economic experiments then being introduced on an experimental basis in Eastern Europe and the **Soviet Union**. In ideological terms there were four basic tenets of revisionism, and thus of Liu's ideology.

- Following the socialization of the means of production in the post-revolutionary period, class struggle is 'extinguished', since classes can no longer be defined by their relationship to property. All people must hence be treated equally in legal and political terms, any further differentiation being based on their functional utility in achieving policy aims, not on class origins.
- Socialism is not merely a brief transition period en route to the communist utopia but a stable and long-term period, with its own laws.
- In the progress of socialism toward ever-higher forms of association, the forces of production essentially set the pace for the relations of production; only after the forces of production have fully matured (in terms of economic productivity) are further changes in the relations of production or the ideological superstructure objectively possible.
- Science and technology are redefined as components of the forces of production rather than the ideological superstructure.

The rehabilitation of Liu Shaoqi in 1980 resulted in a selective synthesis from both pre- and post-1966 versions of his political persona. His original theoretical contributions to communist organization theory have been reaffirmed. Once again acclaimed as classics, some of Liu's main works are broadly disseminated as part of the attempt to enforce organizational discipline and Communist morality. On the whole the **Cultural Revolution** version of Liu has been repudiated (i.e. there is no 'capitalist road' in the CCP, 'line struggle' is a rarity). It is conceded that Liu was willing to make generous concessions to China's capitalist classes in the period immediately after the CCP took power. Liu's ideas are part of a new version of ideological orthodoxy known as Marxism-Leninism-**Mao Zedong Thought**.

A comparison of the materials released during the successive fragments of his public career indicates that he was more orthodox than the ideological renegade criticized during the **Cultural Revolution**, yet also more pragmatic and flexible than the 'iron Bolshevik' depicted in the pre-1966 media. He fully supported the violent seizure of power by the CCP and helped to operationalize it. He also fully supported socialization of the means of production.

Liu emerges as an orthodox Leninist on ideological and organizational issues, albeit one always willing to make pragmatic adjustments, and a man willing to experiment in economic issues.

see also: 1. Overview History of the People's Republic of China; 3. Ideology: Radicalism and Reform; Chinese Communist Party; Cultural Revolution; Deng Xiaoping; Mao Zedong; Mao Zedong Thought; Soviet Union, relations with.

Lowell Dittmer

local government/administration

The PRC state is explicitly unitary in nature. China's leaders are not prepared to grant sub-central units the autonomy required of federal systems. Yet the Chinese state rules a vast territory with a multitudinous population. Under **Mao Zedong**, the Chinese leadership experimented with the role of local (i.e. all sub-central) government and administration. At times the centre controlled even the minutest decision making.

At other times, provinces and even lower levels had powers to make some local decisions. In the post-Mao reform period, many localities have gained significant autonomy, but higher levels still control key local leadership appointments (see **provincial government**).

Basically the Chinese state has four levels of local bureaucratic administration: provinces (*sheng*, numbering 31 in 1997, other than **Taiwan**), prefectures (*diqu*, 334 at the end of 1995), counties (*xian*, 2,143 end 1995) and townships (rural *xiang* or urban *zhen*). Municipal and **minority nationality** equivalents exist at each level. Thus, besides the twenty-two mainland provinces such as **Shandong** and **Sichuan**, the PRC has four provincial-level municipalities (*shi*) (**Beijing**, **Shanghai**, Tianjin and Chongqing) and five provincial-level autonomous regions (*zizhi qu*) (see **minority nationalities policy**). In addition to prefectures, there are prefectural-level municipalities and autonomous prefectures while county-level municipalities, autonomous counties, urban districts and suburban districts are county equivalents. Urban townships and street committees join rural townships at the township level. At each of these four local levels, cadres receive their salaries from the government. Administrative villages exist beneath these four bureaucratic levels. Administrative village cadres receive their salaries from village funds rather than from the government.

Local administration replicates central administration, though the number of organs and employees decreases at each successive level. At all levels the CCP committee remains the key organ of leadership. During the **Cultural Revolution** the CCP secretary usually headed the government, but since the 1980s, these posts are generally held by separate persons. Normally, however, the government leader is also a deputy Party secretary of the local Party committee.

The local Party committees are subordinate to the higher Party committees while the local governments are subject to 'dual leadership'. They are subordinate to both the higher government and to the local Party committee.

Specialized Party offices are also subject to 'dual leadership', being subordinate to the higher-level specialized office and to the local Party committee.

Since the implementation of the post-Mao reforms, local administrations have sought greater autonomy in retaining tax revenues, foreign exchange and the right to approve foreign investment decisions. Such autonomy has developed most rapidly in places with 'preferential policies' like the **special economic zones** and such southern provinces with substantial foreign investment as Guangdong, Fujian and Hainan. **Shanghai**, a key industrial and economic centre and a tax 'cashcow' for the centre, obtained increased autonomy only in 1990 and 1992. Such autonomy allows entrepreneurial local leaders to develop local enterprises and local fiscal income. Yet the centre retains some control of the reins through its power to make key leadership appointments. Similarly, provinces retain control of prefectures through the appointment of prefectural leaders.

Local leaders do have certain powers. For example, local banks, which are supposed to be centrally controlled, often must make loans to localities irrespective of financial prudence because local leaders control the supply of electricity, water, grain, building permits, building materials, jobs for family dependants and school places for children.

Another factor changing post-Mao local administration has been the strengthening of the local people's congresses. In addition to passing local laws and regulations, local people's congresses elect local government leaders. In the post-Mao period three changes have strengthened local people's congresses.

- Provincial and county people's congresses have gained standing committees, which means the people's congresses have a full-time presence in local administration. (Prefectures do not have people's congresses, though prefectural municipalities have both people's congresses and standing committees.)

- Efforts to retire older leaders to the 'second line' have meant many Party and government leaders have shifted to leadership positions in the people's congresses. In order to increase their influence, they have sometimes worked to increase the power of the people's congresses beyond that of a 'rubber stamp'.
- The new **electoral laws** have extended direct election up to county-level people's congresses. Furthermore, the provision of multiple candidates has increased the willingness of voters and of people's congress delegates (when voting for local government leaders and higher-level people's congress delegates) to vote for candidates not endorsed by the local Party committees.

While the changes should not be overstated, the combination of increasing government economic decision-making and the potential for autonomous political decision making by people's congresses has led to some changes. The Zhejiang Provincial People's Congress rejected the centre's choice for provincial governor and elected an alternative, despite the Party-controlled indirect election process for provincial people's congresses. The **Sichuan** Provincial People's Congress has also rejected the Party's nominees for key provincial positions and such rejections are more common at lower levels. Some Chinese supporters of democracy believe these local changes will lead to democratization of the Chinese system, but many other analysts believe this is unlikely in the short term.

see also: Beijing Municipality; Cultural Revolution; electoral laws; Mao Zedong; minority nationalities policy; provincial government; Shandong; Shanghai; Sichuan; special economic zones; Taiwan policy; Tibet Autonomous Region; Xinjiang Uygur Autonomous Region.

J. Bruce Jacobs

Lu Ping

One of Beijing's most influential officials dealing with **Hong Kong** in the 1990s. Lu Ping was born in **Shanghai** in 1927, graduating from St John's University, Shanghai, in 1947. During the 1950s, he worked for the magazine *China Reconstructs* and for the Chinese Welfare Association, which was under the leadership of Sun Yat-sen's widow, Song Qingling.

In 1978, Lu began to participate in the work of the **State Council**'s **Hong Kong** and **Macau** Affairs Office (HKMAO), being promoted to secretary-general in 1984 and three years later to deputy director. In November 1990 Lu was named HKMAO director.

Lu has frequently attacked the British authorities on behalf of Beijing. In 1990, he criticized the **Hong Kong** government for wasting money by building the Chek Lap Kok airport. In 1992, he attacked Governor Chris Patten's political reform proposals so severely that the two have never met again formally. He was present in **Beijing** when **Tung Chee-hwa** received his official appointment as first Chinese chief executive of the **Hong Kong** Special Administrative Region (HKSAR) from Premier **Li Peng** in December 1996 and remained influential on various **Hong Kong** issues, including the reappointment of senior civil servants who could retain their posts beyond 1 July 1997. When Tung toyed with the idea of appointing Ronald Arculli, a member of the Legislative Council, as the Secretary of Justice for the HKSAR, Lu reportedly favoured Elsie Leung Oi-see, a **Hong Kong** member of the **National People's Congress**.

Some **Hong Kong** politicians see Lu as relatively open-minded toward dissenting views. One illustrative example was that Lu listened to the dissenting views of the Bar Association, which opposed the establishment of the provisional legislature in **Hong Kong**, during the Preparatory Committee's consultative session in **Hong Kong** in 1995. On balance, however, Lu is politically conservative, emphasizing the central government's perspectives rather than **Hong Kong**'s autonomy.

see also: Beijing Municipality; Hong Kong; Li Peng; Macau; National People's Congress; Shanghai; State Council; Tung Chee-hwa.

Sonny S. H. Lo

M

Macau

Portuguese territory on the south Chinese coast. In March 1887 China and Portugal signed a protocol formally ceding to Portugal administrative rights over Macau, which had been a Portuguese trading post since the sixteenth century. In 1979 the Chinese and Portuguese ambassadors in Paris reached agreement that sovereignty over Macau should be Chinese, and that in due course the two governments would negotiate the date of returning the territory to China. On 13 April 1987, the PRC and the Portuguese prime ministers formally signed, in **Beijing**, the Sino-Portuguese Joint Declaration on the Question of Macau, stipulating that sovereignty would return to China on 20 December 1999. After that date the Macau Special Administrative Region (SAR) would enjoy a high degree of autonomy on the basis of the **one country, two systems** principle.

Features of Macau during the transition period from 1987 to 1999 include:

- a relatively weak Legislative Assembly;
- a politically fragile democracy movement;
- a civil service heavily influenced by Portuguese and the Portuguese model; and
- a comparatively compliant local Chinese mass media.

The Legislative Assembly, about one-third of the members of which have, since 1976, been directly elected by citizens, is dominated by pro-government and pro-Beijing legislators. Usually the Portuguese governor uses his appointment power to balance the composition of the legislature by appointing local Portuguese – especially the Macanese of mixed Chinese-Portuguese ancestry. While the Macanese dominate the civil service, they are concerned about their future after 20 December 1999, even though the Joint Declaration guarantees respect for Portuguese customs and habits. Although localization of the civil service has been implemented progressively during the transition period, as of 1997 many Portuguese from Portugal still hold the top positions in the bureaucracy. Moreover, there are different interpretations of the term localization. For the Macanese it means promoting local Macanese to the upper levels of the civil service, while the local Chinese regard it as meaning Sinicization, or recruiting and promoting ethnic Chinese rather than the Portuguese and Macanese. Most judges are also Portuguese or Macanese. To localize the **legal system**, the Chinese government has been training experts with mastery over both the Portuguese and Chinese languages and both Portuguese and PRC law.

As of 1997, the local democracy movement, led by intellectuals, is fragile and generally marginalized by the local mass media. The democrats experience difficulty in gaining popular support in elections, because Macau voters tend to be lower-class citizens easily mobilized politically by pro-China and business groups. In the 1996 Legislative Assembly elections, rumours circulated that many voters received bribes from their employers to support political groups which were not only pro-Beijing but even triad-related. However, the Portuguese administration played down the extent of triad influence because this was the last direct election held in Macau under Portuguese rule.

Macau is economically integrated into South China and, since the transition period, its interaction with the Zhuhai **Special Economic Zone** has become more pronounced than before. With the construction of the new Macau airport in 1995 and the expansion of infrastructure projects (like bridges, roads) in the territory, Macau is playing a prominent role in sustaining the momentum of economic modernization in Zhuhai. At the same time, however, economic integration brings new problems, such as cross-border crime which, as of 1997, has become increasingly serious.

Portuguese rule in Macau places more emphasis on harmonious relations with China than did its British counterpart in **Hong Kong**. In the transition period, all Macau governors assume that the path to 'a high degree of autonomy' lies through economic and infrastructural development, rather than through political democratization. In contrast to **Hong Kong**, there is considerable public maladministration in Macau. Corruption is rampant, both in the private and public sectors, and the anti-corruption organs are quite weak. Moreover, there is strong opposition to anti-corruption efforts from the business community and those elites with vested interests.

see also: Beijing Municipality; Hong Kong; legal system; one country, two systems; special economic zones.

Sonny S. H. Lo

Mao Zedong

Chairman of the **Chinese Communist Party** from 1943 to 1976 and China's state president from 1949 to 1959. Born in 1893 into a rich peasant family in Hunan Province, Mao Zedong trained to be a teacher, punctuated by brief military service after the 1911 revolution. Following his graduation in 1918, he went to Beijing where, as a library assistant, he came into contact with a number of influential radicals. In the two years following the May Fourth Movement of 1919, Mao returned to central China, engaging in radical activities which became increasingly Marxist.

In 1921, Mao attended the meeting in **Shanghai** which established the CCP, after which he engaged in the Party's educational and labour organization activities. After 1924, Mao became prominent in the united front between the Guomindang and CCP, serving for a while as an alternate member of the Guomindang Central Executive Committee. In 1925 he headed a Peasant Institute in **Guangzhou** which was important in training activists to enlist support for the Northern Expedition of 1926–7 designed to unite the country. Following the split between the Guomindang and the CCP in 1927, Mao became active in the Autumn Harvest Upris-

ing, after the failure of which he led a guerrilla army to establish a base in Jinggangshan on the borders of Jiangxi and Hunan. Together with Zhu De, Mao eventually moved his base eastwards to Jiangxi where a Chinese Soviet Republic was proclaimed in 1931 with Mao as chairman of its Central Executive Committee (head of state).

During the Jiangxi Soviet period, Mao lost authority over military affairs and the CCP adopted a defensive posture very different from his. Defeat in 1934 resulted in the epic Long March, during which (at the famous Zunyi Conference in 1935) Mao's authority over the Party was said to have been confirmed, though it was consolidated only some time after a base was established in Yan'an and a new united front with the Guomindang was established to resist Japanese invasion. The rectification movement of 1942–4, which celebrated Mao's famous essays 'On Practice' and 'On Contradiction' (1937) in an attempt to sinicize Marxism, cemented Mao's leadership position, reflected in his formal election as chairman of the Politburo and Central Committee Secretariat in 1943. The Seventh **National Party Congress** of 1945 gave pride of place to **Mao Zedong Thought**.

On the founding of the PRC, which Mao proclaimed on 1 October 1949, he assumed the post of chairman of the new Central People's Government Council and the People's Revolutionary Military Council, though **Zhou Enlai** exercised day-to-day management of state affairs and Zhu De commanded the **People's Liberation Army**. At that time, government policy adhered to Mao's concept of the 'people's democratic dictatorship', which prescribed leadership of a 'four class bloc' of workers, peasants, petty bourgeoisie and national capitalists over an 'enemy' (defined as 5 per cent of the population) consisting, among others, of landlords and comprador capitalists. Despite differences with Stalin over the former Comintern policy and Stalin's low opinion of the Chinese revolution, Mao visited Moscow in 1950 and apparently reached a satisfactory *modus vivendi* with Stalin which persisted throughout the **Korean War** (1950–3). At that time Mao's earlier speeches were revised to fit the current situation and the *Selected Works of Mao Zedong* became the CCP's official canon.

In the early years of the PRC, a five-year plan of **Soviet** inspiration was adopted with Mao's blessing, but, by 1955, Mao became impatient with its progress and brought about the rapid collectivization of **agriculture** (see **collective agriculture**) and socialization of **industry** and commerce. While much less disruptive than earlier and similar movements in the **Soviet Union**, the campaigns have been heavily criticized in the official 1980s reassessment of Mao, on the grounds that Mao adopted a voluntaristic approach which neglected the classical Marxist view that changes in the relations of production depend on the prior development of the productive forces.

A temporary period of caution in 1956, as the CCP reacted to Khrushchev's denunciation of Stalin, resulted in the removal of reference to **Mao Zedong Thought** in the Eighth Party Congress **Constitution** and the adoption of a general line which spelt out the principal contradiction in China as existing between the 'advanced socialist system' and the 'backward productive forces'. Mao soon began to oppose that formulation. At the same time he proposed a movement to 'let a hundred flowers bloom, let a hundred schools of thought contend'; but, when the **Hundred Flowers Movement** resulted in anti-socialist sentiments in mid-1957, Mao endorsed the Anti-Rightist Movement which turned on prior critics and soon developed into an attack on what Mao felt to be conservative economic thought. The result was the **Great Leap Forward** of 1958–9, legitimized by Mao's ideas on 'uninterrupted revolution', which saw balance as temporary and imbalance as the normal condition of progress – a view which many orthodox Marxists saw as an 'idealist' affirmation of the human will over economic determinants. The result was an economic disaster.

In late 1958, Mao announced his intention to resign as president, **Liu Shaoqi** formally replacing him in 1959. In that year Mao oscillated between affirmation of measures designed to remedy problems caused by the Great Leap and demands for its revival. When Defence Minister Peng Dehuai criticized the Great Leap at the CCP's Lushan meetings in 1959, Mao had him dismissed and launched a movement against right-leaning elements. There followed a partial revival of the Leap which foundered by 1960 in the midst of economic chaos and famine.

During the period 1960–2, Mao engaged in much theoretical work, retiring to the 'second front' while **Liu Shaoqi**, among others, sought to restore the economy to some sort of stability. Mao began increasingly to react against what he termed 'revisionism' (the use of Marxism to negate Marxism) in the **Soviet Union** and to move against what he saw as a retreat from socialist ideals in China.

In 1962, at the Tenth Plenum of the Eighth Central Committee, Mao returned to the 'first front', declaring that the Party should 'never forget class struggle'. At that time, he put forward a series of ideas, referred to later as 'continuing the revolution under the dictatorship of the proletariat'. While eclectic, there was a new element in his formulations: it held the objects of class struggle not only to be residues of the past society but forces newly generated in society and present in the Party itself.

Mao's pessimistic thinking of the early 1960s led to a series of movements designed to counter capitalism in the countryside, to reform literature and the arts (in which he was aided by his wife Jiang Qing: see **gang of four**) and to emulate the ideological reform which had taken place in the army since **Lin Biao** had replaced Peng Dehuai in 1959. By 1965, Mao's perception of failure in those movements resulted in his view that there was a stratum of 'top persons in authority taking the capitalist road' in the Party – of which **Liu Shaoqi** was eventually to turn out to be the prime representative. The outcome was the **Cultural Revolution** which began in 1966.

During that revolution, Mao revealed himself sometimes as the radical instigator of mass action to reform the Party and sometimes as an orthodox Leninist who maintained central authority. At times he would press for radical action and at other times he would demand stability or even repression by the army. The Red Guards, which he had instigated and encouraged, were eventually seen as superfluous and dispatched to the countryside in the late 1960s. Mao came to see his 'close comrade-in-arms and successor', **Lin Biao**, whom he accused of plotting a coup, as no better than **Liu Shaoqi** – a fact which caused severe depression and contributed to his near-death experiences of 1971. Yet in the 1970s, under the influence of the **gang of four**, Mao repeatedly returned to affirmation of **Cultural Revolution** themes. He died on 9 September 1976, after tacitly endorsing a movement to revive the spirit of the **Cultural Revolution** in the form of 'beating back the adverse wind of reversing previously correct verdicts' and a movement to criticize **Deng Xiaoping**, who stressed Mao's earlier ideas about practical efficacy as the yardstick for policy.

From the perspective of the late 1990s, history has not been kind to Mao. His colleagues (and most spectacularly his doctor Li Zhisui) have revealed a contradictory 'imperial' personality – a person who, in his later years, while usually reigning without ruling, sometimes intervened in politics with dramatic and often disastrous results. The CCP's evaluation of him still follows the 1981 **Sixth Plenum of the Eleventh Central Committee**, which saw him as a great Marxist-Leninist who made serious mistakes in his later years. Among ordinary people, there has been much Mao nostalgia (especially on the centenary of his birth in 1993), because Mao, however imperial, politically ruthless, personally exploitative and sexually outrageous, was not corrupt in the capitalist sense of that word in the 1990s.

see also: 1. Overview History of the People's Republic of China; agriculture; Chinese Communist Party; Chinese Communist Party Central Committee and Politburo; Constitutions; Cultural Revolution; Deng Xiaoping; gang of four; Great Leap Forward; Guangzhou; Hundred Flowers Movement; industry; Korean War; Lin Biao; Liu Shaoqi; Mao Zedong Thought; National Party Congress; People's Liberation Army; Politburo; Shanghai; Sixth Plenum of the Eleventh Central Committee; Soviet Union, relations with; Zhou Enlai.

Bill Brugger

Mao Zedong Thought

According to the 'Resolution' of the **Sixth Plenum of the Eleventh Central Committee** of June 1981, Mao Zedong Thought is 'the product of the integration of the universal principles of Marxism-Leninism with the concrete practice of the Chinese revolution'. Mao Zedong Thought is a 'scientific system' which, while originating with **Mao Zedong**, who most effectively resolved the problem of the adaptation of Marxism-Leninism to Chinese conditions, represents a 'crystallization of the collective wisdom of the CCP'. Many 'outstanding leaders' of the Party had also made contributions to Mao Zedong Thought, not just Mao himself.

With this formulation, the 'Resolution' makes an important distinction between Mao Zedong Thought and the thought of **Mao Zedong**, the individual. While Mao was the foremost figure in the development of Mao Zedong Thought, the fact that he committed a number of serious errors in his later years, in particular the **Great Leap Forward** and the **Cultural Revolution**, meant that not all of his thoughts could be incorporated into Mao Zedong Thought, which is by definition a 'body of correct principles'. The 'Resolution' thus portrays Mao Zedong Thought as an evolving system of thought which encapsulates the correct experience of the CCP and which functions as a guide to action for the Party as it meets new situations requiring new policy initiatives.

While Mao was not, therefore, the only contributor to Mao Zedong Thought, the 'Resolution' credits him with being its originator and with developing a number of fundamental principles and strategies on which the victory of the Chinese revolution and the successful first stage of socialist construction were based. The 'Resolution' emphasizes Mao's correct interpretation of the characteristics of China's revolution before 1949. Mao had interpreted this as a revolution fought against imperialism, feudalism and bureaucrat-capitalism by the masses of the Chinese people, but based primarily on the worker–peasant alliance led by the working class whose consciousness and organization were superior to those of the peasantry. It was necessary for the working class and its vanguard party to lead the peasantry during a protracted armed struggle. According to the 'Resolution', Mao correctly recognized the need for a revolutionary army to fight this protracted armed struggle, and he formulated techniques for transforming what was essentially a peasant army into one that was 'proletarian in character, observes strict discipline and forms close ties with the masses'. Mao similarly developed effective tactics of guerrilla warfare which played a decisive role in China's war against Japan and in the communist victory in the Civil War which followed.

The 'Resolution' continues that, with victory in 1949, Mao laid the foundation for a successful transition to socialism through his establishment of a people's democratic dictatorship, a state based on an alliance of various classes, one which would oversee socialist industrialization and the socialist transformation of private property. Mao correctly recognized that, while the people shared the same fundamental interests, all sorts of contradictions persisted, and it was necessary to distinguish those between the people and the enemy (antagonistic contradictions) from those which existed among the people (non-antagonistic contradictions) and to handle the latter correctly to prevent them from becoming antagonistic.

The 'Resolution' states that Mao perceived the need for an economic strategy suited to the particular characteristics of China's economy, and not based on the experience of foreign countries. He consequently emphasized the importance of **agriculture** as the foundation of the economy, and the need to handle correctly the relationship between **agriculture** and **industry**.

Mao also made an important contribution to Mao Zedong Thought, according to the 'Resolution', through his formulations on Party building. Mao successfully solved the problem of how to establish and develop a Marxist proletarian party in a country in which the peasantry made up the majority of the population and in which the working class was a small minority. He did this by emphasizing the importance of ideological work within the Party, so that Party members, of whatever class background, constantly strove to transform their ideas into proletarian ideas. Mao developed tactics to guide the internal life of the Party. He stressed the need for criticism and self-criticism, and opposed the 'left' approach of 'ruthless struggle and merciless blows' to the settling of internal Party differences.

The 'Resolution' defines the 'living soul' of Mao Zedong Thought as its stand, viewpoint and method, and the essence of these is captured in three basic principles.

- The first is seeking truth from facts, a dialectical materialist approach to gaining knowledge that stresses the importance of practice and a recognition of the existence of contradictions in all things.
- The second is the mass line, which specifies that the Party's relationship with the masses should be premised on the principle of 'from the masses to the masses', a principle which requires Party leadership maintaining close contact with the masses and basing its policies on the interests of the masses.
- The third is independence and self-reliance. While China could not remain in isolation from the rest of the world, its path to development had to be founded on self-reliance, a refusal to allow its national independence to be compromised through submission to pressures from other countries. Mao had correctly emphasized the importance of formulating economic and political strategies in the light of China's own conditions, and had insisted on China's independ-

ence from outside interference. On the basis of independence and self-reliance, China had and would continue to practise peaceful coexistence with other countries in the quest for a genuine internationalism.

The 'Resolution' concludes that Mao Zedong Thought will remain the Party's guide to action 'for a long time to come'. It also stresses that, although Mao wrote many of his important works before 1949, it is important to study them since they contain many important principles and theories which are of universal significance and therefore of relevance to the contemporary problems confronted by China. The 'Resolution' consequently identifies Marxism-Leninism and Mao Zedong Thought as one of the 'four cardinal principles' which constitute the political basis for the unity of the Party and the Chinese people and which guarantee the success of socialist modernization.

The definition of Mao Zedong Thought provided by the 1981 **Sixth Plenum of the Eleventh Central Committee**'s 'Resolution' has remained the basis of the CCP's ideological stance throughout the 1980s and 1990s, and has been reiterated at Party meetings and Congresses. The 'Resolution's' distinction between Mao Zedong Thought, the Party's correct system of thought, and the thought of Mao the individual, has allowed the Party considerable flexibility in ideological matters. The invocation of a sanitized version of Mao's thought as its ideology has allowed the Party leadership to claim political legitimacy through its continued links with Mao and the successes of the Chinese revolution, while leading both the Party and China in a direction very different from that endorsed by Mao during his own lifetime.

see also: agriculture; Cultural Revolution; gang of four; Great Leap Forward; industry; Mao Zedong; Sixth Plenum of the Eleventh Central Committee.

Nick Knight

Marriage Laws

There are two Marriage Laws in the PRC, promulgated on 1 May 1950 and 10 Septem-

ber 1980. The 1950 Marriage Law was the first major law enacted in the PRC, showing its political and social importance for the CCP's revolution. Based on experience from the pre-1949 communist movement and in particular on the Marriage Law of the Chinese Soviet Republic of 8 April 1934, its main stipulations were as follows:

- equality between the sexes;
- the abolition of the 'feudal' marriage system, including the ban on arranged marriages, the remarriage of widows, the taking of foster daughters-in-law, and concubinage or any other form of polygyny;
- the establishment of the minimum age of marriage at 20 for men and 18 for **women**;
- a ban on discrimination against persons born out of wedlock;
- equal rights for husband and wife in the possession and management of family property;
- that both husband and wife may use their own family name;
- that, even when one party insists on a divorce, this 'may be granted only when mediation . . . has failed to bring about a reconciliation';
- the requirement that 'if the spouse of a member of the armed forces on active service insists on divorce, consent must be obtained from the member'; and
- the requirement that authorities in minority areas take account of local customs in making amendments or supplementary regulations.

Although the Family Law of the Republic of China, which came into effect in May 1931, had recognized equality for **women** in some of its clauses, the 1950 Marriage Law was the first in China directly to stipulate equality between the sexes (see **gender equality**). The 1931 Law specified that parties concerned should agree to marriage before betrothal could take place, but did not require both bridegroom and bride to sign the marriage contract. The 1950 Law was thus the first clearly outlawing arranged marriages. The May 1931 Law made no mention of concubinage, which is banned in that of 1950.

The promulgation of the 1950 Marriage Law was followed by a campaign to implement its provisions, reaching a height in 1952. Strong emphasis was laid on abolishing the old system of arranged marriages which had still been the norm in the countryside and on getting the populace to adhere to the minimum ages of marriage. In addition, the divorce rate at first rose greatly as people escaped from loveless unions contracted under the system of arranged marriages. However, after the initial flurry divorce again went out of fashion as traditional mores reasserted themselves.

The 1980 Marriage Law went into effect on 1 January 1981. Its main stipulations varying from the 1950 Law are as follows:

- to raise the minimum age of marriage to 22 for men and 20 for **women**;
- that divorce should be granted 'in cases of complete alienation of mutual affection, and when mediation has failed';
- to forbid a husband to seek divorce from a pregnant wife, or for a year after the birth of the child, but specifically to waive this obligation for wives;
- to ban infanticide;
- to lay down that the husband may become a member of his wife's family or the other way around, as the couple agreed; and
- to obligate both husband and wife to practise family planning and to encourage late marriage and late childbirth.

The reason for the change in the law on divorce was that courts had generally adopted a very strict line in accordance with their view of popular opinion, which was usually not sympathetic to the party applying for the divorce. The demand that both husband and wife practise family planning was associated with a new **population policy** aimed at reducing the growth rate.

Margery Wolf, a Western researcher who interviewed 300 **women** in two cities and four rural areas in 1980–1, found that urban people in general did indeed choose their own spouses according to the law. However, in the rural areas, change had been much slower and less thorough. Her finding was that only 27 per cent of the rural **women** married since 1950 had known their husbands before becoming engaged to them, 29 per cent met them only after becoming engaged, and 33 per cent did not meet them until their wedding day.

An official survey carried out in two counties in Anhui province in the early 1980s found that only 15 per cent of recent marriages were by free choice, 10 per cent had been parentally arranged, and the remainder (75 per cent) had been 'agreed upon' – in other words, the couples had not actively opposed their parents' choice. These figures accord with a belief, widespread both in the West and in China, that the parents generally make the choice of rural marriage partners but it is subject to veto by the partners involved, whereas in the cities it is the other way around – the spouses initiating the choice of partners, which their parents may veto. While this is an enormous advance over the days when rural **women** were not even consulted about their spouse, it falls far short of the real freedom of choice in marriage which the CCP has been trying to implement. As a factor in deciding on a marriage partner, family convenience is much slower to yield to love or other factors in the countryside than in the cities.

In the 1980s, following the new Marriage Law, divorce again developed into a feature of social life in China, especially in the cities. Figures issued by the State Statistical Bureau show that in 1980 there were 7,197,860 registered marriages and 340,998 divorces in all China, or 1 divorce for every 21.1 marriages. However, by 1995, marriages had risen to 9,297,061, but divorces to 1,055,196, showing not only a very substantial rise in divorces but a fall in the proportion of marriages to divorces to 8.81 to 1. In 1995 the province-level unit with the lowest ratio of marriages to divorces was **Xinjiang** (3.1), divorce rates being especially high among the Uygurs of southern Xinjiang. In contrast to the past, it is nowadays usually the **woman** who files for divorce.

These changes are part of a very substantial transformation of society which has accompanied the new politics of China in the 1980s

and 1990s. Although rural society has also changed enormously, the continuities are much more important there than in the cities.
see also: gender equality; population policy; women; Xinjiang Uygur Autonomous Region.

Colin Mackerras

media issues and policy

The media in the PRC have a long history of advocacy, stemming from before 1949 when journalists loyal to the communist cause gathered and reported news and commentary primarily in order to bring about rule by the **Chinese Communist Party** over China. In power, the Party closed existing media run by opponents, and absorbed others into its own media structure. The rulers initially tried to channel all important news, information and influential opinion about politics, society, the economy and morality through channels which they controlled. The media became an integral part of government apparatus, not a separate, let alone independent, part of the nation's political life. They were organized such that each main level of Party organization – central, provincial, autonomous region, municipality and lesser local – had one or more newspapers, as did various other CCP sponsored organizations such as the All-China Federation of Trade Unions, **Central Military Commission** and the Communist Youth League. The CCP-led government also controlled and developed broadcasting stations. Thus media were available for the needs of different levels of administration, controlled by the appropriate Party committee.

In the late 1950s after the **Hundred Flowers Movement**, the CCP used the media as instruments of class struggle. During the **Cultural Revolution** many of the media were closed down and those remaining changed dramatically to accord with the intensely politicized and antagonistic atmosphere of the time. In the early 1970s official public newspapers in China became policy documents and instructional statements rather than containing news. A fairly reliable verbal transmission of news, known to many as *xiaodao*

xiaoxi, developed to fill the vacuum created by the lack of published or broadcast news and information. During politically sponsored campaigns individuals and groups used 'big-character posters' (*dazibao*) in order to circulate their own versions of events.

With the reforms beginning in 1978, the Party adopted new propaganda and information policies in order to win back the disillusioned public as a readership or audience. While the Chinese media were required to promote the CCP's reform policies and report on related issues and events, they underwent a process of reform themselves, with emphasis laid on a professional system of news gathering and circulation, along with a reduction of ideological content in the media. News returned to the media, which became more factual and believable. Economic imperatives also forced the media offices to experiment, innovate and carry paid advertisements, with a view to freeing them from total reliance on government subsidies by making profits. Readership of the CCP organs decreased as the number and variety of papers and magazines catering to different interests increased enormously. Some publications were independent and provided scandalous stories, pornography and other tabloid-style journalism. However, there was also an expansion in the number of more respectable papers, including on scientific and technological subjects, produced with the support of people in official positions but not directly under the supervision of a CCP committee. The Party newspapers continue to compete with a range of publications and programmes containing less political news and more articles dealing with everyday life.

The official media have to be aware of the Party's continuing expectation that they will assist in maintaining national stability and unity, and promote economic development. During the course of reforms in the 1980s and 1990s a major new issue confronted by the serious media is the threat of being sued for libel. As of 1997 there is still no media law for the protection of journalists. Although political interference has lessened enormously as a brake on critical reporting, the threat of libel suits has produced a similar, though much less severe, effect.

Another major new issue in the reform period is private payment to journalists: *youchang xinwen* or 'paid news'. The growth of the market economy has affected the attitude of individual journalists and the people about whom they write. The cost of living has risen significantly and citizens employed in the private sector can earn much higher incomes than public servants. Journalists, who are employed as public servants, spend time moonlighting where money can be made and in some cases succumb to the temptation to write favourable articles for money.

The official PRC media continue to change to suit prevailing political conditions. However, a few principles have remained constant. Bodies such as Party and government organizations, or agencies or social groups directly accountable to the CCP, still effectively control or influence the media. The staff must still act as the 'eyes and ears' of the CCP; they gather news and information into their office, sifting it for appropriate action. They collate and print some of it for internal distribution, publishing or broadcasting only material deemed suitable.

The media continue to be 'mouthpieces' for the CCP. They must carry news of, and official commentary on, the Party's policy decisions and political campaigns, and articles about successful implementation of such policies and programmes. Editors and journalists write with varying degrees of autonomy. Many of the senior editorial staff are CCP members, while socialist practice and the political climate and power structure at any given time can affect what the media publish or broadcast. Published news is not intended to be impartial, both emotional persuasion and selective reporting being acceptable means of reaching and convincing readers or audience. News reports should be factual, but with emphasis on the social or political function of the report. Published news must be topical in a politically timed sense. Critical reporting is usually about

institutions and officials at the same or lower administrative levels compared with that of the reporting medium. In the late 1970s *People's Daily* journalist Liu Binyan carried out much investigative reporting in a climate of major political change in which it suited senior political leaders to allow publication. (Liu was expelled from the CCP in January 1987 on political grounds and in 1988 went to the United States, where he settled.) Some investigative reporting is circulated only within Party political circles, especially where public exposure might make the government look incompetent or even corrupt. Publication of investigative reporting of any substance generally does not occur without the instigation or backing of a powerful political leader. The most spectacular example of this was the slow public exposure and apportioning of blame in the early 1980s for the disaster of the Bohai Number 2 oil rig, which had sunk in November 1979 with the loss of seventy-two lives. There are periods of relative freedom for reporters and editors to publish as they see fit, most dramatically obvious in the months leading up to the **June 4 Incident**. However, Party leaders can still tighten control over the media and their staffs as they see the need.

see also: Central Military Commission; Chinese Communist Party; Cultural Revolution; Hundred Flowers Movement; June 4 Incident; *People's Daily*.

Jennifer Grant

Military Affairs Commission
See **Central Military Commission**.

minority nationalities policy
Policy towards those fifty-five state-recognized ethnic groups which, according to the sample census of 1 October 1995, made up 8.98 per cent of the PRC's total population.

The work of identification, based on Stalin's definition of a 'nationality' which the PRC adopted, took place mostly in the 1950s. Other than the dominant Han, the 1964 census recognized fifty-three nationalities, but by that of 1982 two had been added.

The Chinese Soviet Republic's 1931 **Constitution** allowed secession to those minorities which wanted it. However, the fact that **Japan** was penetrating China's Mongolian areas and encouraging them to secede as pro-Japanese independent states forced **Mao Zedong** to change policy and ban secession.

The basic minorities policy of the PRC has two main arms.

- Areas of minority concentration have the right to autonomy. This means that the minorities enjoy the right to some political control over their own areas. Members of the relevant minority must hold some positions of government, although not necessarily CCP, power. Autonomy also means cultural rights such as the usage of written and spoken languages and the preservation of traditional literatures and arts.
- There is absolute insistence on maintaining 'the unity of the nationalities'. This means a total ban on secessionist activities, the main cases of which have occurred in Tibet and Xinjiang.

The CCP had already set up the Inner Mongolian Autonomous Region on 1 May 1947. During the 1950s and 1960s it established four further province-level autonomous regions, twenty-nine autonomous prefectures and sixty-four autonomous counties or banners, as well as one more prefecture and nearly thirty counties since 1979. The four autonomous regions, with capitals and dates of establishment, are:

- **Xinjiang Uygur Autonomous Region**, Ürümqi, 1 October 1955;
- Guangxi Zhuang Autonomous Region, Nanning, 15 March 1958;
- Ningxia Hui Autonomous Region, Yinchuan, 25 October 1958; and
- **Tibet Autonomous Region**, Lhasa, 9 September 1965 (see **Tibetans**).

Although autonomy remained policy during the **Cultural Revolution** decade of 1966 to 1976, practice was assimilation of the minorities. The reason for this was **Mao Zedong**'s obsession with class struggle as 'the key link'. Religions of all kinds were subject to relentless persecution, while the traditional literatures and arts were suppressed in favour of revolutionary models.

On 15 July 1980, the CCP's mouthpiece *People's Daily* wrote: 'The existence of classes is of much shorter duration than that of nationalities. After the withering away of the former, the latter will remain in existence for a long time'. This signalled a major change in nationalities policy, with autonomy revived and strengthened.

The 1982 **Constitution**'s stipulations on minorities included the following:

- discrimination against minorities or inciting their secession are forbidden;
- minorities practise regional autonomy, on the proviso that 'all the national autonomous areas are inalienable parts' of the PRC;
- minorities have the right to use their own languages and to preserve or reform their own customs, including in government and legal work;
- the administrative head of an autonomous area, although not necessarily the CCP secretary, must be a citizen of one of the relevant minorities;
- regional autonomous areas have the right to administer their own finances and, with the approval of the **State Council**, organize local public security forces; and
- the state must give special assistance to the minorities 'to accelerate their economic and cultural development'.

In addition, the **Constitution** laid down the right of religious belief, but added that such a right may not be used to disrupt public order, provisions which, although not special to the minorities, are particularly relevant to them.

In 1984 the Chinese government adopted a Law on the Autonomy of Nationality Areas, which expanded and strengthened the provisions of the 1982 **Constitution**. It called for efforts to include more minorities in the governments of the national autonomous areas and allowed them to adapt or fail to implement central government laws which did not suit the needs of the autonomous localities. In addition, provided the autonomous organs observed the state's educational direction and PRC law, the 1984 Law allowed them to determine their areas' **education system**, including curriculum content, the language of instruction and student recruitment methods.

Preferential policies towards the minorities expanded. A minority may adopt its own **population policy** or **marriage law**, some of them markedly more permissive than those of the Han. There are special 'nationality schools' and special subsidies and quotas for entry into colleges and universities.

In the late 1980s and in the 1990s the policies of autonomy came under strain when several attempts at secession were made in the minority areas, the most serious being in the **Tibet Autonomous Region** and **Xinjiang Uygur Autonomous Region**. Although these have all been crushed mercilessly, the government has maintained its policy on autonomy.

see also: 6. Peoples of China; Constitutions; Cultural Revolution; education policy and system; Japan, relations with; Mao Zedong; Marriage Laws; *People's Daily*; population policy; State Council; Tibet Autonomous Region; Tibetans; Xinjiang Uygur Autonomous Region.

Colin Mackerras

N

National Congress of the Chinese Communist Party
See **National Party Congress**.

National Party Congress
The highest body of **Chinese Communist Party** power in China. As of the end of 1997 fifteen National Congresses of the CCP have been held since the Party's foundation in 1921; of these eight have been convened since the PRC's foundation. Recent Party **Constitutions** have stipulated that a Congress must be held every five years, though in the past there have sometimes been long intervals between them. Eleven years passed between the Seventh Congress (1945) and the Eighth (1956). A second session of the Eighth Congress met in 1958 but the Ninth did not meet until after the turbulent period of the **Cultural Revolution** (1969). After that, Congresses were held regularly – the Tenth in 1973, the Eleventh in 1977, the Twelfth in 1982, the Thirteenth in 1987, the Fourteenth in 1992 and the Fifteenth in 1997. The 1997 **Constitution** stipulates that congresses may not be postponed 'except under extraordinary circumstances' and may be convened before the due date 'if the Central Committee deems it necessary or if more than one third of the organizations at the provincial level so request'.

The early congresses of the CCP appear to have been appointed by the outgoing **CCP Central Committee** though recent congresses have been largely elected. The process of election, the number of delegates and the constituency represented, however, are determined by the outgoing Central Committee according to its view of the balance of power within the Party and social priorities; for example, in 1982 it stressed the importance of recruiting experts in economics, **science and technology**, **women** and **minority nationalities**. In 1982, Central Committee instructions insisted that elections should be conducted by secret ballot after consultation with Party congresses at every level of the Party structure and that the number of candidates should be greater than the number of persons elected. The 1992 **Constitution** stipulated that the above procedure may be used in formal elections or in preliminary elections designed to draw up a list of candidates for a formal election.

The 2,048 delegates to the Fifteenth Congress were mostly selected in the above manner, though in some cases there were not more candidates than seats and some delegates were in effect chosen by recommendation. For example, there were sixty 'special guests' (veteran leaders who had joined the CCP before 1927) and delegates from the Central Disciplinary Inspection Commission and the outgoing Central Committee who had not stood for election. There were also a number of participants from other political parties and government organizations. Most delegates to the Congress represented local Party organizations (over 70 per cent) though some seats were reserved for representatives of central Party organs. Despite the latter provision, a number of prominent leaders of central organs returned to the provinces to stand for election. Military delegates constituted the remainder.

The formal powers of the National Party Congress, as laid down by the Party **Constitution**, are to:

- hear and examine the report of the Central Committee;
- hear and examine the report of the Central Disciplinary Inspection Commission;
- discuss and decide on major questions concerning the Party;
- revise the **Constitution** of the Party;
- elect the Central Committee; and
- elect the Central Disciplinary Inspection Commission.

The above powers are not very significant in an active sense and there is not much debate on major questions concerning the Party. A body of some 2,000 delegates is not equipped to engage in extensive debate in a meeting which lasts only for one week. Nevertheless, the Congress provides a forum for articulating the position of the CCP on fundamental issues. The Report of the Central Committee, delivered at recent congresses by the general secretary, is an important statement of the Party's political line and outlook for the next five years. It undergoes extensive revision by senior leaders and in the past has often been the subject of much controversy. For many years, debate about the line of the Eighth Party Congress (which apparently was worked out rather hastily in response to developments in the **Soviet Union** and played down the importance of class struggle) was the subject of bitter polemic. **Lin Biao**'s original report, prepared for the Ninth Party Congress, was withdrawn and rewritten on **Mao Zedong**'s instructions. At more recent congresses, the period of preparation has been much longer than before and the line articulated by the political report has reflected the concerns of economic reform, the Fifteenth in 1997 stressing **Deng Xiaoping** Theory of 'building socialism with Chinese characteristics', a 'socialist market economy' and the reform of state-owned enterprises.

The Party **Constitution** has often been revised many times (sometimes also by lower-level Party organs), before it reached the Congress for ratification, and membership of the Central Committee usually largely determined before the Congress met. The Praesidium of the Congress (chosen by the informal top leadership and most significantly the 'core leader') has produced an approved list which has usually been followed. Unlike the case with earlier congresses, however, Congress delegates now have some discretion in the choice of Central Committee members (they can exclude up to 5 per cent of those on the approved list), but the procedure is far less than what one might normally consider to be democratic. More research, however, is needed on how the Politburo (through the Congress Praesidium) orchestrates representation, especially when

one considers that **People's Liberation Army** representation on the 1992 Committee was higher than that proposed by preparatory committees. It appears that, while the power of the Congress to select the Central Committee is somewhat hollow, representation on the Central Committee is not entirely manipulated from a single source.

see also: 2. Government and Institutions; Chinese Communist Party; Chinese Communist Party Central Committee and Politburo; Constitutions; Cultural Revolution; Lin Biao; Mao Zedong; minority nationalities policy; People's Liberation Army; science and technology; Soviet Union, relations with; women.

Bill Brugger

National People's Congress

China's parliament and its highest organ of state, as opposed to Party, power. Except during the years 1965 to 1978, the National People's Congress (NPC) has had a life of five years. The following are the dates of the first eight NPC's First Sessions, together with the number of delegates at each.

1st NPC	15 to 28 Sep 1954	1,226
2nd NPC	18 to 28 Apr 1959	1,226
3rd NPC	21 Dec 1964 to 4 Jan 1965	3,040
4th NPC	13 to 17 Jan 1975	2,885
5th NPC	26 Feb to 5 Mar 1978	3,497
6th NPC	6 to 21 Jun 1983	2,978
7th NPC	25 Mar to 13 Apr 1988	2,970
8th NPC	15 to 31 Mar 1993	2,978

The functions of the NPC are laid down in the four **Constitutions**, these being very similar but not identical. That of 1975 is far less detailed than the other three; and those of 1975 and 1978 give the CCP, not the PRC president, as nominator of the premier of the **State Council**, a post the choice of which all four **Constitutions** allocate to the NPC.

The 1982 **Constitution** lists twenty functions and powers for the NPC. In summary these are:
- amending and supervising the **Constitution**;
- enacting and amending laws;
- electing or dismissing the PRC president and vice-president;

- deciding on, or dismissing, the premier and other members of the **State Council**;
- electing or dismissing various other senior military and legal executives;
- examining and approving the premier's report, the budget and other major government reports;
- approving the establishment of provinces, autonomous regions, and municipalities directly under the central government;
- deciding on questions of war and peace; and
- other functions appropriate to the highest organ of state power.

To pass a resolution normally requires only a simple majority of all NPC deputies. However, an amendment to the **Constitution** requires supporting votes by more than two-thirds of the NPC deputies.

Initiative in framing policies in China belongs to the CCP, not the NPC. On virtually all occasions the NPC follows the CCP. This is why the NPC is usually regarded as a 'rubber stamp' for the CCP. The 1982 **Constitution** provides that NPC deputies 'may not be called to legal account for their speeches or votes at its meetings'. Actually, even in the 1950s there were exceptions to the 'rubber stamp' pattern, one being in 1957 when NPC delegates criticized **Mao Zedong** in relation to the Anti-Rightist Movement. With some inconsistencies, the period of reform since 1978 has seen a general strengthening of the NPC's willingness to resist the CCP leadership. A particularly well-known illustrative case was in 1993 when the First Session of the Eighth NPC asked for over seventy changes to Premier **Li Peng**'s report before finally adopting it. However, even this case does not show the NPC coming anywhere near reversing a policy decision made by the CCP or its leadership.

The NPC should meet annually. When not in session its tasks are undertaken by the NPC Standing Committee, all the members of which the NPC elects. The Eighth NPC of 1993 elected 162 members to its Standing Committee, including 20 **women** and 20 members of the **minority nationalities**. The NPC Standing Committee meets about six times a year, for example, the Seventh NPC Standing Committee meeting thirty-one times over its five-year life from April 1988 to March 1993. Members of the NPC Standing Committee may not hold any post in any of the administrative, judicial or procuratorial organs of the state.

In general the functions of the NPC Standing Committee are similar to those of the NPC itself. However, there are a few which are separate. These include:

- deciding on the appointment and recalling of ambassadors and such plenipotentiary representatives abroad;
- deciding on the ratification and abrogation of treaties and such major agreements with foreign states; and
- instituting titles and ranks for military and diplomatic personnel, as well as instituting state medals and titles of honour.

The NPC Standing Committee is responsible to the NPC and reports to the NPC on its work. Its membership is much smaller than that of the NPC, approximately one in twenty.

The chair of the NPC Standing Committee is among the most senior of state officials. During the period when the position of PRC president did not exist, that is from Liu Shaoqi's dismissal in 1968 until the Fourth **Constitution** of 1982, the NPC Standing Committee chairman acted as head of state. The chairman of the Eighth NPC Standing Committee was **Qiao Shi**.

The day-to-day conduct of NPC affairs is conducted by an even smaller body, the Chair Committee, which consists of the chairman, the vice-chairmen and the secretary-general, with about twenty members. The Eighth NPC Chair Committee had nineteen vice-chairmen, in addition to **Qiao Shi** and the secretary-general.

see also: 2. Government and Institutions; Constitutions; Li Peng; Mao Zedong; minority nationalities policy; Qiao Shi; State Council; women.

Colin Mackerras

New China (Xinhua) News Agency

The state news agency of the PRC. Established in November 1931 as the Red China News Agency (*Hongse Zhonghua tongxun she*), it changed its name to New China News Agency (NCNA) (*Xinhua tongxun she*) in January 1937. It is not to be confused with the China News Agency (*Zhongguo xinwen she*) which provides Chinese-language news services directed toward Chinese-speaking populations outside the PRC.

The agency has offices in all China's provinces, special regions and major cities, which supply domestic news, information and photographs to the head office in **Beijing** (see **media issues and policy**). During certain stages in PRC history, NCNA held a monopoly on the reporting of Chinese political news domestically. Party newspapers (such as the *People's Daily*) were required to carry the official NCNA version when the news involved a government communiqué, statements by CCP leaders, and important domestic news. It was also the major source of foreign news stories for the newspapers attached to the central and provincial committees of the CCP.

NCNA also has offices in many major cities throughout the world. Its overseas branches relay information and news to the central office in **Beijing**. Overseas offices have at various times functioned in diplomatic capacities for the Chinese government, in some cases conducting the normal foreign affairs functions of the Chinese government where formal diplomatic relations had not been established. The NCNA office in **Hong Kong**, for example, functioned for many years on behalf of the Chinese government as more than a news organization.

NCNA produces news and information services for domestic consumption, in the form of news items, formal pronouncements of the CCP and government leaders, and general news. It also collates news and information for publication in its own bulletins which are distributed internally within the Chinese Party and government bureaucracies, and carry different classifications from public to highly restricted. The best known and most widely available of these is the Reference News (*Cankao xiaoxi*) which has been produced since 1931. Apart from news and information supplied by overseas correspondents, Xinhua takes in foreign news services and publications to sift and provide selected articles and summaries for the different levels of restricted internal bulletins for the Chinese leadership.

NCNA produces news services in several foreign languages for foreign consumption, including daily hard copy bulletins in English, French, Arabic, Spanish and Russian. In the 1990s Chinese-language news from NCNA is also carried by some Chinese-language newspapers in countries such as Singapore.

NCNA produces several newspapers and magazines of its own, such as *Fortnightly Chats* (*Banyue Tan*) and *Worldwide Monthly* (*Huanqiu yuebao*), both since 1980. The organization at the head office in **Beijing** includes several departments such as international news, domestic news, news for external services, news photos and sports. There are several other offices and enterprises including the Xinhua Publishing House, China Photograph Service, China Journalism Academy and the China United Advertising Company.

see also: Beijing Municipality; Hong Kong; media issues and policy; *People's Daily*.

Jennifer Grant

new entrepreneurs

The relatively sustained and rapid growth of China's economy during the 1980s and 1990s has created new categories of those who either control or own substantial wealth and thereby have the ability to affect the lives of others. The most publicized of these new economic elites are often originally small-scale **private sector** owner-operators whose businesses have expanded rapidly. However, they also include entrepreneurial financiers and managers in the state and collective sectors; as well as managers and developers of rural and suburban enterprises, and those derived from **local government** activities and 'all-people's' (*quanmin*) enterprises.

The most visible of the new economic elites

are the owner-operators, private entrepreneurs who have developed their own businesses. These owner-operators have been a new departure and a key feature of the reform era, originally, in the early 1980s, regarded by the CCP as rather small-scale entrepreneurs who could be mobilized to meet the demands for flexibility and other demands unmet easily by the planned economy. Thus, the retail sector of the economy rapidly came to be dominated by owner-operators. However, as the state withdrew from direct economic management of enterprises and market reforms were introduced, owner-operators developed larger enterprises in a wider range of activities, notably light **industry**.

The development of rural **township and village enterprises** and **industry** has been only slightly less publicized than the **private sector** within the PRC since 1978. Most of this rural industrial development is actually suburban, located in the rural districts of administratively higher-order cities and urban areas. The boundaries between rural and urban areas were set during the 1950s when in its desire to control urbanization the CCP established different regulatory regimes for **housing**, work and economic management. Suburban villages had always benefited from the availability of both technical inputs to their production and urban markets for their output, and were consequently well placed to take advantage of decollectivization and other aspects of economic reform in the early 1980s.

The economic wealth of these suburban villages is not personal but is wielded collectively on behalf of villages and townships by executives who form an important part of the new economic elite. Though the personal wealth of these new suburban executives is not negligible, their real importance is the economic wealth they control, not least because village enterprises often expand and develop subsidiaries in a largely unregulated way, so that they come to act as conglomerates owned nominally by the village. These new suburban executives, and the new conglomerates they preside over, have for the

most part emerged from the previous collectivized economy. The former agricultural machinery repair workshops have been transformed into light industrial enterprises; village construction departments have moved into property development, and particularly the hotel and hospitality industries; local marketing and supply cooperatives have taken advantage of market reforms and become more specialized as well as economically efficient.

In general, managers of state and **collective sector** enterprises clearly cannot be considered part of the new economic elites, but some have used the opportunity offered by the introduction of market reforms to radically alter their own enterprise structure, or become distinguished formally as 'model managers'. In the state sector, and even in nationally prestigious heavy industrial concerns, some managers have transformed themselves into a form of state **capitalist** by decentralizing their corporations and establishing conglomerates. Managers of 'all-people's' enterprises – owned in principle by other state bodies, economic and otherwise – and those in the **collective sector** have frequently been awarded 'model' status for the achievement of financial independence.

Economic development during the 1980s and 1990s has occurred with a weak and often non-existent financial infrastructure. The need for credit facilities, the provision of ready investment, and the facilitation of both has created considerable space for middlemen and brokers – most obviously in the share-trading houses established in the wake of the fast-growing open exchanges of **Shanghai** and Shenzhen. It has also meant that individuals with relatively liquid funds of their own, or with access to such funds, have been much in demand as potential investors. Both middlemen and investors are an essential part of the new economic environment, and some people have amassed considerable personal wealth.

A final section of the new economic elites have influence rather than access to absolute wealth, though very few could be termed poor. They are the trend-setters: those who constantly appear in the public eye and set the standards, particularly socially, that others follow. Because of their intense concentration on the search for wealth and status the new economic elites are very fashion conscious – in its widest senses beyond just clothes and personal appearance. Though they undoubtedly set the trends for the new middle classes to copy, albeit at a discounted rate, the patterns of conformity for the new economic elites themselves are to be found in the newly emergent 'star culture' created around sports stars, pop music idols, and television personalities; the activities of the '**princelings**'; and at the more local level, the world of the private restaurateur.

see also: capitalists/entrepreneurs; collective sector (non-agricultural); housing; industry; local government/administration; housing; princelings; private sector; Shanghai; township and village enterprises.

David S. G. Goodman

non-governmental organizations

During the 1980s, as the Chinese state moved to free up the economy and to relax direct **Chinese Communist Party** controls over society, it needed mechanisms to bridge the gaps in control that were created. A very large number of associations were established, usually on the government's own initiative, to serve as intermediaries between the state and diverse constituencies and spheres of activity. These range from associations for different sectors of the economy, to **science and technology** associations, religious councils, cultural and social **welfare** groups, and sports associations: the numbers and range keep growing. As of 1993, 1,400 national associations were registered with the central government; 19,600 organizations and branches of organizations were registered with provincial authorities; and more than 160,000 were registered at county level.

These 'non-governmental associations' do not enjoy much autonomy. They must be officially registered, and only one organization is recognized as the representative for each sectoral constituency. Almost all of the associations were established on the initiative of the national government or local authorities, and the operations of all the important ones are subsidized by the state. In addition, their leaders are normally selected by the government and, indeed, are often officials who hold concurrent posts in relevant government agencies. For a number of the associations, moreover, membership is obligatory: thus, a shop owner is required to belong to the government-initiated association for small business people.

In all of these respects, these are 'state corporatist' organizations. Political scientists use the term 'corporatism' to refer to the mechanism whereby a government recognizes one and only one organization as the sole representative of each sector's interests; and 'state corporatism' is the term for a system where the government largely controls these organizations.

In addition to the myriad new Chinese associations that have been registered since 1980, the most important of the 'mass organizations' of Maoist times have survived into the new era. These include the All-China Federation of Trade Unions and the All-China **Women**'s Federation. They are handled today in a state corporatist fashion similar to the new associations.

Under **Mao Zedong**, these 'mass organizations' were intended to serve as 'transmission belts' (or what in China is called the 'mass line'), providing a two-way conduit between the CCP centre and the assigned constituencies: by top-down transmission, mobilization of workers and peasants for increased production on behalf of the nation's collective good; and by bottom-up transmission, articulation of grassroots rights and interests. In reality, however, this notion of a two-way corporatist structure became a charade; directives came down through the structure, but constituent opinion and demands were not allowed to percolate up. During the mid-1950s, for instance, when the peak union federation and some other 'mass organizations' attempted to carry out their ostensible functions by transmitting upward their members' grievances, Mao and the Party leadership promptly slapped them down and dismissed their leaderships. Mao finally lost patience with the sporadic efforts from within the 'mass organizations' to serve as intermediaries, and during the last decade of his rule he dissolved the peak labour union federation altogether. There was to be no 'space' for even the small degree of autonomy implied by state corporatism.

Under **Deng Xiaoping**, the state's grip has been loosened, and many of the associations and 'mass organizations' have indeed been given room to operate as an intermediary between the state and their assigned constituencies. Alongside the freeing up of the Chinese economy, this represents a parallel shift from a CCP command system that dominated directly (for which the word 'totalitarian' was arguably accurate) to one that dominates partly through surrogates (authoritarianism). But at this early stage, what is being witnessed is a gradual devolution of power from the centre that widens the operational space of the 'mass organizations' and of some of the bureaucracies that oversee the associations, rather than the rise of independent associations.

None the less, in some cases the officials who control the associations do lean toward the interests of their constituencies, even occasionally at the expense of the state. This is particularly true where the constituency has a high status or wealth. One such example is the All-China Federation of Industry and Commerce, which counts among its clientele large numbers of the new wealthy private business people.

Strategies have been developed by the officials of such associations to provide their association with a greater degree of independence. The All-China Federation of Industry and Commerce has been engaged, for instance, in establishing local chambers of commerce that come under its umbrella. With the Federation as intermediary, these new chambers become one degree further removed from direct government oversight. Gradually, the associations that are associated with wealth or high professional skills are attaining a measure of autonomy, while many others decidedly are not.

see also: Chinese Communist Party; Deng
    Xiaoping; Mao Zedong; science and
    technology; welfare policy; women.

Jonathan Unger

O

one country, two systems

At once a promise, a slogan and a policy, the phrase originated reputedly with **Deng Xiaoping** himself in the late 1970s as an attempt, quickly rebuffed, to entice **Taiwan** toward reunification. With negotiations over **Hong Kong**'s return formally launched in 1982, the phrase became attached to that process and now embodies in the minds of the **Hong Kong** and mainland public various explicit and implicit aspects governing their relationship until 2047.

First, with both **Taiwan** and **Hong Kong** the phrase was conceived as limited in time: when China drew close to economic parity with **Taiwan** then reunification would proceed smoothly. With **Hong Kong**, a high degree of autonomy and no change in the economic and social system for fifty years after 1997 was promised, then normalized centre–province relations presumably go into effect. Second, the phrase embodied an assumed common nationalism (one country) with two economic and social systems temporarily in place, a developed capitalist society in **Hong Kong** and a developing socialist market society on the mainland. The national issues of defence and foreign affairs rested with the central government; local and economic affairs were the concern of the 'special administrative region' (SAR). Third, politically, **Hong Kong** sends a delegation to the **National People's Congress** and the status of its chief executive was elevated to state leader, an official term in China usually applicable only to people of vice-premier or Politburo member rank and above, which means he officially receives the highest deference in the rank-conscious Chinese hierarchy, above that of provincial leaders. But, while **Hong Kong** might participate in national politics, the phrase as policy explicitly forbade the mainland political model of the entrenched supremacy of the CCP and the dictatorship of the proletariat to apply to **Hong Kong**. At the local level, **Hong Kong** retained a common law **legal system** and a pluralist political system with openly competing political parties, and was promised that at some time during the fifty years, after the second chief executive and Legislative Council were selected, it might choose to go on to a directly elected chief executive and a fully sixty-seat directly elected Legislative Council (up from the thirty directly elected in 2003). **Hong Kong** politicians were forbidden to 'meddle' in mainland affairs, and vice versa, while international economic ties are protected, overseas political ties and influences are curtailed.

The implementing details of the phrase are spelled out in the **Hong Kong** SAR Basic Law promulgated in April 1990.

see also: 9. Taiwan and the Overseas Chinese; Deng Xiaoping; Hong Kong; legal system; National People's Congress; Taiwan policy.

Michael DeGolyer

Overseas Chinese policy

In a broad historical perspective, Beijing's Overseas Chinese policy has been realistic and flexible: realistic because Beijing is not constrained by history; and flexible because it is able to adapt to changes in overseas conditions and China's national interests. The CCP did not come to power in 1949 with any substantial Overseas Chinese support, and, unlike the Nationalist Party (see **9. Taiwan and the Overseas Chinese**), it did not have to feel indebted to Overseas Chinese.

In its early years of rule, being preoccupied with more pressing matters, the CCP gave no high priority to Overseas Chinese issues. Three strands are discernible in the policies the CCP formulated.

- It vaguely inherited traditional obligations of protecting Overseas Chinese.
- It encouraged Overseas Chinese students to study in the PRC.

- Aware of the wealth of Overseas Chinese and the potential to benefit China's economic reconstruction, Beijing appealed to the nationalism of Overseas Chinese for financial support. Famous Overseas Chinese leader from Singapore, Tan Kah Kee, was partly instrumental in the implementation of Beijing's early policy. His business contacts and immense influence in Southeast Asia yielded the new PRC substantial investments.

From 1954, it was clear that Beijing would subordinate its Overseas Chinese policy to foreign policy. This meant integrating Overseas Chinese policy with the 'peaceful coexistence' strategy which followed the **Korean War**. Beijing aimed to resolve Overseas Chinese problems with Southeast Asian countries in order to gain greater diplomatic recognition. Contrary to a theory prevailing at the time that Overseas Chinese were a 'fifth column' for Beijing's subversive activities, Beijing regarded the Overseas Chinese as an impediment to its attempt to develop closer relations with Southeast Asia. To demonstrate its sincerity, Beijing moved swiftly to forge closer relations with Indonesia and on 22 April 1955 the Sino-Indonesian Treaty Concerning the Question of Dual Nationality was signed in Bandung. However, no other Southeast Asian nation followed suit, nor did China win diplomatic recognition from the pro-**Taiwan** countries of the region.

In 1957 Beijing adopted a new policy of disengagement. It slowly disengaged itself from the traditional obligations of protecting Overseas Chinese and providing **education** for the young. This new policy was the product of social and political change both abroad and at home. The continuous process of local orientation saw more and more Overseas Chinese taking up citizenship in Southeast Asian countries and integrating themselves into local communities, rendering diplomatic protection unnecessary. Domestically, the radicalization of Chinese politics in the late 1950s cast Overseas Chinese in a negative ideological light, being a source of capitalist influence. At the same time, the decline of

Overseas Chinese remittances to China no longer justified any ideological concessions given to them. Beijing also withdrew its welcome to young Overseas Chinese to study in the PRC.

By the time the **Cultural Revolution** erupted, China had almost totally withdrawn from traditional obligations towards Overseas Chinese. Attention focused on how to reform and re-educate domestic Overseas Chinese, who were suspected of spreading the pernicious values of capitalism and of being actual or potential running dogs of foreign imperialism. Victimization of the domestic Overseas Chinese became commonplace, with many verbally abused, physically beaten and punished for their overseas connections. Along with intellectuals and other reactionaries, they were condemned as the 'stinking ninth category'.

China's Overseas Chinese policy took a sharp turn after the downfall of the **gang of four** and the rise of the reformers led by **Deng Xiaoping**. The new focus on economic modernization from 1978 found Overseas Chinese, both domestic and external, useful for China's cause. Overseas Chinese money and expertise would be helpful in China's quest for economic power. As the market economy took command, the negative image of Overseas Chinese was transformed, and domestic Overseas Chinese were encouraged to resume their overseas connections, while Overseas Chinese were welcome to visit China. Concessions were given to domestic Overseas Chinese families, with properties confiscated during the **Cultural Revolution** returned, and past wrongs condemned and victims compensated. The result was increased investment from Overseas Chinese communities, especially in **Hong Kong** and Southeast Asia.

The **June 4 Incident** (1989) was unexpectedly positive for Beijing's relations with the Overseas Chinese. As foreigners held back their investments, Beijing succeeded in inducing more Overseas Chinese capital to fill the gap left by the partial Western and Japanese withdrawal. The huge Overseas Chinese investments in Guangdong, Fujian and other coastal provinces are among the main causes for the rapid economic transformation of these regions.

see also: 8. China, the Region and the World; 9. Taiwan and the Overseas Chinese; Cultural Revolution; Deng Xiaoping; education policy and system; gang of four; Hong Kong; June 4 Incident; Korean War; Taiwan policy.

Yen Ching-hwang

P

People's Bank of China

China's most important financial institution, coming under the **State Council**. The People's Bank of China (PBC) began a new life as China's fledgling central bank on 1 July 1995 when the new Commercial Banking Law took effect. Designed to function as the focal institution of a commercially oriented banking system in a market economy context, its ability to fulfil that destiny will be constrained by the overall pace of economic reform. As state-owned enterprises are more completely marketized, the practices, as well as the name, of the old planned economy monobank will gradually be phased out (see **financial policy**).

The old PBC operated under **planning** where money was passive. The plan derived from a few in-kind decisions made by politicians that technicians reworked into lists of final and intermediate targets that they sent to production units as administrative orders. Money wages and prices played only secondary roles for both households and productive enterprises: to ensure they carried out the plan. They also provided accounting checks on enterprise plan fulfilment and were used to influence detailed product- and input-mix decisions. Households paid in paper currency, enterprises by monobank account entries. Monobanks like the old PBC could have kept prices stable by creating only enough cash and credit to finance planned transactions at planned prices, but even under normal circumstances – let alone when war, disaster or major planning errors occurred – they could not always prevent politicians from resorting to inflation. State enterprises' soft budget constraints came largely from having unlimited access to loans, so long as they met plan targets.

Ironically, China's reforms owe much of their success to **Chen Yun**, a committed central planner hostile to marketization. Unlike his Soviet colleagues, Chen resisted pressures to inflate the economy. The reformists therefore inherited an economy that was relatively free of severe inflationary pressures. The benefits of microeconomic reform flowed on to the households, creating a virtuous economic-political circle. As market activity accelerated, the inability of the old monetary arrangements to satisfy normal monetary needs became increasingly burdensome, especially to the more dynamic **private** and **collective sectors**. Secure payment facilities were lacking; capital was unavailable; savings outlets were lacking; insurance and risk spreading facilities were lacking; credit rating was lacking. But reform also weakened the central government's authority and its revenue base, allowing local governments to coerce resident local branches to extend loans to favoured local firms in defiance of central discipline. Inter-enterprise credits, forbidden under **planning**, spread among state enterprises. These debts became uncollectable when credit was tightened (the so-called triangular debt problem). After 1979 China experienced four inflation periods: in 1980, 1985, 1988–9 and 1993–4, each more serious than the previous one.

The outcome of these experiences was a wave of innovations in the **financial** field that sought to end financial repression by offering a wider range of financial facilities and to increase macroeconomic stability by preventing unplanned expansions of money supply. These reforms attempt to commercialize the various state banks by making them profit-oriented and competitive. To enhance competition and upgrade technology, foreign banks were allowed first to set up offices and then branches, and their scope of activities continuously widened, some even trading in *renminbi*, people's currency. From 1980 the national government resumed selling bonds, but whereas at first they were untransferable and sold using administrative coercion, they were later traded freely on well organized competitive secondary markets at fully flex-ible prices. Stockmarkets opened in late 1989 in **Shanghai** and Shenzhen, and trading facil-ities became ubiquitous across China. Similar innovations took place in the areas of insur-ance, negotiable instruments, inter-bank transactions, foreign exchange trading, annu-ities, mortgages, and so on. Even amenities like credit cards and automatic teller machines, unthinkable in the mid-1980s, became common in the 1990s. In just a decade a diversified financial sector capable of ser-vicing the financial needs of its rapidly developing market sector evolved.

Nevertheless, as of 1997, the influence of **planning** still lingers. State-owned enter-prises, overwhelmingly the largest employer, are increasingly unable to compete with col-lectively and privately owned firms. Over-staffed, overburdened with **welfare** responsi-bilities, and often maladministered, they are in decline, with increasing numbers of them technically insolvent. State banks must never-theless extend them open-ended policy loans, since the alternative, bankruptcy, would undermine social order by making their tens of millions of redundant employees un-employed. In lieu of effective social security arrangements, many enterprises are dis-guised dole offices. Making matters worse, state policy dictates that this least efficient sector absorbs ever more of total investment funds. For banks the result is negative inter-est spreads: depositors earn higher interest rates than borrowers pay! The PBC cannot function as a true central bank so long as the activities of the commercial banks it manages must serve to prop up the state-owned sector. Meanwhile it has acquired a reputation as one of the more creative and responsible pol-icy centres in China.

see also: 5. Politics and the Economy: Policy Patterns and Issues; Chen Yun; collective sector; financial policy; planning, eco-nomic; private sector; Shanghai; State Council; welfare policy.

Paul Ivory

People's Daily

The official newspaper of the **CCP Central**
Committee, the *People's Daily* (*Renmin ribao*) is produced in both domestic and overseas editions, the latter for those who live outside China and read Chinese. The domestic edi-tion, distributed mainly within China, uses simplified Chinese characters. However, the overseas edition, which began production in 1985, uses full-form characters, is arranged in a different format, and widely available through printing presses in many places out-side China. It is directed toward **Overseas Chinese** and Chinese citizens working abroad. The *People's Daily* has no relation to the English-language *China Daily*, which is run and produced by the China Daily Pub-lishing House.

For many years of its history the *People's Daily* domestic edition has had a high circula-tion assisted by multiple readers accessing individual copies. Containing news of the CCP's and Chinese government's policies and plans, it has been necessary reading for decision makers and all who want to know what the official line and current views are (see **New China News Agency**). Its editorials are produced and interpreted as the official government view on general and particular issues. At various times, the *People's Daily* has been caught up in, and reflected, political power struggles and political movements (see **media issues and policy**).

Major domestic news, editorials and gov-ernment communiqués are carried on the front page with other news and material inside. International and other foreign news, along with related commentaries, are usually printed on inside pages.

The reporting and editorial staff are organ-ized into several major departments includ-ing theory, commentary, internal politics, science and education, literature and the arts, economics, international, and mass work. The mass work department handles letters and visits from the public. These letters and reports are followed up internally, with collations and summaries sent to depart-ments or people in authority, who have the power to oversee problem solutions. Some of the letters are eventually published in the newspaper as part of its publicity of issues.

Publication of letters occurs when it is deemed the right time politically to deal with the issue publicly.

The newspapers of the provincial and major city CCP committees are similar in organization to the *People's Daily*, and include departments for production of public news reports. They also have mass work departments which function as an extra source of information for the CCP committees and to voice opinions and complaints from the people.

The *People's Daily* also produces *Journalism Front* (*Xinwen zhanxian*), a monthly journal for journalists and editors on professional issues, and publishes the *Market Newspaper* (*Shichang bao*). It also runs the People's Daily Publishing House which publishes various books and other non-newspaper publications.

see also: Chinese Communist Party Central Committee and Politburo; media issues and policy; New China News Agency; Overseas Chinese policy.

Jennifer Grant

People's Liberation Army

The name of China's official armed forces. The People's Liberation Army (PLA), which includes army, navy, air force and strategic missile force, dates its origins from the Nanchang Uprising of 1 August 1927. From its largely guerrilla origins, it developed during the Anti-Japanese War and two civil wars with the Nationalist forces to conquer mainland China and establish and consolidate the PRC under CCP control.

The PLA has always been more than simply a military force. From the beginning, it has been inextricably intermeshed with the CCP. There is a Party hierarchy within the PLA, with corresponding political commissars at each level of the military hierarchy. At the same time, senior military figures hold important positions within the Party organization. Similarly, military personnel hold significant government administrative positions. Indeed, China was under military rule (1949–54) before a civilian administrative apparatus could be established. Likewise,

when Party and government organizations virtually collapsed during the **Cultural Revolution**, it was the PLA which stepped in to restore order and maintain administrative control.

Thus the PLA plays a role in Chinese politics, not only defending the state and supporting CCP rule, but also in determining which individuals hold Party and state leadership positions. While **Mao Zedong**'s dictum that the Party controls the gun, but the gun must not control the Party is adhered to through control of the army by the **Central Military Commission** of the CCP, in reality senior Party figures need the acquiescence (if not support) of their PLA counterparts.

The PLA emerged as a people's army as a result of the doctrine of people's war: it was a lightly armed mass army with close links to the people. This meant that:

- it was to be as self-sufficient as possible so as not to be a drain on the people;
- when not fighting it was expected to help the people in their economic tasks;
- it depended on volunteers from the people for its recruits;
- it relied on logistic support from the people; and
- the people (as militia) would act as auxiliaries in time of war.

The people's war doctrine was essentially defensive, declaring that an occupying army would be forced to extend its supply lines and spread its forces until it was eventually drowned in a sea of people's war. In this way, the PLA could defeat a militarily superior enemy force by trading space for time; employing guerrilla tactics to defeat the enemy piecemeal; and ultimately overwhelming it in conventional battles.

Since 1949, the PLA has experienced tension between maintaining this people's army orientation and moving towards a more conventional professional army. The professional army orientation entailed less emphasis on political education within the PLA and a reduction in its non-military tasks in favour of more stress on training, better weapons and a strategic doctrine which would enable enemies to be repelled in conventional pitched battles. The experiences of the PLA (as 'volunteers') in the **Korean War** revealed the inappropriateness of people's war in that conflict, and saw it move towards professionalism (modelled on the Soviet Red Army) with military aid from the **Soviet Union**. This was symbolized by the introduction of ranks into the PLA in 1955.

After **Lin Biao** replaced Peng Dehuai as minister of Defence in 1959, the PLA moved back towards its people's army orientation. The famous little red book of quotations from **Mao Zedong**, which was brandished throughout the **Cultural Revolution**, was originally published for use within the PLA as part of its drive to restore its level of politicization. By 1964 Mao was putting forward the PLA as a model for emulation in its commitment to socialism. Ranks were abolished in 1965.

After Mao's death, there was a shift back towards a more professional army. Although modernizing the army, or 'national defence', was given the least priority among the **Four Modernizations** (as senior leaders reached the conclusion that China did not face any major strategic threats) there was a clear recognition (especially in the wake of the **Sino-Vietnamese War** of 1979) that the PLA needed more training and modern weapons. This was initially encapsulated in the strategic doctrine of people's war under modern conditions. To some extent this formula can be seen as a compromise – continuing to pay lip-service to the people's war tradition and recognizing that the modernization necessary for its abandonment could not be achieved in the short term, while ultimately pressing for that modernization.

Throughout the 1980s, official budget allocations to the PLA were successively cut, but modernization was pursued within these financial constraints. That is, while funds for new weapons purchases, and even for the daily needs of the troops, were limited, more than 1 million officers and men were demobilized (1985–6) as older commanders were encouraged to retire; regional commands were reduced from eleven to seven; construction and railway units were civilian-

ized; large numbers of soldiers were transferred to the People's Armed Police (see **police force**); higher education standards introduced; and its thirty-six armies were merged into twenty-four combined army corps. The emphasis on professionalism was reflected in a lessening of political education and more attention to training (particularly combined arms exercises), and was symbolized by the reintroduction of ranks in the Military Service Law of 1984.

This divorcing of the PLA from its political role was dramatically reversed in 1989 when martial law was declared and the PLA was called upon to suppress the democracy movement (see **June 4 Incident**). In the wake of this event (and the reluctance of some units to act decisively), political indoctrination and support for the CCP was once more stressed. This, however, has not deflected the modernization process which has continued apace during the 1990s. The lessons of the Gulf War (1991) have seen a shift in the PLA's strategic doctrine to a goal of 'modern (limited) warfare under high-technology conditions'. Military budgets have been increased; further reductions in troop numbers have taken place; rapid response units have been formed and more emphasis has been placed on upgrading weaponry.

By the mid-1990s the PLA ground forces had been reduced to 2.2 million but there were still only a limited number of rapid response units (nine divisions); airborne divisions (three); armoured divisions (eleven) and fully mechanized divisions (two). While the PLA army has some modern units and is a significant regional force, it has been characterized as 'an army with short arms and little legs' because of its limited projection capabilities.

Similarly, although the PLA navy is seeking a 'blue water' capacity, it is unlikely to achieve this until the early part of next century. It has 260,000 naval personnel, 18 destroyers, 37 frigates and 49 submarines, but much of its fleet is obsolete. The air force is also large with a personnel of 470,000, some 470 bombers and over 4,500 fighters. Again, however, the overwhelming majority of its planes are obsolete – no match even for its regional neighbours. Despite purchases (especially from Russia), it is unlikely that the PLA air force will be thoroughly modernized before 2010. At the Fifteenth Party Congress (September 1997) CCP General Secretary **Jiang Zemin** stated that, in addition to the army reduction by one million men in the 1980s, China would further reduce its armed forces by another 500,000 in the next three years.

While the PLA may be greatly inferior to United States forces, it is a growing regional power with a substantial nuclear arsenal. Now that it is totally committed to modernization along professional lines, its capabilities will increase as the Chinese economy continues to grow. Meanwhile, its economic activities have become substantial and its political influence is pivotal.

see also: 2. Government and Institutions; Central Military Commission; Cultural Revolution; Four Modernizations; Jiang Zemin; June 4 Incident; Korean War; Lin Biao; Mao Zedong; police force; Sino-Vietnamese War; Soviet Union, relations with.

Dennis Woodward

planning, economic

The economic planning system adopted during the 1950s was a direct copy of the **Soviet** model. It was based on:

- state monopoly of ownership and distribution;
- the achievement of rapid industrialization through a focus on heavy **industry**;
- the realization of greater regional balance in the distribution of **industry**; and
- the rejection of the market as a mechanism for resource allocation.

Planning implied that all human, material and financial resources should be administratively allocated in order to achieve state-determined targets. At its heart was a process of material balances whereby available resources were calculated and distributed across different activities in order to reach the planned relationships between production, circulation, distribution and consumption, with targets set for all sectors at the end of the planning period.

In practice, plans in China consist of long-term programme documents with a ten- to twelve-year time-frame, five-year plans and annual plans. The shorter the planning period, the more precise its content. The Five-Year Plan is the most important in setting general targets, and annual plans are drawn up to work towards its goals. The Five-Year Plan sets the proportional relationships for the economy, the growth rates, the production targets for **industry** and **agriculture**, the rates of growth in living standards, the scale of investment, technological development goals and so forth. The most detailed of these plans was the First Five-Year Plan (1953–7), which included national, regional and sectoral plans. After 1957, however, the planning system was never able to work as an effective national programme. While the economy was dominated by state controls, it was characterized by much local and short-term planning. The Second Five-Year Plan (1958–62) was interrupted by the **Great Leap Forward** and was never developed beyond a general schema. The Third, Fourth and Fifth Five-Year Plans (1966–70, 1971–5, 1976–80) covered the **Cultural Revolution** period and were formulated only as general programme documents with tentative plan structures. The political and administrative disruptions of the period meant that national, regional and sectoral plans could not be combined into a coherent structure. In addition, political considerations also placed emphasis on the dispersal of **industry** to more remote internal locations under a 'third front' strategy. As a result, annual plans became very important. The Sixth, Seventh, Eighth and Ninth Five-Year Plans (1981–5, 1986–90, 1991–5 and 1996–2000) were all developed during the reform period. Improvements in the administrative system made it possible to define national targets more clearly and implement them better. The administrative decentralization and reductions in the scope of planning, however, resulted in a decline in the proportion of the economy controlled by mandatory planning, an increase in the role of guidance planning and indicative targets, and a rise in the proportion of the economy outside the plan.

Nevertheless, by determining the allocation of state resources, the development of infrastructure and the targets for proportional relationships, the planning system still plays an important role in the management of the economy.

The main characteristics of the planning system as embodied in the First Five-Year Plan model involved target planning for all key activities, a centralized network of hierarchical controls and the subordination of production enterprises to the administrative system. Initially it was also accompanied by large-scale aid from the **Soviet Union** and the adoption of Soviet administrative, scientific and organizational models. Its strategy of heavy industrialization and import substitution also sought to establish a modern industrial base and infrastructure to ensure China's national independence. The implementation of the plan was managed by the State Planning Commission under the **State Council** (see **state economic structures**).

This Commission consulted with the various ministries and regional governments to develop a preliminary comprehensive balance table and indicative control figures. These were then sent downwards through the administrative hierarchies for detailed consideration and the fixing of more precise targets. The results were fed back through the system and, after reconciliation across departments and regions, the plan was formalized and proclaimed.

In a situation of scarcity, the plan was successful in mobilizing resources for particular goals. During the 1950s a substantial industrial system was developed, centring on 156 major large-scale plants built with Soviet aid. Structural change, with a relative decline in **agriculture** and an expansion of **industry** was promoted, and high rates of growth were achieved. There was also a relocation of industry away from the coast and considerable gains in social services and **welfare**. Nevertheless, as the economy grew and became more complex, the requirements for

planning became more demanding. The lack of a reliable statistical base made planning difficult, leading to inevitable bottlenecks and misallocations. By the late 1950s, therefore, **Mao Zedong** and others were becoming critical of many aspects of the plan system. He raised questions about its hierarchical rigidity, its reliance on capital-intensive growth, its tendency to stifle local initiative and its relative neglect of **agriculture**. The **Great Leap Forward** and the **Cultural Revolution** thus incorporated a strong attack on the **Soviet** model for creating a technocratic society and failing to mobilize China's resources. Nevertheless, instead of proposing a shift towards reliance on enterprise autonomy and market integration as a way of allocating resources, Mao promoted a form of regional decentralization within the planned economy, resulting in a hybrid plan system with a mixture of centralized and decentralized elements.

By the late 1970s, the weaknesses of this system had become obvious, paralleling the failings found in other centrally planned economies. They included:

- enterprise inefficiency because of 'soft budget constraints', meaning that they could never be penalized for waste of resources;
- the production of large amounts of poor quality, unwanted goods;
- low technical standards;
- an 'investment hunger', meaning that growth depended on continual increases in new inputs rather than improvements in the efficiency of current input use; and
- a distorted pricing system which protected **industry** and did not reflect relative scarcity.

The reforms after 1978 set out to address both the problems of the planning system and those created by Mao's experiments. After the mid-1980s, they resulted in a progressive decline in the scope and power of the plan and increasing reliance on the market to set prices and to guide resource allocation. Economic decentralization also gave considerable economic authority to both local governments and production enterprises, further limiting the powers of the centre to plan the economy as a whole. Because of the huge size of the state-owned sector and the importance of state investment in the economy, however, central and local planning continued to play an important role in shaping the overall pattern of economic growth.

see also: 5. Politics and the Economy: Policy Patterns and Issues; agriculture; Cultural Revolution; Great Leap Forward; industry; Mao Zedong; Soviet Union, relations with; State Council; state economic structures; welfare policy.

Andrew Watson

police force

In October 1949, the **Chinese People's Political Consultative Conference** passed a law authorizing the formation of a Ministry of Public Security. On 19 October, Luo Ruiqing was appointed minister of Public Security, with the ministry formally established on 1 November. Organizationally, it boasted a nationwide unified structure and its main political role was to defend the state and the CCP.

However, the Chinese police force was significantly different from those in other socialist states. **Mao Zedong** ensured that the influence of **Soviet** advisers within the force was minimal. Much to the irritation of these advisers, the Chinese ended up producing a unique organization that both structurally and 'technically' bore the hallmarks of its Maoist origin. Unlike the **Soviet** police force, the CCP was formally allotted a central role in the organization of the police, reflected in the force's leadership structure. Right down to the county offices, each leadership level within the force has a Party committee overseeing its work. Moreover, the Chinese police adopted a mass-line approach to policing.

Mass-line policing resulted in close ties between the professional police force and such organizations as the neighbourhood committee, the Communist **Youth** League and the All-China **Women**'s Federation. These became auxiliary organizations on which the police could call. They ensured that the force could undertake its huge range

of duties efficiently, despite being so small (only 6.5 officers per 10,000 people in 1993). These duties include everything from fighting fires to registering every resident in the PRC (see **household registration**). In the past, the police even ran the prisons and centres for labour re-education. Since 1983, they are no longer responsible for the **prison system** (the only prison to remain within the purview of the ministry is the infamous Qingcheng prison for political prisoners in **Beijing**), nor are they any longer centrally concerned with counter-espionage work. These areas of work now fall under the jurisdiction of the Ministries of Justice and State Security respectively. While the Public Security Ministry lost those responsibilities in 1983, it picked up the lightly armed military force known as the People's Armed Police, which had been attached to the **People's Liberation Army** (PLA).

Policing in the PRC is closely related to politics. Indeed, the police ran the first large-scale political campaign after 1949, the 1950–3 campaign to suppress counter-revolutionaries, which became the model of virtually all future policing and political campaigns. The only time the police have not been in charge of organizing and running the CCP's campaigns was when the ministry itself became a key victim. In 1967, the then minister of Public Security, Xie Fuzhi (who replaced Luo Ruiqing as minister in 1959) called for 'the worn out' Public Security Ministry to be 'smashed'. Of the thousands who worked there at that time, only forty remained at the end of the purges. In effect, the PLA took over the ministry while all police stations fell under PLA administration. It was not until 1972 that some semblance of order returned, with the purged police cadres gradually rehabilitated and allowed to resume their duties at the ministry.

The fall of the **gang of four** heralded a new era for the Chinese police, a new concern for professionalization becoming one of the hallmarks of the force. There emerged a new emphasis on training, receptivity to foreign methods and concern for forensic detail. At the same time, however, reform also unleashed forces that ended up robbing the police of key conditions upon which much of their earlier strategies were built. Central to this was the declining importance of the **household register** which had been pivotal in ensuring a stable and static population for much of the post-revolution period, and the demise of the neighbourhood security committees.

At the same time the police force faced what they described as a 'tidal wave' of crime. New and increased levels of criminal activity, coupled with less effective policing strategies, resulted in a new target-based form of policing. The police might claim from the early 1980s onwards that they were investing in a new comprehensive management of public security, but in effect they were experimenting with a strategy targeting key types of crime in key places. As a result, professionalization has been subordinate to the old campaign style of policing. The 'severe strike' campaign of 1983 was the main example, but there were similar campaigns against immorality in 1989 (called the campaign against the 'six evils'), and the second 'severe strike' against street crime in 1995–6.

see also: Beijing Municipality; Chinese People's Political Consultative Conference; gang of four; household registration; Mao Zedong; People's Liberation Army; prison system; Soviet Union, relations with; women; youth policy and organizations.

Michael Dutton

Politburo

See **Chinese Communist Party Central Committee and Politburo**.

population policy

China is committed to reducing the growth rate of its population, and in the long term the size of the population itself. It is already the most populous country in the world and its leaders believe that it cannot modernize effectively unless it controls population growth. One of its most widely publicized slogans on the subject is that for each couple to give birth to one child only is a basic policy of the Chinese state.

In the 1950s, **Mao Zedong**'s government advocated rapid population growth, believing that this would make China a powerful and prosperous country and that socialism could solve any resultant ills. In 1957, Mao had Beijing (Peking) University demographer Ma Yinchu heavily criticized for adopting a neo-Malthusian position which claimed that population explosion would bring disaster.

During the **Cultural Revolution**, China's official position was that it was imperialism which spread world poverty, not excessive population growth. At the same time, its government did take measures to reduce growth rates. In 1969 it set up the Birth Planning Leading Group. Fertility rates showed a dramatic fall, being 37.88 and 18.25 per thousand in 1965 and 1978 respectively, the decline being greatest in the rural areas (from 39.53 to 18.91 per thousand in the same two years).

In 1980 the **National People's Congress** formally approved the target of one child per couple for the most populous Han people. Premier **Zhao Ziyang** stated: 'We must take effective measures and encourage late marriage, advocate one child for each couple, strictly control second births and resolutely prevent additional births'. He also denounced the 'criminal activities of female infanticide and maltreatment of the mothers' which had come back again or increased in the Chinese countryside. The peasants continued to demand a son, and in some cases were prepared to kill the first child if a girl, in order to try again for a son. The framers of the 1980 **Marriage Law** had felt it necessary to add a specific ban on infanticide to the 1950 Law. From 1984 the Chinese government began allowing more exceptions to the birth control policy, especially in the countryside, a major reason being to reduce female infanticide.

Just after the announcement of the 1990 census results, the government signalled its intention to tighten policy. On 12 May 1991, the **State Council** and CCP Central

Committee issued a joint 'decision on strengthening family planning work and strictly controlling population growth'.

In October 1995, a variant of the same population policy, having been found successful in Jilin and **Sichuan** Provinces from the early 1990s, was introduced nationwide. In announcing the new policy, called 'three combinations', Minister of the State Family Planning Commission and State Councillor Peng Peiyun said that rural households which adhered strictly to the programme would be given priority in receiving government loans. The essence of the 'three combinations' (combining the family planning programme in rural areas with developing the local economy, improving farmers' living standards and helping them become happier) was to curb population growth in the countryside by making it economically worthwhile for peasant families to have one child only.

The one-child-per-couple has been implemented more flexibly among the **minority nationalities**. Policy varies from one to another among these fifty-five groups, but in general the nearer they are to sensitive borders, and the more sparsely populated the areas where they live, the more flexible policy has been. However, just as in the rest of China, policy has tended to tighten in the 1990s.

The PRC has held four national censuses, in 1953, 1964, 1982 and 1990, all referring to midnight between 30 June and 1 July. The table shows some details from the censuses. The sex ratio is the number of males for every hundred females, while the dependency ratio is the proportion between those of working age and those either below or above it, defining working age as between 15 and 60 for men and 55 for **women**.

A sample survey taken on 1 October 1995

found that the sex ratio of China's population in the zero age group was 116.57. According to the 1993 Annual Population Change Survey, the sex ratio of the population in the zero age group in 1993 was 115.11, being 105.08 in the municipalities or most urbanized areas, and 117.10 in the townships (*zhen*), or most rural regions. The figures for the municipalities are approximately normal, but the overall and township figures suggest fairly widespread underreporting of female births, selective abortion of female foetuses, neglect or abandonment of baby girls and even female infanticide in rural regions.

At a news conference given when the results of the 1990 census were announced, President Zhang Sai of the State Statistical Bureau commented that without the family planning programme there would have been an additional 200 million babies born over the decade preceding the middle of 1990. The natural growth rate of China's population reportedly fell every year from a high point in 1987 (16.61 per thousand) to 1995, when it stood at only 10.55 per thousand. On the other hand, when the policy was first introduced the target was to keep the population within 1.2 billion by the year 2000, but in fact that figure was reached early in 1995. In late September 1995, in which he outlined China's long-term economic targets, Premier Li Peng stated it as an important prerequisite for meeting the targets that the population be kept within 1.3 billion in the year 2000 and within 1.4 billion in 2010.

The policy has been only partially successful, but has nevertheless made a substantial difference to population growth. There is a strong differential between the cities and the countryside, with success being much greater in the former. At the same time, the policy has implied quite a few very serious social problems, but other, even more serious, problems

Year of census	Total	Sex ratio	Dependency ratio
1953	582,603,417	107.57	51.46
1964	694,581,759	105.46	49.40
1982	1,008,175,288	106.3	54.87
1990	1,133,682,501	106.6	60.06

could well emerge without a strong family planning policy.

see also: 6. Peoples of China; Cultural Revolution; Mao Zedong; Marriage Laws; minority nationalities policy; National People's Congress; Sichuan; State Council; women; Zhao Ziyang.

Colin Mackerras

princelings

Term for the offspring of leading state officials. That such people may form a privileged elite based solely on the power and authority exerted by their parents is nothing new in Chinese history, nor are such social formations unique to that country. However, the term princelings (*taizi*) did not emerge until the 1980s. It refers principally to the children and close relatives of senior, central Party and state cadres, especially those who were purged during the **Cultural Revolution** and returned to public prominence in the late 1970s and early 1980s. These veterans worked assiduously to ensure that their reputations were vindicated, and that they were rewarded for their tribulations during the **Cultural Revolution** with senior positions commensurate with their experience and standing within the ruling group. However, their age and, in many cases, poor health militated against their holding their posts for long. Hence, they resorted to a measure time honoured among ruling cliques: using their influence to secure positions of power for their children.

In a society such as China's where the rule of men often substitutes for the rule of law, where influence and connections (*guanxi*) in many instances outweigh the importance of ability and educational qualifications, and where personal relations are the lubricant of political and economic life, it is hardly surprising that family status is a major determinant of an individual's social standing. During the early stages of the **Cultural Revolution** when Red Guard groups were being formed, class background was a key factor determining which faction individuals were likely to join, and the 'children of high-ranking cadres' (*gaogan zidi*) had their own

organization which strictly vetted its members. But during the Maoist period there were periodic and unpredictable campaigns to temper such young people through stints of manual labour on farms and in factories. This was supposed to remind them that the revolution had been fought to liberate the workers and peasants of China, not to create a new red bureaucratic elite. The careers and sacrifices of the two sons of **Mao Zedong** (one of whom died in the **Korean War** while the other worked as a translator) are often contrasted, in private at least, to the wealth and luxury enjoyed by the children of his successors.

No such challenges have faced the elite of post-Mao China. Many of the princelings have undoubted ability and would make their way to the upper echelons of the political-economic-military elite without the assistance of their family connections. However, a great number among them have no special talents, but have been able to use their lineage to obtain power, wealth and influence. The play *If I Were Real* (*Ruguo wo shi zhende*) by Sha Yexin and others (1979) exposed this form of corruption: it concerns a young man who masquerades as the son of a general and finds all doors open to him as if by magic.

With the marketization and internationalization of the Chinese economy the princelings have extended the scope of their operations to **Hong Kong** and overseas. Rumours abound of the amount of the wealth that they and the companies which they operate or advise have invested in property and other portfolios, or have put away in banks and other financial institutions. The lack of transparency in such transactions makes verification of such claims virtually impossible.

From time to time the CCP criticizes certain individuals among the princelings for their dubious activities, and some of the more outrageous abuses are investigated. However, effective action to curb the excesses of this pampered elite becomes virtually impossible when the very people who are carrying out the investigations dare not tread on toes whose owners may have been reared by very powerful and important people. In his efforts to bring to book members of the princelings for their crimes, **Hu Yaobang** offended many senior cadres.

The princelings of the second generation of CCP leaders are today in their fifties and sixties and hold senior positions in the Party-state bureaucracy at the central and provincial levels. They include such well-known figures as the relatives of **Deng Xiaoping**, **Bo Yibo**, Peng Zhen and **Chen Yun**. If they can be said to share a common set of beliefs or a value system the princelings have been seen as advocates and supporters of the 'new authoritarianism' which sees no alternative to the present political system. As such, the fate of the princelings is inextricably tied to that of the CCP.

see also: Bo Yibo; Chen Yun; Cultural Revolution; Deng Xiaoping; Hong Kong; Hu Yaobang; Korean War; Mao Zedong.

Keith Forster

prison system

The Chinese prison system came into being in December 1994. Before that, the penal camps, teams and prisons of China were known collectively as 'reform through labour units'. Despite the name change, this idea of reforming criminals through labour, neither new nor unique to China but with some purchase in certain readings of Marx, still constitutes the key ideological plank of the Chinese prison system.

In the history of Chinese communist penology, the idea of prisons as sites of transformation first appeared in February 1932 when Liang Butai recommended to the Jiangxi Soviet government that they establish institutes of labour persuasion. It was only after 1949 that the name of these institutions was changed, with a fully unified, large-scale and national penal system coming into existence at the Third National Public Security Conference in May 1951. Yet the large-scale nature of this system was less a decision of that meeting than an effect of the campaign to suppress counter-revolutionaries (1950–3), which led to millions being incarcerated. Later, such large-scale incarceration under

the criminal code was thought to be both inappropriate and harsh. Thus developed a close relative of the penal sector, the administrative incarceration system known as reform through education. Like reform through labour, this institution was also born as a result of political campaigning.

The reform through education system came into existence in 1957 to deal with the large number of minor offenders caught in the Anti-Rightist Movement (see **Hundred Flowers Movement**). While those detained were political 'deviants', their errors were regarded as insufficient for a charge of 'counter-revolutionary criminal'. The idea behind the reform through education system was to introduce a form of re-education that would offer a non-stigmatizing space different from, but with the same aims as, the more draconian reform through labour system. Nevertheless, on the basis of the administrative regulations, sentences of up to three years could be imposed, with the possibility of a fourth year's extension. Sentences are imposed not by courts, as is the case in the penal system, but by a reform through education management committee that is made up of people from the local Party and government, the procuratorate, and the **police**.

Reform through education was part of the reform through labour penal system until 1983. In that year, both institutions were transferred from the **police** to the Ministry of Justice and slowly separated. By 1985, official sources suggest that the separation was complete but some Western sources remain doubtful. The Chinese **dissident**, Hongda Harry Wu, suggests that there are between 3 million and 4 million prisoners in the labour camps alone, while official figures put the number of prisoners at around 1.2 million and the number of inmates in administrative detention at 150,000 (1993 figures).

The reasons for detention have changed dramatically since the economic reform process began with far fewer political criminals and far more common criminals. As the nature of the prison population changed, the level of success in reforming inmates began to decline. Recidivism now stalks the Chinese prison sector and offers the ominous sign that as economic reform advances, the ability to transform criminals into useful members of society is proving to be an ever more difficult task.

see also: dissidents; Hundred Flowers Movement; police force.

Michael Dutton

private sector

The private sector in China was suppressed from the mid-1950s until 1978. During that time, private ownership of the means of production was illegal and private employment of labour was seen as exploitation. The only forms of production ownership allowed to exist were state and collective. These policies were based on Marxist theories of class struggle and the creation of value, and on the requirements of the centrally planned economic model.

The revival of the private sector after 1978 was the inevitable consequence of the increased freedoms for market exchange. The process was essentially a pragmatic one, in which the momentum for change tended to move in advance of legal and ideological sanctions. In the absence of rules, peasants began to run shops and services, bought equipment and established small workshops. Some of their activities spread into towns, where the growth of free markets required the emergence of a commercial network. Inevitably, the process also required the CCP to modify its ideological position on the role and nature of the private economy. The CCP abandoned previous orthodoxy, such as the primacy of class struggle, the exploitative nature of wage labour, the ban on private ownership of means of production, and the limits on income differentials, allowing the private sector to become an accepted part of the national economy. Private entrepreneurs were even invited to join the Party. While there was some hesitation and retrenchment in the wake of the **June 4 Incident** (1989), the sector was subsequently reaffirmed and continued to grow strongly.

On coming to power in 1949, the CCP was committed to a process of socialist revolution. During the early transitional stage, however, a mixed economy was tolerated. The assets of the 'bureaucratic capitalists' were confiscated, but the 'national bourgeoisie', defined as those devoted to the growth of an independent Chinese economy and sympathetic to the CCP's cause, were permitted to maintain their private economy. Nevertheless, the CCP moved rapidly to limit the freedoms of private entrepreneurs and to bring them under its direction. State controls over finance and **international trade** determined the macroeconomic framework. The development of trade unions, **labour** laws and enterprise Party committees constrained independent production management. And the 'three-anti' (*sanfan*: suppression of corruption, waste and bureaucracy) and 'five-anti' (*wufan*: suppression of bribery, tax evasion, theft of state property, cheating on state contracts, and stealing state secrets) movements of 1951–2 destroyed the network of government–entrepreneur relationships which had characterized the previous operations of the private sector. Many businesses were fined or closed down and the state increased its powers to intervene. As a result, the proportion of industrial output value from private enterprises dropped from 55.8 per cent in 1949 to 17.1 per cent in 1952. Meanwhile the conversion of many private enterprises into joint state–private firms began the process of nationalization. By 1956, therefore, almost all **industry** and commerce had come under state control. The previous owners continued to receive a small interest payment on their original investment, but that ceased at the beginning of the **Cultural Revolution**. Thereafter, the only private activity that existed was a small number of individual crafts, which were criticized as 'tails of capitalism' and placed under strict limits.

The rural reforms introduced in 1978 breached these foundations by permitting households to own means of production such as tractors, animals, workshops, machinery and transport equipment and by enabling them to invest in enterprises to produce commodities for the market (see **capitalists/ entrepreneurs**). During the 1980s, these reforms spread into the urban economy, and two types of private economy became recognized: the individual economy and the private economy. The individual economy is defined as small owner-operator enterprises, using household labour and resources and employing up to seven labourers. These enterprises are typically shops and restaurants or small-scale handicraft workshops. Employment of up to seven is seen as non-exploitative, though the rationale for this was never fully developed. The private economy refers to larger enterprises which might be owned by individuals, partnerships, or some form of limited liability company. They employ more than seven workers and are clearly capitalist in nature. By the mid-1990s, many of these enterprises employed hundreds of workers and, in some cases, thousands (see **new entrepreneurs**). These two categories are the officially defined components of China's private sector. Apart from private accumulation and investment, the contracting or leasing of collective or state enterprises to individuals also contributed to private sector development by providing a mechanism for privatization of existing assets. In addition, private ownership by foreign investors developed rapidly, especially after 1992.

China's private sector now embraces all forms of economic activity, including manufacturing, commerce and retailing, construction, transport and services such as hairdressing, restaurants, business consulting, credit provision, medical practice, education, law, and entertainment. It is seen as an essential supplement to the planned economy and a means to stimulate economic growth during the 'primary stage of socialism' (see **3. Ideology: Radicalism and Reform**).

Statistics on the size of the private sector are difficult to interpret, since the categories used have changed as the sector has grown. It is estimated that in 1978 there were around 300,000 individual businesses in China, producing a negligible proportion of national output value. In 1992 there were some 15.3 million registered individual businesses, with nearly 25 million employees (compared with a national labour force of around 600 million and an urban workforce of 145 million), and nearly 140,000 registered private enterprises with 2 million employees. In 1980 some 82 per cent of total investment was state-owned, 5 per cent collective and 13 per cent individual. By 1995, only 54 per cent belonged to the state and 16 per cent to collectives. The remainder was owned by a mixture of individual, private, joint and foreign ownership. In 1978, industrial output value was 515 billion *yuan*, of which 76 per cent was state-owned and 24 per cent collective. In 1995 the total was 9,189 billion *yuan*, of which 34 per cent was state-owned, 37 per cent was collective, 13 per cent was individual business and 16 per cent was other forms of ownership, including private business and foreign investment. These figures indicate that the private sector in China was still limited, but they demonstrate its rapid growth and the diversification in ownership which has occurred. The growth of the private sector in China also contributed to the emergence of a 'new rich' stratum, which embraced both private entrepreneurs and those in the Party-state system able to benefit from the reform process.

see also: 3. Ideology: Radicalism and Reform; capitalists/entrepreneurs; Cultural Revolution; industry; international trade; June 4 Incident; labour policy and system; new entrepreneurs.

Andrew Watson

protest movements

A series of movements in China since 1949 characterized by a number of common themes: the demand for greater democracy, respect for human rights, and protest at the dictatorial character of CCP rule. Several of them are discussed individually, specifically the **Hundred Flowers Movement** of 1956–7 and the **Tiananmen Incident** of April 1976.

The downfall of the **gang of four** and the eventual rise to power of **Deng Xiaoping** heightened expectations among many

Chinese that the CCP would now be more sympathetic to democracy and human rights. The democracy movement that emerged in late 1978 to press for these changes staged mass meetings and demonstrations in **Beijing**. It was also responsible for the **Democracy Wall** (in reality the wall in front of **Beijing**'s municipal bus station to the west of the city centre), on which individuals pasted countless posters expressing a wide variety of opinions such as calls for increased political democracy and demands for increased freedom in art and literature. Many unofficial magazines canvassing these issues were distributed openly on the streets. Wei Jingsheng, one of the movement's most prominent activists, called for China's 'fifth modernization – democracy' (see **Four Modernizations**), and another activist, Ren Wending, argued for changes – including a multiparty system, free elections, and an independent judiciary – which would have transformed China into a liberal democracy.

Finding it useful in his struggle against the remaining pro-Maoist radicals within the Party, **Deng Xiaoping** initially gave tacit approval to the democracy movement, which consequently flourished until early 1979. However, fearing the potentially explosive situation created by large numbers of youths returning to the cities following the end of the **Cultural Revolution**, the CCP arrested the movement's most prominent activists and closed down **Democracy Wall**.

The repression of the 1978–9 democracy movement was not as intense or as widespread as the CCP's earlier reactions to protest movements, and a more liberal atmosphere persisted throughout the 1980s. However, the CCP made it clear that it would not relinquish its monopoly of political power, even though it was instituting far-reaching liberalization in the economic realm. The more open intellectual and cultural atmosphere of the 1980s combined with the CCP's resistance to thorough-going political reform created fertile ground for the emergence of a major protest movement aiming at greater democracy and respect for human rights, and a diminution of the CCP's power.

Early indications of this emerged in 1986–7, when students protested in large numbers in many cities, including **Beijing** and **Shanghai**, in support of these goals and in protest against a number of grievances, including official corruption. CCP General Secretary **Hu Yaobang** was forced to resign for resisting demands to suppress this student movement.

During 1988, there was intense and widespread political debate in student and intellectual circles, much of this reported even in the CCP-controlled **media**. Political reforms in other communist countries added to the widespread view that an acceleration of democratic reform was needed in China.

Early in 1989, student activists at Beijing (Peking) University prepared for protest activities to coincide with the seventieth anniversary of the May Fourth Movement of 1919. When **Hu Yaobang** died on 15 April demonstrations occurred over the next few days in **Beijing** and other cities, and were met by considerable **police** violence. This repression drew widespread community support to the student movement and it was this combination of student and community protest which made the 1989 protest movement so explosive and so threatening to the CCP's hold on power.

The *People's Daily* 26 April editorial attempted to stifle the demonstrations by accusing student activists of being 'an extremely small number of people with ulterior purposes' and charged them with establishing illegal organizations; it also called for bans on unlawful parades and demonstrations. The students defiantly reacted by next day holding their largest demonstration since Hu's death in **Beijing**'s Tiananmen Square. Over the next weeks, **Beijing** students organized themselves into an autonomous student union, and called on the government to open a dialogue on the need for increased democracy and an end to corruption.

Demonstrations in Tiananmen grew even more intense after 12 May when students in the Square commenced a hunger strike. In addition, there were demonstrations and student and community unrest in many other cities. The 1989 movement was thus a truly nationwide protest movement and as such represented an extreme threat to the continued dominance of the CCP.

On 20 May, **Li Peng** declared martial law in parts of **Beijing**. His calls for students to clear Tiananmen were largely ineffective, with a strong although declining student presence in the Square continuing. At the beginning of June, four well-known **dissidents** went on hunger strike in Tiananmen Square, while demonstrations continued. However, the movement was suppressed on the night of 3–4 June 1989 (see **June 4 Incident**).

The 1989 democracy movement was the most dramatic of the protest movements in China since 1949 and it encapsulated, although in more intense and widespread form, the calls of earlier protest movements for democratization, freedom and respect for human rights.

see also: 1. Overview History of the People's Republic of China; Beijing Municipality; Cultural Revolution; Democracy Wall; Deng Xiaoping; dissidents; Four Modernizations; gang of four; Hu Yaobang; Hundred Flowers Movement; June 4 Incident; Li Peng; media issues and policy; *People's Daily*; police force; Shanghai; Tiananmen Incident.

Nick Knight

provincial government

There are thirty-one province-level administrative units in the PRC, twenty-two provinces (not including Taiwan), five autonomous regions (see **minority nationalities policy**) and four municipalities.

The highest state, as opposed to Party, body in these units is the people's congress. In provinces and municipalities each is elected by a lower-level people's congress for a term of five years. Among the powers of the province-level people's congresses are to elect or recall the executive heads of the province-level people's governments and their deputies, governors and deputy governors in the case of provinces, regional heads and deputy heads in the case of autonomous regions, and mayors and deputy

mayors in the case of municipalities. The provincial-level people's governments are the executive organs of the people's congresses at the corresponding level and are responsible to them.

The main functions of the province-level people's congresses are to examine and approve the plans for economic and social development, as well as the budgets, of their respective administrative areas. The province-level people's governments carry out administrative work concerning such matters as the economy, education, public health, public security and family planning within their own unit.

During the **Cultural Revolution** the province-level people's governments were abolished and replaced by **revolutionary committees**, each headed by a chair. However, on 1 July 1979 the **National People's Congress** adopted the Organic Law of the Local People's Congresses and Local People's Governments, which came into effect on 1 January 1980. Apart from abolishing the **revolutionary committees**, and hence restoring people's governments and titles such as governor and mayor, the law instituted two major reforms.

- Standing committees are set up for people's congresses at provincial (and county) level, their main functions being to supervise the work of the people's government, people's court and people's procuratorate at the corresponding level; and to appoint or remove functionaries of state organs within their jurisdiction.

- Province-level people's congresses and their standing committees are entitled to draw up and promulgate local statutes in accordance with the specific conditions and needs of the relevant province-level unit, as long as these statutes are in accord with national laws and policies. The effect of this provision is to increase the degree of autonomy enjoyed by the provinces with respect to the central government.

From time to time relations between the centre and the provincial governments have been extremely uneasy. In 1957 and 1958

Mao's regime instituted a decentralization plan which transferred some authority from central to provincial management. The result was the rapid growth of localism, with provinces wanting to build their own self-sufficient industrial complexes. Shortly afterwards, the Central Committee enacted a recentralization programme. This did not overcome a persistent political tug in the 1960s between the centre and those provinces with special economic power.

Localism has reasserted itself in the period of reform, with the central government less able in the 1990s to exercise control over the provinces and province-level authorities than it had once been. The fastest growing provinces, like Guangdong, Fujian, Zhejiang and Jiangsu, enjoyed a disproportionate share of influence in the determination of the state budget. Provincial authorities exercised a surprisingly high degree of mercantilism. It appears from such factors that economic and by extension political power has passed from the centre to the provinces. Such trends do not necessarily mean political separatism among the provinces or the breakup of China, but they certainly suggest that the handling of centre–province relations presents a serious long-term challenge for any central government.

see also: 7. Regional China; Cultural Revolution; local government/administration; minority nationalities policy; National People's Congress; revolutionary committees; Shanghai; Sichuan.

Colin Mackerras

Q

Qian Qichen

China's foreign minister since 1988 and senior CCP leader. Qian Qichen was born in **Shanghai** in November 1928. He joined the CCP in 1942, being active in the student and youth movement in **Shanghai**.

When the PRC was established he quickly became involved in foreign affairs. In 1954 he went to study at the Central School of Communist Youth in the **Soviet Union**, and also served in the Chinese Embassy in Moscow from 1955 to 1963 and again from 1972 to 1974.

Another area of Qian's interest was in the foreign affairs of education. From 1963 to 1964 he was division chief of the Overseas Students Department in the Ministry of Higher Education, and from 1964 to 1969 deputy director of the External Affairs Department in the same ministry.

In 1976 he was transferred to the Ministry of Foreign Affairs becoming vice-minister of Foreign Affairs in 1982. On 12 April 1988, he replaced Wu Xueqian as minister of Foreign Affairs, a position he retained when elected to the **State Council** in 1991 and as vice-premier of the **State Council** at the end of March 1993.

Qian became a member of the **CCP Central Committee** at the Twelfth National Congress in September 1982, retaining that position at the Thirteenth to Fifteenth National Congresses of 1987, 1992 and 1997 respectively. In addition, the First Plenum of the Fourteenth Central Committee elevated him to the Politburo.

In a speech made in Germany on 12 March 1992, Qian outlined 'the basic points of China's foreign policy' as follows.

- China eschews alliances and acts independently;
- China opposes hegemonism and power politics, aiming for world peace;
- China is willing to develop relations with all other countries on the basis of mutual respect for sovereignty and territorial integrity, mutual non-aggression, non-interference in each other's internal affairs, equality and peaceful coexistence; and
- China places emphasis on strengthening cooperation with other developing countries and expanding friendly relations with its surrounding countries.

One of Qian's first major acts as foreign minister was to visit the **Soviet Union** from 1 to 3 December 1988, the first visit by a Chinese foreign minister since **Zhou Enlai**'s in 1956. One of the aims was to prepare for the normalization of relations at the Sino-Soviet summit between Mikhail Gorbachev and **Deng Xiaoping** in Beijing in May 1989. His reaction to the collapse of the Marxist-Leninist regimes in Eastern and Central Europe in 1989 was to doubt that it heralded an end to hegemonism and instability. On the other hand, when the **Soviet Union** collapsed at the end of 1991, he was influential in getting China to recognize the successor states immediately and in developing good relations with them.

Under Qian's tutelage, relations with the **United States** have been uneven. In an article published just after the fortieth anniversary of the PRC's establishment in October 1989, and thus not long after the **June 4 Incident**, Qian attacked 'some Western countries', meaning primarily the **United States**, for constant interference in Chinese internal affairs. 'They keep on talking about "freedom", "equality" and "democracy", but they brazenly pursue hegemonism in handling state-to-state relations', he said. In a speech in New York on 29 September 1995, he warned that China would not budge on regarding **Taiwan** as part of China, because this was a matter involving Chinese sovereignty, territorial integrity and national unity. He welcomed US reaffirmations of its commitment to this one-China policy, but at the same time condemned its government for allowing **Taiwan** President Lee Teng-hui to visit the **United States** in June 1995, demanding that there be no recurrence of such events. He also denounced the recent revival of the 'China threat' theory, arguing that an economically stronger China with improved living standards was a 'contribution to world stability and prosperity, rather than a threat'.

see also: 8. China, the Region and the World; Chinese Communist Party Central Committee and Politburo; Deng Xiaoping; June 4 Incident; Shanghai; Soviet Union, relations with; State Council; Taiwan policy; United States policy; Zhou Enlai.

Colin Mackerras

Qiao Shi

Born in Zhejiang province in December 1924, Qiao Shi joined the CCP in 1940 and worked as an activist in the Party's student underground in **Shanghai** before 1949. From 1950 to 1962, he worked in Party youth affairs in East China and held technician-managerial posts with the Anshan Iron and Steel Company, and the Jiuquan Iron and Steel Company in Gansu Province. In 1963 Qiao was transferred to the International Liaison Department of the **CCP Central Committee** and rose to the post of director in 1982. During this period he travelled abroad extensively.

During 1982–7, Qiao was alternate member and member of the CCP Central Committee Secretariat, director of the General Office and head of the Party's Organization Department, a member of the CCP Politburo (1985), and head of the Leading Group for Rectification of Party Style within Central Departments (1986). In 1986–7, he became vice-premier of the **State Council**, member of the CCP Politburo Standing Committee, and secretary of the Party's Central Commission for Discipline Inspection. He became president of the Central Party School in 1989, in 1991 chairman of the Public Security Supervision Committee, and in March 1993 was elected to the high-profile position of chairman of the **National People's Congress** (NPC) Standing Committee.

Qiao Shi's leading role in the CCP's organizational and staffing, discipline inspection, intelligence and public security spheres has given him considerable influence in intra-Party politics. It has allowed him to build a considerable patronage network and to hold dossiers on all important contenders for authority. He represents the second generation of more educated and urbane Party technocrats in the leadership whose credentials cannot be traced back to the revolutionary struggle or the Long March. At an earlier stage, he had close ties with **Zhao Ziyang** and **Yang Shangkun**, and in the mid-1990s continues a close relationship with fellow CCP Politburo members **Li Ruihuan** and Tian Jiyun. Politically, however, Qiao has adopted a more liberal approach than many of his peers, including Party General Secretary **Jiang Zemin**. For example, he adopted a largely tolerant attitude towards the 1989 student movement, as evidenced by his abstention from a Politburo vote in May that year on whether to send the military into Tiananmen Square (see **June 4 Incident**).

While he has since supported efforts to prevent public debate on the appropriateness of the military response to the student demonstrations, Qiao has resisted full endorsement of **Jiang Zemin**'s ideologically based approaches to fostering patriotism, collectivism and socialism and to curbing corruption by indicating that these issues could be better addressed by enacting more laws and boosting the NPC's status. A supporter of the reform and opening policies, he has advocated promoting checks and balances within the system through using the NPC to supervise the Party and government. He also has differed with Jiang on economic policy, such as the reform of state-owned enterprises which he believes should be subjected to greater market-oriented processes. While in the mid-1990s Qiao and Jiang seemed to have come to a working arrangement built around their mutual desire to preserve Party predominance, and to maintain a representative balance of opinion in the halls of power for the sake of 'managed stability', nonetheless

Qiao lost his position as member of the Politburo Standing Committee at the Fifteenth CCP Congress of September 1997, appearing likely to lose also that of NPC Standing Committee chairman in March 1998. That he still retained some influence, however, was reflected by the elevation of his ally **Wei Jianxing** to the Politburo Standing Committee (ranked sixth of seven members).

see also: Chinese Communist Party Central Committee and Politburo; Jiang Zemin; June 4 Incident; Li Ruihuan; National People's Congress; Shanghai; State Council; Wei Jianxing; Yang Shangkun; Zhao Ziyang.

Donald H. McMillen

R

Red Guards
See **Cultural Revolution**.

revolutionary committees
The radical form of political organization that emerged during the first phase of the **Cultural Revolution**. These committees aimed to undertake leadership functions formerly performed by the CCP which was then under attack for revisionism and elitism. Revolutionary committee members normally came from mass revolutionary organizations, Party cadres and the **People's Liberation Army**. This 'triple alliance' reflected the reduced power of the Party and the increased influence of the cultural revolutionary rebels and particularly the military in Chinese politics. It was often the military that took the initiative in establishing revolutionary committees, although in some local **units** (such as schools, industrial plants and neighbourhoods) the influence of the masses was considerable. The first province-level revolutionary committee was established in Heilongjiang in January 1967, with Guizhou and Shandong following in February, Shanxi in March, and **Beijing** in April.

In February 1967, **Mao Zedong** endorsed the idea of the revolutionary committee. He opposed the attempt by the **Shanghai** radicals (such as Zhang Chunqiao and Yao Wenyuan, both later included in the **gang of four**) to replace CCP leadership with an egalitarian political organization modelled on the Paris Commune. Mao regarded this as 'extreme anarchism', forcing the radicals to convert the **Shanghai** People's Commune into a revolutionary committee based on the triple alliance.

The triple alliance formula inevitably led to tensions between the various members of the alliance, and particularly so between the cultural revolutionaries and the military. However, the actual composition of revolutionary committees varied depending on the local political situation, particularly the relationship between the Red Guards and the local military commanders. In Shanxi, for example, about half the provincial revolutionary committee were Red Guards while the military and cadres made up about one-quarter each; in **Beijing**, the military and cadres were less than one-third of the total membership.

The establishment of revolutionary committees was uneven and only seven of China's provincial level administrative divisions had established them by August 1967. Mao determined that they should be established throughout China by the end of that year, but friction between the military and leftist revolutionary rebels, as well as uncertainties about the composition and function of the revolutionary committee, saw most of the remaining province-level revolutionary committees established only in 1968, and in **Tibet** and **Xinjiang** as late as September of that year. The military was heavily involved in the establishment and operation of these later provincial revolutionary committees, which were then responsible for setting up revolutionary committees at district, county and municipal levels of administration.

Following the Ninth Party Congress of April 1969, the Party began the task of rebuilding its administrative structure. While the revolutionary committees persisted and in some units continued to exert substantial power, their radicalism declined as the Party refashioned itself along Leninist lines. The revolutionary committees, originally intended as a radical form of political administration allowing mass representation in decision making, were either increasingly transformed into institutions for implementing decisions of a strengthened Party leadership or made redundant through the rebuilding of parallel Party committees. In addition, the 'triple alliance' was redefined in the new State **Constitution** of January 1975 as the 'combination of the old, the middle-aged, and the young'. The revolutionary committee was criticized as the tool of the **gang of four** after its arrest in 1976. In June 1979, Peng Zhen announced that, as from January 1980, local people's governments would replace revolutionary committees, thus largely restoring the administrative structure of **provincial** and **local** government which had existed before the **Cultural Revolution**.

see also: 2. Government and Institutions; Beijing Municipality; Constitutions; Cultural Revolution; gang of four; local government/administration; Mao Zedong; People's Liberation Army; provincial government; Shanghai; Tibet Autonomous Region; Xinjiang Uygur Autonomous Region.

Nick Knight

S

Saifudin
See **Seypidin Azizi (Ayze)**.

science and technology
In 1949 the CCP inherited a small modern science and technology system which had been developing since the early years of the twentieth century and which was centred on the Academia Sinica. Most of China's first generation of modern scientists had trained in the United States, with 35,931 students returning to China between 1905 and 1951 after training there. Most of these scientists developed an attitude of non-involvement in politics, so after 1949 being regarded as products of bourgeois society, as individualistic lovers of objective study who were indifferent to politics and the people, and needed re-education.

In 1949 **Chen Boda** visited the **Soviet Union** to study its science and technology system, leading to the implementation of the **Soviet** model in China. This posited a close relationship between science, economic production and politics, and association of science with the masses. **Mao Zedong** saw science as a means of liberation from both nature and traditional culture.

The CCP adopted a leadership role, a new generation of scientists developing a Chinese scientific tradition. The Academia Sinica and the National Academy of Science in Beijing formed the nucleus of the new Chinese Academy of Sciences (CAS). When established in 1949, this had about 20 institutes, but the number grew to 120 by 1966, with a central research secretariat and a system of secretariats within the institutes. Academic departments for planning and overseeing research were created in five areas:

- mathematics, physics and chemistry;
- life sciences;
- earth sciences;
- technical sciences; and
- social sciences.

Research activities were also encouraged in organizations directed by the Ministries of **Health**, **Agriculture** and Defence and in the universities and colleges.

A twelve-year plan for science was drawn up with **Soviet** help in 1956. Personnel was a problem since there were only about 1,600 scientific researchers, some 164,000 engineering and technical personnel and only 191,000 students in tertiary **education** institutions in 1956. Although disrupted by the **Great Leap Forward** and the **Soviet** withdrawal in 1960, many of the aims of the plan were realized. In 1956 the State Technological Commission and the Science Planning Committee were established, merging in 1958 into the State Science and Technology Commission (SSTC). The SSTC became the supreme agency for science administration and policy. Led by Nie Rongzhen, an important political and military figure, it was staffed by administrators lacking scientific education. Centralized control was also exerted over professional scientific societies in 1958 and the Chinese University for Science and Technology was established in **Beijing**.

Also in 1958 the All-China Federation of Scientific Societies and the All-China Association for the Advancement of Scientific and Technical Knowledge were merged into the Science and Technology Association (STA) in an attempt to bridge the gap between professional activities and sources of innovative technology at the grassroots level. Funding of science and technology climbed during the Great Leap period, possibly to 1.54 per cent of the national budget in 1960. In accordance with the decentralizing, mass mobilization policies of the Great Leap there was a proliferation of scientific institutions and activities at the provincial and local level together with the setting up of a network of provincial commissions on science and technology.

During the early 1960s, the failure of the Leap saw some retrenchment and greater emphasis on professional expertise and the importance of life sciences and defence. The first Chinese nuclear test occurred in 1964 and this period saw the breakthrough in insulin production for diabetes. Pressure on professional scientists to remould themselves ideologically declined, with less time spent in political meetings, self-criticism sessions or production activities.

In 1964 a new ten-year science plan showed stresses on consolidation of science, self reliance and more emphasis on serving the agricultural sector. In 1965 funding for science was probably around 1.1 per cent of GNP. In 1966 the plan was interrupted by the **Cultural Revolution** and emphasis again shifted towards 'redness before expertise' for scientists. SSTC Vice-Chairman Han Kuang and CAS Vice-President Zhang Jingfu were criticized at a mass meeting in July 1966; the CAS was disrupted but survived, while the SSTC was dissolved. Scientific activities in most parts of China were severely disrupted; research institutes and universities closed down, professional societies disbanded, scientific meetings discontinued, and many long-term scientific and technological activities abandoned.

Science and technology became part of the mid-1970s succession struggles. This struggle in science centred around a document known as 'The Outline Report on the Work of the Academy of Sciences', the outcome of a month of meetings in 1975 which **Zhou Enlai** had instigated advocating the **Four Modernizations**. In December 1977 Fang Yi, director of the re-established SSTC, reported that the **State Council** had studied and approved the 'Outline Report' but the **gang of four** had tried to sabotage efforts to repair the damage done to science. The fall of the gang released a torrent of criticisms of policies towards science during the 1966–76 decade, with claims that China had fallen ten to twenty years behind the developed nations. By the end of 1977 the **Four Modernizations** had become basic policy. Science and technology was the most important of the four, and the key to the other three.

In 1978 a National Science Conference attended by 6,000 delegates announced plans

for scientific development, with eight priority areas: **agriculture**, energy, materials science, computer science, lasers, space science and technology, high energy physics and genetic engineering. The professional science system regenerated very quickly and by 1980 the mass science system had largely dissolved. Ties revived with the international scientific community. Despite an initial aim to resurrect the pre-1966 **Soviet**-style system, the reform leadership of the 1980s and 1990s moved in a different direction, placing greater emphasis on technology than science, on market mechanisms, on technology transfer and on innovation. Universities re-emerged as centres for science and technology and ties between universities and industry strengthened. China aims at a technological revolution which will allow it to compete with and surpass developed Western nations in the twenty-first century.

see also: agriculture; Beijing Municipality; Chen Boda; Cultural Revolution; education policy and system; Four Modernizations; gang of four; Great Leap Forward; health system; Mao Zedong; Soviet Union, relations with; State Council; Zhou Enlai.

Beverley M. Kitching

Seypidin Azizi (Ayze)

Senior Uygur leader, especially in **minority nationalities** affairs. Known also as Saifudin, he was born in 1915 in Artux County, **Xinjiang**, and later educated at the Central Asian University in Tashkent (1937) becoming a member of the Communist Party of the **Soviet Union**. He participated in the establishment, with Soviet backing, of the Eastern Turkestan Republic in the Yili, Tacheng and Altai districts of northwestern **Xinjiang** in 1944. He served as commissioner of Education during a brief coalition government arranged by Nationalist Party negotiators with the Yili rebels in 1946. He joined the CCP in 1949, and became deputy commander of the **Xinjiang** Military District, a secretary of the Xinjiang CCP Committee and vice-chairman of the **Xinjiang** People's Government.

With the establishment of the **Xinjiang**

Uygur Autonomous Region (XUAR), he became head of the regional government (1955–68). He was an alternate member (1956–69 and 1973–85) and member (1969–73 and 1985–92) of the **CCP Central Committee**, and an alternate member of the CCP Politburo (1973–82). He was vice-chairman (1968–73), then chairman (1973–8) of the XUAR **Revolutionary Committee**, first secretary of the XUAR CCP Committee (1973–8), and first political commissar of the **Xinjiang** Regional Command (1972–7). These positions were occasioned by the removal of the XUAR's CCP power-holder Wang Enmao as a result of the **Cultural Revolution**. However, Seypidin was always shadowed in power by Han CCP and military leaders during this period.

With the fall of the **gang of four** (1976) and with Xinjiang's poor economic performance during the late 1970s, Seypidin was relieved of most of his duties there and, to assuage minority sensitivities, allowed to continue his nationality, united front, and international liaison work from **Beijing**. He had been president of the Chinese Friendship Association with Pakistan (1966–7), and was appointed to head the Egyptian counterpart in 1991. He became honorary president of the Nationality Writers' Association in 1985 and the next year of the Nationality Literatures Foundation. In addition, although advanced in years, Seypidin continued until 1993 to be a vice-chairman of the Standing Committee of the **National People's Congress** (a position he had held since 1954) and became a vice-chairman of the Standing Committee of the **Chinese People's Political Consultative Conference** in 1993.

see also: Beijing Municipality; Chinese Communist Party Central Committee and Politburo; Chinese People's Political Consultative Conference; Cultural Revolution; gang of four; minority nationalities policy; National People's Congress; revolutionary committees; Soviet Union, relations with; Xinjiang Uygur Autonomous Region.

Donald H. McMillen

Shandong

A province of China, located on the lower reaches of the Yellow River. Shandong's land area constitutes 1.6 per cent of China's total, while its population, 87.05 million at the end of 1995, was 7.2 per cent of China's total, making the province the third most populous. With 65 per cent of its area in the plain region, the province is well suited to agriculture, particularly the production of wheat, cotton, soybeans and millet. With its 3,000 kilometre coastline (one-sixth of China's total), Shandong has several deep-water ports such as Qingdao, Yantai, Weihai and Longkou well known for **international trade**. Shandong is also well endowed with natural resources, including gold that ranks number one among China's province-level units in terms of its deposit; and diamonds, petroleum and copper that all rank second. Between 1949 and 1979, Shandong's gross value of agricultural and industrial output (GVAIO) increased at an annual rate of 8.9 per cent. The share of gross value of industrial output (GVIO) in GVAIO rose from 29 per cent to 70 per cent for the same period. The pace of Shandong's economic growth was relatively slow in the early years of the reform. It was in the 1990s that its pace took off to make Shandong one of the fastest developing provinces. The annual growth rate of GVIO for 1990–4 was 40.1 per cent while that for 1978–85 was 12.9 per cent, the figures for GDP being 26.7 and 17.2 per cent respectively. In 1993, only eight provinces managed to mark a per annum growth of GDP higher than 20 per cent over that of 1989, Shandong being fourth behind Zhejiang, Fujian and Hainan, while equalling Guangdong. Furthermore, Shandong's per annum growth rates of GDP, GVAIO GVIO and **international trade** in 1979–94 have all far exceeded the national average. Shandong's agricultural growth has been remarkable with its annual growth rate being three times the national average. Shandong's contribution to China's national income also rose from 6.5 per cent in 1978 to 9.2 per cent in 1993.

Throughout its history, replete with natural disasters, the people of Shandong have tended to be 'anti-outsider'. The province's predominantly Han composition (over 99 per cent) further reinforced its parochialism. Yet, in its relations with the centre, Shandong has rarely been a 'resister'. It ranked thirteenth in its pace of carrying out agricultural cooperativization in 1954–6. Shandong ranked eighth, sixth and seventh, respectively, in its pace of implementing land irrigation, grain purchase and communization policies during the **Great Leap Forward**. In establishing its provincial **revolutionary committee** in 1967, Shandong was the second fastest. In the post-Mao period, too, the province was more compliant than resistant. In implementing agricultural decollectivization, Shandong's pace remained consistent, closely matching the national average. It seems that Beijing is geographically and politically close enough to Shandong to cast a significant shadow over the province's behaviour. The most crucial reward for Shandong's compliance was that the centre permitted a wide latitude in the selection of provincial leaders. Since 1987, all party secretaries and governors were Shandong natives with extensive working experiences in the province. Furthermore, serving as governor seems to have become a prerequisite for the Party secretary position, as the successive cases of Liang Buting, **Jiang Chunyun** and Zhao Zhihao show. The assignment of Wu Guanzheng, a Jiangxi native with no working experience in Shandong, to the Party secretary position in March 1997 constitutes a departure from this pattern. Shandong's fiscal contribution went well beyond budgetary sharing: there were many special levies and funds appropriated from the province, including the State Energy, Transportation and Key Construction Fund, State Budget Adjustment Fund, 'local government loans', 'specific-items remittances' and 'extra fiscal contribution'. Most importantly, as of 1994, only 3.7 per cent of the 5,034 state enterprises in Shandong were owned by the central government. But these enterprises accounted for 34 per cent of the GVIO of the province's state enterprises. Thus, Shandong's annual budgetary remittance of 287 million *yuan* (Chinese dollars *renminbi*) was insignificant

compared to the total size of incomes generated within Shandong but accrued to the central coffer: 16.9 billion in 1994 accounting for 56 per cent of all revenue incomes produced within the province.

In return for its heavy fiscal contribution, Shandong benefited from various preferential policies granted by Beijing. The coastal development strategy considerably benefitted the Jiaodong Peninsula region at the expense of the inland. With the notable exception of **agriculture** in which the inland region reached up to three-quarters of its coastal counterpart, enormous disparities are found in per capita income, GVIO and foreign economic relations. As of 1994, the three coastal cities of Qingdao, Yantai and Weifang accounted for 55 per cent of the province's exports and 60 per cent of its foreign direct investment, while the figures for the four inland prefectures of Heze, Liaocheng, Linyi and Dezhou were only 12.6 and 6.3, respectively. The regional distribution of poverty is another indicator. While the eastern peninsula region had none of its counties designated as poverty-ridden by the central or provincial governments, the middle-belt region had a total of nine and the western region ten.

see also: agriculture; Great Leap Forward; international trade; Jiang Chunyan; revolutionary committees.

Jae Ho Chung

Shanghai

China's largest city and largest port, Shanghai is China's principal industrial centre. With the economic reforms of the 1990s, the city has also become China's 'economic, financial and trade centre'.

The CCP was long ambivalent about pre-1949 Shanghai: it was a 'sink of iniquity', a 'modern city with lopsided development' and yet it was 'the cradle of China's modern **industry** and commerce', 'a window for the spreading of modern Western learning', and 'the forefront of the struggle against imperialism and feudalism in modern times'.

Shanghai was a flourishing port well

before the nineteenth century. During the Ming Dynasty (1368–1644) there were over 1 million people in the area which is now Shanghai Municipality and over 3 million as early as 1816. Shanghai was one of the five ports opened in 1842 by the Treaty of Nanjing.

Much of Shanghai's importance derives from its favourable geographical location near the mouth of the Yangzi River, making it a portal to China's vast central hinterland. Situated on the central coastline, it also has access to ports in both north and south China. With its geographical advantages and good natural port as well as its industrial base, Shanghai is also China's key passageway to the world.

When the CCP captured Shanghai in 1949, the city had a population of about 5 million and was China's key industrial centre. In the mid-1930s Shanghai accounted for about half of China's industrial product. Despite damage from the Japanese invasion, Shanghai still produced one-quarter of China's industrial product in 1949. The population was also relatively highly educated.

Building on its pre-1949 base, Shanghai has remained China's wealthiest province-level unit and an important, relatively efficient industrial centre. The central government kept the 'planned economy' straitjacket on Shanghai until 1992 because of its crucial importance to central government revenues. Prior to the economic reforms, Shanghai provided one-fifth to one-quarter of central government revenue. (With 0.1 per cent of China's area, the 1990 census showed Shanghai Municipality with 13,341,852 people or 1.18 per cent of China's total population.) Thus, when beginning economic reforms in the late 1970s, the centre could not afford to take risks with Shanghai and such other major contributors to central revenue as Jiangsu. Rather it experimented in Guangdong, which provided the centre with less than 1 per cent of its funds.

Shanghai's importance to the centre as a 'cashcow' has continued into the reform period. Shanghai remains the single largest province-level contributor to central revenues and as late as 1992 was the source of

over one-sixth of central government revenues. It is true that Shanghai also received considerable centrally funded investment, but the total accumulated central investment in Shanghai over the period 1950–83 was less than Shanghai's fiscal contribution to the centre in 1983 alone.

The corollary has been that Shanghai has also paid a much larger proportion of its revenues to the centre than any other province-level unit. From May 1949 to the end of 1988, Shanghai paid 83.5 per cent of its fiscal revenues to the centre, retaining only 16.5 per cent for services and the development of Shanghai. As a result of its remaining in the 'planned economy' and ensuring the centre its revenues, Shanghai had poor roads, communications, **housing** and environment as well as a relatively slow growth rate. Unlike Guangdong, which had control over its local revenues, Shanghai had to make appeals to the centre for major investment funds, a process that inevitably slowed growth.

The crux of Shanghai's reform process has been the centre's 'giving' Shanghai 'policies'. Without a policy, Shanghai could not develop. With 'policies', Shanghai has been able to use its various capabilities to progress and develop. In the words of a Shanghai vice-mayor, 'policy is wealth'.

In 1988 the centre allowed Shanghai to use the financial responsibility system, thus enabling it to retain all fiscal revenues above a contracted amount which it provided to the centre. This increased Shanghai's fiscal income, though not by a large amount.

Shanghai's importance to China as a whole with its industrial base, its favourable geographical location, and its numerous and talented human resources in the fields of **science and technology**, economics and finance, and management as well as excellent, numerous quality workers led to the decisions in 1990 to promote Shanghai and its Pudong region. The centre gave Shanghai ten preferential policies including such incentives as tax holidays and relief, encouragement for the establishment of service industries, a free-trade zone and land use for periods of from fifty to seventy years.

The key policy changes occurred, however, in 1992 following **Deng Xiaoping**'s 'inspection tour of the south'. Deng's favourable comments towards Shanghai fundamentally changed the course of reform in the municipality:

> At present Shanghai has all the conditions to move a bit more quickly. In the areas of talented personnel, technology and administration, Shanghai has obvious superiority, which radiates over a wide area. Looking backwards, my one major mistake was not to include Shanghai when we set up the four **special economic zones**. Otherwise, the situation of reform and opening to the outside in the Yangzi River Delta, the entire Yangzi River Valley and even the entire nation would be different.

Shortly afterwards, Shanghai benefited in two ways: it obtained five more 'preferential policies' and tax rates for enterprises in Shanghai were lowered.

The centre's 1992 'policy' gifts have clearly proved crucial to Shanghai's development. After the post-Mao reforms got under way, Shanghai's growth rate was slower than China's national rate. Since 1992 Shanghai's growth rate has exceeded the national rate.

Under reform, Shanghai's economy is restructuring in two key ways.

- The high cost of land and labour in Shanghai has forced its industry to restructure into high technology and high value industry in order to become profitable. Older, less efficient industries lose money and come under increasing competition from other parts of China. As part of this industrial restructuring, heavy industry is becoming increasingly important.
- Shanghai has moved strongly into the tertiary sector. The growth of financial services including foreign banks and the stock, bond and futures exchanges has been especially rapid. Retailing has also developed rapidly since the 1992 reforms.

The reforms have provided Shanghai's leadership with the financial capability to improve the city's infrastructure. Shanghai now has an elevated beltway and an underground, both of which have helped relieve traffic congestion. **Housing** construction and a **housing** reform policy, which has enabled many Shanghai residents to purchase their own accommodation, have improved the **housing** situation in China's most densely populated city.

see also: Deng Xiaoping; housing; industry; science and technology; special economic zones.

J. Bruce Jacobs

Sichuan

Situated in China's southwest, Sichuan is surrounded by **Tibet**, Yunnan, Guizhou, Hunan, Hubei, Shaanxi, Gansu and Qinghai. A particular source of economic strength has been its agricultural output since ancient times, which has won Sichuan a reputation as 'national granary'. The province's aggregate economic performance is not too far behind the provinces of the more advanced coastal areas. Sichuan has a well-developed industrial sector with significant national concentrations of defence-related and nuclear industries. One of China's two space centres is located in Xichang in the southwest corner of the province. Sichuan is also one of China's four major centres for the metallurgical, engineering, electronic and chemical industries. While one of largest provincial economies in China, Sichuan's population, 111.62 million in 1995 and much the largest among China's provinces, means that its per capita economic performance places it among the poorest provinces.

Sichuan was divided into five administrative units immediately after 1949. Four subprovincial governments were established in the north, south, east and west while Chongqing, the former wartime capital of the Nationalist government, kept its special position as a city under the direct leadership of the regional power centre, the Southwest Military-Administrative Committee (SMAC), which controlled the entire southwest region, Sichuan, Xikang, Yunnan, Guizhou and **Tibet**.

In September 1952, the four sub-provincial units were reorganized as one province, while Chongqing remained separate from Sichuan. In 1953, Chongqing was upgraded as a city controlled directly by the central government. In July 1954, when the SMAC was abolished, Chongqing reverted to Sichuan. In 1955, as a result of negotiations between the central and Tibetan governments, Xikang province was abolished, its eastern part being put under Sichuan and its western returning to **Tibet**. In March 1997, the **National People's Congress** formally decided to split Chongqing off from Sichuan to become China's fourth province-level municipality. The decision substantially reduced the province's industrial strength, Chongqing having been by far its main industrial centre.

Local politicians before the **Cultural Revolution** were mainly army leaders and former local underground communists, with a strong presence in the whole region from the 2nd Field Army, led by **Deng Xiaoping** and Liu Bocheng, and Marshal He Long and his 1st Field Army controlling the north and west, about half the province. The tension between the two field armies has exercised an enduring influence on Sichuanese politics.

When Sichuan was reorganized as a province, the Party and government institutions of west Sichuan formed the political core of the new provincial power. Li Jingquan, He Long's political commissar and CCP and government head of west Sichuan, became the secretary of the Sichuan Party Committee, governor of Sichuan and political commissar of the Sichuan Military Region. During the **Great Leap Forward**, Li's loyalty to Mao's radical line won him membership of the Politburo and, later, the post of first secretary of the Southwest Bureau of the Central Party Committee. But the ensuing famine cost the lives of more than 1 million people in Sichuan.

During the **Cultural Revolution**, Li's power collapsed and the province was ruled by military leaders from 1968 to 1975, none of whom could control the situation. In 1975, as part of **Deng Xiaoping**'s attempt to re-establish order in China, **Zhao Ziyang** was appointed provincial Party, government and military leader. The reform was a factor in Deng's dismissal next year, but Zhao survived.

After 1978, Sichuan took a lead in rural economic reform which eventually swept China. **Zhao Ziyang** not only encouraged local Party and government leaders to abolish Mao's egalitarian agricultural system, but also launched reforms in **industry**, aimed at giving more power to managers of state-owned factories.

After Zhao was promoted to the centre, native Sichuanese began to manage the province. Sichuan's position has declined nationally since the 1980s as the central government changed its economic development strategies, granting preferential policies to coastal regions. At the Fourteenth **National Party Congress** (1992), Sichuan lost the Politburo membership that its provincial leaders had held since the 1950s.

The development of Sichuan's economy has been hampered both by its natural and political settings. Remote and isolated, its economy has not been readily integrated into that of China as a whole. During the 1950s this resulted from a deliberate policy which stressed Sichuan's role as a national grain provider. From the late 1950s to the mid-1970s, it was often the interplay between its political leadership and Beijing, rather than provincial concerns, that determined Sichuan's economic development. Industrial development, though large-scale, tended to be defence-oriented and non-productive. With the political changes that led to reform the province found itself responsible for an inefficient and non-productive large industrial sector.

The 1980s and 1990s have again seen the province facing the difficulty of integrating into a national economy characterized by an imbalanced growth strategy, though this time one driven by market forces rather than planned allocations. Its relationships with Beijing and with other parts of China remain prime concerns for Sichuan's leaders.

see also: Cultural Revolution; Deng Xiaoping; Great Leap Forward; industry; National

Party Congress; National People's Congress; Tibet Autonomous Region; Zhao Ziyang.

Lijian Hong

Sino-Indian Border War (1962)

A short war fought from 20 October 1962 until 20 November 1962 in two segments of the Sino-Indian border, Ladakh in the west and the Northeast Frontier Agency (NEFA) in the east.

The *de facto* Sino-Indian border ran along the McMahon line, established at the Simla Conference of 1913–14 and called after Sir Henry McMahon, who led the British delegation at the Conference. While independent India accepted this border, no Chinese authorities had ever done so

During the 1950s relations between China and India were extremely friendly, based on a mutual hatred of imperialism and colonialism. Euphoria reached a height late in 1956, when Chinese Premier **Zhou Enlai** visited New Delhi. During the visit Zhou raised the matter of the McMahon line with Indian Prime Minister Jawaharlal Nehru. A misunderstanding arose and discussion over the border became more acrimonious as the 1950s wore on.

The uprising in Lhasa (**Tibet**) of March 1959 and the subsequent flight of the Dalai Lama to India fuelled the mutual tension. On 25 August 1959 an armed clash occurred at Longju in NEFA, where the alignment of the McMahon line was in dispute. Against Chinese objections, the **Soviet Union** issued a neutral statement on 9 September. **Soviet** leader Nikita Khrushchev was about to hold summit talks with US President Dwight D. Eisenhower in Camp David and did not wish to destroy his chances of a detente with the West, where most people saw the Longju incident as an example of communist aggression.

On 7 November 1959 Zhou wrote to Nehru proposing a meeting and that both Chinese and Indian troops should withdraw from the McMahon line in the eastern sector and the line of 'actual control' in the western. Nehru agreed to the meeting, which took place in New Delhi in April 1960 but failed to solve the border dispute.

Mutual charges of aggression erupted in May 1962. On 20 September a clash occurred north of the McMahon line near the Dhola Post, which the Indians had established on 4 June, casualties resulting on both sides. On 12 October Nehru announced that he had instructed the army to 'free our territory' of Chinese troops.

On 20 October China launched a major offensive in both the eastern (NEFA) and western (Ladakh) sectors. They gained quick victories, taking the town of Bomdi La in western NEFA on 18 November, Indian resistance collapsing by 20 November. The same day, China announced a unilateral ceasefire, adding that all Chinese troops would withdraw behind the 'line of actual control' of 7 November 1959.

Although China won the war so decisively, the effects for its international relations were disastrous. Nehru and Zhou continued to try to patch up their differences, but in fact relations between their countries were so poisoned that they have never fully recovered. The first Indian Ambassador to China since the early 1960s presented his credentials in July 1976. Relations did not revert to 'normal' until Rajiv Gandhi visited Beijing in December 1988, the first time for an Indian prime minister since Nehru in October 1954.

There was also a serious impact on Sino-**Soviet** relations. The Chinese were furious at the equivocal position the **Soviet Union** took in its statement of 9 September 1959 over the Longju incident. A *People's Daily* editorial of 27 February 1963 denounced the statement as the first time in history that a socialist country had supported a capitalist one (India) against a 'fraternal socialist country' (China) in a case of armed provocation.

see also: People's Daily; Soviet Union, relations with; Tibet Autonomous Region; Zhou Enlai.

Colin Mackerras

Sino-Vietnamese War (1979)

Sino-Vietnamese relations have long been coloured by a chequered history of Chinese suzerainty, and ethnic and territorial disputes. The unified Socialist Republic of Vietnam, formally established in 1976, increasingly turned to the **Soviet Union** for aid and support in its quest for national reconstruction and sub-regional dominance. In November 1978, Hanoi signed a twenty-five-year Treaty of Friendship and Mutual Assistance with the **Soviet Union**, and on 25 December, a matter of days after Beijing and Washington had announced that they would establish diplomatic relations, launched an invasion of Cambodia, which had been headed by the Chinese-backed Khmer Rouge regime under the notorious Pol Pot.

In December 1978 and January 1979, **Deng Xiaoping** made a visit to the **United States**, during which he warned against Vietnam's aggressive behaviour. On 17 February 1979, China launched a seventeen-day-long punitive attack on northern Vietnam, involving some 250,000 troops along a 720-kilometre front. Beijing claimed at the outset that it would be a 'limited and brief operation', along the lines of the **Sino-Indian Border War** of 1962. It justified the move as defensive, based on constant Vietnamese intrusions into Chinese territory over the preceding months and on Hanoi's ill-treatment of ethnic Chinese. Underlying these claims was Beijing's sense of betrayal and humiliation for Vietnam's ingratitude for supplies valued at US$15 billion to 20 billion in economic aid to Vietnam in 1950–78 and for some 300,000 Chinese technicians who had supported its war against the French and, later, the Americans. In addition, China was furious at Hanoi's perceived involvement in Moscow's 'China encirclement strategy'.

The performance of the **People's Liberation Army** (PLA) in the conflict was not as effective as **Deng Xiaoping** and other Chinese leaders had hoped, and although its troops initially advanced swiftly they became bogged down by a lack of modern weapons and by the Vietnamese troops' avoidance of major battles. While laying siege to a northern provincial capital at Lang Son in early March, Beijing proposed peace talks, and on 5 March it summarily announced the withdrawal of PLA troops. The next day, Vietnam agreed to peace talks, and by 16 March all Chinese forces had been withdrawn.

The Chinese suffered some 46,000 casualties in the conflict, and its estimated cost was about US$1.36 billion, which proved to be a drag on China's **Four Modernizations** drive. Coincidentally, this strengthened Deng's hand at home by lending additional credence to his emerging policies of reform and opening. The war did show that China was able to act on threats and that it did not fear the **Soviet Union**. On the other hand, the need for drastic modernization of the PLA also became evident.

Beijing's gambit also raised renewed fears of a continuing 'China threat' in Southeast Asia, just at the time it was trying to cultivate better relations there as part of its attempts to break '**Soviet** hegemonic encirclement' and to 'protect' other regional states from an 'expansionist' **Soviet**–Vietnamese strategy. China's support of the deposed Khmer Rouge and other anti-Vietnamese groups in Cambodia kept that conflict raging for another decade, and also further underlined China's continued willingness to support 'anti-government' struggles in the region. These regional perceptions of China as a source both of stability and threat continue to coexist.

see also: 8. China, the Region and the World; Deng Xiaoping; Four Modernizations; People's Liberation Army; Sino-Indian Border War; Soviet Union, relations with; United States policy.

Donald H. McMillen

Sixth Plenum of the Eleventh Central Committee

The Sixth Plenum of the Eleventh Central Committee of the CCP was held in Beijing from 27 to 29 June 1981. This Plenum was very significant for two main reasons.

First, the Plenum adopted the 'Resolution on Certain Questions in the History of our Party since the Founding of the People's Republic of China', a wide-ranging evaluation of the Party's history since 1949 and **Mao Zedong**'s role in it. The 'Resolution' had been written by a drafting group headed by Hu Qiaomu under the guidance of the **CCP Central Committee**'s Politburo. **Hu Yaobang, Chen Yun** and **Deng Xiaoping** contributed revisions to early drafts of the 'Resolution', and its content came to reflect the perspective of Deng and his supporters on post-1949 Party history, as well as their growing power within the Party. **Deng Xiaoping** had criticized early drafts of the 'Resolution' for being excessively critical of **Mao Zedong** and **Mao Zedong Thought**, arguing that Mao's mistakes after 1957, and particularly during the **Cultural Revolution**, had to be judged against his positive contributions both before and after 1949. Deng recognized the need to link the Party's continuing claim to legitimacy to Mao's achievements and the positive dimensions of his thought.

The 'Resolution' adopted by the Sixth Plenum consequently states that Mao's contributions to the Chinese revolution far outweighed his mistakes, and that 'his merits are primary and his errors secondary'. Singled out for praise is Mao's leadership of the CCP before 1949 and his contribution to the first seven years of socialist transformation after 1949. However, from 1958, **Mao Zedong** became impatient for quick results in economic development and socialist transformation, and began to commit 'Left' errors, such as the **Great Leap Forward** and widening the scope of class struggle in the early 1960s. This set the scene for the **Cultural Revolution**, defined by the 'Resolution' as lasting from 1966 to 1976. The **Cultural Revolution**, initiated and led by Mao, was 'responsible for the most severe setback and the heaviest losses suffered by the Party, the state and the people since the founding of the People's Republic'. The 'Resolution' is also extremely critical of the role played in the **Cultural Revolution** by the **Lin Biao** and Jiang Qing 'cliques', as well as the continuation of 'Left' errors by **Hua Guofeng** in the two years following Mao's death and the arrest of the **gang of four** in 1976. These 'Left' errors were corrected by the **Third Plenum of the Eleventh Central Committee** in December 1978.

The 'Resolution' of the Sixth Plenum praised Mao for his integration of Marxism-Leninism with the practice of the Chinese revolution in the years before 1949, an integration which gave rise to **Mao Zedong Thought**. The 'Resolution' emphasizes that **Mao Zedong Thought**, the guiding ideology of the CCP, is a scientific system of thought not equivalent to the thoughts of Mao, the individual, some of which were clearly in error. Rather, **Mao Zedong Thought** is a 'crystallization of the collective wisdom of the **Chinese Communist Party**'. In other words, it is a system of thought to which other Party leaders made contributions. The 'Resolution' defines the 'living soul' of **Mao Zedong Thought** as seeking truth from facts, the mass line, and independence and self-reliance, and asserts that **Mao Zedong Thought** will remain the Party's guide to action 'for a long time to come'.

The 'Resolution' has remained the CCP's authoritative interpretation of its history during and immediately after the Mao years. It stands in the tradition of the 'Resolution on Some Questions in the History of Our Party' adopted by the Seventh **National Party Congress** in April 1945 which affirmed **Mao Zedong**'s dominance of the CCP and the correctness of his line in previous intra-Party struggles.

Second, the Sixth Plenum is also significant as it saw the demotion of **Hua Guofeng** to the position of Central Committee vice-chairman. Since Mao's death, Hua had occupied the positions of chairman of the Central Committee and chairman of the **Central Military Commission**. His loss of these two positions and his demotion to vice-chairman of the Central Committee reflected the growing dominance of **Deng Xiaoping** and his supporters within the Party. **Hu Yaobang** was elevated to the position of chairman and **Zhao Ziyang** vice-chairman of the Central Committee. Deng took over the position of chairman of the **Central Military Commission**. The Standing Committee of the Politburo elected at the Sixth Plenum included **Hu Yaobang, Ye Jianying, Deng Xiaoping, Zhao Ziyang, Li Xiannian, Chen Yun** and **Hua Guofeng**.

The Communiqué of the Sixth Plenum stated that the election of the leading members of the Central Committee was instrumental in strengthening collective leadership and was a return to the Yan'an tradition of speaking out freely and inner-Party democracy, a criticism of the one-man style of leadership which had been practised under Mao during his later years and by **Hua Guofeng** during his period as chairman of the Central Committee.

The Sixth Plenum of the Eleventh Central Committee stands as one of the CCP's most important Plenums. Its 'Resolution' laid the foundation for the Party's subsequent theoretical and ideological work, and the change of leadership which occurred at it reinforced the power of **Deng Xiaoping**.

see also: Central Military Commission; Chen Yun; Chinese Communist Party; Chinese Communist Party Central Committee and Politburo; Cultural Revolution; Deng Xiaoping; gang of four; Great Leap Forward; Hu Yaobang; Hua Guofeng; Li Xiannian; Lin Biao; Mao Zedong; Mao Zedong Thought; National Party Congress; Third Plenum of the Eleventh Central Committee; Ye Jianying; Zhao Ziyang.

Nick Knight

Song Ping

Major leader with influence in such crucial areas as cadre management, and follower of **Chen Yun**'s line. Born in **Shandong** Province in 1917, Song joined the CCP in 1937 and was **Zhou Enlai**'s secretary in the 1940s.

In September 1953, Song was appointed vice-minister of Labour and in November 1954 as a member of the then powerful State Planning Commission (SPC). In April 1958, he was promoted as SPC vice-minister. In 1960, he concurrently served as the director of the Northwest China Bureau's Regional Planning Commission and deputy director of the Third-Front Construction Commission.

Having disappeared during the early years of the **Cultural Revolution**, Song resurfaced in 1970, rising to serve concurrently as Gansu's first Party secretary, chairman of its **Revolutionary Committee**, First Political Commissar of the Gansu Military District, and a **CCP Central Committee** member (since 1977). This was the decade-long period during which Song cultivated relationships with many members of his 'Gansu Faction', notably **Hu Jintao** and Hou Zongbin.

Having mastered the management of provincial affairs, Song moved back to Beijing as vice-minister of the SPC in 1981. In June 1983, he was promoted to State Councillor and minister of the SPC. Song's political fortunes rose in tandem with the intermittent re-emergence of the more conservative policy line, which happened to coincide with the fall of two designated successors of **Deng Xiaoping**. In June 1987, in the aftermath of **Hu Yaobang**'s fall from power, Song was appointed the head of the Central Organization Department under the **CCP Central Committee** and in November he was elected to the Politburo of the Thirteenth Central Committee. Just after **Zhao Ziyang** was disgraced over the **June 4 Incident** in June 1989, Song was again promoted to the Standing Committee of the Politburo, a position he kept until 1992.

Even after retiring from formal positions, Song continued to exert enormous influence over key personnel matters. He has also served as chairman of the China Family Planning Association.

see also: Chen Yun; Chinese Communist Party Central Committee and Politburo; Cultural Revolution; Deng Xiaoping; Hu Jintao; Hu Yaobang; June 4 Incident; revolutionary committees; Shandong; Zhao Ziyang; Zhou Enlai.

Jae Ho Chung

South China Sea

Bounded by China to the north, **Taiwan** and the Philippines to the east, Indonesia and Malaysia to the south and, in the west, Vietnam and Thailand, this region contains the most disputed and most strategically sensitive body of water in the world. The oil lifelines of **Japan**, South Korea and **Taiwan** pass through the shoal and island strewn waters while the major trade routes of China, South Korea, **Taiwan**, Singapore and **Japan** with

Australia, the countries of the **Association of Southeast Asian Nations (ASEAN)**, southern Asia, Africa and Europe converge on two major access controlling straits in the west, the Malacca which passes under Singapore, and the Sunda, through the Indonesian archipelago, while **Taiwan**, a disputed province of China, lies athwart the sea lanes on the east.

Historically, China viewed the area both as its own and as a troublesome source of piracy and foreign intrusion. In the seven voyages of Zheng He during China's era of predominance in the early 1400s, a fleet of some 300 ships established diplomatic and trade relations throughout the area, only to be abandoned by imperial edict in 1433. The arrival in 1557 of first Portuguese, then increasingly throughout the seventeenth and eighteenth centuries Spanish, Dutch, French, British and American traders forced imperial focus on Guangdong and Fujian Provinces in the vain attempt to hold European intrusion at bay. By the early nineteenth century the sea became dominated by European imperial powers and remained under the control of European and US naval forces until the late twentieth century. As late as 1996 the US Seventh Fleet demonstrated in the South China Sea and the Pacific off **Taiwan** as a warning to China against invasion.

In the Law on the Territorial Waters and Contiguous Areas of the PRC (February 1992) China (re)asserted claims suspended more than 500 years earlier, and began to re-establish a blue water navy and to build airstrips and outposts on the Spratly and Paracel Islands. This law defines the Xisha (Paracels), Nansha (Spratlys), Dongsha (Pratas Bank), Zhongsha (Macclesfield Bank) and Penghu (Pescadores) islands in the South China Sea and the Diaoyutai (Senkaku) islands in the East China Sea as integral parts of China, with air and water sovereignty claims drawn in a continuous line outward from the islands for the 12-mile zone of territorial waters and the 200-nautical-mile economic zone allowed in international law. China also claims the right accorded to archipelago nations to extend the lines of maritime sovereignty contiguously from the outer edge of the territorial and economic zones back to the mainland; thus China has claimed over 800,000 square kilometres of ocean and virtually all the South China Sea as territorial waters. It asserts the right to 'inspect' vessels passing through and technically insists that submarines surface and fly their national flag and other naval vessels obtain permission before passage. While restrictions on naval forces have not been enforced, the UN's International Maritime Organization has reported that 'piracy' by Chinese vessels, often crewed by **People's Liberation Army** uniformed personnel and sometimes enforced by gunfire, has grown in frequency since 1991 to become quite a serious problem. China and Vietnam have had numerous armed clashes over claims in the 1980s and 1990s while in 1996 the Philippines and China sparred over aptly named Mischief Reef. Of the fifteen new boundaries laid out by the 1992 law, twelve are disputed.

In 1992 the ASEAN Ministerial Meeting made a 'Declaration on the South China Sea' which called for settlement of claims by 'peaceful means, without resort to force'. In March 1995 in Senate Resolution S R 97, the US Senate called on the president to reiterate that, while the United States took no position on any claim, it fully supported the 1992 ASEAN Declaration, urging peaceful resolution of disputes and a freezing in place of the status quo. China has continued its buildup of air and sea forces in the region, consolidating control of shipping lanes. US and other naval forces which enforced international rights of passage by frequent ship visits to **Hong Kong** became much less able, and less frequently, to assert international free passage. While China has repeatedly insisted on its intent to resolve disputes peacefully, and has invited joint development of marine, oil and mineral resources, it has insistently held to its claims of sovereignty.

see also: Association of Southeast Asian Nations; Australia; Hong Kong; Japan, relations with; People's Liberation Army; Taiwan policy; United States policy.

Michael DeGolyer

Soviet Union, relations with

This entry includes the PRC's relations with the Soviet Union and the successor Commonwealth of Independent States (CIS). These relations have been marked by great instability, moving from close and friendly to extremely hostile and back to cordial.

In February 1950, Moscow and Beijing signed a thirty-year Treaty of Friendship, Alliance and Mutual Assistance, with attached protocols, thus aligning the PRC with the Soviet Union and providing China with loans (initially US$300 million) and technical assistance (by 1953–4 some 400,000 scientists and technicians and 6,000–35,000 military advisers). For a period, Moscow also retained joint ownership of the Changchun Railway, its stocks in **Xinjiang** enterprises, and the right to use Dalian and Lüshun as naval bases, the last Soviet troops not being withdrawn from Lüshun until 1955. After China sent troops to the **Korean War**, China had to pay Moscow US$1.35 billion for supplies.

At the Twentieth Congress of the Communist Party of the Soviet Union (CPSU) in 1956, Nikita Khrushchev delivered a secret speech denouncing Stalin's personality cult and announcing a policy of peaceful coexistence with the West. This angered **Mao Zedong** on both policy and leadership grounds, and was followed by the erosion of the alliance and China's decision to take its own path to socialism.

Escalating polemics led Moscow to recall 1,390 technicians from China and cut all aid in 1960. In October 1961, **Zhou Enlai** walked out of the Twenty-Second CPSU Congress. During the early 1960s, Beijing accused Moscow of fomenting armed clashes along their increasingly militarized 4,150-mile border and claimed some 1.5 million square miles of territory seized by Russia under the unequal treaties. China criticized Khrushchev for 'capitulationism' following the 1962 Cuban Missile Crisis and the signing of the 1963 Limited Test-Ban Treaty. Soviet aid now gone, China developed its own nuclear weapons programme, testing its first device in 1964. In March and August 1969 armed clashes occurred along the border at the Ussuri River in the northeast and in **Xinjiang** in the west. Sino-Soviet contention for leadership in the world communist movement and for influence in the **Third World** also intensified.

After Moscow's invasion of Czechoslovakia in 1968, China attacked both US and Soviet imperialism. Fears of a possible Soviet pre-emptive nuclear strike led to tunnel-digging throughout China. Significantly, Beijing also began a reassessment of its relations with the **United States**.

In November 1978, Vietnam signed a security agreement with Moscow. In December, with Soviet support, Hanoi invaded Cambodia, overthrowing the pro-China Pol Pot regime. In January 1979, Beijing abrogated the 1950 Sino-Soviet treaty and in February China launched an attack against Vietnam (see **Sino-Vietnamese War (1979)**), one reason being its participation in Moscow's campaign of 'encirclement' against China. Meanwhile, to China's fury, Soviet troops occupied Afghanistan at the end of 1979.

In 1980, **Deng Xiaoping** outlined 'three obstacles' to Sino-Soviet rapprochement:

- Soviet support for Vietnam's occupation of Kampuchea (Cambodia);
- the Soviet presence in Afghanistan; and
- Soviet troops along the Sino-Soviet and Sino-Mongolian borders.

In his Tashkent speech of March 1982, Leonid Brezhnev acknowledged Chinese sovereignty over **Taiwan** and proposed discussions to improve bilateral relations. In December 1984, First Deputy Chairman of the Soviet Praesidium Ivan Arkhipov visited Beijing and concluded a series of economic agreements, including the renewal of cross-border trade. In March 1985, Vice-Premier **Li Peng** attended the funeral of Soviet leader Konstantin Chernenko, meeting successor Mikhail Gorbachev. These were clear signs of a rapprochement.

Gorbachev's Vladivostok speech of 28 July 1986 was a key step in this process, since he specifically agreed to resolve the 'three obstacles' to improved relations with China. In May 1987, Moscow announced the removal of a mechanized division from Mongolia and in 1988 the Geneva agreement on Afghanistan provided for Soviet withdrawal, the last troops being removed in February 1989, and Gorbachev offered further efforts to resolve the Cambodian imbroglio.

In mid-May 1989, Gorbachev's China visit symbolized the normalization of Party-to-Party relations, but was overshadowed by the student demonstrations in Tiananmen Square (see **June 4 Incident**). To many of the protesters, his programme of openness with democratization represented a model which China should emulate – a view not shared by most CCP leaders. Gorbachev suggested only that there might be greater dialogue between the protesters and authorities.

In April 1990, **Li Peng** visited a Soviet Union in the throes of disintegration amidst rising ethno-nationalism. In **Jiang Zemin**'s return visit to Moscow in May 1991, he stated that Sino-Soviet relations were based on the 'five principles of peaceful coexistence' but could not return to the situation which had prevailed in the 1950s. He stressed the importance of stabilizing the Eurasian region through agreements defining the eastern and western borders between the two states. In the event two such agreements followed, in May 1991 and September 1994, although by the time of the second the Soviet Union had collapsed.

When the Soviet Union disintegrated into the loose Commonwealth of Independent States (CIS) in December 1991, Foreign Minister **Qian Qichen** immediately proclaimed the friendship of the Chinese people for all the peoples of the new republics as well as an intention to develop relations with them on the basis of non-interference. In January 1992, a delegation led by Minister of Foreign Economic Relations and Trade **Li Lanqing** toured Russia, the Ukraine and the Central Asian republics to develop economic and technical cooperation. Russian President Boris Yeltsin's visit to China in December 1992 confirmed the cooperative nature of relations with the signing of a Joint Declaration on the Basis of Relations providing that neither side should join any military or polit-

ical alliance against the other nor harm the sovereignty or security interests of the other.

Premier Li Peng made a four-nation, ten-day Central Asian tour in April 1994 to solidify working relations with these states and to counter any support for separatist groups in **Xinjiang**. In fact, the upsurge in trade along the borders brought with it a heightened contact between kindred ethnic groups which was tinged by Islamic and ethno-nationalist sentiments.

In April 1996, Yeltsin's visit to China was hailed by Beijing as the culmination of a new 'strategic partnership' of equality, mutual confidence and mutual coordination, according to which each side would inform the other about their military exercises and would not target or attack one another. While the two sides reiterated their strict observance of the principles set forth in the Joint Statement of December 1992 (reconfirmed in September 1994), this arrangement fell short of a new military alliance against the US, due largely to Russian reluctance to place obstacles in the way of access to Western trade and technology.

In 1985, when the trend towards normalization of relations was gathering momentum, trade between China and the Soviet Union stood at $US1.9 billion (3 per cent of China's total trade). By 1993, the volume of trade between China and Russia reached US$7.68 billion (an increase of 23–5 per cent over 1992), while trade with other states of the former Soviet Union stood at US$1.34 billion (an increase of 40 per cent over 1992). China had become Russia's second biggest trading partner after Germany, while Russia ranked seventh among China's trading partners. The generally more prosperous economic conditions on the Chinese side of the borders probably had positive spin-offs so far as local public satisfaction and security there were concerned. In 1994, trade slowed somewhat, in part due to tighter CIS regulations and fees and Chinese efforts to assure that trade was not accompanied by contraband, illegal immigration, and/or any other potentially hostile phenomena.

Following the Soviet Union's demise,

China also sought defence technology and expertise from the successor states, partly as a less expensive source of weaponry and expertise and as a counter to US power and perceived 'neo-containment'. This included the purchase and delivery of twenty-two Sukhoi advanced-fighter aircraft and a series of military exchanges and dialogues. In Shanghai in April 1996 and in Moscow in April 1997 the presidents of China, Russia, Kirgizstan, Tajikistan and Kazakhstan signed two communiqués demilitarizing the China–CIS borders. China also reaffirmed its support for Russia's admission to the **Asia-Pacific Economic Cooperation** community. Interestingly, Russia stated that it would not establish official relations nor enter into official contacts with **Taiwan**, although in December 1996 it opened a representative office there (**Taiwan** had established a similar office in Moscow in 1993) and agreed to begin air links with the island in 1997.

In sum, by 1997 relations between China and the states of the former Soviet Union were generally cordial and businesslike, and while they would continue to be influenced by domestic developments and bilateral issues they would not be conducted in a vacuum nor would they fail to be coloured by history and proximity.

see also: 8. China, the Region and the World; Asia-Pacific Economic Cooperation; Deng Xiaoping; Jiang Zemin; Korean War; Li Lanqing; Li Peng; Mao Zedong; Qian Qichen; Sino-Vietnamese War; Taiwan policy; Third World policy; United States policy; Xinjiang Uygur Autonomous Region; Zhou Enlai.

Donald H. McMillen

special economic zones

Inspired by the success of export processing zones in **Taiwan** and Asian countries, China officially decided in August 1980 to establish special economic zones (SEZs) in Guangdong and Fujian Provinces. The decision to establish the SEZs had the blessing of **Deng Xiaoping**, who always defended them in the face of criticism from those who either opposed the SEZ concept or were critical of their perform-

ance. In terms of achieving their objectives, the SEZs have had mixed results. In the mid-1990s, the special privileges enjoyed by the SEZs have also come under criticism from the leaders of inland provinces.

Three of the original four SEZs (Shenzhen, Zhuhai and Shantou) are located in Guangdong, the fourth (Xiamen) being in Fujian Province. They were chosen for their close proximity to **Hong Kong** or **Taiwan** (see **Taiwanese–PRC trade and investment**), as well as for being a safe distance away from the major population centres where the old centrally planned economy was to remain in operation for the foreseeable future. On 13 April 1988, the **National People's Congress** adopted a resolution upgrading Hainan Island to the status of a province and a SEZ, and it thus became the fifth and largest such zone.

In addition to the objectives of attracting foreign capital and technology which are common to most export processing zones, China's SEZs were also intended to serve two other functions. These were:
- to inspire **Hong Kong** and **Taiwan** confidence in China by creating economic buffer zones practising quasi-capitalist economic policies; and
- to use these zones as laboratories for economic reform where market-oriented policies could be tried out with a view to introducing successful examples in other parts of the country.

Given their controversial nature and the uncertain political climate of post-Mao China, the SEZs were not immediately popular with all factions of the Party. While those ideologically opposed to the open-door and economic reform policies were naturally unhappy with the decidedly non-egalitarian policies adopted by the SEZs, even some reformers had serious reservations about them. To many within China, the SEZs were the modern manifestations of colonialism and imperialism. Supporters of the SEZ policy were, however, at pains to explain the differences between the treaty ports of the pre-revolutionary days and the modern SEZs under the control of a Leninist state. The latter were an important part of a strategy to make China richer, stronger and more powerful so that it would never again have to suffer humiliation at the hands of the imperialists.

Nevertheless, there was intense debate among Party ideologues and academics about the exact social and economic character of these zones: over whether they were socialist or capitalist in character. A conference which the Shenzhen Economic Society organized in April 1984 concluded that the social and economic character of the SEZs should be treated as two separate issues. The social character of the SEZs was said to be socialist 'beyond any doubt', but economically they were described as 'comprehensive entities' involving multiple economic forms, but with state capitalism as the leading component.

What has proved most impressive about the SEZs is the sheer speed and scale of their development, especially that of Shenzhen with its resemblance to **Hong Kong**. Between 1980 and 1995, over 18 per cent of China's US$120 billion in actual foreign investment went to the five SEZs. However, not all the SEZs developed at the same speed or in the same manner. Shenzhen was clearly the pacesetter in infrastructure development and in attracting foreign direct investment. Others struggled to catch up with Shenzhen. But it had also come under close scrutiny from the SEZ detractors. They pointed to its failure to generate a foreign currency surplus and alleged that it was growing at the expense of other cities and provinces. To be sure, huge amounts of domestic funds were diverted from other regions in the country to be invested in the SEZs. There was hardly any Chinese province which did not set up shop in Shenzhen to take advantage of its liberal economic environment. There were also numerous reported cases of Chinese money being recycled back into Shenzhen by state-owned companies as foreign capital to take advantage of the generous conditions offered by the SEZs to foreign investors.

In January 1992, **Deng Xiaoping** included Shenzhen and Zhuhai SEZs in his famous 'inspection tour of the south' to shore up support for his liberal economic policies. Yet even his authority did not prevent the leaders of central and western provinces from later calling for the SEZs' privileges to be rolled back. They blamed the preferential treatment given to the SEZs and other coastal regions for their own relative underdevelopment, and called for SEZ-like policies to be allowed in the interior.

see also: 1. Overview History of the People's Republic of China; 5. Politics and the Economy: Policy Patterns and Issues; Deng Xiaoping; Hong Kong; National People's Congress; Taiwan policy; Taiwanese–PRC trade and investment.

Pradeep Taneja

State Council

China's main administrative organ of government and the functional centre of state power, equivalent to the Central People's Government. The composition, functions and powers of the State Council are laid down in the four **Constitutions**. In essence these are very similar to each other where the State Council is concerned, although the level of detail is very different. The State Council came into existence in September 1954, with the adoption of the first **Constitution**.

The State Council consists of the premier, vice-premiers, state councillors, ministers in charge of ministries or commissions, the auditor-general and the secretary-general. The membership has ranged from a minimum of thirty to over one hundred. The State Council usually meets about once a month. There is, however, a more select body, consisting of the premier, vice-premiers, the state councillors and the secretary-general, which holds executive meetings more frequently.

The term of office of the State Council is the same as that of the **National People's Congress** (NPC), which is five years. The State Council is responsible to the NPC, which elects its members. The First Session of the Eighth NPC chose as members of the State Council for the period 1993 to 1998 **Li Peng** as premier, four vice-premiers, namely **Zhu Rongji**, **Zou Jiahua**, **Qian Qichen** and **Li**

Lanqing, eight state councillors and forty-one ministerial officials.

The premier of the State Council has the function of presiding over the work of the State Council. Up to the late 1990s, four men had occupied the position. Together with their date of election by the NPC these are:

- **Zhou Enlai**, 27 September 1954, already premier of the State Council's predecessor since October 1949;
- **Hua Guofeng**, 5 March 1978, but in fact became acting premier on 3 February 1976 following the death of **Zhou Enlai** the preceding month, being confirmed in the position by the Politburo on 7 April 1976;
- **Zhao Ziyang**, 10 September 1980; and
- **Li Peng**, 9 April 1988, the NPC Standing Committee having approved both Zhao's resignation as premier and Li's appointment in an acting capacity on 24 November 1987.

Under the 1982 **Constitution**, the premier, vice-premiers and state councillors are not allowed to serve more than two consecutive five-year terms.

The functions and powers of the State Council include:

- adopting and enacting administrative rules and regulations;
- submitting proposals to the NPC or its Standing Committee;
- 'exercising unified leadership' over the ministries and commissions subordinate to it;
- drawing up and implementing the plan for national economic and social development and the state budget; and
- conducting foreign affairs and managing China's national defence.

Subordinate to the State Council are a range of ministries, state commissions and the **People's Bank of China**. The number of ministers in charge of ministries or state commissions elected by the Seventh NPC in 1988 was thirty-seven and by the Eighth in 1993 thirty-eight, the responsibilities of the relevant bodies from the two NPCs being very similar but not identical. The 1982 Constitution provides for an auditing body attached to the State Council, which must be independent, 'subject to no interference by any other administrative organ or any public organization or individual'.

Ministries under the State Council include those of Foreign Affairs, Civil Affairs, Finance, Labour, Railways, Justice, Communications, Culture, Agriculture and several in the industrial sphere. In the period of reform since 1978 the State Commissions include the State Nationalities Affairs Commission, the State Science and Technology Commission, and the State Family Planning Commission. In June 1985 the NPC Standing Committee replaced the Ministry of Education with the State Education Commission. This change came at the same time as major educational reforms were announced and implied a higher importance for **education** in China's overall modernization programme.

In addition to the ministries and commissions there are numerous units, administrative offices, subordinate institutions and bureaux. Their functions are wide-ranging, and include the State Statistical Bureau, the State Environmental Protection Bureau, the Civil Aviation Administration of China, the **New China News Agency** and the Chinese Academies of Sciences and Social Sciences.

In March 1993 the NPC approved a plan to streamline the State Council and its administrative structures. The plan envisaged that the size of government staff would be cut by about one-fifth and that the number of subordinate units, offices and bureaux would be sharply reduced.

Although China's state structure suffered enormously during the **Cultural Revolution**, the State Council was relatively stable. The reason for this was **Zhou Enlai**'s negotiating, administrative and stabilizing influence at the time, and his ability to weave his way through **Mao Zedong**'s policies and instructions, minimizing the damage they caused without angering Mao.

In the period of reform the influence of the State Council has tended to increase. The reason for this is the primacy of economic issues during the period. Among the thirty-seven and thirty-eight ministries and commissions subordinate to the State Council, as elected by the Seventh and Eighth NPCs in 1988 and 1993 respectively, twenty were directly economic in nature.

see also: 2. Government and Institutions; Constitutions; Cultural Revolution; education; Hua Guofeng; Li Lanqing; Li Peng; Mao Zedong; National People's Congress; New China (Xinhua) News Agency; People's Bank of China; Qian Qichen; Zhao Ziyang; Zhou Enlai; Zhu Rongji; Zou Jiahua.

Colin Mackerras

state economic structures

After 1949, China's state economic structure was based on state ownership of the means of production and administrative **planning** for the allocation of resources. It was thus a system of ownership and a system of economic production. The structure was shaped by the centralized pattern of commissions and ministries under the **State Council**, with their hierarchy of subordinate offices and enterprises, and by the economic departments of provincial and municipal governments, with authority within their territorial area. The responsibilities for economic policy and control of state enterprises were shared between the central hierarchies and the local governments, with shifts in the balance of authority at various times. The **planning** model adopted in the 1950s tended to emphasize centralization, while **Mao Zedong** promoted greater decentralization. As a result, state enterprises have experienced mixed lines of control. Matters like personnel and production planning tended to come under provincial leadership, and material planning and investment were more commonly controlled from the centre.

The policy of separating administration and economic enterprises after 1978 led to a reduction in the role of state agencies in direct production management. The remaining powers of those agencies, however, provided the opportunity for corruption by some economic officials. The reforms also increased the level of provincial autonomy *vis-à-vis* the centre. In addition, the growth of market forces created a need for new legal and institutional mechanisms to manage a market

economy. Nevertheless, the role of state economic structures remains dominant, and many state agencies have attempted to resist the erosion of their authority.

The main features of the state economic structures were established during the 1950s and the broad outline has remained much the same since that time. The **State Council** stands at the apex and controls a number of commissions and ministries for developing and implementing economic policies. Ministries exist for a variety of economic sectors, including **agriculture**, commerce, **international trade**, **industries**, finance and so forth. Over time these ministries have been merged, or separated, or had revisions in their range of responsibilities. The most significant economic agencies have been the State Planning Commission (SPC), the State Economic Commission (SEC), the State Structural Reform Commission (SSRC) and the State Economic and Trade Commission (SETC).

For most of the period after 1949, the SPC was the most powerful of all the commissions. It was responsible for long-term **planning**, for determining the allocation of resources and for integrating the plans of the central departments and the provincial authorities. During the 1980s, it came under **Zhao Ziyang** and advocated reform policies which contrasted in details with those promoted by the SEC under **Hu Yaobang**. By the mid-1990s, the development of market forces had tended to reduce the SPC's direct influence over economic activity. It was also losing economic authority to the newly established SETC. Nevertheless, it still retained considerable importance, especially in developing long-term plans.

The SEC was charged with overseeing the implementation of annual plans and with the supervision of the work of the economic ministries. In 1982 it absorbed a number of other commissions and bureaux, and then became associated with policies promoted by **Hu Yaobang**. In April 1988, the SEC was absorbed by the SPC, further enhancing the importance of the latter.

The SSRC was established in May 1982

under **Zhao Ziyang**. Its duties were to design reform policies and procedures and to carry out research into the needs of economic reform. It became a major 'think tank' for reform ideas, though its influence has varied with the importance of the political leaders associated with it.

The SETC was first established as an office in the spring of 1992 under **Zhu Rongji**, with the aim of replacing the SPC as the key unit for economic management. Guided by Zhu's strong technical emphasis in economic management, it expanded quickly, with eleven vice-directors and eleven departments looking after each of the major economic sectors. It began to play an important role in determining policies for macroeconomic management and for new initiatives such as the establishment of stock exchanges. At its March 1993 session, the **National People's Congress** increased the SETC's authority to take over functions from some of the economic ministries. The SETC thus appeared to be evolving into the key economic administrative structure, and **Zhu Rongji** was reported as arguing that it should become the Chinese equivalent of the Japanese Ministry of International Trade and Industry.

see also: agriculture; Hu Yaobang; industry; international trade; Mao Zedong; National People's Congress; planning, economic; State Council; Zhao Ziyang; Zhu Rongji.

Andrew Watson

T

Taiwan policy

China's fundamental policy towards Taiwan is that China retains sovereignty over the island, which remains an inalienable part of China. In the words of the 1993 Chinese White Paper on Taiwan, 'Every sovereign state has the right to use any measures which it considers necessary, including military measures, to protect its sovereignty and territorial integrity'.

Taiwan is an island of 36,000 square kilometres located 200 km off the southeast China coast with a population of 21 million (1994). Over 98 per cent of the island's population are Han Chinese whose ancestors came from the Chinese mainland (see **minority nationalities policy**). Nine indigenous tribes account for the remainder of the population.

China's relationship with Taiwan has a variegated history. In 1683, the Manchus successfully incorporated Taiwan into the territory ruled by their Qing Dynasty (1644–1911), but their control over the island remained relatively loose and concentrated in the coastal plains. After the Sino-French War of 1884–5, the Qing government moved to strengthen Taiwan militarily and administratively, making Taiwan a separate province in 1887. However, the Qing court ceded Taiwan to **Japan** following the Sino-Japanese War of 1894–5.

In an effort to develop Taiwan as a granary, the Japanese colonial rulers established and maintained public order with a penetrating administrative system backed by a strong police force, Taiwanese being permitted only limited political activity. Yet the Japanese improved public health and primary education, built roads and railways and developed some processing industry. When Taiwan was returned to China in 1945, the island had a much higher living standard than the Chinese mainland.

The then ruling Nationalist Party took over Taiwan and exploited the island's wealth.

The exploitation and corruption sparked resentment leading to the 28 February 1947 Incident, a series of demonstrations which the Nationalists brutally suppressed. Some 20,000 Taiwan leaders died, creating a massive social and political divide between the Nationalists and local Taiwanese. When the Nationalists lost the mainland to the CCP, they shifted their government to Taiwan where it survived against heavy odds, due in large part to US naval protection. For their part, the Nationalists used the breathing space that the protection afforded to implement reform and make Taiwan a 'model province'.

The Beijing CCP and Taibei Nationalist governments both claimed to be the sole legitimate government of China and each declared Taiwan an integral part of China. The PRC decisively rejected the Taibei Nationalist government's claim to represent the Republic of China. Two separate, hostile governments existed, each vowing to destroy the other. Thus, until the end of 1978, China declared it would 'liberate' Taiwan militarily.

Taiwan clearly loomed large in the Chinese decision to establish diplomatic relations with the **United States** at the end of 1978. The Communiqué of the **Third Plenum of the Eleventh Central Committee** explicitly tied the establishment of diplomatic relations with the **United States** to reunification:

> The Plenum believes, with the normalization of Sino-American relations, the return of our sacred territory Taiwan to the bosom of the Motherland and the prospect of achieving the great undertaking of reunification has already come one step closer.

A week later, on New Year's Day 1979, the Standing Committee of the **National People's Congress** issued a 'Letter to Taiwan Compatriots', which enunciated the new policy:

Our national leaders have already shown their determination definitely to consider present circumstances in completing the great undertaking of reunifying the Motherland. When solving the problem of reunification, they will respect Taiwan's present situation and the opinions of various groups of people in Taiwan, and use fair and reasonable policies and methods to assure the people of Taiwan do not suffer losses.

The 'Letter' also announced that the Chinese would cease shelling the Nationalist-held offshore islands.

Under **Deng Xiaoping's** personal leadership, the Chinese evolved the policy of **one country, two systems**. This provided that, after unification, Taiwan's 'social and economic system, lifestyles, and foreign investment will not change. The military will become local militia'. In September 1981, NPC Standing Committee Chairman **Ye Jianying** called for negotiations with the Nationalists over Taiwan, stating that after reunification, Taiwan could enjoy a high degree of autonomy and retain its own armed forces.

Taiwan responded slowly and suspiciously to China's 'peaceful reunification' initiatives. However, in 1987 Taiwan allowed its own residents to visit the Chinese mainland. The result was that millions of Taiwanese visited China and trade between the Chinese mainland and Taiwan increased rapidly. **Taiwanese–PRC investment** grew exponentially with Taiwan becoming China's largest foreign investor. (Many investments from the **United States**, **Japan** and **Hong Kong** are actually Taiwanese capital.)

China's Taiwan policy contains a fundamental contradiction. While China emphasizes that 'peaceful reunification is an established policy of the Chinese government', it refuses to forgo the possibility of using military power to reunify Taiwan with the mainland. The result has been policy conflict within the Chinese leadership. President **Jiang Zemin** has urged a more 'moderate' policy towards Taiwan as exemplified in

his 'Eight Points' of January 1995. However, when the **United States** issued a visa to Taiwan President Lee Teng-hui for a 'private visit' in June 1995, the 'hard-liners' led by the Chinese military claimed the 'moderate' policy had failed. The 'hard-liners' then implemented a policy of military threats, which reached a climax during the Taiwan presidential election campaign of March 1996. Although the threats aimed to intimidate Taiwan's voters into opposing President Lee, he received an overwhelming mandate, enabling the 'moderates' to criticize the 'hard-liners'. While the 'hard-line' policy has failed, its advocates still remain influential because of the importance of the military in Chinese politics.

see also: 9. Taiwan and the Overseas Chinese; Deng Xiaoping; Hong Kong; Japan, relations with; Jiang Zemin; minority nationalities policy; National People's Congress; one country, two systems; Taiwanese–PRC trade and investment; Third Plenum of the Eleventh Central Committee; United States policy; Ye Jianying.

J. Bruce Jacobs

Taiwanese–PRC trade and investment

Since the mid-1970s PRC–Taiwan economic relationships have progressed from virtually nil to China's replacing the **United States** as Taiwan's leading trade partner, with thousands of Taiwanese firms operating on the Chinese mainland (see **Taiwan policy**). From 1950 to 1977, owing to hostilities between the two, any exchanges were through smuggling. Then Taiwan permitted imports of herbal medicines and agricultural products through **Hong Kong**. In 1979, China called for resumption of shipping, post and commerce, but Taiwan responded with the 'three no's' policy forbidding contact, talks and communication, a policy that it did not relax fully until 1988. China, in that period, first offered then withdrew preferential entry for, and purchase of, Taiwan goods and treatment to Taiwanese to buy PRC goods. Despite this, trade increased, from US$21.5 million in 1979 and US$235 million in 1980 to US$811 million in 1986.

Meanwhile, pressures on Taiwanese manufacturers grew steadily; worker rights to bonuses, wage costs and land prices increased, restrictions were imposed on overtime work, environmental protection regulations were more tightly enforced, and young workers eschewed 'dirty' factory work in favour of white-collar jobs. In order to remain competitive, labour-intensive industries began moving overseas, especially to Southeast Asia. That it was political restrictions which prevented more than small amounts of investment in China, where the shared language and culture facilitate rather than obstruct, is manifested in the sea change which occurred in 1987–8. Factors in the change at that time were the lifting of restrictions on foreign exchange and on most Taiwan residents to visit relatives in China, as well as the death of President Chiang Ching-kuo in January 1988 and the accession as his successor in that post of Vice-President Lee Teng-hui. Funds invested in China from Taiwan quadrupled and from **Hong Kong** doubled, much of the latter actually being Taiwanese funds. In 1990, Taiwan in essence legalized both trade with and investment in China, which, in tandem with the growing attraction of the domestic Chinese, led to an even greater flood of investment there from US$100 million in 1987 to US$1.4 billion in 1991 and US$3.4 billion in 1992. In the first three quarters of 1996, Taiwan invested a total of US$4.634 billion in the PRC, and there were tens of thousands of Taiwanese firms there.

Although Taiwan has been a leading investor in Vietnam since the early 1990s, the opening of the PRC has largely signalled a shift away from investments in Southeast Asia.

Trade and investment figures must be treated cautiously, but they are indicative. Trade figures are distorted by the amount of raw materials and semi-finished products that flow between the two; many goods sold by Taiwan firms are manufactured with Taiwanese raw materials in both Taiwan and China. Not all investments are made public, especially in Taiwan, and PRC figures on Taiwanese investment may reflect originally tendered rather than actual invested amounts. Moreover, investment figures stated on operating permits are sometimes inflated.

These economic exchanges have been driven by both economic and political factors. From the PRC side, initially the most important consideration was the utilization of Taiwan's capital and expertise to develop its economy. A subsidiary interest was political. PRC President **Yang Shangkun** stated in December 1990, 'Strive to develop cross-Straits relationships. . . . Use economics to drive politics, and the people to drive officials in guiding cross-Straits communications to further unification of the motherland and the **Four Modernizations**.'

Despite this, the early 1990s were marked by the submergence of politics in cross-Straits relationships, with both sides setting up semi-official bodies to deal with each other. Moreover, both sides stated that trade should be between the people rather than through official bodies. That state of affairs was shattered by Lee Teng-hui's visit to the **United States** in June 1995, which was deemed by Chinese authorities as a step toward Taiwan independence. Since that time, recovery of Taiwan has assumed greater urgency than previously, and Taiwanese business operators in China have felt threatened by some central government moves.

On Taiwan's side, businesses have been moved by economic factors, but the government more by politics. In the 1980s, more and more people, especially those originally from the mainland, made clandestine visits to the PRC via various Southeast Asian cities. Officials recognized the need for some industries to relocate in China, but they were also cognizant of the danger of the 'hollowing out' of Taiwan's industrial core and the need to maintain a technological edge over the PRC. They thus offered assistance to industries which could be saved by technical upgrading and acted to prevent investment in large-scale, high-technology companies, such as the naphtha cracking plant proposed by Formosa Plastic. Since the increase in cross-Straits tensions in 1995, Taiwan has attempted to limit further Taiwanese business operations in China, especially in response to crises such as that created by South Africa's decision, announced by Nelson Mandela in November 1996, to switch its diplomatic recognition from Taiwan to the PRC in 1997, but it also acknowledges that businesses are moved much more by market than political forces.

see also: 9. Taiwan and the Overseas Chinese; Four Modernizations; Hong Kong; Taiwan policy; United States policy; Yang Shangkun.

David Schak

telecommunications
See **transport and telecommunications**.

Third Plenum of the Eleventh Central Committee
The Third Plenum took place from 18 to 22 December 1978. It is generally regarded as the meeting which introduced the 'period of reform' and of **Deng Xiaoping**.

Although **Hua Guofeng** presided over the Third Plenum and remained the CCP chairman until the middle of 1981, **Deng Xiaoping**'s ideas are visible in all its decisions.

The most important of these were:

- to modernize China as rapidly as possible;
- to concentrate energy on advancing **agriculture**;
- to rehabilitate Peng Dehuai and several others;
- to declare a high evaluation on the discussion over whether practice is the sole criterion for testing truth;
- to reinterpret the **Tiananmen Incident** of 1976;
- to open the way for total negation of the **Cultural Revolution**, following at the **Sixth Plenum of the Eleventh Central Committee**;
- to establish a strong socialist **legal system**; and
- to make several important leadership changes.

The **Sixth Plenum** of mid-1981 recorded the view that the Third Plenum 'marked a crucial

turning point of far-reaching significance in the history of our Party since the birth of the People's Republic'. It gave numerous reasons for its view, among them that it eliminated leftist errors and made 'the strategic decision to shift the focus of work to socialist modernization'. In addressing troops on 9 June 1989, just after the **June 4 Incident**, **Deng Xiaoping** still appealed to the principles and policies of the Third Plenum of the Eleventh Central Committee as 'correct', especially those of reform, modernization and 'opening to the outside world'.

Of the six main decisions the first stands out for its significance, and is above all what leads observers to regard the Third Plenum as the beginning of the period of reform. One of the extracts in the Plenum's communiqué which stresses modernization runs as follows:

> Now is an appropriate time to take the decision to close the large-scale nationwide mass movement to expose and criticize **Lin Biao** and the '**gang of four**' and to shift the emphasis of our Party's work and the attention of the people of the whole country to socialist modernization. ... Socialist modernization is therefore a profound and extensive revolution.

Zhou Enlai and **Hua Guofeng** had earlier laid emphasis on '**Four Modernizations**', of **agriculture**, **industry**, national defence and **science and technology**. These were now to be pushed much more vigorously than had happened up to that time.

The communiqué allocated much space to **agriculture**. It propounded the principle of 'to each according to work', rather than to need, thus opening the way for a strengthening of material incentives. Although the communiqué specifically declared that the right of ownership by the people's communes must be protected by state laws, in fact the overall thrust of the Plenum's decisions led towards giving greater play to private and family initiative, and the people's communes were later abandoned.

Those rehabilitated included several who had suffered from **Mao Zedong**'s policies, especially during the **Cultural Revolution**. They included, apart from Peng Dehuai, Tao Zhu, **Bo Yibo** and **Yang Shangkun**.

The decision on practice as the sole criterion of truth and the statement on the **Cultural Revolution** both downgrade the **Cultural Revolution**'s notion that class struggle is the key link in all activities and governing all decisions (see **3. Ideology: Radicalism and Reform**).

The Plenum described the **Tiananmen Incident (1976)** as a series of 'entirely revolutionary actions'. This was the precise opposite of the official verdict at the time that 'a counter-revolutionary political incident' had taken place. Since it was **Mao Zedong** and the **gang of four**, the principal supporters of the **Cultural Revolution**, who had been responsible for that verdict, the Third Plenum's reversal was an implied negation of the **Cultural Revolution** and criticism of Mao.

The formal leadership decisions were as follows:

- to elect **Chen Yun** as an additional vice-chairman of the **CCP Central Committee**;
- to elect Deng Yingchao, **Hu Yaobang** and **Wang Zhen** as further members of the Politburo; and
- to elect a Central Commission for Discipline Inspection, which would be headed by **Chen Yun**.

Other than **Deng Xiaoping**, the main winner from the Plenum was thus **Chen Yun**, whose economic and other policies are enshrined in its decisions. The main aim of the Central Commission for Discipline Inspection was to prevent and eliminate corruption within the Party. This has not prevented corruption from worsening greatly in the period of reform.

The **Cultural Revolution** had produced a devastating effect on the **legal system**. The Third Plenum communiqué ordained that a new **legal system** should be established and followed. It stated that 'there must be laws for people to follow, these laws must be observed, their enforcement must be strict and law-breakers must be dealt with'. Despite shortcomings, law occupies an incomparably more important place in the period of reform than it did in the preceding years.

Although foreign relations are not mentioned among the highlighted decisions listed at the beginning of the communiqué, the document itself praises China's recent performance in the area and, in particular, the normalization of relations between China and the **United States**, which had been announced just two days before the Plenum began. The policy direction of the Plenum was undoubtedly towards 'opening to the outside world', a slogan heard repeatedly in China during the period of reform.

see also: 1. Overview History of the People's Republic of China; 3. Ideology: Radicalism and Reform; agriculture; Bo Yibo; Chen Yun; Chinese Communist Party Central Committee and Politburo; Cultural Revolution; Deng Xiaoping; Four Modernizations; gang of four; Hu Yaobang; Hua Guofeng; industry; June 4 Incident; legal system; Lin Biao; Mao Zedong; science and technology; Sixth Plenum of the Eleventh Central Committee; Tiananmen Incident (1976); United States policy; Wang Zhen; Yang Shangkun; Zhou Enlai.

Colin Mackerras

Third World policy

After 1949, China identified itself, despite its links with the **Soviet Union**, as a member of the non-aligned world and a champion of anti-colonialist struggle and national liberation. However, China competed with India in obtaining recognition as a leader of the 'Third World' of developing states. At the Bandung Conference of 1955, **Zhou Enlai** enunciated the 'five principles of peaceful coexistence' which became popular in the foreign policies of China and many other states.

With the deepening of the Sino-**Soviet** rift in the 1960s, Beijing practised a 'dual adversary' foreign policy, criticizing both **United States** and **Soviet** hegemonism. From December 1963 to February 1964, **Zhou Enlai** made a highly visible tour of African states to court influence among them as a fellow Third World state. During this period, China sent economic experts and limited aid to several such regimes, including Tanzania. This strategy was also designed to challenge and erode both US and **Soviet** influence there, sow the seeds for trade and mutual economic assistance, and show support for anti-colonial struggles.

China remained supportive of Third World causes in the 1970s, despite its push towards the West. **Mao Zedong**'s famous 'three worlds theory' was in large measure designed to forge an international united front to counter perceived **Soviet** encirclement in the region. China supported the anti-hegemonist and economic redistributionist efforts of all states from the Third World (and many of those in the Second World) against the dominance and exploitation of the **United States** and the **Soviet Union**, which constituted the First World.

In the post-1976 period, with the slow resolution of regional conflicts such as those in Indochina and Afghanistan and the initiation of the reform policies, China's emphasis has shifted away from the Third World. Especially after the **June 4 Incident** Beijing renewed its rhetoric championing of Third World interests as part of its 'independent' foreign policy stance. On some issues, such as opposition to the universalistic view of human rights, China finds its interests as consonant with those of much of the Third World. Yet China has largely disqualified itself as a Third World country by what it has come to espouse and practise in its modernization drive.

see also: 8. China, the Region and the World; June 4 Incident; Mao Zedong; Soviet Union, relations with; United States policy; Zhou Enlai.

Donald H. McMillen

Three Gorges Dam

On 3 April 1992 the **National People's Congress** formally approved the construction of the Three Gorges Dam, and work began in December 1994. The project has aroused unprecedented interest both within China and abroad. Its foreign critics have variously described it as an 'ill-conceived megaproject',

'environmental disaster' and 'a Chinese Love Canal, Chernobyl and Three Mile Island rolled into one'. Many Chinese intellectuals have also voiced serious concerns about the viability and safety of the dam. The project has been criticized on environmental, economic and strategic grounds.

Ever since Sun Yat-sen first proposed the idea in 1919, China's leaders have wanted to build a gigantic dam in the spectacular Three Gorges area to harness the country's longest river, the Yangzi. In the mid-1940s, the US Bureau of Reclamation cooperated with the Nationalist government of Chiang Kai-shek in assessing potential hydroelectric sites on the Yangzi. Soon afterwards, however, the Nationalists lost control of mainland China. The idea of building a dam in the Three Gorges area was revived after the CCP's victory, but the huge cost of the project and lack of technological skills deterred **Mao Zedong**'s government.

With the period of reform and modernization, a feasibility study was conducted in 1986 with financial help from the Canadian government. The World Bank also provided funds for evaluating environmental aspects of the project. After a series of studies by Chinese experts, the leaders made up their minds to go ahead with the construction of the dam. There was, however, considerable opposition in the **National People's Congress**. In the final vote to endorse the project, 177 of the 2,633 deputies present voted against the motion to proceed while 664 abstained.

The sheer size of the project and the sums involved are staggering. The scheme, which incorporates the world's biggest hydropower station and ship-lift with a series of five consecutive ship locks, would cost US$28 billion, according to 1997 Chinese government estimates. When completed in 2009, the power station will have a generating capacity of 84.7 billion kilowatt/hours a year, or about 10 per cent of China's total power supply. Over 1 million people in Chongqing Municipality and Hubei Province are being moved from their homes and villages to new townships. Many peasants fear the relocation as this could mean learning to grow new crops or abandoning farming altogether when shifted to an even less hospitable terrain. At the same time, many peasant families, accustomed to living in traditional-style homes, are being resettled in modern four-storey houses shared by several households, forcing drastic changes in lifestyles.

Purely from the energy requirements point of view, the project appears to make sense. China's burgeoning economy has already made it the third largest energy consumer and the fourth largest user of electricity in the world. It is true that on a per capita basis, China's energy consumption is still very low, a typical Chinese household consuming less than 0.03 per cent of the energy used in the average North American home. Yet considering the potential for development of China's economy, the country's appetite for energy use is insatiable.

In 1989, as the events leading up to the **June 4 Incident** were gaining momentum, a group of Chinese scientists, journalists and other intellectuals launched a rare campaign to lobby the government decision makers to abandon the plans for the construction of the dam. To provide the **National People's Congress** deputies and other influential public figures with alternative information, they compiled and released a book containing strong arguments against the project. Led by prominent journalist Dai Qing, this group constituted a 'green' movement in the relatively more tolerant times just prior to the **June 4 Incident**. Dai Qing was arrested later in 1989 and detained for ten months, and the book was banned. Nevertheless, Dai Qing remains a strong critic of the project, and was awarded the highly prestigious Goldman Environmental Award in 1993.

The Three Gorges project has also drawn a great deal of criticism from environmental groups outside China. The World Bank has been reluctant to lend funding to the project. In May 1996, the US Export-Import Bank also turned down requests for financing by some major US corporations seeking to participate in the project. Unsure of its viability and afraid of a backlash from voters, most West-

ern governments have so far tried to keep a distance from the project. Under these circumstances, the Chinese government has been forced to rely on domestic sources for funds to construct the dam and related works.

see also: June 4 Incident; Mao Zedong; National People's Congress.

Pradeep Taneja

Tiananmen Incident (1976)

The climax of major demonstrations in Tiananmen Square in the centre of Beijing and elsewhere in mourning for **Zhou Enlai**.

On 25 March 1976 **Zhou Enlai**, who had died on 8 January, was attacked as a capitalist roader in the Shanghai newspaper *Wenhui bao*, sparking immediate protesters in his favour. On 28 March protesters in Nanjing openly attacked the **gang of four** with slogans criticizing them and the *Wenhui bao* article being stuck on trains going to Shanghai. By the end of the month, wreaths in Zhou's honour began appearing in Tiananmen Square, followed shortly by large-scale demonstrations. The Festival of the Dead (Qingming), when traditionally Chinese honoured the dead and swept the graves of their ancestors, was approaching, giving added point to the surge of affection and respect for the late premier.

This movement gave rise to numerous epitaphs and poetry, some explicitly and strongly hostile to the **gang of four**, who watched the demonstrations with growing anxiety and fear. They believed, rightly, that **Deng Xiaoping** was encouraging the demonstrations to further his own political ends, and to counter theirs. Meanwhile, similar demonstrations were taking place in other Chinese cities, including Hangzhou, Nanjing and Taiyuan. In the evening of 4 April the Politburo, which was dominated by the **gang of four**, decided to suppress the mourning and, with **Mao Zedong**'s approval, sent militia into the Square and cleared it of epitaphs and wreaths.

On 5 April, in defiance against this action, thousands of demonstrators surged into the Square. The **gang of four**'s representatives clashed with Zhou's supporters. At one point the crowd overturned a car and set it on fire. The climax came in the evening when 'workers' militia' came out in force from the direction of the Imperial Palaces to the north of the Square and suppressed the demonstration. They beat people to the ground and took away bleeding demonstrators. Hundreds were arrested and an equal number wounded, some seriously, although it is not certain how many, if any, were actually killed. By the next morning, the Square had been cleaned up, to remove any sign of the troubles.

The radical faction immediately had the events condemned as a 'counter-revolutionary political incident'. They blamed **Deng Xiaoping** and had him dismissed from his posts, although **Mao Zedong** would not agree to his expulsion from the CCP, and had **Hua Guofeng**, at that time on their side, appointed premier. Despite the **gang of four**'s interpretation, these were, in the first instance, the first truly spontaneous demonstrations held under the PRC (see **protest movements**). They were celebrated as expressions of freedom and were regarded as the origin of a progressive April Fifth (*Siwu*) Movement, with parallels to the May Fourth (*Wusi*) Movement of 1919. On 14 November 1978, the Beijing Municipal CCP Central Committee changed its verdict on the Incident, giving it formal endorsement. The next month, the **Third Plenum of the Eleventh Central Committee** described the demonstrations in Tiananmen Square as 'entirely revolutionary actions'. In his famous article 'The Fifth Modernization', which was posted on the **Democracy Wall** on 5 December 1978, famous **dissident** Wei Jingsheng referred to the movement in saying 'now democracy and prosperity, so earnestly sought by those who shed their blood at Tiananmen, seem soon to be realized'. Although **Deng Xiaoping** was shortly to have Wei imprisoned for his views, the two men did agree in giving a positive evaluation to this incident.

see also: Democracy Wall; Deng Xiaoping; dissidents; gang of four; Hua Guofeng; Mao Zedong; protest movements; Third Ple-

num of the Eleventh Central Committee; Zhou Enlai.

Colin Mackerras

Tiananmen Massacre (1989)
See **June 4 Incident**.

Tibet Autonomous Region
The least populous but, other than **Xinjiang**, the largest in area of China's province-level units, the Tibet Autonomous Region (TAR) is located in China's southwest with an area of 1,228,400 square kilometres.

Not including the army, the population of Tibet, as given in the two censuses since the TAR was established, is:

- 1982: 1,863,623, of whom 921,238 male and 942,385 female, and 94.97 per cent belonged to the Tibetan and other **minority nationalities**;
- 1990: 2,196,010, of whom 1,098,694 (50.03 per cent) male and 1,097,316 (49.97 per cent) female, and 2,096,346 (95.46 per cent) were **Tibetans**.

The reincorporation of Tibet into China was formalized through the Agreement for the Peaceful Liberation of Tibet of 23 May 1951, which specified that:

- Tibet would become part of the PRC;
- the Tibetan people would exercise national regional autonomy under the central government and enjoy freedom of religion;
- reform would be carried out through consultation; and
- the central government would handle external affairs.

Following this Agreement, the first contingent of Chinese troops arrived in Lhasa on 9 September 1951.

In March 1959 a major uprising against Chinese rule erupted in Lhasa, which Chinese troops under Zhang Guohua suppressed quickly but with very heavy casualties and lasting bitterness to ethnic relations. One result was the flight of the Dalai Lama to India, who immediately renounced the 1951 Agreement and attacked the 'invading Chinese troops' for forcing it upon his government (see **Sino-Indian Border War (1962)**).

In April 1959 the **National People's Congress** in **Beijing** resolved to implement 'democratic reform' in Tibet, including the emancipation of serfs. The former administrative system and the relative autonomy of the 1950s both disappeared.

The TAR was formally established on 9 September 1965. However, when the **Cultural Revolution** broke out the next year, persecution of Tibetan Buddhism and attacks on other aspects of Tibetan culture reached an unprecedented height, with massive destruction of the monasteries and suppression of Tibetan arts and lifestyle.

In May 1980 a delegation from the central government, led by General Secretary **Hu Yaobang**, visited Tibet. Very shocked at conditions, the central government announced six reform measures, including:

- the effective implementation of the policy of autonomy, with rejection of all policies inappropriate to Tibet's local conditions;
- the revival of Tibetan culture, education and science, provided socialist principles were not directly contravened; and
- the commitment that over two-thirds of government functionaries should be full-time cadres of Tibetan nationality within two or three years.

The 1980s saw immense improvements in Tibet. However, the quota of over two-thirds was probably not reached until the early 1990s. A 1996 figure put the proportion at 70 per cent.

Despite the more tolerant policies, the wish for an independent Tibet has persisted, especially among the clergy, as has Chinese determination to suppress secessionism. From 27 September to 6 October 1987 demonstrations on behalf of independence took place, leading the Chinese authorities to send in more troops to suppress the demonstrators, police beating up monks and casualties resulting. Early in March 1989, further riots occurred to mark the thirtieth anniversary of the 1959 uprising, the worst since that time. There was serious violence between police and demonstrators and looting of Han Chinese houses and shops. On 7 March the Chinese authorities reacted by imposing martial law, for the first time in the PRC.

In Lhasa there were anti-government demonstrations late in May 1993, especially on 24 May when up to 3,000 Tibetans rioted. The initial cause was inflation, and police kept their distance until slogans changed into calls for Tibetan independence, even then using tear gas, not lethal weapons, to disperse the crowds. In May 1996 the official Tibetan press called for increased crackdowns on armed secessionist terrorism. The call was prompted by clergy-led protests against local officials' attempts to ban the display of pictures of the Dalai Lama. At the large Ganden Monastery some 60 kilometres outside Lhasa police broke up demonstrators, reportedly killing two monks.

Apart from police action, the other Chinese government method of persuading **Tibetans** against the wish to split from China is to modernize the economy and raise living standards, while at the same time allowing what cultural freedom it judges will not threaten secession. It inaugurated sixty-two construction projects, including mainly infrastructure, such as water supply, electricity, roads, power, telecommunications, schools and hospitals. On the thirtieth anniversary of the founding of the TAR in September 1995, the government announced many figures showing economic and social improvements. These included:

- 285 industrial enterprises employing over 20,000 workers, with a 1994 industrial output value twelve times that of 1964;
- a highway network of 20,000 kilometres, reaching four-fifths of townships; and
- a life expectancy of 63.4 years compared with 36 before 1951.

see also: 6. Peoples of China; Beijing Municipality; Cultural Revolution; Hu Yaobang; minority nationalities policy; National People's Congress: Sino-Indian Border War; Tibetans; Xinjiang Uygur Autonomous Region.

Colin Mackerras

Tibetans

A people inhabiting Southwest China, recognized by the Chinese state as one of its fifty-five **minority nationalities**, and known for their unique and strong culture, a crucial part of which is Tibetan Buddhism. Of all fifty-five minorities the Tibetans have caused most political embarrassment to the PRC because of the international movement for their status as an independent nation-state and the persistent opposition to Chinese policy and rule found among them.

Figures from the four PRC censuses show the number of Tibetans as 2,753,081 (1953), 2,501,174 (1964), 3,847,875 (1982) and 4,593,072 (1990). The 1990 census showed less than half living in the **Tibet Autonomous Region** (2,096,346), and the great majority of the remainder in the four provinces of **Sichuan** (1,087,510), Qinghai (911,860), Gansu (366,718) and Yunnan (111,414).

The pre-1949 Xikang Province, which contained a substantial Tibetan population, was abolished in July 1955, the territory east of the Yangzi being absorbed into **Sichuan** later the same year and, in 1956, the territory to its west into Tibet. The great majority of Tibetans in **Sichuan** live in Ganzi Tibetan, Liangshan Yi and Ngawa Tibetan Autonomous Prefectures, set up respectively in 1950, 1952 and 1953.

The great majority of Qinghai's Tibetans inhabit the six autonomous prefectures of Yushu, Haibei, Hainan, Haixi, Huangnan and Golog, all established in 1951, 1953 or 1954. Gansu and Yunnan have one Tibetan autonomous prefecture each, respectively Gannan, established in October 1953, and Diqing, September 1957. Tibetans know those Tibetan territories of Yunnan and the former Xikang as Kham, those of Qinghai and Gansu as Amdo.

The 17-point Agreement of May 1951 (see **Tibet Autonomous Region** TAR) covered only those regions in Tibet itself, not the other Tibetan areas, where socialist reform was imposed on an unwilling population. A place of special importance politically was Chamdo, in Xikang Province until its abolition in 1955 and then in Tibet. There anti-Chinese violence broke out in the early 1950s, with long-lasting bloody rebellion spreading over many of the Kham areas, and for a while in Amdo as well. These rebellions, undertaken by guerrilla and conventional warfare, were suppressed with great bloodshed by Chinese troops, which also suffered considerable casualties. It was mainly refugee Khampas who led the rebellion in Lhasa in 1959.

All Tibetan areas suffered cultural and religious persecution during the **Cultural Revolution**. Early in 1988 reports circulated that disturbances in one of Qinghai's Tibetan areas in December 1987 had demanded its incorporation into Tibet. However, the main political incidents since 1987 involving Tibetans have been focused on Lhasa, not Tibetan areas outside the TAR.

In April 1982 the Chinese government began negotiations with the Dalai Lama's representatives over the future of Tibet. But each side began with assumptions so different that the negotiations got nowhere. In particular, the Chinese assumption was that the TAR and other Tibetan areas currently in China would remain inalienable territories of China, whereas the Dalai Lama's representatives wanted not only an independent Tibet but also one which would include, apart from the TAR, the whole of Qinghai province, as well as parts of Gansu, **Sichuan**, Yunnan and **Xinjiang**. Meanwhile the Dalai Lama himself has made proposals stopping short of total Tibetan independence in speeches given in Strasbourg in July 1988 and London in July 1996. In the first his main point was that whereas China might take responsibility for Tibet's foreign affairs, Tibetans should enjoy full self-rule in domestic matters. In the second he stated that what he was striving for was not independence but 'genuine self-rule for Tibet' and reiterated his willingness to start negotiations with China 'without any preconditions'. He repeated this formula many times in the following period.

One of the charges which the Dalai Lama and his representatives make most often against the Chinese is that 7.5 million Chinese live in Tibet, with the result that there are more Chinese than Tibetans there. But according to figures derived from the 1990 census, there are about 1.5 million Han

Chinese in all those territories classified as Tibetan autonomous places, which are home to the overwhelming majority of China's Tibetans. Although the territory classified as part of Tibet by the Dalai Lama but not as a Tibetan autonomous place in the census is comparatively small, it does include some significant populous areas, perhaps the most important being the capital of Qinghai Province, Xining, and the nearby counties of Haidong in Qinghai, the combined population of which, in the 1990 census, came to 2,995,536 of Qinghai's total of 4,456,946.

see also: 6. Peoples of China; Cultural Revolution; minority nationalities policy; Tibet Autonomous Region; Xinjiang Uygur Autonomous Region.

Colin Mackerras

township and village enterprises

Township and village enterprises (TVEs) are rural non-agricultural enterprises located in villages and small towns and owned by rural people, either collectively or privately. Among the most dynamic sectors to emerge from the post-1978 reforms, they operate outside the plan system and in response to market forces. They transformed the structure of the rural economy and also profoundly influenced China's **industry** and **international trade**. In addition, the TVEs created a new community of rural entrepreneurs and workers reliant on market development and committed to further economic reform.

The origins of the TVEs lie in the small-scale industries and enterprises developed to support agriculture in the people's communes before 1978. These produced inputs for agricultural production, processed agricultural raw materials, and made local handicraft products. Operating in a plan environment, however, they were not able to compete with urban **industry** or to produce for market consumption. Yet by 1978 they numbered around 1.5 million, employed some 28 million rural labourers and provided a pool of technical and managerial skills in the countryside.

The rural reforms stimulated dramatic TVE growth. The introduction of household farm-ing enabled households to plan **labour** use efficiently and also made them sharply aware of their opportunity costs. The large increases in state purchase prices meant rises in incomes and savings, and in capital for rural investment. The opening up of the free market system provided a source of inputs and of demand for products. The market was thus the catalyst which encouraged a shift of rural investment towards profitable non-agricultural activities.

After the official 1984 decision to promote the growth of TVEs, the sector expanded rapidly, especially in labour-intensive manufacturing such as textiles, food-processing, construction materials and raw material extraction.

The rapid growth absorbed **labour** out of **agriculture** and pushed the overall structure of manufacturing in China towards labour-intensive activities, in which China has a natural comparative advantage. Over time it also shifted China's exports towards a heavy focus on labour-intensive products, and thereby influenced production in other countries which found it difficult to compete.

The problems facing further TVE development in the 1990s were a concentration in the coastal regions (about two-thirds of all enterprises and over 70 per cent of profits), a shortage of capital, and a lack of clarity in property rights. The regional concentration was creating significant disparities in rural incomes. The shortage of capital was an obstacle to further rapid growth and improvement in technology; the ownership structure meant that **collective** enterprises were often run in the interests of local government rather than in the most efficient way. Moreover, individual peasants could not realize their rights as **collective** owners. Government policies were thus encouraging more TVE development in the interior and promoting forms of shareholder ownership. The next stage of development required more open and equal competition between state enterprises and TVEs by the removal of remaining administrative barriers between the two.

By 1995, there were over 22 million TVEs (excluding the very small and informal).

They operated in all economic sectors and had some 129 million employees (28 per cent of the rural labour force). Of these enterprises, only 1.6 million were owned collectively by townships and villages, but these employed close to half the workers and produced nearly 60 per cent of the output value. They were thus larger in scale and more capital intensive than the privately owned TVEs. Around 75 per cent of output was industrial manufacturing. The output value of TVEs was about 77 per cent of total rural output value. They generated slightly over a quarter of rural per capita incomes, and in the more developed areas, as much as 80 per cent. By the mid-1990s, therefore, they produced around 20 per cent of total GDP, approaching 40 per cent of national industrial value-added, and between a quarter and a third of all of China's exports. In addition, they were attracting a growing proportion of foreign investment. The TVEs were thus a key sector in the economy as a whole and represented a new force in the political economy of China's development.

see also: agriculture; collective agriculture; collective sector; industry; international trade; labour policy and system.

Andrew Watson

trade

See **international trade**.

transport and telecommunications

As a developing country, China has faced major problems of infrastructure development. In 1949, the road and rail systems were totally inadequate. This was particularly the case for north–south communications, symbolized by the absence of any bridges across the Yangzi River. Telecommunications were also very limited. As a result, investment in transport and telecommunications has been an important element of development programmes.

Before the economic reforms began, the transport shortage was managed by plan allocations. The controls over **population** movement and the absence of rapid and flexible market interaction also served to limit

demand. After 1978, the rapid growth of the economy and the increasing mobility of people and commodities placed great strains on the transport infrastructure, which is now seen as a major bottleneck. The need for greater speed of communication also saw a sharp rise in the needs for telephone, telegram and, more recently, fax services. In general, improvements have been fastest in the coastal zones, and large areas of the interior still face significant constraints.

Transport
After 1949, the Ministry of Railways took over the railway system and administered it through twenty regional bureaux. Inland waterways and coastal shipping, which formed a major transport network in the traditional economy, especially in the south, came under the Ministry of Transport, which operated them through a combination of state and collective enterprises. In general, larger scale and more modern technology enterprises were state-owned.

Sea shipping was controlled through a state-owned company under the Ministry of Transport. Roads also came under the Ministry of Transport, though much of the practical administration was at the local provincial level and below. Aviation was managed through the Civil Aviation Bureau under the **State Council** and operated through six regional bureaux. Pipeline transport, primarily for oil and natural gas, began to develop during the 1960s under the Ministry of Petroleum.

Within this framework, the railways acted as the key system for the movement of goods. In general, the existence of sharp boundaries between regions and administrative systems was an obstacle to the growth of integrated transport services and tended to increase the costs of trans-shipment between systems.

Investment in the transport network after 1949 was substantial. The railway network increased from 22,000 km in 1949 to 51,900 km in 1980. New lines were built, the length of double-tracking was extended, and major bridges across the Yangzi and Yellow Rivers were constructed. Passengers rose from 13 billion person/kilometres to 138.3 billion and freight from 18.4 billion tonne/kilometres to 571.7 billion. Over the same period, the road system grew from 80,000 km to 888,000 km, the inland river routes from 73,600 km to 108,000 km, and the airline system from 11,400 km to 191,700 km. In 1980, the railways carried 27 per cent of passenger traffic and 46.3 per cent of freight, and the roads 65 per cent of passengers and 31.6 per cent of freight. This represented a shift of passenger traffic to roads (though the distance per passenger was lower than by rail) and a shift of freight towards rail. In addition, pipelines were around 10,600 km in 1980 and carried over 63 per cent of crude oil transport.

Despite this substantial growth, the extent of transport services remained limited, and this became very clear when the economic reforms created a substantial market for all forms of transport. Transport of goods for the free markets competed with goods distributed under plan allocations. The movement of people for commercial transactions increased, and this was augmented during the 1980s with a demand for domestic tourism and a substantial movement of contract labour between the countryside and the cities. By the early 1990s it was estimated that there were up to 80 million people in the 'floating' population, and cities such as **Beijing** could have as many as 1 million outsiders in residence every day.

The huge growth in transport demand created competition between the market and plan allocations. Extra fees could be charged for market goods while plan allocations went unfulfilled. The growth also stimulated **collective** and individual enterprise, especially for road haulage and local transport. While the railway network remained state-run, the ownership of road haulage services and small-scale river transport was diversified. The airline system was reorganized as a number of competing regional airlines. Investment in roads also increased substantially, and local governments used road tolls as a means of financing road investment and supplementing revenue. Meanwhile, the prices of transport also rose considerably.

Under the plan system, prices had been kept low in order to reduce industrial costs. As the reforms increased the focus on economic efficiency, the transport systems came under pressure both to improve profitability and to generate funds for reinvestment. Prices rose, though plan rail prices remained low.

As a result of this growth in demand, investment in transport rose, especially in roads and airlines. By 1995, the railway network had grown to 54,600 km, the roads to 1.157 million km and aviation routes to 1.129 million km (including 348,000 km of international routes). Pipelines had also grown to 17,200 km. Railway passenger/kilometres had risen to 354.6 billion and freight to 1,287 billion. In comparison, road passenger/kilometres were 460.3 billion and freight was 469.5 billion. In terms of ratios, rail accounted for about 9 per cent of passengers and 13 per cent of freight, while roads accounted for 88 per cent of passengers and 76 per cent of freight. The figures thus indicated a marked shift towards road transport, especially for shorter distances and in the rural economy, where private and **collective** haulage services formed an important element in the **township and village enterprise** system. This shift was reflected in the increase in the number of road vehicles from 1.36 million in 1978 to 10.4 million in 1995.

Despite this impressive growth, transport remained a substantial bottleneck. The provision of transport infrastructure remained a public good, financed from government revenue. Investment had to compete with all the other demands on the national budget, and implementation of investment plans was not always realised.

In the Seventh Five-Year Plan (1986–90), for example, transport investment was only 12 per cent of total investment and only 2,300 km of the planned 3,600 km of new railways were completed. Demand continued to exceed supply. There was also considerable scope to improve transport efficiency through such matters as containerization, bulk transport and the formation of integrated transport companies across administrative boundaries. The situation was particularly difficult in the inland provinces which received less emphasis under the preferential policies for coastal development.

As a result of the political pressures on the central government caused by the uneven regional development, by the mid-1990s the regional bias in policies had given way to a sectoral emphasis. Transport received greater priority, with stress on development in the western regions. The Ninth Five-Year Plan (1996–2000) called for an extension of the railways to 68,000 km and the roads to 1.23 million km.

Telecommunications

Before 1978, the main form of personal communication in China was the postal and telegraphic system under the Ministry of Posts and Telecommunications. Access to telephones was primarily institutional or through public services, private telephone numbers being very limited. In part this situation reflected the limits on non-official business. From 1952 to 1978, the number of subscribers rose only from 295,000 to 1,192,000, an increase of around 12 per cent per year. By 1995 the number had risen to 32,636,000, growing at 155 per cent per year.

The dramatic acceleration reflected the impact of the market economy, the growth in personal telephone use and the substantial investment in telephone systems. By 1995, 72 per cent of telephone subscribers were residential. As a result, the number of telephones per 100 people had risen from 0.43 in 1980 to 4.66 in 1995. In addition, new services such as fax machines also began to grow.

According to official statistics, the number of faxes sent rose from around 1 million in 1991 to 4.4 million in 1995. Given the relative underdevelopment of the network before 1978, much of the new investment was in new technology, including fibre-optic cables, automatic exchanges and mobile systems. The Ninth Five-Year Plan thus emphasized the use of optical cables, microwave and satellite communication and synchronized digital systems.

Overall this rise in telecommunications represented a fundamental change in the operation of economic and administrative networks and in the capacity for individual communication. Changes of this kind meant a massive increase in the circulation of information and in the potential for all types of interaction, both nationally and internationally.

see also: Beijing Municipality; collective sector; population policy; State Council; township and village enterprises.

Andrew Watson

Tung Chee-hwa

On 11 December 1996, Tung Chee-hwa was selected as China's first chief executive of the **Hong Kong** Special Administration Region (HKSAR), having received 320 votes from the 400-member selection committee which **Beijing** established for this task.

Tung was born in 1937 in **Shanghai**, being the son of C. Y. Tung. The elder Tung established a shipping company in **Hong Kong** in 1941, and two more companies on the mainland in 1946–7. After the CCP took power in 1949, the Tung family followed the defeated Nationalist Party to **Taiwan**, taking all assets with them. In later decades, the Taiwan-based business grew as its ships became the prime carriers of US goods to Asia, particularly during the Vietnam War. Tung Chee-hwa took over the family business as chairman of Orient Overseas International in 1979, three years before his father died.

In the mid-1980s the business ran into significant financial difficulties due to a serious recession in the global shipping industry. After being turned down by the **Taiwan** authorities, Tung obtained US$120 million in funding support from a China-backed syndicate headed by **Hong Kong** business tycoon Henry Fok Ying-tung. It is likely that a good part of this capital input came from a contingency fund set up by the **New China News Agency** in **Hong Kong** with the approval of the central government. The family business survived the crisis and Tung started to invest in China shortly thereafter. Now basing his business operations in **Hong Kong**, in March 1989 Tung visited **Shanghai** where he met the municipality's CCP Secretary **Jiang Zemin**. Tung's China investments were in the food and beverage industry, but also included joint ventures in shipbuilding and a 23 per cent share of the US$1.5 billion Oriental Plaza shopping centre in **Beijing**'s Wangfujing district (a project in which another **Hong Kong** tycoon, Li Ka-shing, holds a 64 per cent investment through his flagship Cheung Kong).

Tung's involvement in **Hong Kong** politics began in 1985 when he was appointed a member of the Beijing-selected Basic Law Consultative Committee. In March 1992, China appointed him a member of the first batch of forty-four **Hong Kong** affairs advisers, and in the same year Governor Chris Patten appointed him to the Executive Council on the recommendation of Hong Kong Bank chief Sir William Purves. In February 1993, Tung was appointed a member of the **Chinese People's Political Consultative Conference** (the first executive councillor ever to serve on this body). In January 1996, Tung was named vice-chairman of the Preparatory Committee for the HKSAR and when this group was later in **Beijing Jiang Zemin** singled him out for a handshake photograph.

In June 1996, Tung resigned from the Executive Council, and in September publicly announced his chief executive candidacy. In the nomination process in mid-November, he garnered 206 nominations, far more than the other two successful candidates, Yang Ti-liang (82) and Peter Woo Kwong-ching (54). The local reaction to his selection in December 1996 was positive, since his reputed integrity and the range of ties he cultivated over the years with business and government leaders in **Taiwan**, the **United States**, **Japan**, the United Kingdom, **Hong Kong** and the PRC provided him with a great degree of credibility as a leader of **Hong Kong** under Chinese sovereignty.

see also: Beijing Municipality; Chinese People's Political Consultative Conference; Hong Kong; Japan, relations with; Jiang Zemin; New China News Agency; Shanghai; Taiwan policy; United States policy.

Donald H. McMillen

U

Union of Soviet Socialist Republics (USSR)/Commonwealth of Independent States (CIS), relations with
see **Soviet Union, relations with**.

unit

The unit (*danwei*) was the organizational module of Chinese society under the economic **planning** system whose persisting influences affect social and economic development under reform. From the start of grain rationing in the mid-1950s, unit membership gave one access to food, whether 'collective grain' raised in one's commune, brigade or team and distributed in-kind to members, or to 'state grain' sold to those with ration cards at grain stores for cash. Together with the **household registration (*hukou*)** system, units formed a comprehensive internal passport system for regulating mobility and facilitating general political control. (In existing residential areas, these control functions were shared with local governments and police agencies.)

Although myriad variations existed to suit varied social and economic circumstances, the ideal type of unit was a large state-owned industrial enterprise of the 1970s like **Beijing**'s famous Capital Steel Mill. In such units the ideal member was a worker who was born to parents working in that unit in one of its hospitals, who was educated in its primary and middle schools, who paid a nominal rent to live in one of its flats with a co-worker spouse, who made daily purchases in its shops, banked in its credit cooperative and on retirement drew a pension from it. All these subsidies and outlays were treated as current **labour** cost charged against current sales revenues. Should anyone aspire to enter university or pursue a political career, the case would be decided by the Party and mass organization (**Women**'s Federation, Communist **Youth** League), bodies that paralleled

the unit's functional bureaucratic structure. With the help of its public security office, one's daily political behaviour would be recorded in the unit's personal files (*dang'an*). One's children and grandchildren would ideally inherit one's position in the unit.

The word 'unit' has obvious military connotations, but the aspirations towards comprehensiveness, closedness and permanency that it connotes derived from a variety of practical and ideological sources. For the many units that began as new industrial complexes built with **Soviet** aid, social infrastructures had to be planned and installed along with the industrial plant. Household registration and collective responsibility, both well established traditions in Chinese policing, acquired new functions once 'class identity' (*chengfen*) and 'social origin' (*chushen*) labels were assigned to everyone in the early 1950s. By effectively attaching the peasants to the soil, the grain distribution system functioned as a fiscal device for assuring the agricultural surpluses needed for industrialization. At the ideological level, Marxism incorporated currents of syndicalist idealism that structured propaganda from above and periodically resurfaced as populist pressures from below.

Despite these appeals, units proved politically unstable because they were closed and juxtaposed theoretical egalitarianism with actual inequality. Wages and social benefits all depended on specific units' incomes, which varied greatly, producing large inter-unit inequalities. State-owned urban enterprises did better than **collective** ones, and centrally owned better than locally owned. Among rural **collectives**, those with better natural conditions, lower population densities or laxer enforcement of leftist policies, did better than others. Intra-unit inequalities were equally marked. In industrial units several types of underprivileged employees, such as temporary or contract workers, toiled alongside regular workers for lower wages and without fringe benefits or hope of promotion. Among regular workers large differences in pay and privileges separated apprentices from master workers. In the communes, permanently stigmatized and privileged classes emerged. The tumultuous conflicts of the **Cultural Revolution**, though blurred by momentary personal and political factors, generally reflected interest conflicts between citizens systematically advantaged or disadvantaged by the unit system.

Reform exposed the economic defects of the unit system. Setting aside the general economic problems of central **planning**, units wasted workers by blunting **labour** markets. Lifetime job tenure, age-based promotion, and chronic overstaffing eliminated marginal incentives for effort, while a unit's veto over transfers prevented efficient workers from being hired away. New growth since reform has overwhelmingly been concentrated in family-owned, private or **collective** units unburdened by unit traditions, while the large state-owned units have become chronic loss-makers, kept solvent only by ever escalating subsidies. The unit tradition thus forms a major obstacle to further economic reform.

see also: Beijing Municipality; collective agriculture; collective sector; Cultural Revolution; household registration (*hukou*); labour policy and system; planning, economic; Soviet Union, relations with; women; youth policy and organizations.

Paul Ivory

United Nations policy

The admission of the PRC to the United Nations (UN) in October 1971 marked a shift in its policy towards the world body from one of resentment and indifference to one of participation and support. Before 1971 the China seat was occupied by the Republic of China (**Taiwan**), a founding member since 1945.

Shortly after the establishment of the PRC (1949), its Ministry of Foreign Affairs announced that it would retain the right to take its rightful place at an appropriate time in all international organizations, including the UN, its seat having been usurped by **Taiwan**. Fresh from victory over the Nationalists, the PRC was trying to establish its international legitimacy. However, the outbreak of the **Korean War** in June 1950 and China's entry into the war impeded its effort to acquire international recognition. The UN condemned China as aggressor and the Security Council passed a resolution to send a multilateral force, led by the **United States**, to intervene. China entered a period of acrimonious relationship with the UN, accusing it of being a puppet or instrument of imperialism controlled by the US.

China's later efforts to join the UN and other major international organizations in the late 1950s and the 1960s were foiled mainly by the US. In frustration China depicted the UN as a 'dirty international political stock exchange in the grip of a few big powers' in 1965 and called for an alternative, revolutionary international organization. Turning its attention to the **Third World**, China supported the Non-Aligned Movement, although it has never been a member.

For every year since 1950 China's membership application to the UN was debated and voted upon. With decolonization and the rise of small states, a UN of 59 states in 1950 became one of 128 by 1971. China's support from the communist and non-aligned developing countries gained momentum during the 1950s and 1960s. In 1971 China finally won the two-thirds majority support (76 for, 35 against, with 17 abstentions) for membership, **Taiwan** feeling obliged to leave the world body. In subsequent years China gained entry to a host of organs and specialized agencies of the UN system. In 1980 it became a member of the World Bank and the International Monetary Fund.

Although it still did not belong to the **World Trade Organization**, in 1996 China was a member of over forty-four UN organs, specialized agencies and commissions and increasingly involved in various UN activities. Beijing plays host to regional offices of the UN Development Programme, the United Nations Educational, Scientific and Cultural Organization, the United Nations High

Commission for Refugees and the World Health Organization.

China's position with respect to UN peace-keeping operations has changed from antagonism in the 1950s and 1960s to antipathy in the 1970s, and then to active cooperation and participation in the 1980s and 1990s, indicative of China's cooperative behaviour in international relations and political socialization into the global system.

The critical point came in December 1981 when, for the first time in its history, China voted in favour of a UN resolution sanctioning the extension of the mandate of its peace-keeping forces in Cyprus. The first time that China sent peace-keepers to join UN operations was in 1992 when it dispatched 47 military observers and an engineering battalion of 400 men to Cambodia.

In marking the UN's fiftieth anniversary in 1995, an editorial in *China Daily* said that the UN was 'the most representative and authoritative international organization in the world' and 'its functions are irreplaceable'. The paucity of well-trained diplomats and bureaucrats, financial constraints, and China's political culture still limit its contributions towards the UN system, especially in the area of agenda setting. However, being one of the five permanent members of the Security Council with a veto power, China can maintain a strong say in matters of importance to the UN.

In sum, China's policy towards international organizations in general and the UN in particular has changed largely from system-transforming to system-conforming. The world body has proved to be a convenient forum for China to voice its global concerns and to express its world-views.

see also: 8. China, the Region and the World; Korean War; Taiwan policy; Third World policy; United States policy; World Trade Organization.

Gerald Chan

United States policy

China's policy towards the US has gone through some fundamental changes since 1949: from hostility in the 1950s and 1960s, to rapprochement in the 1970s, and to normalization and adjustments from the 1980s onwards. In the 1990s China is trying to seek a good, stable working relationship with the US based on its Five Principles of Peaceful Coexistence in general and the three communiqués signed with the US in particular, Foreign Minister **Qian Qichen** expressing the hope that the two countries 'will enhance confidence, reduce trouble, expand cooperation, and avoid confrontation.'

For China, relations with the US form its most important bilateral relationship; to the US, the China relationship is second in importance only to the Japanese in Eastern and South Asia. With the rise of China's political and economic powers, Sino-American relations have assumed an increasingly prominent place in US Asian policy. China recognizes a cordial relationship with the US as helpful for its modernization goals.

China's policy towards the US can be viewed in the context of China's overall foreign policy. Since 1949 China's foreign policy goals have been to safeguard its national security, to preserve its sovereign and territorial integrity, and to achieve speedy development and modernization, in that order. In the first two decades after its establishment, the safeguarding of its national security was paramount.

China's first major conflict with the US was the **Korean War** of 1950–3. This war helped to cement China's uneasy alliance with the **Soviet Union**, an alliance that was forged by the top Chinese leadership, with **Mao Zedong** at its helm, when it decided to side with the **Soviet Union** against the US. The **Korean War** was the first serious threat to the PRC's national security, and the US became its top enemy.

After the outbreak of the war, the US dispatched its Seventh Fleet to patrol the Taiwan Strait and poured military assistance into South **Korea**, **Japan** and **Taiwan** in order to contain a growing perceived threat from China and the **Soviet Union**. China saw the deployment of the Seventh Fleet as a second serious threat to its security and sovereignty.

In 1958, a military crisis developed from China's shelling of Quemoy and Matsu, two Taiwanese-held offshore islands near China's Fujian Province, and reciprocal shelling from **Taiwan** across the Strait. China has continued to blame the US for separating **Taiwan** from the motherland.

The deterioration in Sino-American relations during the 1950s and 1960s can be seen in terms of the big power triangle involving the US, the **Soviet Union** and China and in terms of domestic politics in both countries. China's military alliance with the **Soviet Union** and its ideological bond with the communist world meant that the capitalist and imperialist US remained its top enemy. This situation eased somewhat after the split between China and the **Soviet Union**. The split became open in the mid-1960s, culminating in border clashes in 1969. The excesses of the **Cultural Revolution** in the late 1960s obliged China to begin new foreign policy initiatives.

China began to espouse its 'three worlds theory', first enunciated by **Mao Zedong** in February 1974 and publicly stated by **Deng Xiaoping** before the **United Nations** General Assembly two months later. According to the theory, the US and the **Soviet Union** belong to the First World; the developed countries in the West, including **Japan**, Canada and those in Europe to the Second World; and the developing countries in Asia, Africa, and Latin America to the **Third World**. China has always maintained, even up to the mid-1990s, that it belongs to the **Third World**. In this theory China put the two imperialist superpowers at odds with the Third World, and hence with China, despite the beginning of a rapprochement between the US and China.

Richard Nixon's visit to China in the last week of February 1972 marked a new chapter in Sino-American relations. The Shanghai Communiqué signed towards the end of his visit has remained one of the three communiqués that govern Sino-American relations. The second communiqué was signed in December 1978 to establish diplomatic relations on 1 January 1979. The third, signed in August 1982, made specific reference to the US sales of arms to **Taiwan**, which would 'not exceed, either in qualitative or in quantitative terms, the level of those supplied in recent years since the establishment of diplomatic relations between the US and China'.

The **June 4 Incident** of 1989 set back Sino-American relations temporarily without much upsetting the basic structure of the relationship in the longer run. The issue of **Taiwan** has remained one of the most intricate stumbling blocks in the bilateral relationship in the post-Cold War era. The visit of President Lee Teng-hui of **Taiwan** to the US in June 1995 infuriated China, which responded by testing missiles and holding military exercises in the Taiwan Strait in July and August 1995 and again in March 1996, the later incident occurring just ahead of the first presidential election in **Taiwan**. The escalation of tension across the Strait brought the US Seventh Fleet near Taiwanese waters. Other sources of conflict include China's nuclear proliferation and sales of arms, its human rights record, disputes over trade and the protection of intellectual property rights, and China's application to join the **World Trade Organization**.

At the **Asia-Pacific Economic Cooperation** meeting held in Manila in November 1996, Chinese President **Jiang Zemin** and US President Bill Clinton agreed to exchange state visits in 1997 and 1998.

see also: 8. China, the Region and the World; Asia-Pacific Economic Cooperation; Cultural Revolution; Deng Xiaoping; Japan, relations with; Jiang Zemin; June 4 Incident; Korea, policy on; Korean War; Mao Zedong; Qian Qichen; Soviet Union, relations with; Taiwan policy; Third World policy; United Nations policy.

Gerald Chan

W

Wan Li

Senior leader who played a critical role in transforming the system of **collective agriculture**. Loyal to **Deng Xiaoping**, Wan is known for his economic pragmatism.

Born in Dongping County, **Shandong**, in 1916, Wan joined the CCP in 1936 and served the revolution actively. After transfer to **Beijing** in 1952, he served as vice-minister, and later minister, of Urban Construction. In 1958, he was appointed secretary of the **Beijing Municipal** Party Committee and vice-mayor. In 1966, he fell from power as a 'bourgeois reactionary'.

Wan re-emerged in 1971 as a member of the **Beijing** Party Committee's Standing Committee and in 1973 was designated as a vice-chairman of the **Beijing Municipal Revolutionary Committee**. In 1975 Wan became minister of Railways, effectively terminating several railway strikes. In 1977 he became Anhui Provincial Party secretary, Deng being determined to eliminate the influence of the **gang of four** in a province notorious for factional strife. Wan condemned the **Dazhai** model and paved the way for household responsibility systems. He:

- conducted thorough examinations of problems associated with the **collective** system;
- allowed experimentation with grassroots innovations; and
- protected provincial and local officials from criticism from the centre.

After transfer to **Beijing** in 1980, Wan continued to support rural reform through membership of the **CCP Central Committee** Secretariat, as vice-premier, and as director of the State Agricultural Commission, for example by producing such policy documents as that of September 1980 which legitimized the household-based responsibility systems. In 1982 and 1987 respectively Wan was appointed to the Politburos of the Twelfth and Thirteenth Central Committees.

Wan is also known for his liberal views on political reform. As early as 1984, he supported the idea that the Chinese Writers' Association should democratically elect its own leaders. Wan called for more independence for universities and research institutes in their curriculum and finances. Elected chairman of the **National People's Congress** (NPC) in April 1988, he advocated a more open and democratic work style for the legislature.

In 1989, during his visit to the **United States** just before the **June 4 Incident**, Wan opposed martial law but, probably due to loyalty to Deng, changed position upon return to China, publicly announcing his support for martial law.

Though retiring from the NPC chair late in 1992, Wan's influence remains strong.

see also: Beijing Municipality; Chinese Communist Party Central Committee and Politburo; collective agriculture; Dazhai; Deng Xiaoping; gang of four; June 4 Incident; National People's Congress; revolutionary committees; Shandong; United States policy.

Jae Ho Chung

Wang Zhen

A leading CCP leader, especially in **Xinjiang**, Wang was born in Hunan Province in 1908, and joined the CCP in 1927. To 1934, he was successively a minor CCP secretary, a participant in various peasant revolts and eventually troop leader in units commanded by He Long. After taking part in the Long March (1934–5), he was made commander of a brigade in the 8th Route Army which conducted land reclamation at Nanniwan – later extolled as a model of army self-sacrifice, self-reliance and service to the people. In 1949, he became the commander of the 1st Field Army Group, which liberated **Xinjiang**, and in the early 1950s served as commander and political commissar of the **Xinjiang** Military District, as well as several leading posts in the

Northwest Military Region. Subsequently, he was commander and political commissar of the People's Liberation Army (PLA) Railway Corps.

Wang held several leading CCP posts in **Xinjiang** after 1949, was a **CCP Central Committee** member (1956–85), a CCP Politburo member (1978–85), president of the Central Party School (1982–7) and vice-president of the Central Advisory Committee (1985–7). His governmental posts included minister of State Farms and Land Reclamation (1956–67), vice-premier of the **State Council** (1975–80) and vice-president of the PRC (from 1988 to his death in March 1993). In 1988 he was elected as a **Xinjiang** deputy to the Seventh **National People's Congress** and to its Praesidium. In his later years, Wang made several visits abroad, particularly to **Japan** (as honorary president of the China–Japan Friendship Association).

Wang Zhen's status in the Northwest, and particularly in **Xinjiang**, was reflected in his advocacy of firm CCP, and Han, rule and integrational policies in the **minority nationality** border regions as well as in his leadership of PLA and Production and Construction Corps units involved in reclamation-production, control and security in such areas. His subordinates, especially Wang Enmao, continued to dominate **Xinjiang** affairs with but a brief hiatus during the **Cultural Revolution**. Wang was one of the few leading cadres to survive the **Cultural Revolution** basically unharmed.

An avid supporter of the 'four cardinal principles', which **Deng Xiaoping** put forward in 1979 and which demanded continued CCP dominance (see **3. Ideology: Radicalism and Reform**), Wang Zhen was referred to as one of the Party's 'eight immortals'.

see also: 3. Ideology: Radicalism and Reform; Chinese Communist Party Central Committee and Politburo; Cultural Revolution; Deng Xiaoping; Japan, relations with; minority nationalities policy; National People's Congress; People's Liberation Army; State Council; Xinjiang Uygur Autonomous Region.

Donald H. McMillen

Wei Jianxing

Senior CCP leader, from 1992 a member of the CCP Politburo and the Secretariat member in charge of trade unions, **youth** organizations and **women**'s affairs, as well as secretary of the Party's Central Commission for Discipline Inspection, a position once held by the powerful Party elder **Chen Yun**. In September 1997, the Fifteenth Central Committee's First Plenum elected him to the Politburo Standing Committee, thus making him among the most powerful people in China.

Born in January 1931, Wei joined the CCP in 1949. He graduated from the Dalian Institute of Engineering in 1952 and his interests and experience were, for a time, largely confined to industrial work, a career path enhanced by his study of industrial management in the Soviet Union from 1953 to 1955. It was only in 1981 that he began a more political career after training at the Central Party School the previous year. He was soon appointed mayor of Harbin, an extremely important industrial city. At the Twelfth **National Party Congress** (1982) he was elected an alternate member of the **CCP Central Committee** and vice-chairman of the All-China Federation of Trade Unions (see **labour policy and system**), becoming chairman of its executive committee in 1993.

In 1984 Wei was promoted as deputy head of the Party's Organization Department. Although the reason is unclear, it is notable that since then he has sometimes taken over positions previously held by **Qiao Shi**. Thus, he succeeded Qiao as head of the Organization Department (July 1985 to July 1987) and, more notably, secretary of the Central Commission for Discipline Inspection from the Fourteenth **National Party Congress** (1992). Most important of all was his replacement of Qiao on the Politburo Standing Committee.

Clearly Wei was increasingly Qiao's right-hand lieutenant handling matters concerning public security, law and order, and disciplining corrupt Party and government officials. His appointment as minister of Supervision (1987) was merely another indicator of his portfolio within Qiao's 'political and **legal** system' responsible for law and order and legal institutions. It was probably not accidental that after **Jiang Zemin** dismissed Chen Xitong, a Politburo member and leading figure of **Beijing Municipality**, Wei Jianxing became the natural candidate to govern the national capital. While continuing his leading political and legal role, he also served concurrently as CCP secretary of **Beijing Municipality** from April 1995.

see also: Beijing Municipality; Chen Yun; Chinese Communist Party Central Committee and Politburo; Jiang Zemin; labour policy and system; legal; National Party Congress; Qiao Shi; women; youth policy and organizations.

Warren Sun

welfare policy

In China welfare includes such items as **labour** protection, retirement and old-age pensions, funeral and disaster relief, and benefits for disabled people, orphans, ex-servicemen and the families of CCP martyrs and disabled veterans. Welfare is handled by the Ministry of Civil Affairs.

Before the reforms of the 1980s, the primary avenue through which welfare was channelled was the workplace **unit**. In the countryside the 'five guarantees' (*wubao*) provided welfare for elderly people with no children to support them, orphans, disabled people and others, the 'five guarantees' being food, clothing, medical care and **housing**, and burial expenses for elderly people or education for orphans. In the cities a major function of the trade unions within the **units** was to look after and administer welfare for the workers (see **labour policy and system**). Although **Cultural Revolution** policy demanded improvements in welfare, in practice, the movement's damaging effect on the trade unions produced the reverse effect.

The state has continued to regard welfare as among its responsibilities in the reform period. Article 45 of the 1982 State **Constitution** gives PRC citizens 'the right to material assistance from the state and society when they are old, ill or disabled'. It continues:

The state develops the social insurance, social relief and medical and **health** services that are required to enable citizens to enjoy this right. ... The state and society help make arrangements for the work, livelihood and education of the blind, deaf-mute and other handicapped citizens.

However, the period of reform has brought about major changes in policy and administration. The demise of the people's commune in 1983 removed the main agent of welfare distribution in the countryside (see **collective agriculture**), and the 'five guarantees' system was seriously affected, although it has survived, with the number of persons receiving benefits from this scheme falling from 2.75 million in 1985 to 2.5 million in 1995. In 1985 the Ministry of Civil Affairs authorized the province-level administrative areas to take over responsibility for welfare policies and programmes which had previously been the preserve of the central government. In 1986 the government decided to allow relief funds to be used for investment, and not merely direct aid. As far as possible, the poor would receive tax relief in preference to outright grants. Although in accordance with the principle of making relief funds productive and designed to reduce the escalating government welfare bill, the new policy signalled a substantial change in the rural social welfare system towards forcing self-reliance among the peasants.

Among the decisions adopted by the Third Plenum of the Fourteenth Central Committee in November 1993 was one to establish a multi-layered social security system. Different arrangements would apply in urban and rural areas, with the extent of social security protection depending on local development levels. The new system is funded by a combination of the state, enterprises and individuals themselves. There appear to be two basic aims: to maintain social stability but at the same time shift the balance of funds required further away from the state and towards collectives and individuals.

The new system required the introduction of pensions and benefits into all urban enterprises, even privately owned ones. It aimed to guarantee basic material life needs of workers who had become unable to work or ceased employment for reasons such as age, sickness, industrial injury or retrenchment, the last allowing people some bridging relief while they retrained for another job or entered private business. Employees must set aside a small proportion of their salaries, the precise percentage varying from place to place, which they place into an insurance premium. By the middle of 1995, 87.5 million employees and 20.32 million retirees were participating in the scheme.

Social welfare institutions include convalescent homes, orphanages, urban social welfare homes, rural homes for elderly people and homes for disabled veterans. Some of these are still run by the departments of the Ministry of Civil Affairs at various levels, but the majority by communities, with the gap between the numbers in the two kinds of administration widening, especially in terms of personnel. In 1985, of a total of 29,100 social welfare institutions, 1,584 were run by Civil Affairs departments and employed 43,695 people, while 27,516 institutions were community-run, employing 66,452 people. In 1995, the total was 43,074 institutions, of which 2,182 were government-run, with 59,484 employees, the corresponding figures for the community-run institutions being 40,892 and 117,166.

Although the figures suggest significant improvements, there are still major problems in China's welfare system. The general privatization of society has reduced the government's ability to enforce welfare provisions in individual organizations. Welfare is enormously better in the cities than the countryside, with the vast bulk of funds spent on the former, even though most people live in the latter. The main improvements are also in the cities. While the urban social welfare homes rose greatly in number between 1985 (4,433) and 1995 (18,450), the number of homes for elderly people in the villages actually fell from 23,622 in the former year to 23,201 in the latter, and while it is true that the proportion of the **population** shifted over

the same period towards the urban areas, the rural people remained in a large majority in 1995.

In the mid-1990s China was accused of human rights abuses following publicity given in the West to appalling conditions in some Chinese orphanages. It was alleged that nurses had 'got rid of' children in one of them in **Shanghai**, evidence being cited from a staff member who had actually worked there. The Chinese authorities responded by denying the reports strongly, impugning the honesty of the staff member and taking foreign diplomats and others to visit the orphanage.

see also: collective agriculture; Constitutions; Cultural Revolution; health policy; housing; labour policy and system; population policy; Shanghai; unit.

Colin Mackerras

women (organizations, political role)

Chinese women have been a particular focus of attention since 1949, with the new government officially prescribing **gender equality** and involving itself strongly in women's issues. Activities relating to women have officially been in the hands of a state-sponsored women's organization, the All-China Women's Federation. In the post-Mao reform era, its main activities have been in the areas of combating gender discrimination in the workforce, **labour** protection, the protection of women's legal rights, giving women practical training, and improving their self-image. Since the mid-1980s, the Federation's monopoly of 'women's work' (*funü gongzuo*) has been challenged by nascent autonomous women's organizations, particularly women's study centres. While women played an expanding – though still limited – role in mainstream politics during the Maoist era, their participation at some levels has declined during the post-Mao period.

Chinese women were mobilized for, and promised equality through, the CCP's revolution. Officially, all that remained to be done after the revolution, following the overthrow of capitalism and class oppression, was the implementation of the state's guarantee of **gender equality** and the eradication of feudal ideas. In such a situation, there was ostensibly no need for a separate women's movement and no conflict between the Women's Federation's dual role of acting as the 'transmission belt' for Party policy and as the representative of women's interests.

Overall, as Emily Honig and Gail Hershatter concluded, the Women's Federation has 'remained a top-down, government-sponsored organization, rather than one independently formed by women'. It has continually adjusted its own pronouncements and activities in accordance with changing central policy. For example, the Federation heralded Engels's formula for women's emancipation in the late 1950s when female **labour** was deemed necessary for the **Great Leap Forward**, but changed its focus to women's domestic role in the resulting recession of the early 1960s. Disbanded in the **Cultural Revolution** along with other mass organizations, its revival in 1978 coincided with the official switch from the gender egalitarianism of the **Cultural Revolution** to the subordination of women's productive role to that of being wives and mothers. At the Fourth National Women's Congress in September 1978, China's women were told that they 'form the main force in logistics. Among them are women child care and **education** workers, salesclerks, cooks, street sweepers, nurses, barefoot doctors and other service personnel'. Subsequent congresses (in 1983, 1988 and 1993) only reiterated these sentiments.

The Women's Federation has not merely been a tool of changing state policy. It has also acted as a pressure group when women's interests have been overly subordinated to what are perceived as national priorities by the male-dominated leadership. The Federation's major focus of concern during the post-Mao era has been the negative effects of China's modernization programme on women. It has drawn continuing attention to the problem of employment discrimination against women ever since a group of female Beijing (Peking) University graduates com-

plained to then Federation President Deng Yingchao in early 1983. The Federation's most active and, to some extent, effective action in recent years has been its opposition to the widely canvassed suggestion (made even by some male CCP officials) that married women should 'return home' to make way for unemployed young people. The Federation waged a strong campaign in its publications and also exerted direct pressure on the government to drop this suggestion, denouncing it as a reflection of feudal thinking and counter to the achievement of women's emancipation. It also objected to proposals that women take 'prolonged maternity leave' (up to three years) to help solve the unemployment problem, insisting that any such leave should be voluntary.

The major practical outcome of the Federation's concern has been the 'protection' of women already in the workforce, rather than success in outlawing discrimination against female employment. The replacement of the Maoist slogan 'Anything a man can do, a woman can do too' by renewed attention to 'the special **labour** difficulties caused by women's physical characteristics' has included new Women's Federation-endorsed **labour** regulations. The 1988 Women Workers and Employees' Labour Protection Regulations, hailed as the first comprehensive law on working women's **labour** protection in China, forbade women from working in mines and doing severe physical labour, and gave pregnant women varying degrees of protection from having to do overtime or night shifts. However, the regulations proved difficult to implement (for example, in textile factories where over 65 per cent of workers are female) and have had the characteristic deleterious impact on female employment options.

In the field of domestic and sexual politics, the Federation's stress has been on the protection of women's **legal** rights. Since the early 1980s it has drawn attention to, and denounced, increasing domestic violence against women, the revival of female infanticide and the selling of women. Provincial and local branches of the Women's Federation conducted a number of surveys revealing the extent of these problems. At the same time, the Federation has been the major activist and publicist for the one-child policy, initiated in 1979, which was the basic cause of some of these problems (see **population policy**).

The Federation has also played an important role at the micropolitical level through its wide organizational network: by the mid-1990s it had over 98,000 full-time employees at national, provincial, municipal, county and township levels. Activities range from running literacy classes and training programmes for women in poor areas to enable them to participate in the private economy, to establishing legal consultancy services aimed at ensuring that women are fully informed of their rights regarding **marriage** and divorce. The Federation also places considerable emphasis on raising women's self-image, mainly through organizing classes and meetings in the effort to increase female participation in the political arena.

The Federation's high-profile public activities accelerated in the early 1990s. It was active in the formulation of the 1992 Law on the Protection of the Rights and Interests of Women which spelt out women's rights in politics, culture, **education**, work, property, person and family life. The Federation hailed the law as a major advance in the promotion of women's rights and publicized it widely in its network of women's newspapers and magazines: *Chinese Women's Newspaper* (*Zhongguo funü bao*) and *Chinese Women* (*Zhongguo funü*) at the national level, and a large number of provincial magazines. It was also heavily involved in the promotion of Chinese women's rights in the period leading up to the Fourth World Conference on Women, held in Beijing in September 1995. Major government documents in which it played a major role included the February 1994 *Report of the PRC on the Implementation of the Nairobi Forward-Looking Strategies for the Advancement of Women* and the June 1994 document *The Situation of Chinese Women*.

In all its activities, however, the Women's Federation has continued to be constrained by overall state policy. Indeed, it has been a major publicist for the renewed stress on women's domestic role at the expense of equal participation in the workforce. Its magazines are little different from many women's magazines in the West, covering the familiar subjects of child care, cooking, beauty and fashion, and featuring advertisements associating women with domestic appliances and beauty products. Competing for readers in a highly competitive market, *Chinese Women* and other Federation-sponsored magazines have themselves been in the vanguard of featuring glamorous cover-girls, contributing to the overall images of women as decorative and even as sex objects.

In the relatively liberal atmosphere of the post-Mao era, the Federation has not been exempt from the questioning and criticism directed at most official policies and organizations. First, it was criticized, like other 'mass' organizations, for indulging in rhetoric rather than practical action to solve women's everyday problems. Second, new feminist voices began challenging the Federation's official monopoly on women's issues, setting up separate women's study groups. By the late 1980s some sixteen tertiary institutions in China had already introduced women's studies courses. Feminist academic Li Xiaojiang, Head of the Women's Research Centre at Zhengzhou University, which has played a leading role in the development of women's studies, edits a series of publications on women's issues and has herself written such books as *Women's Future* (*Nüren de chulu*). A number of small independent women's associations have also been established with varying links to the official Women's Federation.

The second major aspect of women's political activities has been their participation in mainstream Chinese politics. The 1954 Constitution stated that women were to 'enjoy equal rights with men in all spheres of life'; this specifically included political life (in addition to their domestic, economic, social and cultural life). Women's participation in politics increased substantially during the Maoist era. Their representation on the **National People's Congress**, for example, increased from 12 per cent in 1954 to 17.8 per cent in 1964 and 22.6 per cent in 1975. Similarly their representation on the **CCP Central Committee** increased from 4.1 per cent of members in 1958 to 7.6 per cent in 1969 and 10.3 per cent in 1973. A substantial proportion of the increases at both national and lower levels occurred during the **Cultural Revolution** decade when the CCP not only intensified its rhetoric about gender equality but introduced mandatory quotas for female political representation at different levels.

During the post-Mao era, women's participation in mainstream politics has shown mixed tendencies. While maintaining or even increasing their role at some areas of lower level politics, women have had a declining level of representation in more senior ranks. For example, female representation at the 1993 **National People's Congress** was 21.03 per cent of the total, only slightly down on 22.6 per cent at the 1975 Congress. But their representation on the Congress's standing committee fell from 25.1 per cent in 1975 to only 9 per cent in 1983, although it had subsequently increased slightly to 12.7 per cent by 1993. While the proportion of women members of the CCP reached over 15 per cent in the mid-1990s, their representation on the important **CCP Central Committee** had declined to 6.4 per cent, below its level of the late 1960s. Some 32 per cent of all people working in government organs were women, but the proportion of female ministers and vice-ministers was only 6.6 per cent.

In the mid-1990s the Women's Federation summarized the overall situation of women in Chinese politics as 'one low, three fews' (*yi di san shao*): a low proportion of women engaged in politics and few women at higher levels, in top positions and in key sectors. The Federation's research institute reported that this was as true of local level politics as of national politics, with women constituting only 3.8 per cent of heads or deputy heads of townships and small towns, and 5.9 per cent of county heads or deputy heads.

While the role of women in Chinese politics is on a par with, or even greater than, that in many countries, the discrepancies between male and female participation have provoked concern not just from the Women's Federation but from some male officials and the general media. The customary explanations of Chinese women's failure to achieve political equality, along with other aspects of **gender equality**, focus on the burden of their reproductive and child-care role, and the persistence of 'feudal' attitudes of male supremacy (among women as well as men) which impede women's educational and career prospects, including their political prospects. The overall decreased representation of women in politics in the post-Mao era is seen as an outcome of the shift towards a market economy, with women bearing the brunt of enterprise redundancies, an emphasis on women's domestic role, and the decline of ideological imperatives (including the abolition of affirmative action) for women's involvement in politics.

Renewed efforts to increase women's political participation include the establishment of official targets and programmes to train women officials. The proclaimed objectives, to be achieved by the year 2000, are to raise the proportion of women in people's congresses at all levels, to have a woman vice-premier or state councillor, to expand female participation in the leadership at all levels (from village to provincial), and to increase the proportion of women in management and on policy-making bodies.

see also: Chinese Communist Party Central Committee and Politburo; Cultural Revolution; education policy and system; gender equality; Great Leap Forward; labour policy and system; legal system; Marriage Laws; National People's Congress; population policy.

Beverley Hooper

World Trade Organization

The World Trade Organization (WTO) was established in January 1995 as the institutional framework for the continuation of the General Agreement on Tariffs and Trade

(GATT). Its goal is to encourage further liber-alization of trade under GATT rules and to provide the mechanisms for managing trade agreements and settling disputes. A founding member of GATT in 1948, China withdrew in 1950.

China's deepening involvement in the world economy after 1978 was marked by admittance to the International Monetary Fund and the World Bank in 1980 (see also **Asia-Pacific Economic Cooperation (APEC)**). In 1986 China applied for readmis-sion to the GATT and negotiated for mem-bership over the next ten years. The key negotiation issues were:

- whether China might join as a 'develop-ing' country and thus have a longer period of adjustment, with special provi-sions such as the right to control in trade in the event of a balance of payments crisis;
- how fair and open the China market might be, given the transitional nature of the Chinese economy; and
- the extent to which China would honour intellectual property rights.

After failing to become a founding member of the WTO in 1995, China's enthusiasm for membership waned slightly but the applica-tion remained in place. Politically, the more conservative forces in China tended to be less enthusiastic, especially given the perception that outsiders were using the process as a means of influencing domestic development. China's exclusion also delayed entry for **Taiwan**.

From China's point of view, the gains of membership included easier access to world markets, especially for its **labour**-intensive products, large potential gains in **inter-national trade**, and better mechanisms for settling trade disputes. The need to obtain most-favoured-nation status from the **United States** on an annual basis would also be removed. Gains for the rest of the world included reduced tariffs and protection by China and further consolidation of China's reform process. Obstacles to membership included US efforts to link WTO membership to political issues and China's concern at the adjustment costs that the removal of protec-tions and subsidies might bring to domestic manufacturing and agriculture. China's accession was also seen as a precedent for membership by other former centrally planned economies. As of October 1997, China had still not joined, and the need per-sisted to find some special compromise between developed and developing country status resolving both China's and the rest of the world's concerns.

see also: Asia-Pacific Economic Cooperation; international trade; labour policy and sys-tem; Taiwan policy; United States policy.

Andrew Watson

Wu Bangguo

The vice-premier charged with reform of state-owned enterprises, Wu Bangguo is closely associated with President **Jiang Zemin** and the so-called '**Shanghai** Faction' in China's central-level politics.

Born in Anhui in 1941, Wu joined the CCP in 1964 and graduated as an electronics engineer from Qinghua University in 1967. During 1968–82 he worked as an engineer and manager in **Shanghai**'s electronics industry before a short stint in the Telecom-munications Bureau of the **Shanghai** Muni-cipal Government during 1982–3.

From 1983 to 1994, Wu rose steadily in the Party hierarchy of **Shanghai** Municipality. Elected a member of the Standing Committee of the Municipal Party Committee in 1983, he became a deputy secretary in 1986 as well as an alternate member of the **CCP Central Committee**. In 1991 he became secretary of the **Shanghai** Municipal Party Committee (succeeding Vice-Premier **Zhu Rongji** who had followed President **Jiang Zemin**) and became a member of the powerful Politburo in 1992. Wu thus served as an important member of the technocratic **Shanghai** leader-ship which finally promulgated reform in 1990–2.

In 1994 Wu Bangguo was transferred to the centre and formally elected vice-premier at the **National People's Congress** of 1995, with special responsibility for reforming China's inefficient and costly state-owned enterprises. Many observers saw the relatively large number of votes opposing Wu and another nominee for vice-premier, **Jiang Chunyun**, as a criticism of President **Jiang Zemin**. Some believe Wu Bangguo was President **Jiang Zemin**'s preferred choice as successor to Premier **Li Peng** (whose term ends in 1998), but, as of 1997, Wu's star has dimmed owing to the difficulties China has faced in reforming state-owned enterprises. At the First Plenum of the CCP's Fifteenth Central Committee on 19 September 1997, Wu retained his seat on the Politburo, but failed to gain elevation to the Poliburo's Standing Committee, reducing the likelihood of his becoming premier in 1998.

see also: Chinese Communist Party Central Committee and Politburo; Jiang Chunyun; Jiang Zemin; Li Peng; National People's Congress; Shanghai; Zhu Rongji.

J. Bruce Jacobs

X

Xinjiang Uygur Autonomous Region

The largest in area of China's province-level units, Xinjiang lies in the country's far northwest and is largely inhabited by non-Han Islamic peoples.

Becoming a province in 1884, this resource-rich, desert and mountain region constitutes one-sixth of China's area, or 1,660,400 square kilometres. Its peoples belong to the Uygur, Kazak, Uzbek, Kirgiz, Tajik, Tatar and Hui **minority nationalities** of China, with the 1990 census showing the total population of 15,156,883 at 37 per cent Han. In the nineteenth and early twentieth centuries it remained a cauldron of intrigue between the Chinese, Russian and British empires, of violent separatist struggles against Han rule, with manipulative (and manipulated) local warlords and separatist rebellions persisting into the twentieth century.

On 25 September 1949 the Guomindang military commander in Xinjiang surrendered to units of the **People's Liberation Army** (PLA) 1st Field Army Group led by **Wang Zhen**. Many of the Han troops in Xinjiang were subsequently demobilized into 'Production and Construction Corps' (XJPCC) units for reclamation work. In October 1955, the Xinjiang Uygur Autonomous Region was established, with five autonomous districts (*zhou*) and six autonomous counties (*xian*). Central subsidies were required to maintain the region's economic stability and development.

Xinjiang's integration into the Chinese state has never been easy. Infrastructural linkages with eastern China have remained tenuous. The region's peoples have remained restive, with over 60,000 Kazaks and Uygurs fleeing to the **Soviet Union** in 1962. Later, the region's 5,400-km border with the **Soviet Union** was militarized as relations soured to the point of armed clashes. Beijing-recognized anti-Han incidents persisted at Aksu, Baren and Kaxgar in the Tarim Basin in the south and in Ürümqi from the mid-1980s to the mid-1990s, raising fears among many in CCP and PLA circles of ethno-nationalist militancy and **Soviet**-style disintegration. In 1996, an exiled opposition group called the United Revolutionary National Front claimed that numerous Muslim-inspired separatists were still being executed by Chinese authorities despite China's April agreement with Russia, Kazakhstan, Kirgizstan and Tajikistan which established a 440-km demilitarized zone straddling the border. Early in February 1997, very serious rioting broke out in Yining, northwestern Xinjiang, and on 25 February, the same day as **Deng Xiaoping**'s funeral, three time-bombs planted on buses in the capital Ürümqi killed nine people and wounded seventy-four, according to official figures.

After 1949, the CCP maintained its power in Xinjiang almost exclusively through a Han- and military-dominated and heavily subsidized authoritarianism. Few non-Han cadre have ever held positions of real authority in Xinjiang – with those holding high nominal positions often being criticized as 'jackals serving the Han'. While non-Han governmental cadres tend to predominate in quantitative terms, the majority of CCP, PLA and XJPCC leading posts were left in the hands of Han cadres. Burhan Shahidi, a Tatar, **Seypidin Azizi**, a Uygur, and the current (as of 1997) incumbent Ablait Abdurexit, a Uygur, have held the chairmanship of the regional people's congress at different times, but only briefly did a non-Han, Seypidin, hold the top CCP position. The regional CCP head in 1997 was a Han, Wang Lequan. A few have risen to high posts in **Beijing**, largely in **minority nationalities** affairs – such as Ismail Amat, minister of the State Nationalities Affairs Commission. Socially and culturally the local people lead lives quite distinct from those of the Han, and they retain some ties with ethnic cousins in the states of Central Asia.

During the most turbulent days of the **Cultural Revolution**, the long-serving CCP leader in Xinjiang, Wang Enmao, attempted to restrain extremism imported by Han Red Guards from other areas and revolutionary dictates from Beijing to prevent widespread ethnic and economic chaos which would endanger the region's security. Wang subsequently was removed for his 'regionalist tendencies', only to be brought back to Ürümqi in the post-1976 period as a senior CCP adviser.

From the 1960s, thousands of Han youth and other elements like unemployed workers, dissidents and criminals were 'resettled' in Xinjiang from cities such as **Shanghai**. Since the 1980s, a tide of 'drifters', that is persons escaping poverty and job market saturation in their home areas, have arrived in Xinjiang attracted by the new opportunities offered by booming border trade under socialist market conditions accompanied by the completion of the railway linking the region, and China, with Kazakhstan. All have brought with them Han habits and beliefs, thus adding to social tensions.

While locals hold that Chinese Marxism, like its **Soviet** counterpart, is largely a spent force, they concede that assertive Chinese nationalism is alive and well. For the estimated 9 million to 10 million Muslims this is a threat to a way of life which is deeply imprinted by hundreds of years of Islamic influence. With much of China's previous communist practice now discredited, it is easy to see how Islam in combination with capitalism could provide a dynamic ideological and economic ethic in Xinjiang. Increased cross-border trade has further blurred the political map of the region, a fact which concerns the PLA and People's Armed **Police** whose security brief must address an 'enlarged domestic community'. Incompetent or corrupt administrators only feed such concerns.

Concerned by these trends, Premier **Li Peng** made a four-nation, ten-day Central Asian tour in April 1994, seeking assurances that Islamic or separatist elements would receive no support. He promised economic cooperation, including soft loans, to promote a 'New Silk Road' of trade. At the end of September 1997 Li also signed an agreement in Almaty, capital of Kazakhstan, to exploit two of the largest oilfields in the Caspian Basin and undertook that China would build a long pipeline into Xinjiang. This policy of 'containment through economics' is made possible by the economic boom within China. Xinjiang's buoyant economy, with GDP increasing more than 10 per cent annually, has underlined the perception that things there are better than on the other side of the frontier.

From the mid-1990s China has cooperated with foreign firms to develop the petroleum reserves, estimated at 10 billion tons, in the Tarim Basin and planned to develop related transportation and processing infrastructures. These could bring both economic growth and stimulate the region's further integration into the Chinese economy and state. The question remains whether the local people either favour the exploitation of their resources through these initiatives or believe that they would reap reasonable benefits from them.

see also: 6. Peoples of China; Beijing Municipality; Cultural Revolution; Deng Xiaoping; Li Peng; minority nationalities policy; People's Liberation Army; police force; Seypidin Azizi; Shanghai; Soviet Union, relations with; Wang Zhen.

Donald H. McMillen

Xu Jiatun

Director of the **Hong Kong** branch of the **New China News Agency** (NCNA) from April 1983 to January 1990 and influential in **Hong Kong**–PRC relations over that time.

In 1950, Xu was a secretary of the CCP in Fuzhou, capital of Fujian Province. In 1954 he was Party secretary in the Nanjing Municipal Government. One year later, Xu was named a deputy secretary of the CCP Committee of Jiangsu Province. In 1958, he was promoted to be deputy governor of Jiangsu. During the

Cultural Revolution in 1968 Red Guards stripped him of his posts. However, he was rehabilitated in 1970, becoming vice-chairman of the Jiangsu **Revolutionary Committee**.

The first impression of Xu when he became NCNA director in April 1983 showed him as a strong advocate of the Chinese position on the question of sovereignty in a context where that position was still not universally accepted. However, with the passage of time, his views lost stridency and he appeared as a liberal-minded CCP official responsible for **Hong Kong** affairs. He not only publicly praised the capitalist system, but also met frequently with the business and social leaders in **Hong Kong**, giving an impression that he favoured regular communication with the upper classes rather than the working classes in **Hong Kong**.

During the **protest movement** of 1989, Xu was a supporter of Party General Secretary **Zhao Ziyang**. Xu even imitated Zhao's action, going out of the NCNA office in **Hong Kong** to shake hands with demonstrators who supported the student protesters in **Beijing**. After the **June 4 Incident**, Xu argued with the hard-line officials responsible for **Hong Kong** affairs, saying that the PRC should win the hearts and minds of the **Hong Kong** people instead of using the Basic Law to restrict political activities. He even wrote a report concerning a proposal made by a group of **Hong Kong** business people, who suggested that Britain might continue to administer **Hong Kong** after 1 July 1997 by paying a 'rent' of £10 billion. **Lu Ping** and Zhou Nan criticized Xu's action as 'unpatriotic'. **Li Peng** and other senior Chinese leaders stopped consulting Xu after the **June 4 Incident**, an indication that he was politically isolated.

After his escape from China to the US in April 1990, Xu wrote his memoirs on **Hong Kong**, an indispensable work on China's policy toward **Hong Kong**. He also wrote a long article entitled 'Tentative Commentary on Peaceful Evolution', in which he argued that capitalism and socialism had influenced each other and that any evolution in the two kinds of system should be directed only at the well-being of humankind.

see also: Beijing Municipality; Cultural Revolution; Hong Kong; June 4 Incident; Li Peng; Lu Ping; New China News Agency; protest movements; revolutionary committees; Zhao Ziyang.

Sonny S. H. Lo

Y

Yang Shangkun

Born in 1907 in Shuangjiang, **Sichuan**, Yang Shangkun was influential within the CCP before being purged during the **Cultural Revolution**. Closely associated with **Deng Xiaoping**, Yang rose to prominence after his rehabilitation in the late 1970s to hold senior Party, military and government positions (including president of the PRC) before his dismissal in 1992.

Yang attended middle school in Chengdu and joined the Communist Youth League in 1925. He then studied at the Sino-French Institute in Chongqing (1926), at the time a Nationalist Party training establishment working closely with the CCP, which he joined in 1926. He worked under **Zhou Enlai** in **Shanghai** before spending 1927–31 at the Sun Yat-sen University, Moscow.

Yang was part of Wang Ming's 'returned student faction' in the CCP. He worked in the CCP underground in **Shanghai** (1931–2) before making his way to the Chinese Soviet Republic (Jiangxi Soviet), set up in November 1931. He served (under Zhou) as director of the Political Department of the 1st Red Army during 1933–7 except for the period of the Long March (1934–5). He joined Peng Dehuai's 3rd Army Corps in 1934 as its political commissar and served as deputy director of the Central Executive Committee's Revolutionary Military Council in 1935.

During the period of the Anti-Japanese War, Yang was secretary-general of the 8th Route Army headquarters in Yan'an. After 1949, he played a significant role as head of the General Office of the **CCP's Central Committee** and, in particular, as head of intelligence of the General Secretariat (after its establishment in 1956). His office (the Party's 'nerve centre') processed all central directives and documents as well as administering the Party archives. Yang also supervised the State Security Ministry.

Yang was a standing committee member of both the second and third **Chinese People's Political Consultative Conference** (CPPCC, 1954–64) and was also elected as a **Sichuan** deputy and standing committee member of the Third **National People's Congress** (NPC) in 1964. He was elevated to the **CCP Central Committee** at its Eighth Congress in 1956.

Yang was removed from his posts during the early stages of the **Cultural Revolution**. However, at the **Third Plenum of the Eleventh Central Committee** (December 1978) he was exonerated and rehabilitated. His initial appointments (1978–80) were to Party and military positions in Guangdong.

In 1979, Yang was restored to the CPPCC as a standing committee member and to the **CCP Central Committee**. He remained on the Central Committee until October 1992, also serving on the Politburo for most of this period (1982–92). Yang joined the Fifth NPC in September 1980 as a vice-chairman of its standing committee and went on to serve on the Sixth and Seventh NPCs, including a period as President of the PRC from April 1988 until his dismissal (confirmed at the Eighth NPC in 1993).

Most importantly, Yang was appointed as secretary-general of the Party **Central Military Commission** in July 1981 and was its first vice-chairman from September 1982 until October 1992. In this position, he oversaw the **People's Liberation Army**'s rectification and modernization and was a key adviser and confidant of **Deng Xiaoping**. Yang was also a prominent figure in the **June 4 Incident** of 1989. His downfall in 1992 appears to have been due to a falling out with Deng as a result of machinations over the succession.

see also: Central Military Commission; Chinese Communist Party Central Committee and Politburo; Chinese People's Political Consultative Conference; Cultural Revolution; Deng Xiaoping; June 4 Incident; National People's Congress; People's

Liberation Army; Shanghai; Sichuan; Third Plenum of the Eleventh Central Committee; Zhou Enlai.

Dennis Woodward

Yao Yilin

Yao Yilin held some of the most important posts in the Chinese Party and state during the post-Mao era with special responsibilities in the economic sphere. While supporting many key reform programmes, he was identified with the **planning** apparatus and the cautious approach of his mentor, **Chen Yun**.

Born in Anhui in 1917, Yao was one of many idealistic students drawn to the CCP's cause by the struggle against Japan. He participated in the December Ninth Movement (1935) against Japanese aggression in Beijing, and joined the CCP the same year. He subsequently worked in both the underground and base areas of North China. With the start of the civil war in 1946, Yao became part of an important cohort of educated Party members who specialized in economic affairs. After the establishment of the PRC he was appointed a vice-minister of Trade in 1949 and to subsequent positions including minister of Commerce from 1960 to the **Cultural Revolution**. Though cast aside as revisionist, the need for economic expertise saw Yao recalled in 1973 as first vice-minister of Foreign Trade.

With the end of the Maoist era Yao became one of the many technically competent younger leaders systematically promoted under **Chen Yun**'s personnel reform. The early critical appointment was as secretary-general of the Finance and Economics Commission set up under Chen in 1979 which took the crucial first steps in promoting economic reform. His performance in this and other duties (most notably as head of the State Planning Commission) led to his promotion to alternate Politburo status in 1982, full membership in 1985, and to the Standing Committee of the **CCP Central Committee**'s Politburo in 1987. While Yao's 1987 promotion in no way represented a challenge to **Deng Xiaoping** or the general thrust of reform, his cautious inclinations soon brought him into conflict with Party General

Secretary **Zhao Ziyang**'s rapid growth policies which contributed to unprecedented inflation in 1988, and apparently together with Premier **Li Peng** he succeeded in convincing Deng of the need to rein in the economy. He then became a key figure shaping the policies of retrenchment, yet in a period where Yao and **Li Peng** carried the greatest weight in economic matters considerable reforms were still made, as in developing domestic financial markets and selective price reforms. Yao formally retired in 1992 and died two years later.

see also: Chen Yun; Chinese Communist Party Central Committee and Politburo; Cultural Revolution; Deng Xiaoping; Li Peng; planning, economic; Zhao Ziyang.

Frederick C. Teiwes

Ye Jianying

Born in 1896 in Mei County, Guangdong, Ye took part in most of the major turning points in the history of the CCP until his death in 1986. Throughout his career, he held important army, Party and government positions.

He graduated from the Yunnan Military Academy and was a foundation instructor at the Whampoa (Huangpu) Military Academy. He commanded a division during the Northern Expedition (1926–7) and helped plan and participated in the Nanchang Uprising (1 August 1927), regarded as the birthdate of the **People's Liberation Army** (PLA).

Ye secretly joined the CCP in 1927 and in December of that year played a key role in the failed Guangzhou Uprising. Forced to flee, he made his way to **Shanghai** and thence to Moscow where he studied military science (1928–31). He later joined the Chinese Soviet Republic in Jiangxi, where he held positions as head of the Red Army School and as a member of the Revolutionary Military Council. He took part in the Long March, siding with **Mao Zedong** against Zhang Guotao (1935).

Ye was involved (with **Zhou Enlai**) in the negotiations over the Xi'an Incident in 1936. During the Anti-Japanese War he was chief of staff of the 8th Route Army. He was a member of the **CCP's Central Committee** over 1945–85.

Ye assumed the positions of mayor and chairman of the municipal Military Control Commission when the PLA took **Beijing** in January 1949. He then took part in commanding the campaigns to liberate Guangzhou and Hainan Island and became a key figure in the Guangdong military, Party and administrative hierarchy in 1949–54, holding positions as mayor of Guangzhou, governor of Guangdong and commander of the South China Military Region.

When ranks were introduced into the PLA in 1955, Ye became one of the ten marshals appointed. He was elected as a deputy to the First, Second and Third **National People's Congresses** and was chairman of the Standing Committee for the Fifth (1978–83). His influence increased during the **Cultural Revolution**, and he was brought into the Politburo in late 1966, serving on its Standing Committee between 1973 and 1985. As a senior Party and army figure, he played a crucial role after the death of Mao (including helping in the removal of the **gang of four**) until he retired from all posts in 1985.

see also: Beijing Municipality; Chinese Communist Party Central Committee and Politburo; Cultural Revolution; gang of four; Mao Zedong; National People's Congress; People's Liberation Army; Shanghai; Zhou Enlai.

Dennis Woodward

youth policy and organizations

China's youth generation has been a particular focus of attention throughout the PRC period. Youth policy is implemented through the Communist Youth League (CYL, the youth wing of the CCP) and more broadly through the All-China Youth Federation. In the post-Mao era the government has both stressed the importance of youth for China's modernization efforts and become increasingly concerned about mounting youth problems, ranging from unemployment and crime to moral laxity and political alienation.

China's youth generation is officially defined as the 14–25 age group and accounts for over one-quarter of the country's total population (25.73 per cent according to the 1990 census). The Chinese government and the CCP have regarded youth as the group in the forefront of both revolution and modernization. In 1957 **Mao Zedong** proclaimed: 'You young people, full of vigour and vitality, are in the bloom of life. ... China's future belongs to you'. Young people were mobilized in the 1950s to be in the forefront of creating the 'New China'. In the mid-1960s they were singled out by Mao and labelled as Red Guards to carry out the **Cultural Revolution**, shattering the existing CCP and bureaucratic structure. In subsequent years some 16 million young urban people were sent to the countryside to 'learn from the peasants'. During the post-Mao era, young people have been identified as the most important generation for China's modernization policies. In official terminology: 'Whether China's modernization succeeds will depend largely on young people'.

Youth policy is promulgated through general Party and government organs, and more specifically through youth organizations. The CYL was founded as the Socialist Youth League of China in 1922, became the New Democratic Youth League in 1949, and finally the CYL in 1957. Both before and since the revolution it has acted as a training ground for future CCP members and as an instigator of Party policy towards youth. The CYL recruits young people from 18 to 25, having over 60 million members in the late 1990s. The second major youth organization, the All-China Youth Federation, was founded in 1949 as the General Federation of All-China Democratic Youth and given its present name in 1958. It is officially described as 'a united organization for all youth bodies, with the CYL as its core'. Organizations it represents include the CYL, the All-China Students' Federation, the Chinese Young Men's Christian Association and the Young Women's Christian Association, the Chinese Association of Young Entrepreneurs, the Chinese Youth Volunteers' Association, and the youth federations of the individual provinces, autonomous regions and centrally administered municipalities.

A number of other organizations and

networks help to formulate and publicize youth policy. The Youth and Juvenile Research Institute, originally the research wing of the CYL, was established within the Academy of Social Sciences in 1980. It analyses current youth issues and problems, undertakes surveys of youth attitudes, publishes an internal journal *Youth Studies* (*Qingnian yanjiu*) and advises the CYL and government on youth policy. A wide-ranging publications network, mostly under the control and management of the CYL, publishes newspapers and magazines specifically directed at young people. These include *Chinese Youth News* (*Zhongguo qingnian bao*) and *Chinese Youth* (*Zhongguo qingnian*) at the national level, together with regional publications such as *Beijing Youth News* (*Beijing qingnian bao*), *The Youth Generation* (*Qingnian yidai*) (Shanghai) and *The Golden Generation* (*Huangjin shidai*) (Guangzhou).

Government policy towards the youth generation has focused on inculcating socialist values and support for, or at least obedience to, the CCP. Throughout the history of post-revolutionary China, a major strategy has been the creation of youth role models who incorporate ideal socialist values. The best known of these was the selfless young soldier Lei Feng, who denied all personal interests, dying in April 1962 in the service of 'New China' aged 22. Lei Feng and other youth models were publicized through youth organizations, schools and universities (see **education policy and system**) and the media, as well as being the subject of national political campaigns.

In the post-Mao period, youth policy has been directly associated with problems resulting from the economic reforms, China's increasing openness to the outside world, and general social liberalization. While many of these problems are not limited to one generational group, young people have been the most susceptible to, and the most affected by, the new influences. Economically, they were particularly hard hit by the rationalization of the state sector, with the 'youth awaiting work' (*daiye qingnian*) issue eventually giving way to an acknowledged unemployment

problem. Socially, a major official concern has been the rising level of youth crime, with people under 21 accounting for up to 70 per cent of all crimes committed. Political dissent, particularly among university students (see **protest movements**), has challenged the actual social fabric, culminating in the **June 4 Incident** (1989).

More generally, there has been a high level of official concern about young people's values, in particular how they conduct their everyday economic, social and personal lives. Officials and sometimes the older generation frown on them for their excessive interest in material gain, as demonstrated by their extreme enthusiasm for the latest consumer goods. Young people are also criticized for their developing youth culture, ranging from rock music to bars and fashion fads, as well as for their increasingly relaxed attitudes to personal and even sexual relations. Much of this behaviour is officially blamed on Western 'bourgeois influences' coming into China. Foreign television programmes, films and magazines, contact with foreigners, and growing access to global **media** and communications networks, are creating a youth generation which is increasingly part of an international youth culture.

The major official reaction to these developments has been a renewed effort to persuade young people to adhere to 'socialist' values, with a stress on hard work, concern for others, and 'clean living'. The campaign to 'learn from Lei Feng', initially pushed in the mid-1960s following an instruction issued by **Mao Zedong** in March 1963 to 'learn from Comrade Lei Feng', was revived in the 1980s, and again in the early 1990s following the **June 4 Incident**. There have also been a number of other, though less enduring, youth role models, such as the young soldier Zhang Hua, who died in 1982 while trying to rescue an elderly peasant from a pit of nightsoil. While the official press reported an 'upsurge of enthusiasm' to learn from Lei Feng and other official role models, Chinese surveys of secondary school and university students have revealed cynicism and even ridicule of the campaigns, with young people citing famous athletes and performers, as well as historical and even fictitious characters (both Chinese and Western), as their main role models.

Youth policy makers continue to urge youth to 'follow the theory of building socialism with Chinese characteristics and subject themselves to the Party's leadership'. But they have also recognized the declining appeal of such admonitions. Increasingly they have stressed the importance of 'China's traditional values' to the extent of urging young people to revive the once-condemned Confucian values of diligence and respect for their parents. Young people have also been a major target of the appeal to Chinese nationalism and patriotism as the major values to lead China into the twenty-first century. In **Li Peng**'s words, young people should 'love the motherland and carry forward the glorious tradition of patriotism'. Efforts have also been made to link socialism and patriotism, with young people being told that 'to love the motherland, one must love socialism'. Although officials and the **media** cite youth's enthusiasm for political involvement and even for socialism, there continues to be a wide gap between media rhetoric and the results of surveys undertaken by research organizations in China. While China's young people are undoubtedly enthusiastic about living in a modernizing and increasingly consumer-oriented society, they show few signs of enthusiasm for the government's policies in the ideological realm.

see also: Cultural Revolution; education policy and system; June 4 Incident; Li Peng; Mao Zedong; media issues and policy; protest movements.

Beverley Hooper

Z

Zhang Wannian

Senior Chinese general. Zhang Wannian, born in August 1928, native of Longkou County, **Shandong** Province, was executive deputy chairman of the **Central Military Commission** (CMC) as of 1997, making him the highest-ranking professional soldier in the **People's Liberation Army** (PLA) and in actual daily control of China's armed forces, outranking even **Chi Haotian**, together with whom he was promoted to the Politburo by the First Plenum of the Fifteenth Central Committee (19 September 1997).

General Zhang began his military career as an infantry man in 1944, being one of the few Anti-Japanese War veterans still active in the PLA as of 1997. In the 1950s and 1970s he studied for a total of five years in the PLA Military Academy, this systematic academic training convincing him of the importance of advanced military science and technology. In 1968 he became the youngest divisional commander of the time, commanding the 127th division of the 43rd Army. Many regard the division as the best in the PLA: it originated from the bodyguard battalion for Sun Yat-sen and has counted three PLA marshals among its commanders, including **Lin Biao**. The association with the division won him participation in the Ninth **National Party Congress** (1969) and acquaintance with several PLA elders of great influence, including Yang Dezhi and Xiao Ke.

General Zhang survived the **Cultural Revolution**. In 1978 he was promoted as deputy commander of the 43rd Army and two years later, commander. Between 1982 and 1985 he was deputy commander of the Wuhan and Guangdong Military Regions, becoming commander of Guangdong Military Region in 1987. In 1990 he was transferred to the Ji'nan Military Region and stayed there till 1992, when he was appointed as the PLA's chief of the general staff and as a member of the CMC. In both roles he was active in revising PLA defence strategy from **Deng Xiaoping**'s slogan 'fighting people's war under modern conditions' to the post-Deng notion, espoused in particular by **Liu Huaqing**, of 'fighting a modern high-tech war'.

Later, General Zhang took personal charge of reforming the PLA's training programmes, reordering its research and development priorities and redeploying its troops in the post-Cold war era. As the representative of the CMC, he coordinated the series of combined military exercises near the Taiwan Straits in March 1996. The post-Deng CCP leadership, with its emphasis on the military and technological aspects of PLA modernization, has placed great value on General Zhang's professional expertise and attitudes towards civilian government.

see also: Central Military Commission; Chi Haotian; Cultural Revolution; Deng Xiaoping; Lin Biao; Liu Huaqing; National Party Congress; People's Liberation Army; Shandong.

You Ji

Zhao Ziyang

A provincial official during the Maoist period, Zhao Ziyang reached national prominence in the post-Mao era as a key figure in the process of economic reform. As premier and then Party general secretary, Zhao led efforts on the 'first front' of comparatively younger officials responsible for day-to-day affairs to speed up the reform of the economy. Once Zhao shifted roles from premier to general secretary in 1987, he came into increasing conflict with other economic officials over both policy and turf. Zhao apparently was already in political decline when the **Beijing** democracy movement began in spring 1989, and his comparatively accommodating stance toward the protesters led to further challenges to his leadership. His refusal to back

Deng Xiaoping's decision to invoke martial law led to his replacement as general secretary by **Jiang Zemin**.

Born in Henan in 1919, Zhao joined the CCP in 1938 and held a series of civilian Party posts during the revolutionary period in the Hebei-**Shandong** and Hebei-**Shandong-Henan** Border Regions. In 1949 Zhao was apparently assigned to **Lin Biao**'s 4th Field Army and subsequently wound up in Guangdong with those forces. Zhao then held a series of Party posts up to the **Cultural Revolution** in the South China sub-bureau, the Guangdong provincial apparatus, and in the early 1960s the Central-South bureau, in all cases working closely with Tao Zhu. Clearly Zhao had become one of China's most important local officials, and in the years just before the **Cultural Revolution** he participated in Tao's comparatively leftist policies. This, however, did not save him during the **Cultural Revolution**, and he was purged in 1967 together with Tao who had briefly become one of the highest-ranking leaders in **Beijing**. By 1971, however, Zhao reappeared as Party secretary in Inner Mongolia, and in 1972 was transferred back to his Guangdong base in a similar position, rising to first secretary in 1974. Late in 1975 he assumed the even more sensitive post of first CCP secretary of **Sichuan**, where he avoided political problems at the time of **Deng Xiaoping**'s removal through a judicious echoing of the official line on Deng.

Zhao's initial prominence in the post-Mao period was largely a result of his activities in **Sichuan** where, like **Wan Li** in Anhui, he was at the forefront of developing reform policies. Yet Zhao's significance was recognized even before he launched **Sichuan**'s reforms, arguably due to his position as leader of China's most populous province, when he was elected an alternate member of the **CCP Central Committee**'s Politburo at the Eleventh Party Congress in 1977. With reform taking hold, Zhao received further promotions to full Politburo status in autumn 1979 and then to Standing Committee membership in early 1980 when he was transferred to Beijing and took over day-to-day charge of the **State Council**. This was fully acknowledged the following September when he was named premier. Zhao's key role in economic reform was also seen in his taking over responsibility as head of the Party centre's finance and economics small group from **Chen Yun**, although Chen initially remained the most important economic policy maker and Zhao shared many of his views. With time, however, economic reform went beyond Chen's cautious preferences and Zhao became the main architect in this area, as with the landmark 1984 decision on urban reform (see **1. Overview History of the People's Republic of China**). As premier, Zhao was broadly aligned with the reform advocacy of Party General Secretary **Hu Yaobang**, but Zhao was both more concerned with economic than political reform and chafed at Hu's tendency to interfere in economic matters, especially since one of the reforms advocated by both Hu and Zhao was the separation of Party and state functions. In this context, when Hu was in political trouble at the end of 1986, Zhao joined in the criticism which led to Hu's resignation. Given his preference for economic matters, Zhao sought to avoid replacing Hu, but as the remaining senior figure on the 'first front' he had no choice. Because of his effort to guide economic policy from the Party leadership, Zhao soon encountered difficulties with Premier **Li Peng** and State Planning Commission head **Yao Yilin**, who both preferred more cautious policies to Zhao's expansionary inclinations. When inflation got out of control in mid-1988, Li and Yao succeeded in convincing **Deng Xiaoping** of the need for retreat, thus seriously undermining Zhao's authority. It was in this context that Zhao sought accommodation with student demonstrators in spring 1989, in the process taking the unprecedented step of failing to endorse the leader's position, thus ensuring his removal from office. Subsequently Zhao lived under a comfortable form of house arrest in **Beijing**.

see also: 1. Overview History of the People's Republic of China; Beijing Municipality; Chen Yun; Chinese Communist Party

Central Committee and Politburo; Cultural Revolution; Deng Xiaoping; Hu Yaobang; Jiang Zemin; Li Peng; Lin Biao; Shandong; Sichuan; State Council; Wan Li; Yao Yilin.

Frederick C. Teiwes

Zhou Enlai

Zhou Enlai was one of the most prominent of all **Chinese Communist Party** leaders, second only to **Mao Zedong** in popular consciousness if not actual importance. A leading revolutionary from the early 1920s, Zhou often had an ambiguous relationship with Mao in the 1920s and 1930s, but thereafter became one of his most loyal and skilful followers. In the post-1949 period Zhou survived all political twists and turns, although not without a major setback at the time of the **Great Leap Forward**. Zhou's role focused on governmental affairs as premier with particular attention to foreign affairs, where he deeply impressed a remarkable array of foreign interlocutors, while in his self-designated role as assistant to Mao he engaged in some dubious activities for such a widely respected figure during the **Cultural Revolution**. Nevertheless, Zhou's reputation was such that his death in 1976 served as the occasion for the anti-**Cultural Revolution** protests of the **Tiananmen Incident** that year.

Born in Jiangsu in 1898, Zhou began his comparatively extensive foreign experience by studying in Japan in 1917–19. Upon returning home in the wake of the May Fourth Movement of 1919, Zhou engaged in political work before departing for Paris in 1920 where he soon became a leading figure in the new French branch of the CCP. Zhou also spent time in England and Germany before returning home in mid-1924, where he assumed a key role in the new united front between the Nationalists and the CCP. Of particular importance was his position as political director of the Whampoa (Huangpu) Military Academy where he forged ties with many future leaders of the Red Army. This became critical when the Nationalists turned on the CCP in 1927, and Zhou became a major leader of the Nanchang Uprising of August 1927.

Over the next six years Zhou, who had already attained Politburo membership in spring 1927, was one of the foremost leaders of the CCP in both the **Hong Kong** and **Shanghai** underground and the Jiangxi Soviet. By 1929 he was one of the top two CCP leaders with Li Lisan in **Shanghai**, and in that capacity clashed with Mao, who was developing his own strategy in Jiangxi. Zhou, however, also clashed with Li and as a result was in Moscow when Li's disastrous revolutionary offensive failed in mid-1930. Thus Zhou was able to retain a key position when Li was disgraced and he cooperated with the new Returned Student leadership of Wang Ming which was installed by the Comintern in early 1931. In this role Zhou again came into conflict with Mao, replacing him as political commissar of the 1st Front Army, but Zhou handled the matter diplomatically by expressing the wish that Mao would soon return to his post. Later, when the military tactics of the Returned Students failed and the communist forces began the Long March, Zhou offered significant support, although less crucial than that of others, to Mao at the 1935 Zunyi conference which saw Mao attain *de facto* military leadership. Despite close cooperation with Mao over the next three years, Zhou nevertheless sided with Wang Ming concerning the nature of the united front in 1938, finally accepting Mao's views in 1939. Although fully loyal to Mao from that point, Zhou only obtained a top role in the emerging Maoist leadership after making excessive self-criticisms during the rectification campaign in 1943–4, ranking third in the Politburo selected in 1945 after Mao and **Liu Shaoqi**. During the united front after 1937 and the civil war from 1946 Zhou played a crucial diplomatic role in dealing with the Nationalists and **United States** representatives.

With the PRC established Zhou became premier and concurrently foreign minister. He played an important role in economic affairs, especially in 1956–7 in guiding the programme of 'opposing rash advance' which was necessary after the dislocations caused by the 'little leap forward' in early

1956. In this Zhou was unusually bold in shaping policy and actively engaging Mao, persuading him of the need for caution. But when Mao changed his mind in late 1957 and launched the **Great Leap Forward**, he also scathingly criticized Zhou and others. Zhou soon lost his foreign ministry post, engaged in another round of excessive self-criticism, and in June 1958 felt compelled to offer his resignation as premier. This was rejected, but from that time on he redoubled his efforts to understand Mao's meaning before acting.

This stood Zhou in good stead during the **Cultural Revolution** when he retained his rank while **Lin Biao** replaced **Liu Shaoqi** as the successor to Mao. While generally regarded as a moderate during this tumultuous period, and Zhou did attempt to moderate the movement in several key respects, it is now clear that he totally supported Mao not only in such measures as the 'flying leap' in economic policy in 1969–71, but also in overseeing the special case groups which persecuted many of his longstanding comrades. Yet with the dramatic fall of **Lin Biao** in 1971, Zhou attacked **Cultural Revolution** leftism, initially with Mao's support although by 1973 drawing his criticisms. In this period Zhou also was critical in implementing Mao's new diplomatic design, deeply impressing US President Richard Nixon and his foreign policy adviser Henry Kissinger during Sino-American rapprochement.

From 1973 he suffered dual blows, physically from cancer and politically from the attempts of the **gang of four** to undermine his standing with Mao. At the time of his death on 8 January 1976 Zhou was identified in the public mind with the old guard leadership headed by **Deng Xiaoping**. The **Tiananmen Incident** (1976) was the result of shunting Deng aside, as well as a popular demonstration honouring Zhou and expressing disgust with the **gang of four** and the **Cultural Revolution**.

see also: 1. Overview History of the People's Republic of China; Chinese Communist Party; Cultural Revolution; Deng Xiaoping; gang of four; Great Leap Forward; Hong Kong; Lin Biao; Liu Shaoqi; Mao Zedong; Shanghai; Tiananmen Incident (1976); United States policy.

Frederick C. Teiwes

Zhu Rongji

One of China's senior leaders and a member of the central group in succession to **Deng Xiaoping**. He became a vice-premier of the **State Council** in April 1991 and a member of the Standing Committee of the **CCP Central Committee**'s Politburo in October 1992, being confirmed on that supreme body, in the third place, at the time of the Fifteenth **National Party Congress** (September 1997). In March 1993, he was appointed the senior vice-premier and given charge of controlling the overheating economy. By 1997, his efforts to limit money supply, promote fiscal and financial reform, control investment and rein in credit had engineered a 'soft landing' for an economy that had been in danger of spiralling out of control.

Zhu was born in October 1928 in Hunan. He graduated as an electrical engineer from Qinghua University and was assigned to work in industrial ministries in the 1950s and 1960s. According to some reports, he was criticized during the Anti-Rightist Movement (see **Hundred Flowers Movement**) of 1957 for liberal views. He emerged in 1978 as the director of the Industrial Economics Institute of the Chinese Academy of Social Sciences. In the early 1980s he moved to the State Economic Commission (SEC), where he was linked to the development of reform policies. From 1983 until 1988, he was a vice-minister of the SEC and also a permanent director of the China International Trust and Investment Corporation. In late 1987 he became a deputy secretary of the **Shanghai** CCP committee and was mayor of **Shanghai** from 1988 to 1991, taking over the role of **Shanghai** Party secretary when **Jiang Zemin** moved to join the central leadership after the **June 4 Incident** (1989). Zhu was prominent in managing a relatively peaceful end to the **Shanghai** student protests of that year.

During his time in **Shanghai**, Zhu was well known as a reformer with good technical management skills. He was reported to be on the CCP's moderate wing, earning the name 'one-chop' Zhu because of his brisk, no-nonsense approach and his keenness to cut through bureaucratic processes to achieve quick decisions. This decisiveness, which tended to create resentment among those affected by his policies, also characterized his approach to his work in the central government.

Zhu's success in **Shanghai** and his reputation as a reformer lay behind his appointment as vice-premier in 1991. He soon became known as the economic 'tsar'. He was director of the **State Council** Economy and Trade Office in 1992–3 and president of the **People's Bank of China** 1993–5. Largely because of his strong management, China was successful in achieving more stable economic growth in 1997. The difficulty he faced in implementing his investment squeeze of July 1993 and the fiscal and financial reforms of 1994, however, underlined the growing complexity of economic leadership in China. His emergence as number three in the leadership hierarchy at the Fifteenth **National Party Congress** of 1997 made him the most likely successor to **Li Peng** as premier, an appointment due in March 1998.

see also: Chinese Communist Party Central Committee and Politburo; Deng Xiaoping; Hundred Flowers Movement; Jiang Zemin; June 4 Incident; Li Peng; National Party Congress; People's Bank of China; Shanghai; State Council.

Andrew Watson

Zou Jiahua

Appointed one of China's vice-premiers in April 1991, Zou Jiahua's main responsibilities have been in the areas of planning, basic investment policy and machine-building industries.

Zou Jiahua was born in October 1926. He joined the Red Army's New 4th Army in 1944 and was a local district Party secretary by 1946. From 1948 to 1955 he studied engineering in Moscow, and on his return to China was appointed as deputy manager of the Shenyang Number 2 Machine Tool Plant. He then joined the First Ministry of Machine Building and was director of its Machinery Research Institute and subsequently deputy director of its Machinery Research Academy. In the early 1980s he became prominent in the national defence industries, rising to be minister of Ordnance Industries. He then moved to be minister of the Machine Building Industry Commission and minister of Machinery and Electronics Industry. From the late 1980s to 1993, he was minister for the State Planning Commission. At various times he has also been a senior member of quality control, production safety and technology committees. Since 1993, he has been vice-chairman of the **Three Gorges** Construction Engineering Committee.

As his list of appointments makes clear, Zou has worked primarily within his area of engineering expertise. His early history in the CCP has also meant that he has played an important role in Party activities within the various ministries. His image within China is primarily one of technical rather than political leadership.

see also: Planning, economics; Three Gorges Dam.

Andrew Watson

Further Reading

For reasons of space this list of further reading makes no attempt to be comprehensive. It is designed to assist users to find up-to-date further reading on the topics covered in the dictionary, for which reason the emphasis is on recent works, with none published before 1980. The list covers only books in the English language and only those which focus on the PRC.

General

Baum, Richard (ed.) (1980) *China's Four Modernizations: The New Technological Revolution*, Boulder, CO: Westview Press (Has accounts of the state of, and policies on, technology and modernization in China in the late 1970s. Topics include the modernization of industry, industrial science, technology transfer and national defence).

Benewick, Robert and Wingrove, Paul (1988) *Reforming the Revolution: China in Transition*, London: Macmillan (A general treatment of China in the 1980s with coverage of politics, the economy, health delivery, family, education, literature and foreign relations).

—— (1995) *China in the 1990s*, London: Macmillan (A general treatment of China in the 1990s with some similarities to the preceding volume in terms of approach, coverage, authorship and style, but with some completely new chapter subjects, such as on civil society, gender and population).

Breslin, Shaun (1996) *China in the 1980s: Centre–Province Relations in a Reforming Socialist State*, London: Macmillan (Takes a mainly economic and political approach to the study of relations between the centre and provinces, arguing (p. 11) that 'rather than creating a more market rational economic system, reform has instead produced a national economic structure that is characterized by provincial autarky').

Brugger, Bill and Reglar, Stephen (1994) *Politics, Economy and Society in Contemporary China*, London: Macmillan (Designed especially for students, this book is in two parts:

(1) overviews of PRC history; (2) themes such as 'state and countryside', 'law and policing', 'family and gender relations' and 'minority nationalities').

Cheng, Joseph Y. S. (ed.) (1989) *China: Modernization in the 1980s*, Hong Kong: Chinese University Press; Sydney: Allen & Unwin Australia (This multi-authored book outlines China's policies and realities in the political, foreign relations, economic, educational, social welfare and literature fields).

China Information (Leiden), *The China Journal* (Canberra) and *The China Quarterly* (London) are the three English-language scholarly journals consistently providing solid studies of all aspects of contemporary China, with the last including a useful quarterly chronicle.

Ching, Frank (ed.) (1994) *China in Transition*, Hong Kong: Review Publishing Company (Contains journalistic articles originally appearing in the *Far Eastern Economic Review*, one of the best and most important weeklies dealing with Eastern Asia. Fields covered include the economic, foreign affairs, legal and social).

Dietrich, Craig (1994) *People's China: A Brief History*, 2nd edn, Oxford: Oxford University Press (This is a chronological descriptive history of the PRC down to the early 1990s, with some background history of the pre-1949 CCP and personalities).

Dwyer, Denis (ed.) (1994) *China: The Next Decades*, London: Longman (A general survey of China's economic and social policies and conditions since 1949, with the emphasis on the 1980s and 1990s. Topics covered include population, economic reform, urbanization, the environment, water resources and health care).

Gittings, John (1990) *China Changes Face: The Road from Revolution, 1949–1989*, 2nd edn, Oxford: Oxford University Press (This book, first published in 1989, traces the struggle between two forms of socialism from 1949 on, the second edition adding a harshly critical chapter on the 1989 crisis).

Goodman, David S. G. (ed.) (1997) *China's Provinces in Reform: Class, Community and Political Culture*, London: Routledge (A significant study of several province-level units).

Goodman, David S. G. and Segal, Gerald (eds) (1994) *China Deconstructs: Politics, Trade and Regionalism*, London: Routledge (An important study of several Chinese province-level units and their domestic and foreign linkages, as well as of regionalism and its implications).

Hsu, Immanuel C. Y. (1982) *China Without Mao*, Oxford: Oxford University Press (Deals with the period 1976–81, covering the fall of the gang of four and the rise of Deng Xiaoping. Section 4 of this book deals with the Four Modernizations detailing the major problems and consequences of rapid modernization).

MacFarquhar, Roderick (1987, 1997) *The Origins of the Cultural Revolution, 1: Contradictions among the People 1956–1957, The Origins of the Cultural Revolution, 2: The Great Leap Forward 1958–1960*, and *The Origins of the Cultural Revolution, 3: The Coming of the Cataclysm, 1961–1966*, New York: Columbia University Press (A classic trilogy examining in great detail elite interaction over the pre-Cultural Revolution decade. Emphasizes elite conflict, but with a much more dominant Mao emerging by Volume 3 in comparison to Volume 1).

MacFarquhar, Roderick and Fairbank, John K. (eds) (1987) *The Cambridge History of China, Volume 14: The People's Republic, Part 1: The Emergence of Revolutionary China, 1949–1965*, Cambridge: Cambridge University Press (The first volume of *The Cambridge History* on the PRC, covering politics, economics, culture, education and foreign relations).

Mackerras, Colin and Yorke, Amanda (1991) *The Cambridge Handbook of Contemporary China*, Cambridge: Cambridge University Press (Includes a chronology, a gazetteer and biographies, as well as chapters covering such matters as the economy, population, minority nationalities, education and culture).

Mackerras, Colin, Taneja, Pradeep and Young, Graham (1994) *China Since 1978: Reform, Modernisation, and 'Socialism with Chinese Characteristics'*, Melbourne: Longman Cheshire, New York: St Martin's Press (Designed as a textbook for university students, this book focuses on the period of reform, covering historical background, population, law, the economy, the environment, social welfare and foreign relations).

Maxwell, Neville and McFarlane, Bruce (eds) (1984) *China's Changed Road to Development*, Oxford: Pergamon (Includes extensive treatment on economic and social policy and conditions in China since 1976).

McCormick, Barrett and Unger, Jonathan (eds) (1996) *China After Socialism: In the Footsteps of Eastern Europe or East Asia?*, Armonk, NY: M. E. Sharpe (While the core of the book is China, it is comparative, seeking comparisons and contrasts with the Soviet Union and other states of East and Central Europe, with the emphasis being on politics and economics).

Zhou, Kate Xiao (1996) *How the Farmers Changed China: Power of the People*, Boulder, CO: Westview Press (Argues strongly that the farmers have been the major force driving economic and social reform in China).

Foreign Relations

Barnett, A. Doak (1985) *The Making of Foreign Policy in China*, Boulder, CO: Westview Press (A seminal study of the actors and processes involved in Beijing's formulation of foreign policy).

Chen, Jian (1994) *China's Road to the Korean War: The Making of the Sino-American Confrontation*, New York: Columbia University Press (Takes a wide-ranging look at the foreign relations implications of China's decision to enter the Korean War, including the ramifications for Taiwan).

Dittmer, Lowell and Kim, Samuel S. (eds) (1993) *China's Quest for National Identity*,

Ithaca, NY: Cornell University Press (Takes up the roles of national identity, nationalism, ideology and personality in Chinese foreign policy).

Foot, Rosemary (1995) *The Practice of Power: U.S. Relations with China Since 1949*, Oxford: Oxford University Press (Takes up various aspects of US policy on China, showing how domestic politics and other factors helped or hindered attempts to isolate, confront or engage with China).

Goncharov, Sergei N., Lewis, John W. and Xue Litai (1993) *Uncertain Partners: Stalin, Mao, and the Korean War*, Stanford, CA: Stanford University Press (Based on Soviet archives and newly available Chinese documents, this book focuses on the early stages of the PRC's relations with the Soviet Union and the implications for the Korean War).

Hamrin, Carol Lee (1993) *China and the Challenge of the Future*, Boulder, CO: Westview Press (Takes up the domestic context of Chinese foreign policy).

Harding, Harry (ed.) (1984) *China's Foreign Relations in the 1980s*, New Haven, CT: Yale University Press (Covers topics such as the relationship between domestic and foreign politics, China in the international economy and the PRC as a regional power).

—— (1992) *A Fragile Relationship: The United States and China Since 1972*, Washington, DC: Brookings Institution (A thorough description and analysis of Sino-American relations, taking a basically chronological approach, from 1972 to 1991, but introducing detailed themes for each period as well).

Harris, Stuart and Klintworth, Gary (eds) (1993) *China as a Great Power: Myths, Realities and Challenges in the Asia-Pacific Region*, Melbourne: Longman, New York: St Martin's Press (A collection of essays dealing primarily with Beijing's relations with particular global regions or states across a range of topics).

Hoyt, Edwin P. (1990) *The Day the Chinese Attacked: Korea, 1950: The Story of the Failure of America's China Policy*, New York: McGraw-Hill (Focuses on relations

between China and the US over the period from the end of the Second World War until the end of the Korean War in 1953 and includes an account of the Korean War).

Kent, Ann (1993) *Between Freedom and Subsistence: China and Human Rights*, Hong Kong: Oxford University Press (The best detailed treatment of the controversial issue of human rights and its role in China's foreign relations. Most of the eight chapters take a chronological approach, with the focus on the period from 1979 to 1991).

Kim, Samuel S. (ed.) (1989) *China and the World: New Directions in Chinese Foreign Relations*, 2nd rev. edn, Boulder, CO: Westview Press (Covers both theoretical issues and China's relations with specific countries, such as the US and Soviet Union, and categories such as the Third World).

Mackerras, Colin (ed.) (1996) *Australia and China, Partners in Asia*, Melbourne: Macmillan (Takes up numerous aspects of this bilateral relationship, including political and economic factors, as well as immigration and education, with the emphasis on the period 1985 to 1995).

Robinson, Thomas W. and Shambaugh, David (eds) (1995) *Chinese Foreign Policy, Theory and Practice*, Oxford: Clarendon (Takes a wide-ranging look at PRC foreign policy, taking up theoretical issues and some of China's bilateral and regional relationships).

Ross, Robert S. (1988) *The Indochina Tangle: China's Vietnam Policy 1975–79*, New York: Columbia University Press (Considers the Indochina problems, and especially China's involvement, chronologically, with extensive use of primary sources from China and various other countries).

—— (1995) *Negotiating Cooperation, The United States and China, 1969–1989*, Cambridge: Cambridge University Press (Discusses the processes of negotiation despite ongoing sources of conflict, among which Taiwan was the most important).

Short, Philip (1982) *The Dragon and the Bear: China and Russia in the Eighties*, New York: William Morrow (Traces Sino-Soviet relations from 1949 to 1981, including commentary on Chinese and Soviet society and politics).

Spurr, Russell (1988) *Enter the Dragon: China's Undeclared War Against the U.S. in Korea, 1950–51*, New York: Newmarket (Concerns China's participation in the Korean War, and the military campaigns of the war, especially for the first years).

Swaine, Michael D. (1995) *China: Domestic Change and Foreign Policy*, Santa Monica, CA: Rand Corporation (A well-argued and accessible study concerning the impact of foreign relations on domestic decision making in China, the author's expectation being mainly continuity both in domestic and foreign affairs until the end of the twentieth century).

Tan Qingshan (1992) *The Making of US China Policy: From Normalization to the Post-Cold War Era*, Boulder, CO: Lynne Rienner (Covers processes in the formulation of US China policy, as well as several crucial issues, such as Taiwan, arms sales, trade and most-favoured-nation status. It concludes that US political institutions and public opinion are crucial to policy and that the complexity of the relationship should not be reduced to the assertion of balance of power).

Yahuda, Michael (1983) *China's Foreign Policy After Mao: Towards the End of Isolation*, London: Macmillan (Provides an analytical account of developments in China's foreign policy, attempting to distinguish between the geopolitical and societal dimensions of China's foreign relations).

Domestic Ideology, Law, the Military, Policing and Politics

Baum, Richard (1994) *Burying Mao: Chinese Politics in the Age of Deng Xiaoping*, Princeton, NJ: Princeton University Press (An extremely detailed analytical description of the development of Chinese politics from the death of Mao Zedong in 1976 to 1993).

Black, George and Munro, Robin (1993) *Black Hands of Beijing: Lives of Defiance in China's Democracy Movement*, New York: Wiley (An account of the democracy movement of 1989, with the focus on selected prominent activists who took part in it).

Brady, James (1982) *Criminal Justice in Post-Mao China*, London: Academic Press (Takes up the relationship of criminal justice to social order issues, adopting a perspective hostile to the post-1978 economic reforms).

Chen, A. H. Y. (1992) *An Introduction to the Legal System of the People's Republic of China*, Singapore: Butterworth Asia (This book provides a systematic account of the legal system of the PRC covering its history, constitutional structure, sources of law, major legal institutions, as well as the basic concepts and principles of procedural and substantive law).

Du Xichuan and Zhang Lingyuan (1990) *China's Legal System: A General Survey*, Beijing: New World Press (Focuses on the legal system of the 1980s from the official Chinese point of view).

Dutton, Michael (1992) *Policing and Punishment in China*, Cambridge: Cambridge University Press (About half this book is devoted to the question of household registration; it also focuses on the reform through labour system).

Goodman, David S. G. (1986) *Centre and Province in the People's Republic of China, Sichuan and Guizhou, 1955–1965*, Cambridge: Cambridge University Press (Dealing with two provinces in Southwest China, this book gives a detailed analysis of the interaction between Sichuan and the centre in the 1950s and 1960s).

—— (ed.) (1997) *China's Provinces in Reform: Class, Community and Political Culture*, London: Routledge (An important study of several province-level units).

Goodman, David S. G. and Segal, Gerald (1991) *China in the Nineties, Crisis Management and Beyond*, Oxford: Clarendon (A substantially revised edition of *China at Forty*, published by the Oxford University Press in 1989, this book focuses on politics and foreign relations of China in the 1980s and early 1990s, taking account of the crisis of mid-1989).

International Institute of Strategic Studies (1995) *The Military Balance, 1994–1995*,

London: Brasseys (An authoritative assessment of the People's Liberation Army's military capabilities).

Joffe, Ellis (1987) *The Chinese Army After Mao*, Cambridge, MA: Harvard University Press (This gives a good account of the early stage of modernization of the People's Liberation Army, dealing with military doctrine and army–civil relations as well as weaponry, but also covers the historical background).

Kuiken, Kees (1993) *Soldiers, Cops, Bannermen: The Rise and Fall of the First Communist Police State 1931–1969*, Groningen, Netherlands: Wolters-Noordhoff Academieprijs (Weakened by the fact that it is based largely on English-language material with occasional references to Taiwanese sources, this book is, however, the only book-length study of contemporary Chinese policing available).

Lam, Willy Wo-Lap (1995) *China After Deng Xiaoping: The Power Struggle in Beijing since Tiananmen*, Singapore: Wiley (A blunt but extremely well informed account of factional divisions and personal rivalries in the Chinese leadership and their likely impact on China following Deng Xiaoping's death).

Lee, Ngok (1989) *China's Defence Modernisation and Military Leadership*, Sydney: Australian National University Press (A detailed account of the early phase of People's Liberation Army modernization after Mao. Good on defence strategy and weaponry, but also deals with issues of Party–army leadership relations).

Leng, S. C. and Chiu, H. D. (1985) *Criminal Justice in Post-Mao China: Analysis and Documents*, Albany, NY: State University of New York Press (This book studies the development, organization, and functioning of the criminal justice system in post-Mao China by examining both the formal aspects of criminal justice, and the extra-judicial organs and sanctions that shape criminal justice).

Lieberthal, Kenneth (1995) *Governing China*, New York: Norton (A good introduction to the formal and informal processes of governing China).

Liu Binyan (1990) *China's Crisis, China's Hope*, trans. Howard Goldblatt, Cambridge, MA: Harvard University Press (A journalistic account of contemporary China, focused around the democracy movement of 1989 by one of China's best known reporters).

Lo, Carlos Wing-hung (1995) *China's Legal Awakening: Legal Theory and Criminal Justice in Deng's Era*, Hong Kong: Hong Kong University Press (This book illustrates that the establishment of a formal criminal justice system and the development of an embryonic socialist theory of law in Deng's China reflect a genuine and widespread legal awakening).

MacFarquhar, Roderick (ed.) (1994) *The Politics of China, 1949–1989*, Cambridge: Cambridge University Press (Mainly chapters by leading scholars drawn from Volumes 14 and 15 of *The Cambridge History of China*).

McCormick, Barrett (1990) *Political Reform in Post-Mao China: Democracy and Bureaucracy in a Leninist State*, Berkeley, CA: University of California Press (The focus is on government and economic policy in China since 1976, with the accent on the tension between democracy and the bureaucratic state).

O'Brien, Kevin J. (1990) *Reform without Liberalization: China's National People's Congress and the Politics of Institutional Change*, Cambridge: Cambridge University Press (Has sections on the origins of the National People's Congress before 1949, under Mao Zedong and under Deng Xiaoping. It discusses systemic changes under Deng, describing them (p. 157) as 'fitful and uneven, unexpected and incomplete').

Potter, Pitman B. (ed.) (1994) *Domestic Law Reforms in Post-Mao China*, Armonk, NY: M. E. Sharpe (The primary focus is on economic and civil law, but with attention given also to cultural background and the role of law to legitimize CCP rule).

Seymour, James (1987) *China's Satellite Parties*, Armonk, NY: M. E. Sharpe (Deals with China's government under the People's Republic, with the focus on six of those parties other than the Chinese Communist Party termed 'democratic parties').

Sun Yan (1995) *The Chinese Reassessment of Socialism, 1976–1992*, Princeton, NJ: Princeton University Press (A rich analysis of the reassessment of socialism and types of socialist system in official ideology and among critical Marxists under Deng Xiaoping).

Swaine, Michael (1992) *The Military and Political Succession in China*, Santa Monica, CA: Rand Corporation (A good analysis of army–Party relations and the influence of the People's Liberation Army on Party leadership).

—— (1994) *The Modernization of the Chinese People's Liberation Army*, Seattle, WA: National Bureau of Asian Research (A very good analysis of progress in defence modernization).

Townsend, James R. and Womack, Brantly (1986) *Politics in China*, 3rd edn, Boston, MA: Little, Brown (Covers such issues as political structure, organization and processes, with substantial focus on political ideology; originally published in 1973, it has been extensively updated).

Unger, Jonathan (ed.) (1991) *The Pro-Democracy Protests in China: Reports from the Provinces*, Armonk, NY: M. E. Sharpe (Takes a sympathetic look at the manifestations of the democracy movement of 1989 not merely in Beijing, the focus of most of the literature, but in the provinces of the northeast, the interior, the South China Coast and the Yangzi Delta).

Wang, J. C. F. (1992) *Contemporary Chinese Politics: An Introduction*, 4th edn, Englewood Cliffs, NJ: Prentice Hall (A textbook rich in detail on government).

White, Gordon (1993) *Riding the Tiger: The Politics of Economic Reform in Post-Mao China*, London: Macmillan (Deals with the political and social economy of post-Mao China, covering such areas as the failure of the Maoist development state and the politics of agrarian and industrial reform, as well as the social impact of economic reform).

White, Lynn T. III (1989) *Policies of Chaos: The Organizational Causes of Violence in China's Cultural Revolution*, Princeton, NJ: Princeton University Press (A highly scholarly study of the Cultural Revolution, analysing its causes, nature and processes).

Wu, Hongda Harry (1992), *Laogai: The Chinese Gulag*, trans. Ted Singerland, Boulder, CO: Westview (More than anyone else, Harry Wu has brought the problems of the Chinese prison sector to the attention of international critics; the reform through labour system is the focus of this work).

The Economy

Becker, Jasper (1996) *Hungry Ghosts: China's Secret Famine*, London: John Murray (An extremely damning account of the great famine of 1958–62, which is argued to have been man-made and, unique in Chinese history, to have affected all parts of China).

Bramall, Chris (1993) *In Praise of Maoist Economic Planning: Living Standards and Economic Development in Sichuan since 1931*, Oxford: Clarendon (Deals with regional and income inequalities and economic policy and conditions, with the focus on Sichuan province and some material on the period since 1976).

Bucknall, Kevin (1989) *China and the Open Door Policy*, Sydney: Allen & Unwin (Deals with trade, foreign investment and foreign aid from 1949 to near the date of publication, the focus being on the period since 1978, with a chapter on the special economic zones).

Byrd, William A. and Lin Qingsong (eds) (1989) *China's Rural Industry: Structure, Development, and Reform*, New York: Oxford University Press for the World Bank (Covers industrial and economic policy and rural industries, with a focus on the period since 1976).

Christiansen, Flemming and Zhang Junzou (eds) (1997) *Village Inc.: Chinese Rural Society in the 1990s*, Richmond, Surrey: Curzon Press (Argues that local government in rural China has corporatist characteristics and can be conceptualized as a hybrid of market forces and collective management).

Crane, George T. (1990) *The Political Economy of China's Special Economic Zones*, Armonk,

NY: M. E. Sharpe (Adopting a 'political structuralist' approach to the study of China's special economic zones, this book uses the special economic zones as examples of economic policy decision-making in China).

Findlay, Christopher, Watson, Andrew and Wu, Harry X. (eds) (1994) *Rural Enterprises in China*, London: Macmillan, New York: St Martin's Press (Covers issues in rural enterprises, analysing problems, achievements, reason for the rapid growth, and prospects for the future).

Hinton, William (1990) *The Great Reversal: The Privatization of China, 1978–1989*, New York: Monthly Review Press (His focus on agriculture in the 1980s, Hinton attacks the reform policies and the privatization they involve).

Huang, Yasheng (1996) *Inflation and Investment Controls in China: The Political Economy of Central–Local Relations during the Reform Era*, Cambridge: Cambridge University Press (This very thorough study of the major and controversial issue of centre–local relations argues that no decline in central control has resulted from the decentralization of economic and fiscal resources, with political institutions remaining basically unaffected by economic reform).

Ikels, Charlotte (1996) *The Return of the God of Wealth: The Transition to a Market Economy in Urban China*, Stanford, CA: Stanford University Press (A very thorough look at Guangzhou in the period of reform. The book is multifaceted, covering numerous aspects of the city's life, and gives some attention to its history).

Jacobson, Harold K. and Oksenberg, Michel (1990) *China's Participation in the IMF, the World Bank and GATT: Towards a Global Economic Order*, Ann Arbor, MI: University of Michigan Press (Covers China's foreign economic relations, especially its involvement with the International Bank for Reconstruction and Development, the International Monetary Fund and the General Agreement on Tariffs and Trade).

Jao, Y. C. and Leung, C. K. (eds) (1986) *China's Special Economic Zones: Policies, Problems and Prospects*, Hong Kong: Oxford University Press (Written mainly by Hong Kong scholars this book has three parts: (1) the physical environment; (2) the political and legal framework; and (3) economic and management perspectives).

Kraus, W. (1991) *Private Business in China: Revival between Ideology and Pragmatism*, London: Hurst (A comprehensive account of the private sector development during the 1980s).

Lardy, Nicholas R. (1983) *Agriculture in China's Modern Economic Development*, Cambridge: Cambridge University Press (Takes up such matters as planning, prices, living standards and the prospects for further reform; emphasizes the uneven performance and uncertain future).

—— (1992) *Foreign Trade and Economic Reform in China, 1978–1990*, Cambridge: Cambridge University Press (A wide-ranging analysis of the relationship between China's foreign trade reforms and domestic economic reform).

Liew, Leong (1997) *The Chinese Economy in Transition From Plan to Market*, Cheltenham, UK and Brookfield, MO: Edward Elgar (About 'the transformation of China from a planned to a market economy' (p. 3), this book analyses the economic reforms introduced under Deng Xiaoping. It focuses on three broad areas of the Chinese economy: agriculture, industry and macroeconomic management, and adopts an interdisciplinary approach, with attention given to political as well as economic problems).

Lin, Justin Yifu, Fang Cai and Zhou Li (1996) *The China Miracle: Development Strategy and Economic Reform*, Hong Kong: Chinese University Press (An accessible account of the reform process and current issues in the Chinese economy).

Luk, Shiu-hung and Whitney, Joseph (eds) (1993) *Megaproject, A Case Study of China's Three Gorges Project*, Armonk, NY: M. E. Sharpe (Focuses on the ecological issues of the dam, with some attention also to resettlement and other matters. Calls for the Chinese government to undertake greater consultation and research before proceeding with construction).

Naughton, Barry (1995) *Growing out of the Plan: Chinese Economic Reform 1978–1993*, Cambridge: Cambridge University Press (A clear and insightful overview of the key issues and trends in China's reform process, with focuses on industry and macroeconomic policy).

Perkins, Dwight and Yusuf, Shahid (1984) *Rural Development in China*, Baltimore, MD: Johns Hopkins University Press for the World Bank (A critical but basically favourable account of the changes in China's rural economy since 1949; covers such matters as the dual economy, agricultural production, organizational changes, income distribution, and health care).

Pomfret, Richard (1991) *Investing in China: Ten Years of the Open Door Policy*, Hemel Hempstead: Harvester Wheatsheaf, Ames, IA: Iowa State University Press (Takes the story of foreign investment in the PRC from the beginning of the reform period to 1989).

Riskin, Carl (1987) *China's Political Economy: The Quest for Development since 1949*, Oxford: Oxford University Press (A comprehensive survey of China's economy for the period 1949–85, providing an insightful account of how the various sectors of China's economy developed).

Shirk, Susan (1993) *The Political Logic of Economic Reform in China*, Berkeley, CA: University of California Press (A sophisticated analysis of the politics of economic reform; Chapter 4 is particularly useful in its analysis of the way leading bodies are selected.

Young, Susan (1995) *Private Business and Economic Reform in China*, Armonk, NY: M. E. Sharpe (Based on a doctoral thesis, this book deals with the revival of the private sector in China in the 1980s and its social and political context; it includes the factor of state control and an assessment of the private sector).

Society, Minorities, Culture and Education

Banister, Judith (1987) *China's Changing Population*, Stanford, CA: Stanford University Press (Covers such issues as fertility decline, mortality, late marriage and birth planning; this scholarly book focuses on the post-Mao period).

Barnett, Robert and Akiner, Shirin (eds) (1994) *Resistance and Reform in Tibet*, London: Hurst (Deals with the modern history and culture of Tibet, taking a generally strongly anti-Chinese line. Calls for greater attention to Tibetan studies).

Chan, Anita, Madsen, Richard and Unger, Jonathan (1992) *Chen Village: The Recent History of a Peasant Community in Mao's China*, Berkeley, CA: University of California Press (A study of the social and political impact of the communes in one village).

Cleverley, John (1991) *The Schooling of China, Tradition and Modernity in Chinese Education*, 2nd edn, Sydney: Allen & Unwin (Provides a very good and clear account of the Chinese education system, including its achievements and problems, this second edition including an account of the implications of the 1989 crisis).

Croll, Elisabeth (1981) *The Politics of Marriage in Contemporary China*, Cambridge: Cambridge University Press (Examines the changes in marriage in the PRC from 1949 to the late 1970s, including such matters as the criteria governing choice of spouse, age of marriage and its ritual and ceremonial forms).

Education Atlas of China (1995) Shanghai: Shanghai Science and Technology Press (An excellent graphic account of Chinese education and the Chinese educational system, with much statistical and spatial information).

Gilmartin, Christina K., Hershatter, Gail, Rofel, Lisa and White, Tyrene (1994) *Engendering China: Women, Culture and the State*, Cambridge, MA: Harvard University Press (On a range of issues relating to women and gender in China, this book focuses on the period since the sixteenth century, about half of it on the PRC).

Goodman, David S. G. and Hooper, Beverley (eds) (1994) *China's Quiet Revolution*, Melbourne: Longman Cheshire (The focus is on the changing social structure and new social forces, such as private entrepreneurs and the social elite, with emphasis on wealth, status and power).

Heberer, Thomas (1989) *China and its National Minorities, Autonomy or Assimilation?*, Armonk, NY: M. E. Sharpe (Deals with problems of identification, the issue of autonomy, the case of Yunnan province, population policies and religion).

Honig, Emily and Hershatter, Gail (1988) *Personal Voices: Chinese Women in the 1980's*, Stanford, CA: Stanford University Press (A comprehensive analysis of women's private and public roles, containing both overall assessments and a wealth of articles translated from Chinese newspapers and magazines).

Hooper, Beverley (1985) *Youth in China*, Harmondsworth: Penguin (An examination of the lives of China's youth generation in the early years of the post-Mao era, dealing with young people's personal as well as their working lives).

Jacka, Tamara (1997) *Women's Work in Rural China, Change and Continuity in an Era of Reform*, Cambridge: Cambridge University Press (The most comprehensive study of the effects of the policies of reform on rural women since 1978).

Judd, Ellen R. (1994) *Gender and Power in Rural North China*, Stanford, CA: Stanford University Press (A close study of gender relations in three Shandong villages, based on field work carried out from 1986 to 1990).

Kane, Penny (1987) *The Second Billion: Population and Family Planning in China*, Ringwood, Victoria: Penguin (Gives detailed coverage of the development of the PRC's population policies, reaching the conclusion that China's population policy succeeded in its main aims).

Lee, Chin-Chuan (ed.) (1990) *Voices of China: The Interplay of Politics and Journalism*, New York: Guilford Press (Based on presentations made at a conference held in October 1989, this book contains good material on PRC media issues up until 1989 and covers American reporting on China).

—— (ed.) (1994) *China's Media, Media's China*, Boulder, CO: Westview (Covers issues of China's media policy and practice, including its intimate relationship with politics).

Leung, Joe C. B. and Nann, Richard C. (1995) *Authority and Benevolence: Social Welfare in China*, Hong Kong: Chinese University Press (Although with substantial historical background information, the focus is on the period of reform, including evaluation of welfare programmes, administration, eligibility and other factors).

Mackerras, Colin (1994) *China's Minorities, Modernization and Integration in the Twentieth Century*, Hong Kong: Oxford University Press (Covers the minorities from the points of view of policy, economy, population and foreign relations, over half focused on the PRC).

Orleans, Leo A. (1980) *Science in Contemporary China*, Stanford, CA: Stanford University Press (Beginning with short chapters on science in China's past and China's science policy and organization, this book continues with accounts of various scientific disciplines, such as mathematics, physics, chemistry, astronomy and environmental science).

Peng Xizhe (1991) *Demographic Transition in China, Fertility Trends since the 1950s*, Oxford: Clarendon (A comprehensive study of fertility trends in China, including reference to the impact of reform).

Pepper, Suzanne (1990) *China's Education Reform in the 1980s, Policies, Issues, and Historical Perspectives*, Berkeley, CA: Institute of East Asian Studies, University of California (A wide-ranging study of Chinese education in the 1980s, including historical background and commentary on the aftermath of the 1989 crisis).

Simon, Denis Fred and Goldman, Merle (eds) (1989) *Science and Technology in Post-Mao China*, Cambridge, MA: Harvard University Press (Other than an introduction, this book has four parts: (1) historical precedents; (2) the reorganization of science and technology; (3) the application of science and technology reforms; (4) technology transfer).

Wang Jiye and Hull, Terence H. (eds) (1991) *Population and Development Planning in China*, Sydney: Allen & Unwin (A thorough study of China's population policy and practice, with emphasis on various aspects of economic and social development in the 1980s).

Wang Yeu-Farn (1993) *China's Science and Technology Policy: 1949–1989*, Aldershot: Avebury (The four parts are (1) analytical concepts; (2) a chronological account of China's science and technology policy from 1949 to 1980; (3) discussion of the reform period of the 1980s; (4) analysis of science, technology and modernization).

Wong, Linda and MacPherson, Stewart (1995) *Social Change and Social Policy in Contemporary China*, Aldershot, UK and Brookfield, MO: Avebury (Covers the social ramifications of reform since 1978, including social welfare and security, education, health, gender, housing and social policy).

Wu Dingbo and Murphy, Patrick D. (eds) (1994) *Handbook of Chinese Popular Culture*, Westport, CT: Greenwood (The emphasis here is on bibliography and literature review, rather than scholarly critique or theoretical analysis).

Biography

Bachman, D. M. (1985) *Chen Yun and the Chinese Political System*, Berkeley, CA: Center for Chinese Studies, University of California (A thoughtful study of the career and politics of one of the CCP's most influential leaders of the 1950s, and late 1970s and early 1980s).

Bonavia, David, *Deng* (1989) Hong Kong: Longman (This biography of Deng Xiaoping traces his career from childhood to the mid-1980s, evaluating his role as reformer, statesman, commander-in-chief, and thinker).

Bryan, John and Pack, Robert (1992) *The Claws of the Dragon: Kang Sheng: The Evil Genius behind Mao and his Legacy of Terror in People's China*, New York: Simon & Schuster (Based on declassified US archives and a PRC biography of Kang with restricted domestic circulation, this book by an Australian diplomat and US journalist is the first scholarly biography of Kang published in the West).

Fang, Percy Jusheng and Fang, Lucy Guirong J. (1986) *Zhou Enlai: A Profile*, Beijing: Foreign Languages Press (Although reflecting official attitudes toward Zhou, a revealing sketch of one of the CCP's most renowned figures which is particularly valuable in the absence of serious biographies of the former premier).

Goodman, David S. G. (1994) *Deng Xiaoping and the Chinese Revolution: A Political Biography*, London: Routledge (A thickly documented and detailed account of Deng's career from his birth in 1904 to 1992, concluding that Deng was probably China's most successful economic modernizer but a less successful political reformer).

Hamrin, Carol Lee and Zhao, Suisheng (eds) (1995) *Decision-Making in Deng's China: Perspectives from Insiders*, Armonk, NY: M. E. Sharpe (Containing accounts by Chinese who actually worked in the Chinese bureaucracy in the 1980s, this book analyses the nature of, and processes of change in, the Chinese system at that time).

Li Zhisui (1994) *The Private Life of Chairman Mao: The Inside Story of the Man Who Made Modern China*, London: Chatto & Windus (A revealing but controversial inside account of Mao's political and personal behaviour by his personal physician. Excellent for the atmosphere of Mao's court, but full of dubious claims and interpretations).

Phathanothai, Sarin (1994) *The Dragon's Pearl*, New York: Simon & Schuster (Includes a vivid account of Liao Chengzhi, the author being his ward).

Shambaugh, David L. (1984) *The Making of a Premier: Zhao Ziyang's Provincial Career*, Boulder, CO: Westview Press (A detailed study of Zhao Ziyang's career as a provincial official prior to becoming premier in 1980).

Teiwes, Frederick C. (1990) *Politics at Mao's*

Court: Gao Gang and Party Factionalism in the Early 1950s, Armonk, NY: M. E. Sharpe (A detailed case study of the first leadership purge of the post-1949 period which elaborates the nature of court politics during the CCP's alleged 'golden age' in the early and mid-1950s).

—— (1993) *Politics and Purges in China: Rectification and the Decline of Party Norms 1950–1965*, 2nd edn, Armonk, NY: M. E. Sharpe (A classic analysis of elite politics from the founding of the PRC to the Cultural Revolution. Systematically undermines the 'two-line struggle' model of elite conflict while providing a detailed picture of a Mao-dominated polity).

Teiwes, Frederick C. with Sun, Warren (1994) *The Formation of the Maoist Leadership: From the Return of Wang Ming to the Seventh Party Congress*, London: Contemporary China Institute (An innovative study of the factors leading not only to the rise of Mao Zedong to undisputed leadership of the CCP, but also of those affecting the selection of the key leaders supporting the new chairman).

Teiwes, Frederick C. and Sun, Warren (eds) (1993) *The Politics of Agricultural Cooperativization: Mao, Deng Zihui, and the 'High Tide of 1955'*, Armonk, NY: M. E. Sharpe (A collection of translated materials together with an analytic introduction illustrating Mao's ability to single-handedly overturn the Party consensus on agricultural cooperativization. Revises accepted interpretations of this debate).

—— (1996) *The Tragedy of Lin Biao: Riding the Tiger during the Cultural Revolution 1966–1971*, London: Hurst (A detailed examination of the rise and fall of Lin Biao which demolishes conventional views of an ambitious politician engaged in a bitter power struggle with Mao. Lin is instead revealed as someone content with an inactive albeit honoured position who was thrust into a leading role by Mao and subsequently cast aside for reasons having little to do with any desire for greater power).

Terrill, Ross (1980, 1993) *A Biography: Mao*, Sydney: Hale & Iremonger (This biography of Mao Zedong attempts to place the emphasis on Mao as a person. It portrays him as a man of contradictions, prejudiced and changeable but dedicated to the ideology of the Chinese revolution).

Ting Wang (1980) *Chairman Hua: Leader of the Chinese Communists*, Montreal: McGill-Queen's University Press (A valuable if not completely accurate biography of China's transitional leader following Mao's death by a leading Hong Kong China watcher).

Yang Zhongmei (1988) *Hu Yaobang: A Chinese Biography*, Armonk, NY: M. E. Sharpe (A well-documented biography of leading post-Mao reformist Hu Yaobang by a former Cultural Revolution activist living abroad).

Hong Kong and China Outside the PRC

Buckley, Roger (1997) *Hong Kong: The Road to 1997*, Cambridge: Cambridge University Press (Focuses on the history of Hong Kong from 1945 to 1995, and includes a chapter on its likely future as a special administrative region of the PRC).

Cheng, Joseph Y. S. and Lo, Sonny S. H. (1995) *From Colony To SAR: Hong Kong's Challenges Ahead*, Hong Kong: Chinese University Press (The many authors, based in Hong Kong, take a careful and multi-faceted look at Hong Kong's recent past, present and future in the period around the transfer of sovereignty to the PRC. Topics covered include politics, law, infrastructure and many aspects of the economy).

Jacobs, J. Bruce (1993) *Taiwan*, Sydney: Asia-Australia Institute, University of New South Wales (A brief, but excellent, introduction to Taiwan).

Klintworth, Gary (ed.) (1994) *Taiwan in the Asia-Pacific in the 1990s*, Sydney: Allen & Unwin (Focuses on Taiwan's foreign economic relations, especially in the Pacific area).

—— (ed.) (1995) *New Taiwan, New China: Taiwan's Changing Role in the Asia-Pacific Region*, Melbourne: Longman Australia (A study of Taiwan focusing on the importance of China in Taiwan's recent development).

Lo Shiu Hing (1995) *Political Development in Macau*, Hong Kong: Chinese University Press (Analyses Macau's political development since the 1970s, concluding that, despite the differences between the two, political convergence will occur between Hong Kong and Macau's political systems, with Hong Kong's polity moving towards Macau's).

McMillen, Donald H. and DeGolyer, Michael E. (eds) (1993) *One Culture, Many Systems? Politics in the Reunification of China*, Hong Kong: Chinese University Press (Discusses the interplay of domestic political development and Chinese reunification activities concerning Taiwan, Hong Kong and Macau).

Shambaugh, David (ed.) (1995) *Greater China: The Next Superpower?*, Oxford: Oxford University Press (Deals with economic foreign relations within the Pacific, notably those of China, Taiwan and Hong Kong since the mid-1970s).

Wang Gungwu (1992) *Community and Nation: China, Southeast Asia and Australia*, Sydney: Allen & Unwin (A series of essays by a distinguished historian covering a range of topics connected with the role of the Overseas Chinese, especially those of Malaysia and Indonesia, as well as some on foreign relations and other matters).

Yahuda, Michael (1996) *Hong Kong China's Challenge*, London: Routledge (Assesses the Sino-British negotiations leading up to agreement on the transfer of Hong Kong sovereignty to China, and the likely impact on Hong Kong and China).

Index